GW00771266

IVA BABAJA
Icograda Vice President 2007-2009

Design as a potent agent of change

I had the great privilege of being the observer of Icograda at the 2008 jury of the European Design Awards and was impressed not only by the quanitity and quality of the works presented, but also by the jurying process itself - a concept of a jury comprised of design editors brought the level of discussion and judging to a stunningly high standard.
This year showed a record number of submissions, a clear proof that this award, albeit a young one, has already managed to command great respect within the European Design Community.
One could argue that it is precisely this award that helped unify our perspective of European Design and offered a comprehensive overview of its development and challenges. In a globalised world, where the balance between local specificity and global unification is becoming increasingly questionable, this is an important step.
But perhaps more importantly, the fact that around 1000 works entered this year also gives me hope at this point in time when the world is struggling with a massive financial crisis. The fact that designers did not take the back-seat but instead produced such a high number and quality of entries is a remarkable thing. It shows a hope that design is finally understood as a potent agent of change, a force that can help us rebuild and reshape the world and this should be an encouragement for all of us to embrace this responsibility.

EUROPEAN DESIGN HALL OF FAME

2009 | Adrian Frutiger
2008 | Javier Mariscal
2007 | Erik Spiekermann

TABLE OF CONTENTS

TABLE OF CONTENTS

PACKAGING

ILLUSTRATIONS

SELF PROMOTION

VARIOUS

JURY PRIZE

INDEX

JUDGING COMMITTEE

JACEK MROWCZYK *(Poland)*

Co-founder, editor of the graphic design section.

Jacek Mrowczyk, born in Krakow in 1972. Graphic designer, graduated from the Academy of Fine Arts in Krakow in 1998 (Poland). Lecturer in the Department of Visual Communication at the AFA in Krakow (1999-2007). Awarded several prizes and special mentions (inter alia at the 18th International Biennial of Graphic Design in Brno, Czech Republic in 1998 and at the 16th Biennial of the Polish Poster in Katowice, Poland in 1999).

Co-founder and editor of a Polish design quarterly 2+3D. He received his Doctor of Art from the Academy of Fine Arts in Krakow in 2005. Jury member of national and international graphic design competitions. Author of several articles about design and a Polish Dictionary of Typographic Terms. Member of the Polish Graphic Design Association (STGU) and Association Typographique Internationale (ATypI). A Fulbright scholar at the Cooper-Hewitt National Design Museum in New York, USA (2001/2002) and a Kosciuszko Foundation scholar at the Rhode Island School of Design in Providence, USA (2006/2007).

Assistant professor at the Academy of Fine Arts in Katowice (Poland). Visiting teacher in the Rhode Island School of Design in Providence (USA).

2+3D grafika plus produkt

www.2plus3d.pl

PETER BANKOV *(Russia)*

Editor in chief

Peter Bankov was born in 1969. He graduated from Minsk Art College in 1988 and Moscow State Polygraph Institute in 1993.
1996 – he organized [kAk) magazine. Now it's one of the key points of graphic design creative progress by forming of energetic communicational space among its audience. Peter Bankov is "Design Depot" (www.designdepot.ru) founder and creator director.

Awards: Victoria National Award at the "Design" All-Russian exhibition-competition (1997, 1998, 2001), 1st diploma at the "Grahit" Moscow Festival (1998), Diploma of the Russian Union of Designers and Special prize of the "Design and Advertising" exhibition (1999), 2nd Award at the "Press Prize" Festival (2000), 1st Award (2003), 2nd Award (1999, 2001, 2003), 3rd Award (two times in 2002) at the Moscow International Festival Advertising, 1st Award (two times in 2004), 2nd Award (2004,2005), 3rd award (2004), Gold, Silver (2006) at the Kiev International Festival of Advertising , two Golden medals and Bronze medal (2005, 2008), Gold and Silver (2007) at the "ADCR Award" competition, 3rd Award at the Identity: Best Of The Best 2006; 3rd Awards at the Moscow International Festival Advertising Red Apple (2007, 2008), 1st Prize at ProdExpoPack 2007, 1st and 2nd Award at the XI Federal Competition of Annual Reports of RTS Stock Exchange (2008).

[kAk)

www.kak.ru

MARIOS LINAKIS *(Greece)*

Creative Director

Marios Linakis was born in Athens in 1972. He studied Graphic Design at Brighton University and received his Master of Arts in Communication design from Central St. Martins College of Art & Design in London in 1995.

Since then he has designed for creative agencies in Athens specializing in web design. In 2001 he cofounded {Linakis + Associates} providing online as well as classical design solutions. He has taught typography and graphic design at AKTO School of Art & Design in Athens and has contributed as speaker or lecturer to design conferences and forums in Greece and abroad.

Marios is the recipient of Greek and international design awards and has taken part in judging committees in Greece. Since 2001 Marios has been contributing a regular column on web design for +design. Marios is a member of the Chartered Society of Designers.

+design

www.designmag.gr, www.linakis.com

MICHEL CHANAUD *(France)*

Editor & Art Director

Leader and founder of the company Pyramyd which publishes the French magazine Étape: In 1989, Michel Chanaud launched the French magazine Étapes and Pyramyd Editions.

Formed in visual creation in the Ensad, he made his first weapons in interior architecture, scenography and design. He continued his career as a graphic designer freelance journalist especially for projects of packaging and in advertising creation. Before founding his publishing society, he started a graphic studio of creation.

During last years, he created a center of training in graphics. He also has extended the range of its publications, with the first magazine on the design of animation published, the DVD magazine DESIGNFLUX. Moreover, he is the editor of a hundred books on the design, like the collection D&D - design&designer – or like Émergence, a volume on young creation.

étapes

www.etapes.com

MARTIN LENGAUER *(Austria)*

Head of Communication, designaustria

Born in 1969. He studied philosophy, philology, political and communication science. Free lance journalist, founder and CEO of "die jungs kommunikation", a Vienna-based PR-agency. "die jungs" offer full service in public relations, text-production, media-conception and event-management for private, public, cultural, scientific and non-profit enterprises. Among them many design-related companies as well as the "designforum Vienna" and "designaustria", the umbrella organisation of Austrian designers, where Martin leads the communication department.

He also holds a teaching position in public relations at the University of Vienna. designaustria issues a quarterly, the "DA mitteilungen", which addresses all designaustria members as well as the Austrian design community.

designaustria & DA mitteilungen

www.designaustria.at

THIERRY HAUSERMANN *(Switzerland)*

Editor and Art Director

Based in Morges/Lausanne, Switzerland, IDPURE magazine was founded by Thierry Hausermann in 2004. Dedicated to the provision of cutting edge, contemporary and personalized graphic design culture, Thierry emphasizes personal involvement in design and artistic projects like IDPURE. Thierry believes that graphic design should serve and support the needs of products or messages, which can only be achieved through up-close collaboration and understanding between clients and graphic/product designers, artists, etc. Thierry's motivation is to discover new talents and explore the possibilities of presenting them in IDPURE.

Thierry followed a one year program at ESAA (école supérieure d'arts appliqués) in Vevey, Switzerland, than studied a 4 year graphic design program at ERACOM (école romande d'arts et communication) in Lausanne, Switzerland, where he graduated in 1986. Thierry also pursued a course of studies at the Academy of Arts of San Francisco for 1 year in 1997. In addition to the graphic designer piece, he is an editor, a writer and a project manager.

idpure

www.idpure.ch

JUDGING COMMITTEE

RUDOLF VAN WEZEL *(The Netherlands)*

Publisher

Rudolf van Wezel (1956) studied publishing at the Frederik Muller Academy in Amsterdam and has worked in the Dutch Publishing industry since 1982.

Rudolf founded BIS Publishers in 1986. BIS is an international publisher in the field of graphic design, communication, product design, fashion and architecture. BIS publishes about 25 titles per year and most of them are in English and distributed all over the world. BIS has published Items Magazine, the Dutch national design magazine, for 15 years but sold this title to another Dutch publisher in 2007.

Rudolf also co-founded Frame Publishers and Mark Publishers. Frame is the international interior and design magazine that become a global player with a vast international distribution. Frame is now also available in licensed editions in Turkish, Russian and Chinese. Mark is the international Architectural magazine by the makers of Frame. Mark won the 2008 European Design Award for best magazine design. Rudolf started Graphic Magazine on international graphic visual culture in 2006. In the fall of 2009 Graphic will be revamped under a new name.

In 2008 Rudolf founded the Creative Company Conference which is an international yearly conference on creativity, innovation and entrepreneurship in Amsterdam.

Graphic

www.bispublishers.nl
www.framemag.com
www.mark-magazine.com
www.creativecompanyconference.com

SILVIA SFLIGIOTTI *(Italy)*

Member of the editorial board

Silvia Sfligiotti is a designer, educator and design writer based in Milano. She's a founding partner at Alizarina, a graphic and new media design studio. Silvia is co-author of three books on Italian graphic and type design; the most recent is Italic 2.0: contemporary type design in Italy (2008).

In 2008 she co-curated the Multiverso conference and exhibition during the Icograda Design Week Torino. She teaches typography and history of graphic design at the Scuola Politecnica di Design and is project leader for Visual Communication at the Faculty of Design and Art of the Free University of Bozen. She also lectured at international conferences and several Italian universities and design schools. Silvia is on the editorial board of «Progetto Grafico» since 2007, and she regularly contributes to the magazine; her articles were also published in other design magazines such as «Abitare», «Typo» and «Artlab».

Progetto Grafico

www.aiap.it/progettografico

BETTINA SCHULZ *(Germany)*

Chief editor

Bettina Schulz (born 1974 in Munich) has been editor-in-chief of the international journal novum World of Graphic Design since 2001. She joined the editorial staff of the magazine in 1994. Mrs Schulz also works as a freelance writer and editor for national and international magazines and for a range of clients in different sectors.

Bettina Schulz already serves on a number of design juries (e.g. for red dot communication design award, for the Best of Corporate Publishing Award, for the MfG competition of the Bundesverband Druck, Monaco de Luxe Packaging Award, Canon Pro Fashional Award, Adobe Photoshop Award, twice-yearly diploma awards presentation at the U5 Academy) and is co-founder of the »Creative Paper Conference« (www.creative-paper.de) in Munich.

novum World of Graphic Design

www.novumnet.de

LINDA KUDRNOVSKÁ *(Czech Republic)*

Editor-in-chief

Linda Kudrnovská (born 1977) is a design writer and theoretician. She is the Editor-in-Chief and one of the founding members of TYPO, a Prague-based magazine focused on design and typography.Having studied graphic design and illustration, she graduated in theory of culture and history of art at the Faculty of Fine Arts, Charles University, Prague. Ever since, she has been a member of the editorial board of the TYPO Magazine; she also regularly contributes to a number of other periodicals.

TYPO

www.magtypo.cz

EDUARDO BRAVO *(Spain)*

Editor

Born in Madrid in 1973. Graded in Law by the UAM he has always working in the world of the communication. He has been scriptwriter, TV producer, journalist, jury in different advertising and graphic design contests and, since 2001, he works in Visual magazine and Blur Ediciones. He is also biographer and expert in the live and works of Spanish filmmaker Santiago Lorenzo.

Visual

www.visual.gi

ÖMER DURMAZ *(Turkey)*

Editor-in-chief

Ömer Durmaz (born in 1974) is the editor-in-chief, co-founder and art director of GRAFIK TASARIM magazine. Grafik Tasarim was founded in 2006 and is the only magazine in Turkey dedicated to graphic design and communication design. It aims is to promote greater design consciousness within Turkish society, introducing the best examples of graphic design, typography and art direction from Turkey and around the world.

Ömer started his graphic design career in 1993 and began to work as a full time designer in 1997. He graduated from the Dokuz Eylul University Faculty of Fine Arts Graphic Design Department in 1999 and has been a full-time lecturer at the same university since 2002. He is the author of several articles about graphic design and is a member of the Turkish Graphic Design Association (GMK).

Grafik Tasarim

www.grafiktasarim.com.tr

IDENTITY

GOLD
BRAND LOGO

TITLE
Points of view
COMPANY
Vidale-Gloesener Sarl
CLIENT
Fondation de l'Architecture et de l'Ingénierie
DESIGNER
Tom Gloesener
ART DIRECTOR
Silvano Vidale
COUNTRY
Luxembourg

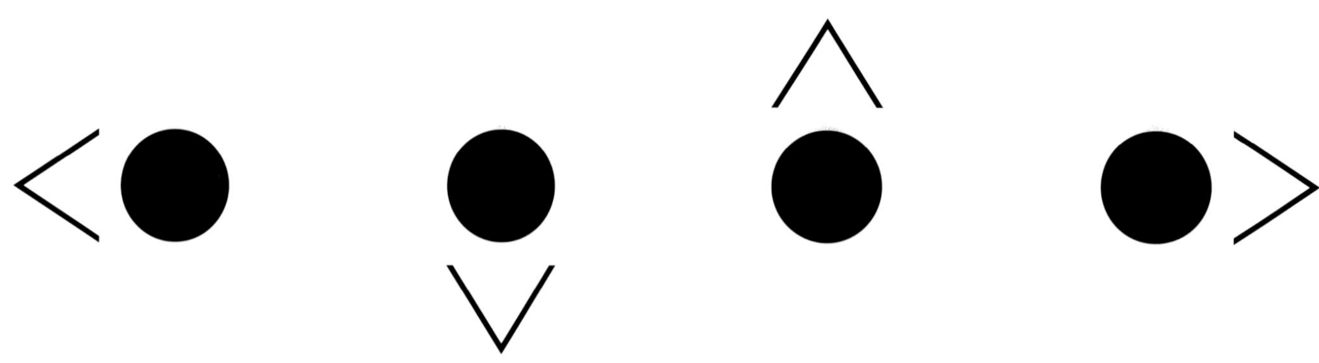

Points of view. 4 questions. 44 answers.

The Fondation de l'Architecture du Luxembourg is a platform for architectural debate, and seeks to retain a critical perspective on the discipline and on the built environment. The logo created by Vidale-Gloesener for the 2008 Venice Biennale symbolises the idea of different viewpoints brought together by four questions put to 11 architects. This design, which is unafraid of being simple in order to express an idea of architectural criticism, ultimately swayed a majority of the jury. This approach allows a strong contrast with the city of Venice. The logo is used in minimalist manner, is easy to memorise, and invites visitors to look differently at the idea of the viewpoint, which is wholly appropriate to architecture.

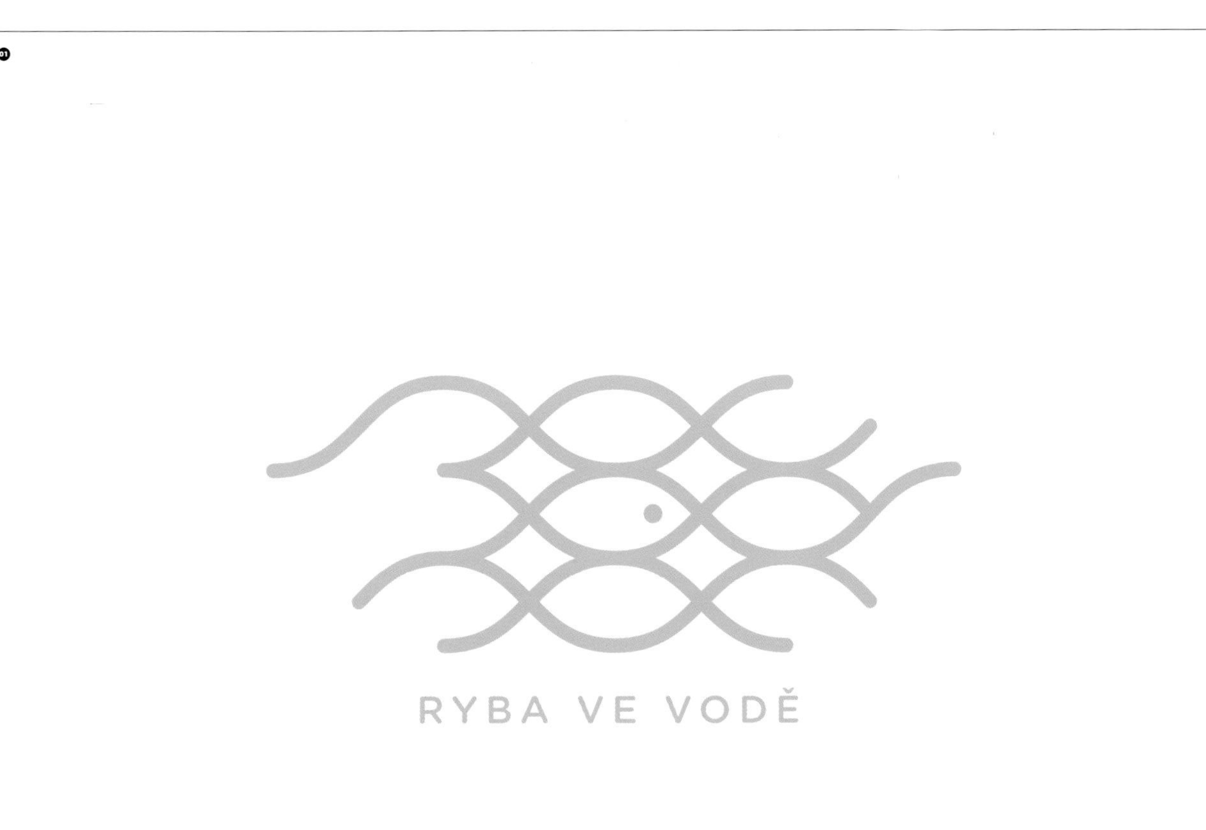

SILVER
BRAND LOGO

01.
TITLE
Ryba ve vode
(A Fish in the Water)
COMPANY
Jan Sabach Design
CLIENT
Perfect Crowd
DESIGNERS
Jan Šabach
ART DIRECTOR
Jan Šabach
WRITER
Jaroslav Cír not Jan Šabach
URL
www.rybavevode.cz
COUNTRY
Czech Republic

02.
TITLE
Stiftung Warentest
COMPANY
KMS TEAM GmbH
CLIENT
Stiftung Warentest
DESIGNER
Birte Helms
Lars Breitenfeldt
CREATIVE DIRECTOR
Knut Maierhofer
DESIGN DIRECTOR
Helena Frühauf
ACCOUNT DIRECTOR
Eva-Maria Schleip
COUNTRY
Germany

BRONZE
BRAND LOGO

01.
TITLE
Alps and Arts
COMPANY
graphic design
CLIENT
Alps and Arts GmbH
COUNTRY
Switzerland

02.
TITLE
Platonos 08
COMPANY
the design shop
CLIENT
Dry Honey
COUNTRY
Greece

03.
TITLE
Relax in Cyprus
COMPANY
beetroot design group
CLIENT
Cyprus Architect Accotiation
COUNTRY
Greece

04.
TITLE
Precious pineapple
COMPANY
Manuel Galdón Morcillo
CLIENT
Conagrican, S.L.
COUNTRY
Spain

01

02

03

04

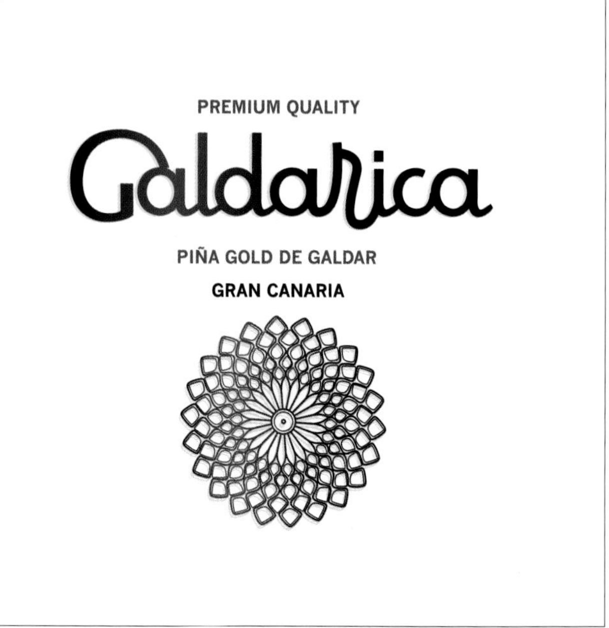

ápla

M11

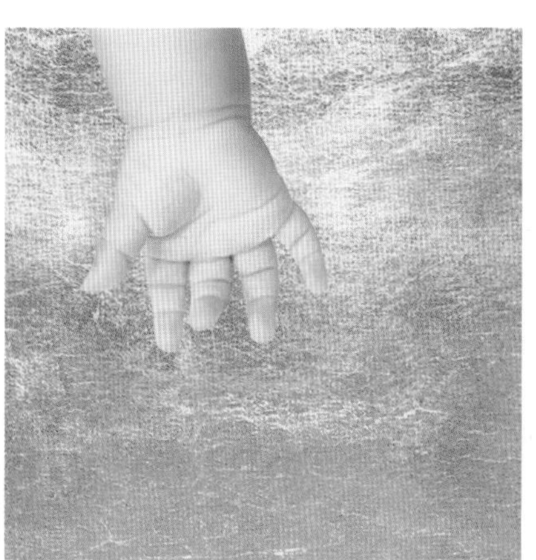

JOURNALISTIC TELEVISION
AWARD **ILARIA ALPI**
XV EDITION

XVT

FINALIST
BRAND LOGO

01.
TITLE
apla
COMPANY
Colibri
CLIENT
Mono Catering
COUNTRY
Greece

02.
TITLE
Italianzoomer Robot Logo
COMPANY
Kut communications
CLIENT
Italianzoomer
COUNTRY
Italy

03.
TITLE
M11
COMPANY
Vidale-Gloesener Sarl
CLIENT
SEO S.A.
COUNTRY
Luxembourg

04.
TITLE
Goldenes Händchen
COMPANY
motterdesign
CLIENT
Dorn photographer
COUNTRY
Austria

05.
TITLE
COP15 Copenhagen UN Climate Change Conference 2009
COMPANY
NR2154
CLIENT
Ministry of Foreign Affairs of Denmark
COUNTRY
Denmark

06.
TITLE
Ilaria Alpi journalistic television award
COMPANY
Stefano Tonti Design
CLIENT
Ilaria Alpi Association
COUNTRY
Italy

SILVER
COMPANY LOGO

01.
TITLE
Grün macht Frölich
COMPANY
Speck Visuelle Kommunikation
CLIENT
Dipl.-Ing. Klaus Detlev Fröhlich
DESIGNER
Dominic Speck
Daniel Kremin
Matthias Müller
PHOTOGRAPHER
Lisa Lenneper
COUNTRY
Germany

01

SILVER
COMPANY LOGO

02.
TITLE
Werner Sobek
COMPANY
Buero Uebele Visuelle Kommunikation
CLIENT
prof. Werner Sobek
DESIGNER
Buero Uebele Visuelle Kommunikation
CREATIVE DIRECTOR
Beate Kapprell
DESIGN DIRECTOR
Andreas Uebele
COUNTRY
Germany

03.
TITLE
Mercedes Urquijo
COMPANY
virgen extra
CLIENT
Mercedes Urquijo
DESIGNER
Ismael Medina
CREATIVE DIRECTOR
Ismael Medina
Sebas Cangiano
COUNTRY
Spain

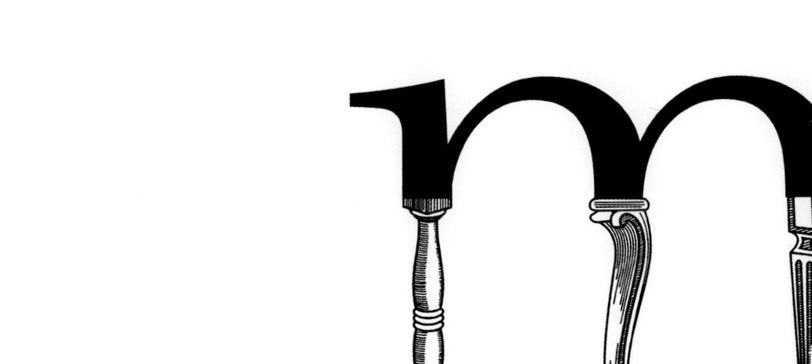

BRONZE
COMPANY LOGO

01.
TITLE
Heaven Scent Retail Store
COMPANY
Claudia Graphic Design Studio
CLIENT
Heaven Scent
COUNTRY
Norway

02.
TITLE
Idékorpset
COMPANY
Kirk & Holm
CLIENT
Idékorpset
COUNTRY
Denmark

03.
TITLE
Swisscom
COMPANY
Moving Brands
CLIENT
Swisscom
COUNTRY
United Kingdom

04.
TITLE
Moebeltischlerei Anabith
COMPANY
Kreative Visualisierung
CLIENT
Moebeltischlerei Anabith
COUNTRY
Austria

01

02

03

04

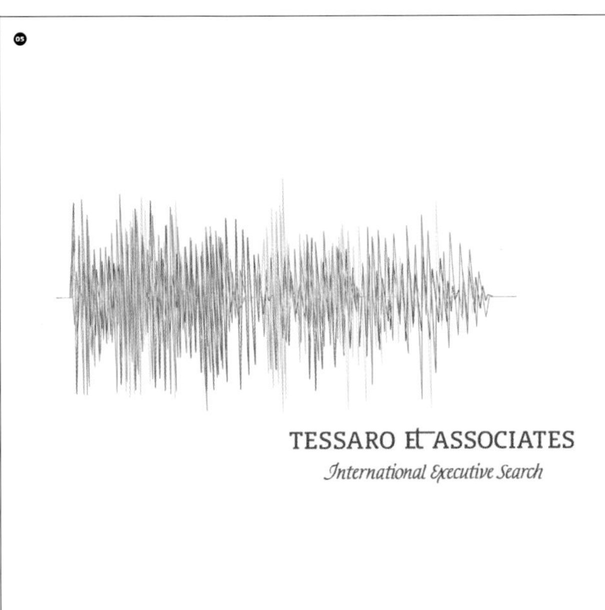

BRONZE
COMPANY LOGO

05.
TITLE
Tessaro
COMPANY
Fuenfwerken Design AG
CLIENT
Teessaro & Associates
COUNTRY
Germany

06.
TITLE
Diplom-Geologen Firchow & Melchers GbR
COMPANY
labor b designbüro
CLIENT
Diplom-Geologen Firchow & Melchers GbR
COUNTRY
Germany

07.
TITLE
Mindshare
COMPANY
Moving Brands
CLIENT
Mindshare
COUNTRY
United Kingdom

08.
TITLE
Fjällpuben
COMPANY
Stylt Trampoli AB
CLIENT
Grupp f12
COUNTRY
Sweden

GOLD
BRAND IMPLEMENTATION

TITLE
Impakt festival 2008
COMPANY
Lava grafisch ontwerpers
CLIENT
Impakt
DESIGNER
Ruben Pater
ART DIRECTOR
Ruben Pater
ILLUSTRATOR
Ruben Pater
COUNTRY
Netherlands

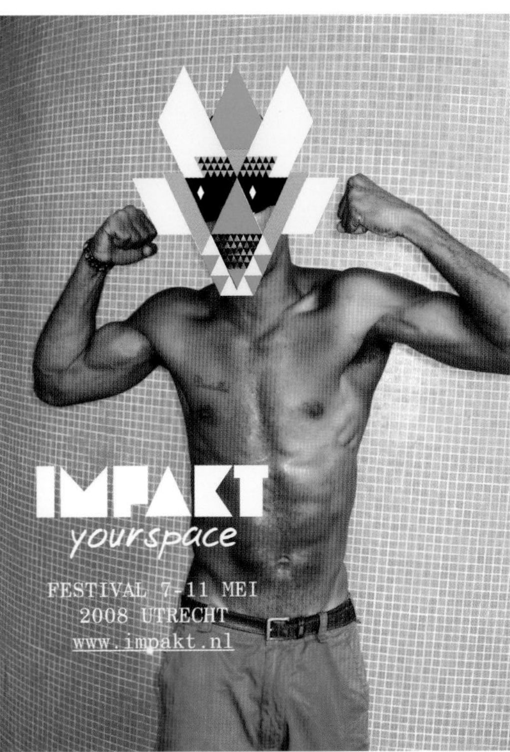

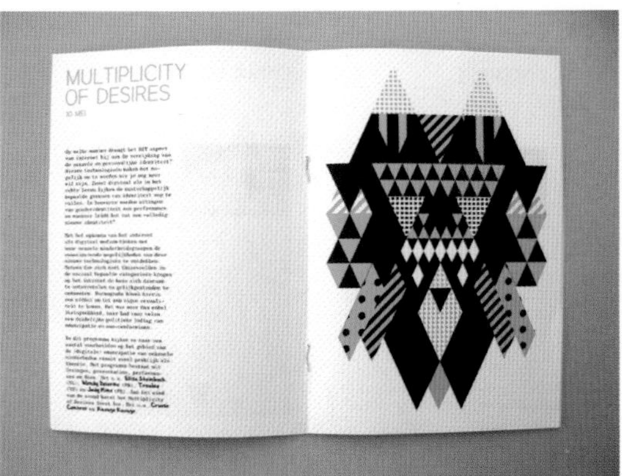

An original idea and system: these are the two points that struck us about Lava's project. The system, based on multi-coloured masks composed of triangles, allows all the festival actors – public included – to be incorporated. The posters, flyers and visuals are devised from photos of mundane everyday characters in which everyone wears masks. In this visual solution, the masked-ball theme blends jauntily with Web 2.0 avatars. The impression that there is a talent behind every mask knits perfectly with the festival concept. We particularly enjoyed this fluid identity and this implementation, which plays with the over-strict rules of traditional branding and heralds the more playful, interactive ones of the future.

GOLD
BRAND IMPLEMENTATION

TITLE
Beyondrisør
COMPANY
Bleed
CLIENT
Beyondrisør
DESIGNER
Astrid Feldner
ILLUSTRATOR
Astrid Feldner
URL
www.beyondrisor.no
COUNTRY
Norway

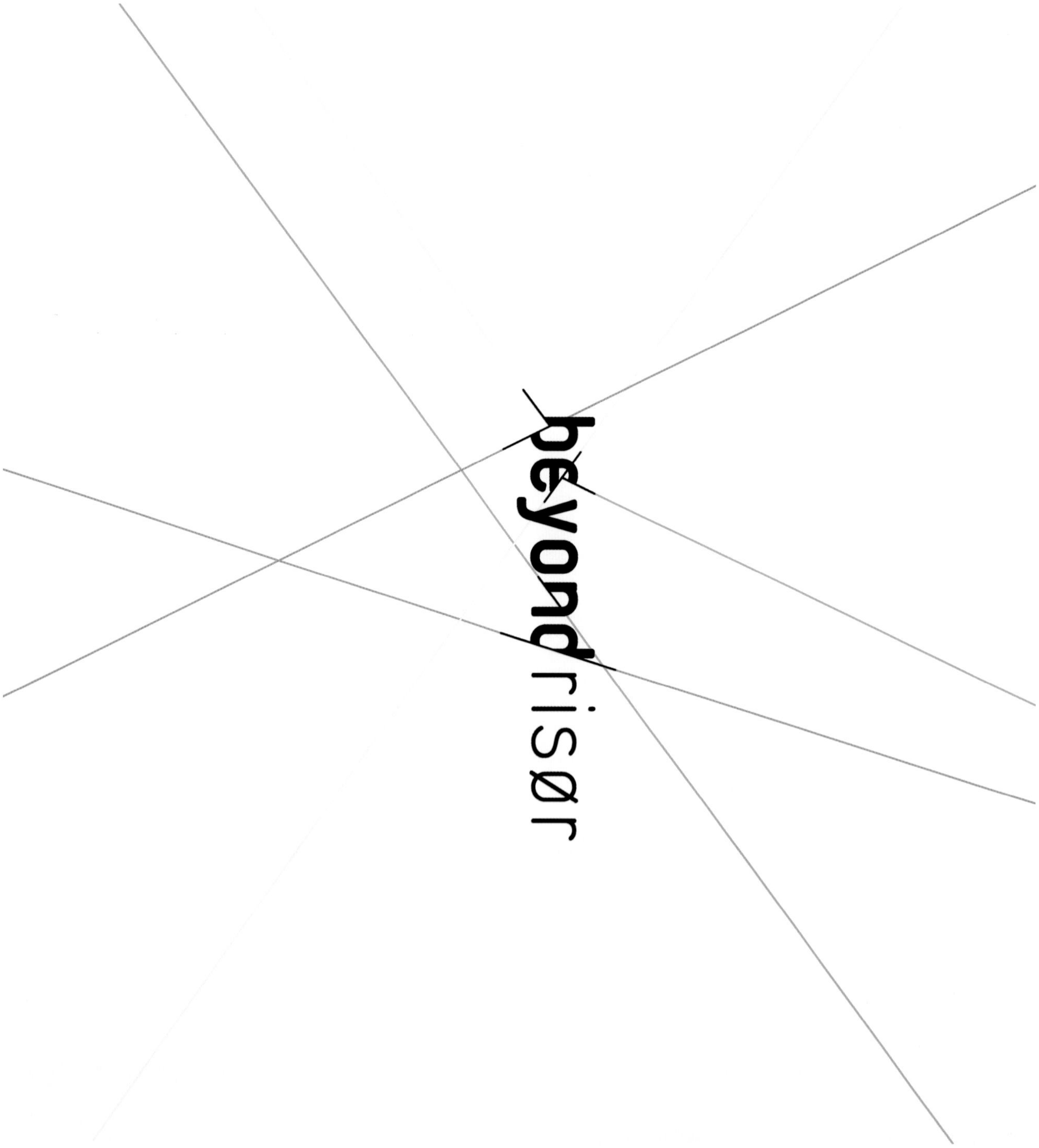

beyondrisør

Bringing business and design together is the aim of Beyondrisor. This implementation is as much a challenge as the event design. The rationality of business and design's greater instinctiveness often struggle for mutual understanding. The exemplary character of this work merits prolonged attention. It perfectly handles simplicity and functionalism. The graphic system, based on type and a cut-out, opens up a vast realm of possibility and allows numerous applications.

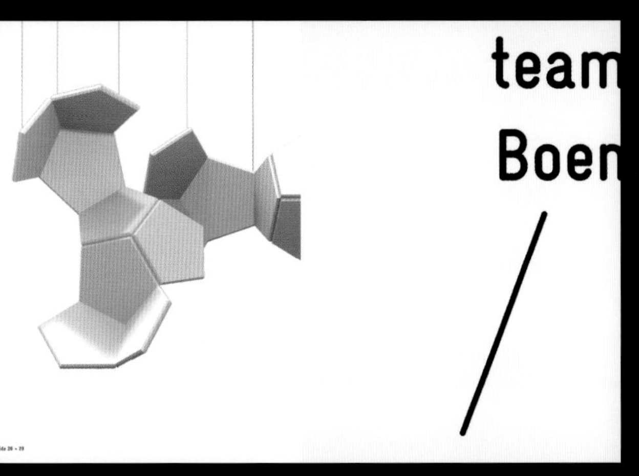

Boen

Boens historie er en historie om mennesker. Lojale og arbeidsomme mennesker med pågangsmot og kjærlighet til naturen. **Boens** historie går tilbake til 1600-tallet. Allerede i 1641 var to sager i drift ved **Boen**fossen i Topdalselva i Kristiansand. I over 350 år har altså menneskene på **Boen** forvaltet og foredlet trevirke. Kvalitet og grundighet har hele tiden vært viktige drivkrefter i arbeidet.

Boens historie er også en historie om oppfinnsomhet og nytenkning. Fra mølle til sagbruk. Fra gårdsdrift til parkettproduksjon. Hele tiden har menneskene på **Boen** vært levende opptatt av å komme videre, finne de beste løsningene, de beste produktene. Og hele tiden har respekten for naturressursene vært en grunnleggende del av **Boens** kultur og historie. Råvarene er og har alltid vært selve utgangspunktet for **Boens** eksistens. En respektfull omgang med naturens ressurser har derfor preget menneskene i bedriften gjennom alle tider.

Kvalitet er en av **Boens** kjerneverdier, og ligger til grunn for all vår råvarebehandling, produksjon og service. **Boens** kvalitetsbegrep blir til i møtet mellom norsk tradisjon for treforedling, litauisk flittighet og tysk grundighet.

Boen assosieres med høy kvalitet. I Sør- og Mellom-Europa er parkettlegging et eget fagområde, og **Boen** har alltid hatt, og har, en tett dialog med disse miljøene. Håndverkernes erfaringer og tilbakemeldinger bidrar til at vi hele tiden kan forbedre og videreutvikle våre produkter. **Boens** produkter distribueres og forhandles gjennom et nettverk av samarbeidspartnere over store deler av verden.

beyondrisør
12. og 13. juni 2008

SILVER
BRAND IMPLEMENTATION

TITLE
The Øya Festival, Oslo.
COMPANY
The A.K.I.G.A
CLIENT
The Øya Festival
DESIGNER
Are Kleivan
ART DIRECTOR
Are Kleivan
CREATIVE DIRECTORS
Are Kleivan
Arnt Olaf Anderssen
DESIGN DIRECTOR
Are Kleivan
ILLUSTRATOR
Are Kleivan
OTHER
Arnt Olaf Anderssen
URL
www.kleivan.net
COUNTRY
Norway

MIDDELALDERPARKEN, OSLO
5.–9.AUG
ØØØYYYAAA!
N.E.R.D.(US)
TURBONEGRO PERFORMING APOCALYPSE DUDES
KAIZERS ORCHESTRA
MY BLOODY VALENTINE(IE/UK)
GRINDERMAN
ANE BRUN
RAGA ROCKERS
SONIC YOUTH(US)
INGRID OLAVA
IRON & WINE(US)
SIGUR ROS(IS)
CUT COPY(AU) · JAMIE LIDELL(UK) · ANIMAL ALPHA · EL CUERO · DIPLO(US) · GIRL TALK(US) · JOSÉ GONZALES(SE) · LARS HORNTVETH M/KORK · INGRID OLAVA · KUNG FU GIRLS · HOWL · ISIS(US) · KID SISTER & A-TRAK(US) · LYKKE LI(SE) · MOGWAI(UK) · THE NATIONAL(US) · OKKERVIL RIVER(US) · SUNN O)))(US) · THOM HELL · SUPERSILENT M/ NILS PETTER MOLVÆR · YEASAYER(US) · LUKESTAR
BURAKA SOM SISTEMA(PT) · CASIOKIDS · COLISEUM(US) · DARK MEAT(US) · DISKJOKKE BAND · THE DODOS (US) · ELEPHANT9 · FAT FREDDY'S DROP(NZ) · FLEET FOXES(US) · GERILJA · GRAND ISLAND · EL GUINCHO (ES) · HEALTH(US) · HOLY FUCK(CA) · KONONO NO. 1(DRC) · LAMA · LIGHTSPEED CHAMPION(UK) · THE MAE SHI(US) · MASTER PIECE OF CAKE · MODDI · JANELLE MONAÉ(US) · STELLA MWANGI · THE NIGHT MARCHERS (US) · NO AGE(US) · PIRATE LOVE · ROGER GRÆSBERG & THE ANTI-MUSIC BONANZA · SILJE NES · THE SWORD(US) · TOMMY TOKYO & STARVING FOR MY GRAVY · SIGH & EXPLODE · TRULS AND THE TREES
OYAFESTIVALEN.COM
+ MANGE FLER! FØLG WEB FOR OPPDATERINGER!
DAGSBILLETTER 565,- +avgift
www.billettservice.no · 815 33 133 Med forbehold om programendringer
IKEA · djuice · PEPSI MAX · VG · Sony Ericsson
ØYA OSLO
myspace a place for friends · nrk P3

2008

SILVER
BRAND IMPLEMENTATION

TITLE
Expatcenter identity
COMPANY
Silo / Fabrique Communicatie en Design
CLIENT
Gemeente Amsterdam
DESIGNER
Silo / Fabrique Communications and Design
PROJECT MANAGER
Merijn Hillen (Fabrique)
COUNTRY
Netherlands

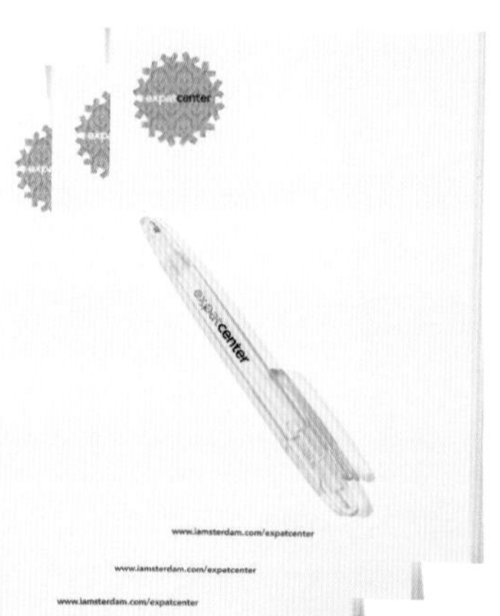

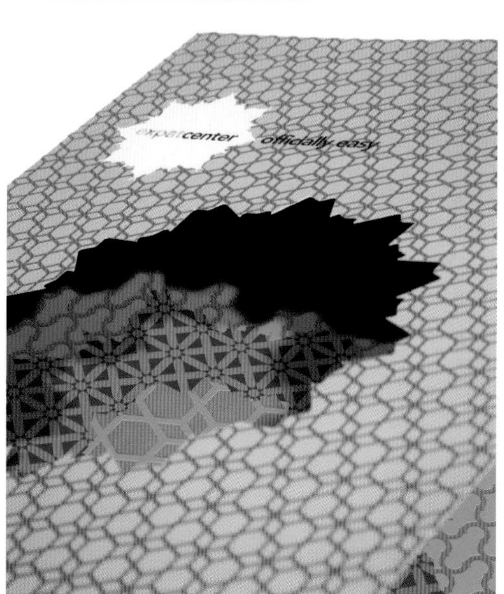

expatcenter
expatcenter

BRONZE
BRAND IMPLEMENTATION

TITLE
Multiverso - Icograda Design Week Torino 2008
COMPANY
zup associati srl
CLIENTS
Icograda
Aiap
Icograda Design Week
COUNTRY
Italy

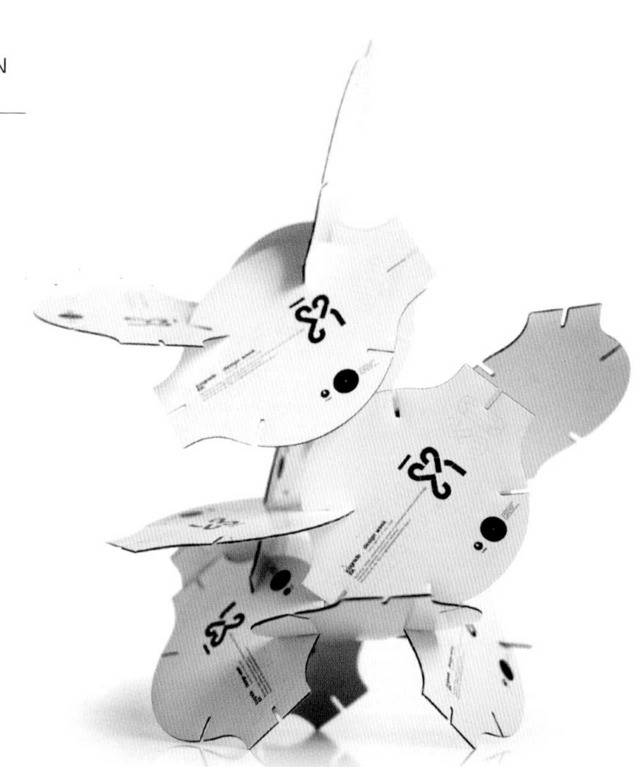

icograda
IDA
design week
torino, italia • 13-19 october, 2008

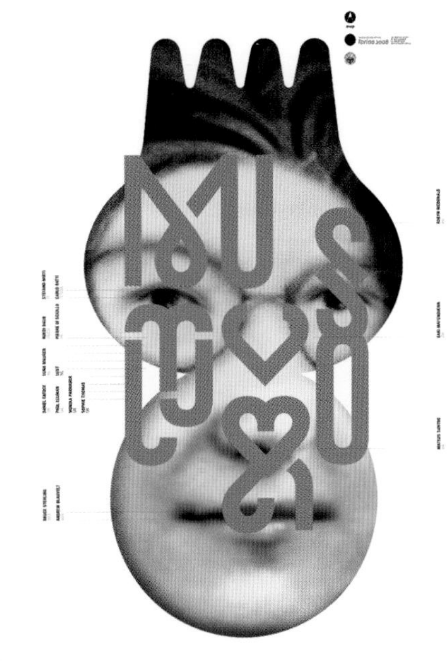
icograda
IDA
design week
torino, italia • 13-19 october, 2008

icograda
IDA
design week
torino, italia • 13-19 october, 2008

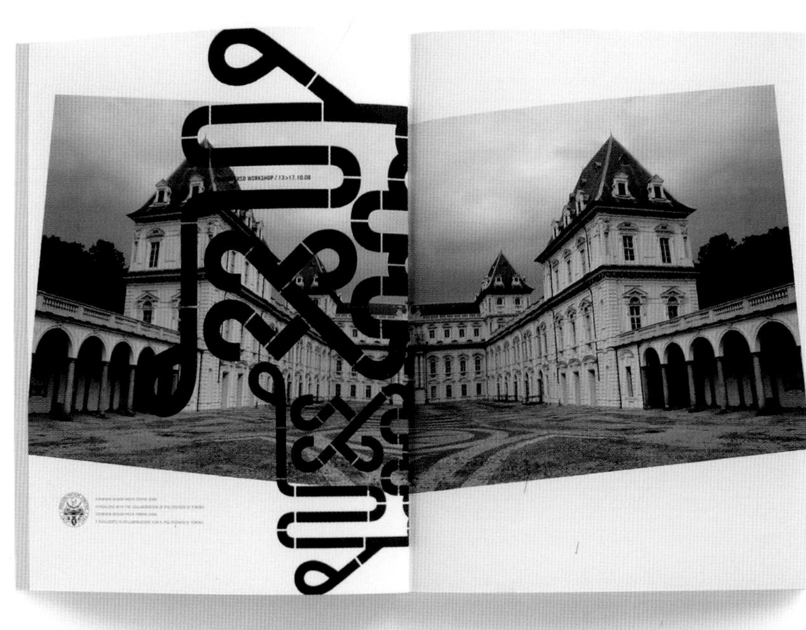

BAUR
R

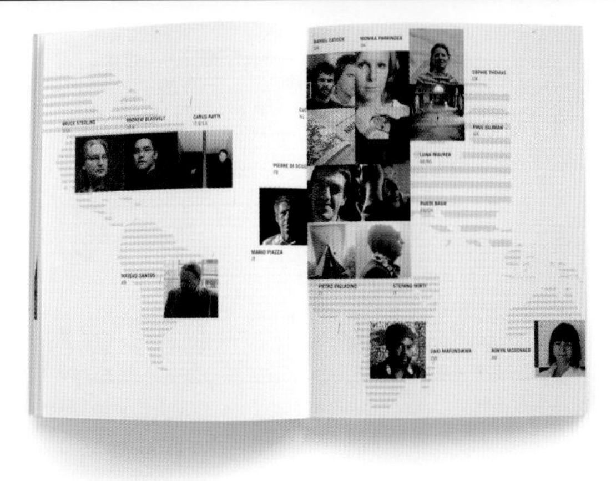

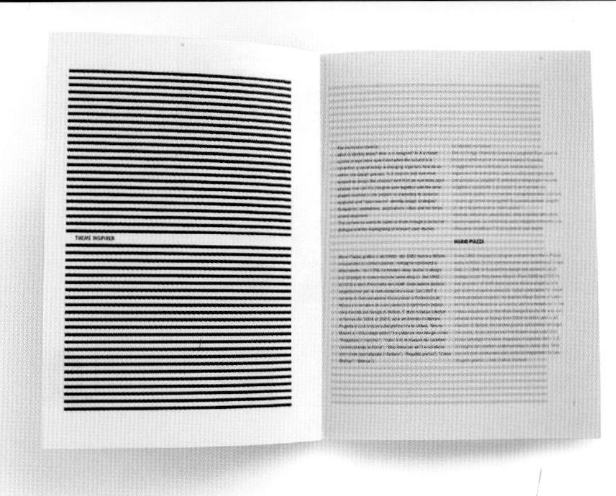

BRONZE
BRAND IMPLEMENTATION

TITLE
Relax in Cyprus
COMPANY
beetroot design group
CLIENT
Cyprus Architect Accotiation
COUNTRY
Greece

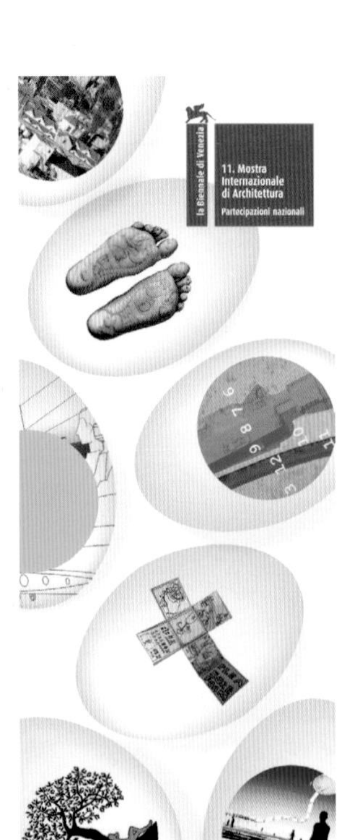

ARCHITECTURAL CONSCIOUSNESS
easy over
SUNSANDSEX

SLOW DOWN
think FREE

take it easy
think FREE
11. Mostra Internazionale di Architettura
Partecipazioni nazionali

curated by Sir Peter Cook
11TH INTERNATIONAL
CYPRUS
at
ARCHITECTURE
EXHIBITION
VENICE
La Biennale .08
IN CYPRUS
RELAX
AS
ARCHITECTS
REINTERPRET
Spazioeventi
Libreria Mondadori
September 14
to November 23

BRONZE
BRAND IMPLEMENTATION

TITLE
Ivan Hair Salon
COMPANY
G
CLIENTS
Ivan Foulidis
Ageliki Kotsifakou
URL
www.ivanhairsalon.gr
COUNTRY
Greece

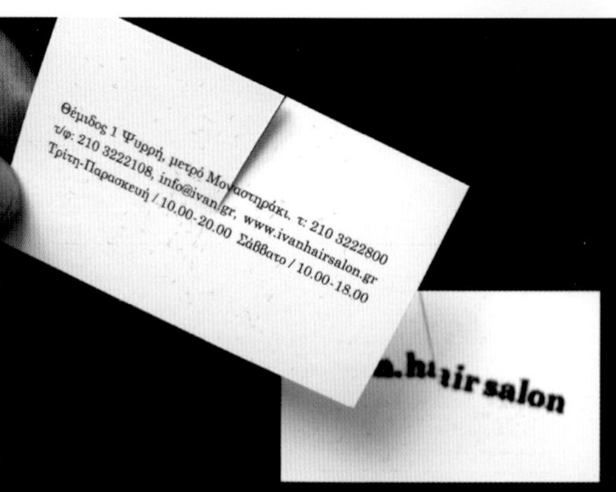

ivan.hair salon

ivan.hair salon

ράκι. τ: 210 3222
ρὸ Μοναστηww.ivanhairsalo
o@ivan.gr,

BRONZE
BRAND IMPLEMENTATION

TITLE
FD4K'08
COMPANY
Hakobo
CLIENT
Festival of Dialogue of Four Cultures
URL
www.4kultury.pl
COUNTRY
Poland

Festiwal Dialogu Czterech Kultur '08
Wer bist du?

Festiwal Dialogu Czterech Kultur '08
5-12 września Łódź
Kto ty jesteś?

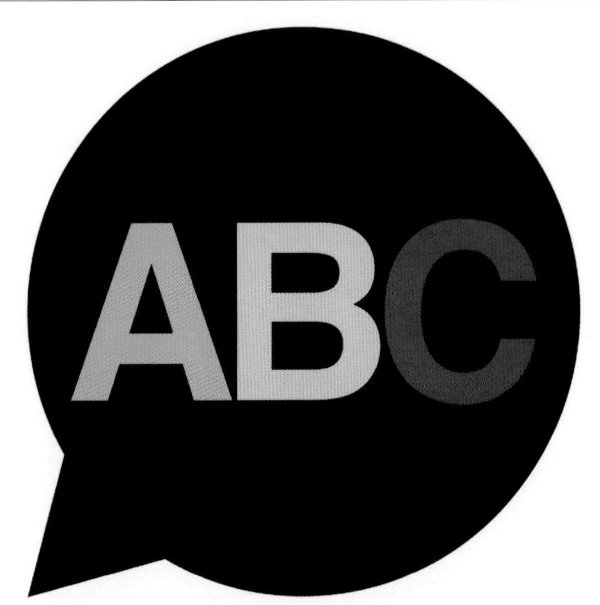
ABC
Projekt linii kreatywnej materiałów graficznych dla Festiwalu Dialogu Czterech Kultur 2008 Hakobo WWW.HAKOBO.ART.PL
KOLORY MOTYWY GRAFICZNE ZASTOSOWANIE KROJE CZCIONEK

Festiwal Dialogu Czterech Kultur '08
Master &Monster
05-28/09/2008

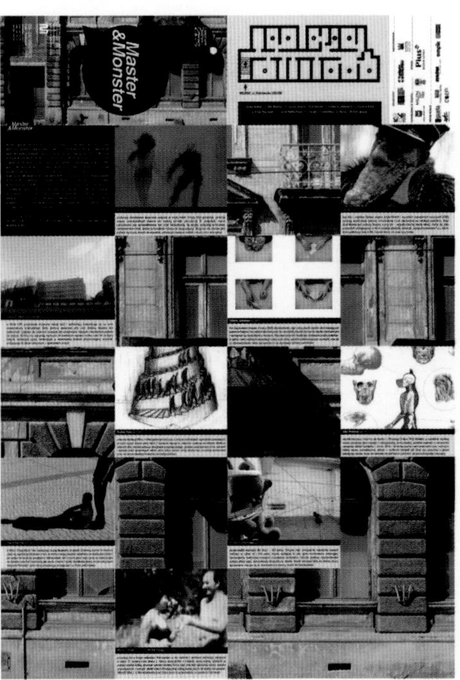
Master &Monster

Fathers

Kto ty jesteś?
Festiwal Dialogu Czterech Kultur '08
Ojcowie
Ты кто такой?
Wer bist du?

Festiwal Dialogu Czterech Kultur '08
4kultury.pl
FESTIWAL DIALOGU CZTERECH KULTUR
Kto ty jesteś?
Ты кто такой?
Wer bist du?

Janusz Korczak
08-11/09/2008

BRONZE
BRAND IMPLEMENTATION

TITLE
Visual Arts in Greece 3
COMPANY
dolphins // communication design
CLIENT
State Museum of Contemporary Art
COUNTRY
Greece

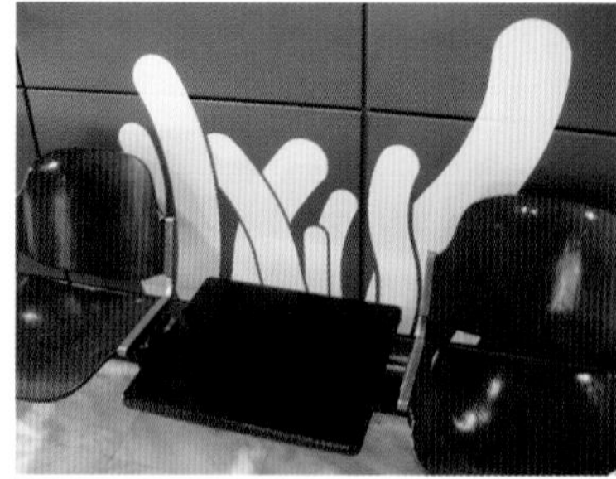

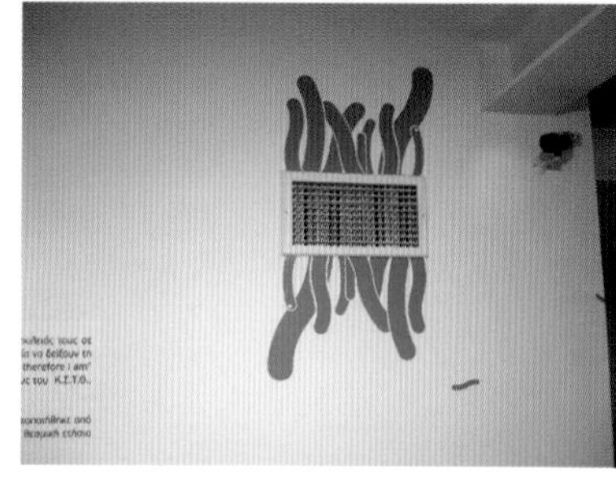

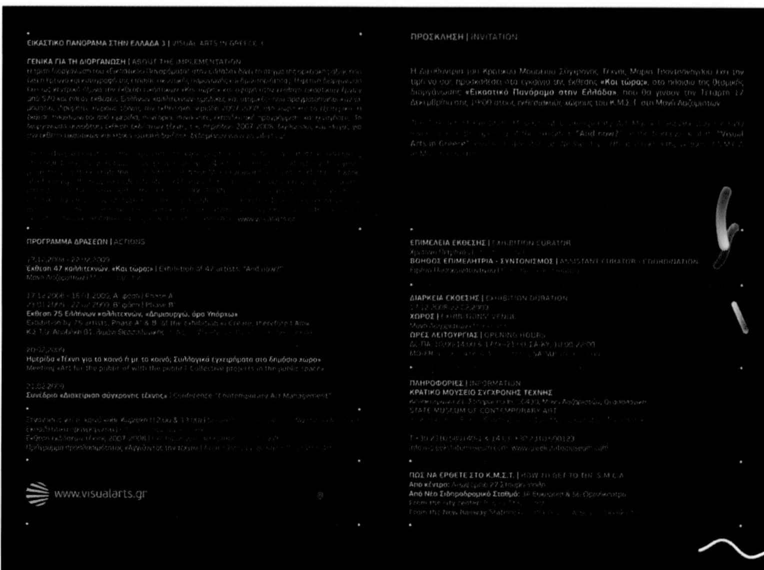

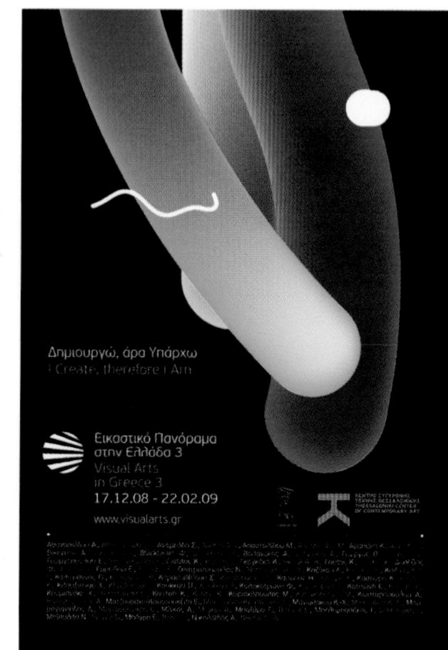

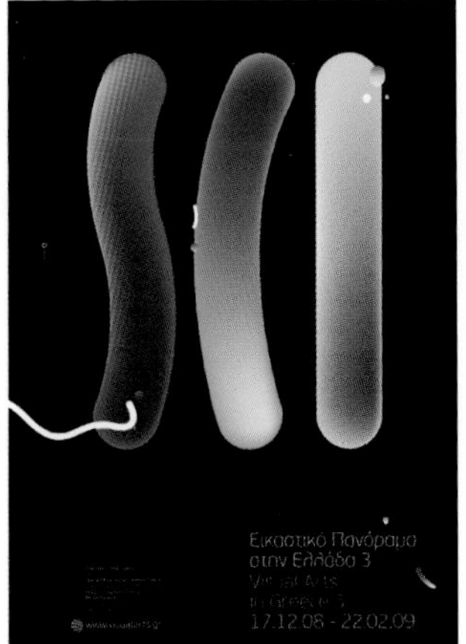

Εικαστικό Πανόραμα
στην Ελλάδα 3
Visual Arts
in Greece 3
17.12.08 - 22.02.09

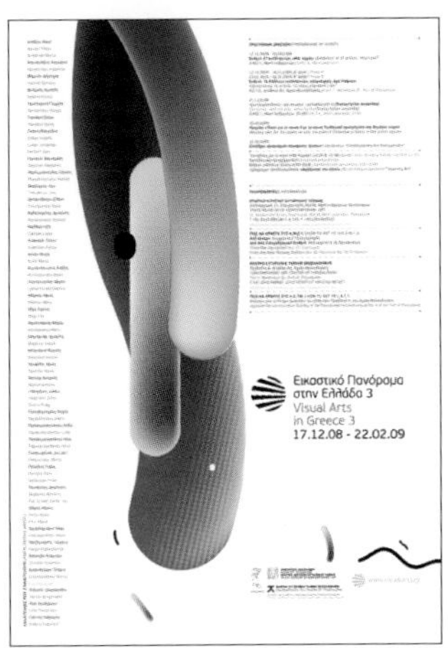

Εικαστικό Πανόραμα
στην Ελλάδα 3
Visual Arts
in Greece 3
17.12.08 - 22.02.09

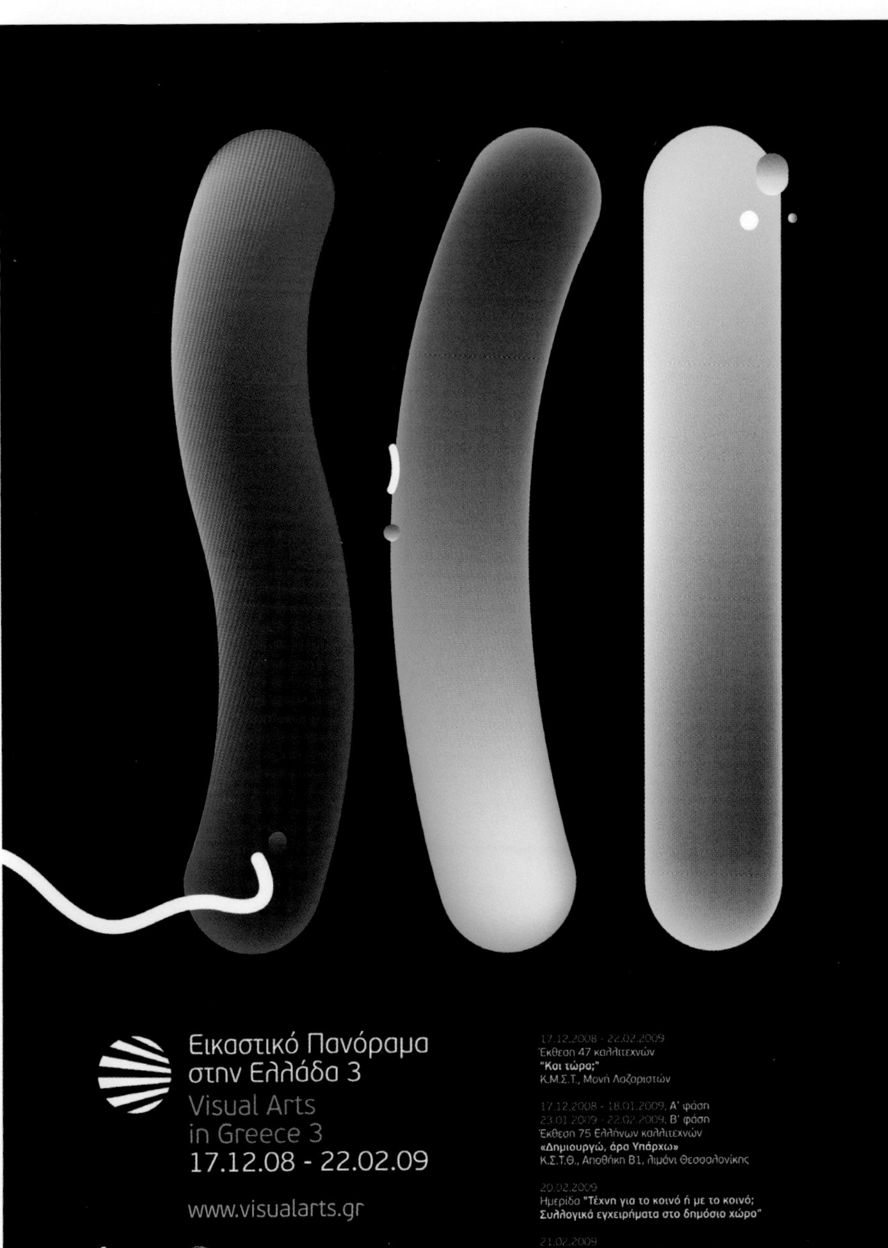

Εικαστικό Πανόραμα
στην Ελλάδα 3
Visual Arts
in Greece 3
17.12.08 - 22.02.09
www.visualarts.gr
ΥΠΟΥΡΓΕΙΟ ΠΟΛΙΤΙΣΜΟΥ
MINISTRY OF CULTURE
ΚΡΑΤΙΚΟ ΜΟΥΣΕΙΟ ΣΥΓΧΡΟΝΗΣ ΤΕΧΝΗΣ
STATE MUSEUM OF CONTEMPORARY ART
ΚΕΝΤΡΟ ΣΥΓΧΡΟΝΗΣ ΤΕΧΝΗΣ ΘΕΣΣΑΛΟΝΙΚΗΣ
CONTEMPORARY ART CENTER OF THESSALONIKI
Το Κ.Μ.Σ.Τ. και το Κ.Σ.Τ.Θ. επιχορηγούνται από το Υπουργείο Πολιτισμού
17.12.2008 - 22.02.2009
Έκθεση 47 καλλιτεχνών
"Και τώρα;"
Κ.Μ.Σ.Τ., Μονή Λαζαριστών
17.12.2008 - 18.01.2009, Α' φάση
23.01.2009 - 22.02.2009, Β' φάση
Έκθεση 75 Ελλήνων καλλιτεχνών
«Δημιουργώ, άρα Υπάρχω»
Κ.Σ.Τ.Θ., Αποθήκη Β1, λιμάνι Θεσσαλονίκης
20.02.2009
Ημερίδα "Τέχνη για το κοινό ή με το κοινό;
Συλλογικά εγχειρήματα στο δημόσιο χώρο"
21.02.2009
Συνέδριο "Διαχείριση σύγχρονης τέχνης"
Ξεναγήσεις για το κοινό κάθε Κυριακή
Εκπαιδευτικά προγράμματα
Έκθεση εκδόσεων τέχνης 2007-2008
Πρόγραμμα προσβασιμότητας "Αγγίζοντας την τέχνη"

Εικαστικό Πανόραμα
στην Ελλάδα 3
Visual Arts
in Greece 3
17.12.08 - 22.02.09

Εικαστικό Πανόραμα
στην Ελλάδα 3
Visual Arts
in Greece 3
17.12.08 - 22.02.09
www.visualarts.gr

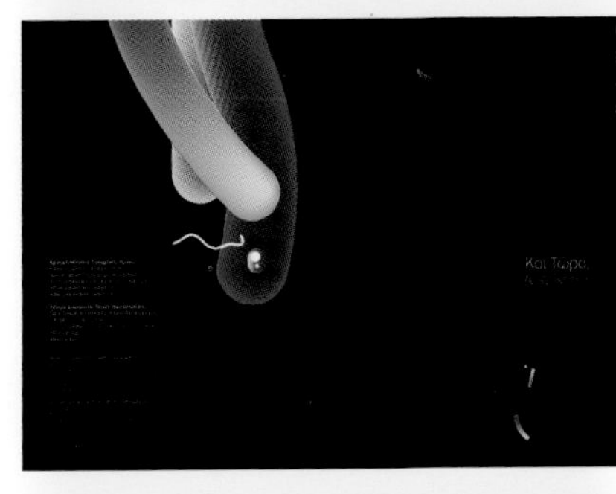

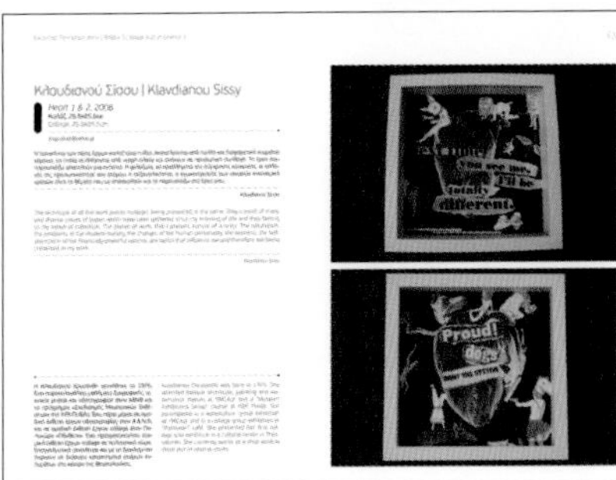

BRONZE
BRAND IMPLEMENTATION

TITLE
Regione Umbria
COMPANY
bcpt associati srl
CLIENT
Regione Umbria
COUNTRY
Italy

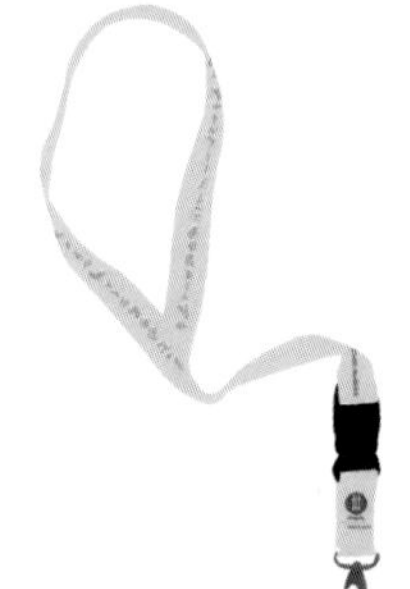

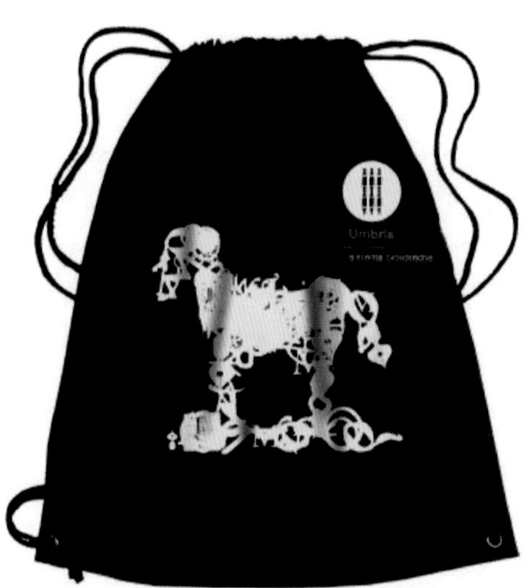

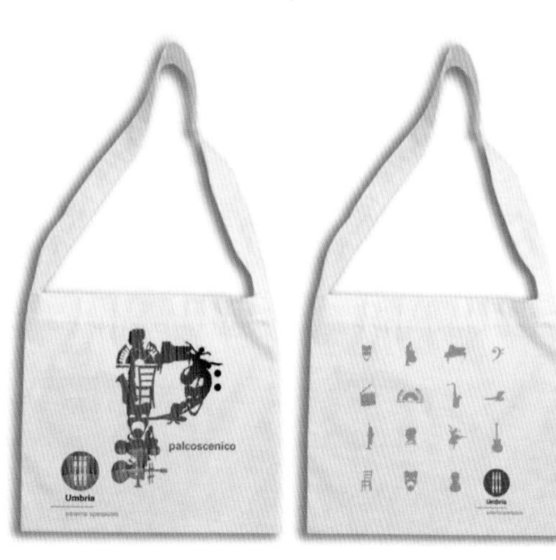

Umbria
sistema musei

H_2O
Umbria

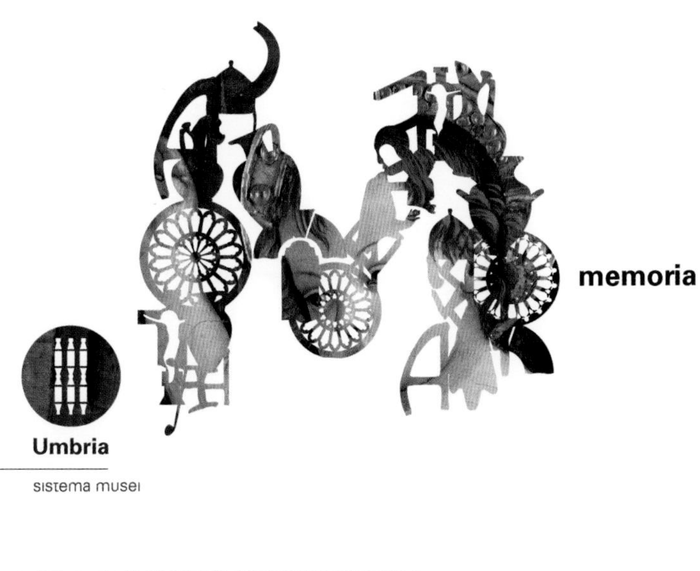
memoria
Umbria
sistema musei

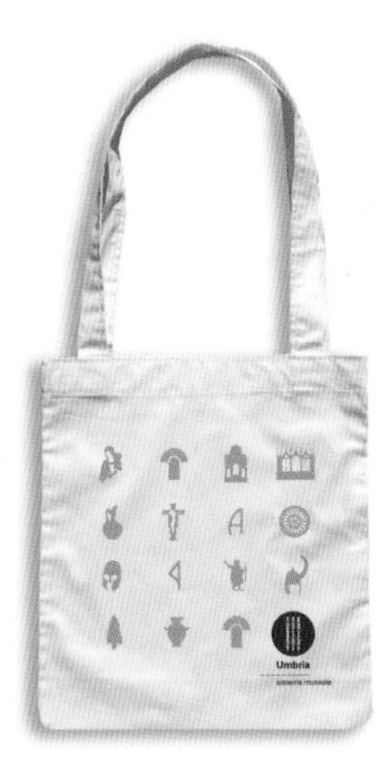

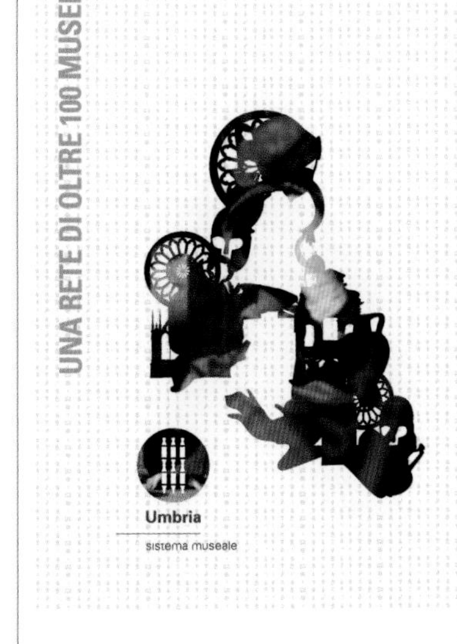
UNA RETE DI OLTRE 100 MUSEI
Umbria
sistema museale

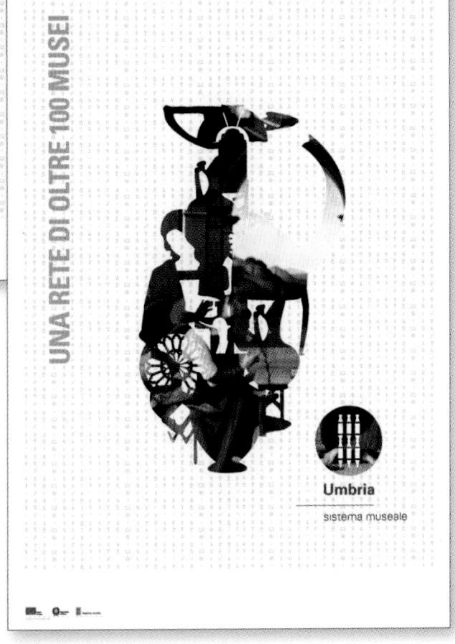
UNA RETE DI OLTRE 100 MUSEI
Umbria
sistema museale

UMBRIA AND ITS MUSEUMS
Umbria

UNA RETE
DI OLTRE 100 MUSEI
Umbria

BRONZE
BRAND IMPLEMENTATION

TITLE
Wortbruch (Word mine)
COMPANY
Rosagelb – Pinkyellow
CLIENT
Wortbruch project group
COUNTRY
Germany

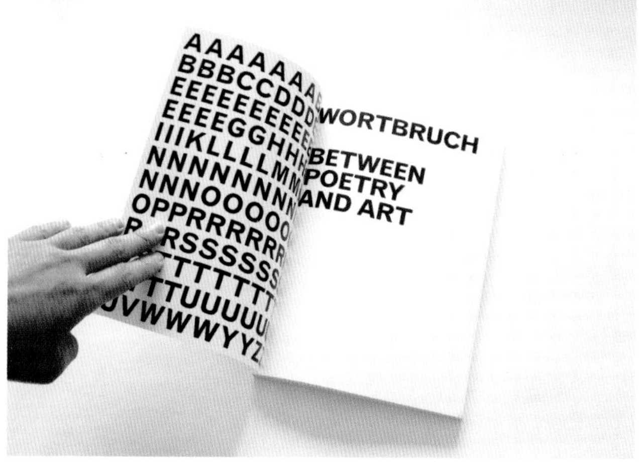

AAAAAAABBB
BBCCDDDEEEEE
EEEEEEEEEEE
GGHHIIIIIKLL
LLMMMNNNNN
NNNNNNNOOO
OOOOPPRRRR
RRRRRRSSSS
SSSSSTTTTT
TTTTTTUUUUU
UUVWWWYYZZ

Wortbruch – Between Poetry and Art Internationales Symposium 10.10.–1.11.2008 in Frankfurt

BRONZE
BRAND IMPLEMENTATION

TITLE
FreeDesigndom

COMPANY
Solar Initiative

CLIENTS
Premsela
Dutch Platform for Design and Fashion

URL
www.freedesigndom.com

COUNTRY
Netherlands

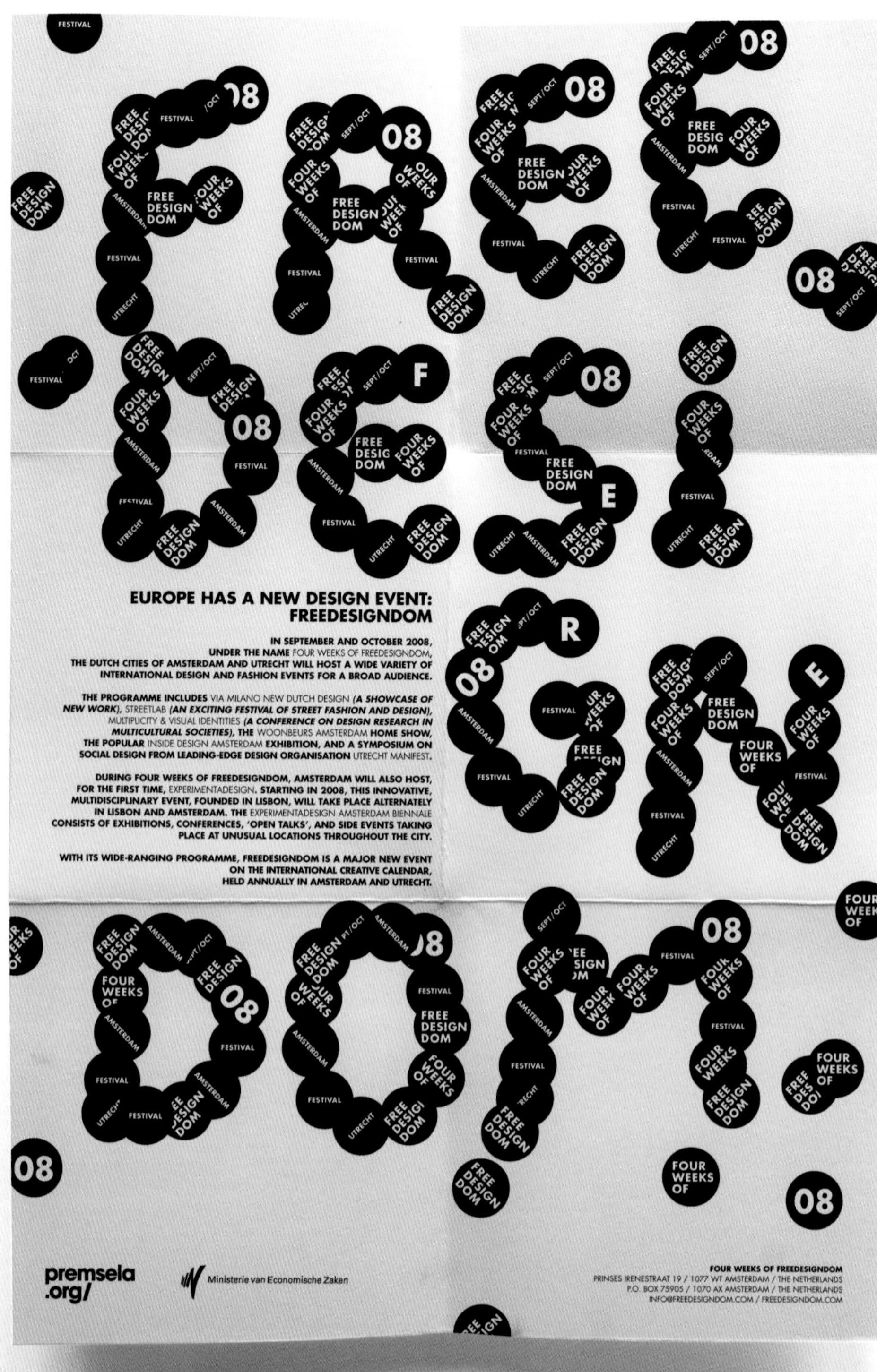

Solar Initiative
Oliver Helfrich
'sGravenhekje 1A
1011 TG Amsterdam
The Netherlands

Onderwerp
1e onderwerpregel
2de onderwerpregel

Datum
10 januari 2008
Afdeling
Management
Onze referentie
SJK / KvdL91006.01

Aanhef,

Guerillandio dit, quisis dunt acillandip endrerc iliquisl dolore ver aute duissit praessi tie tionse dit luscing enim dolore con hendrer sit la adidrerc illiquisl dolore ver aute duissit praessi tie tionse dit iuscing enim dolore con hendrer sit la adiat vel ulla facilla adit am, se consectet adipisim vendionsed tet, consequisi. Obor suscillandre velent vero el delessi at vel ulla facilla adit am, se consectet adipisim vendionsed tet, consequisl. Obor suscillandendrer sit la adiat vel ulla facilla adit am, se consectet adipisim vendionsed tet, consequisi. Obor suscillandre velent vero el delessi.Sisaim in vel ipit ullaorpero consenis do do con henis nos aut acidui tiniat, quismodion henim zzriure rostrud te dolenibh ex esequi euissequat, quat at.
Ing euipit autpat. Num ipit estrud deliquatue do eniam quat vendit volorperatet nibh eliquissi et loreraestie dolum veliqui tat nis niamcon enim dolore minismolent nostie veliquisim eros et, quisim iriustismod te faccum dolore eum ip etue dionse tie veliquisit augait, quis et adit lutpatem veliquamet, sit veniamconum volobore min verat nit luptatis dolesto od min vel utat aliquatue vendipisim zzriliqui exer suscidunt augiati onulpute velendi amconsent la faccum dolese dolortissis del Ing euipit autpat. Num ipit estrud deliquatue do eniam quat vendit volorperatet nibh eliquissi et loreraestie dolum veliqui tat nis niamcon enim dolore minismolent nostie veliquisim eros et, iurerat nonsequ ipiscidunt vel in eum quat. Lis nim veliqui siscips ustrud enliqui tatisi ut praessi.Ing euipit autpat. Num ipit estrud deliquatue do eniam quat vendit volorperatet nibh eliquissi et loreraestie dolum veliqui tat nis niamcon enim dolore minismolent nostie veliquisim eros et.
An henis estrud dolorer iureet lut ilit eum iurer alis nonsenim nostio dunt luptat wisl.
It velis autpat praessequam et adigniam, conse molorti ssenibh ent alis ad er sustismod magnim dolesto erosto od dolore essi te tat.

Hoogachtend,

Naam
Functie

FESTIVAL
08
FOUR WEEKS OF
FREE DESIGN DOM
UTRECHT
SEPT/OCT

EUROPE HAS A NEW DESIGN EVENT:
FREEDESIGNDOM

IN SEPTEMBER AND OCTOBER 2008,
UNDER THE NAME
FOUR WEEKS OF FREEDESIGNDOM,
THE DUTCH CITIES OF AMSTERDAM
AND UTRECHT WILL HOST
A WIDE VARIETY OF INTERNATIONAL
DESIGN AND FASHION EVENTS
FOR A BROAD AUDIENCE.

VANESSA VAN HOUTUM
PROJECT MANAGER

T +31 (0)20 34 49 449
F +31 (0)20 34 49 443
M +31 (0)6 413 154 34

FREEDESIGNDOM
PRINSES IRENESTRAAT 19
1077 WT AMSTERDAM
THE NETHERLANDS
P.O. BOX 75905
1070 AX AMSTERDAM
THE NETHERLANDS

VANESSA@FREEDESIGNDOM.COM
FREEDESIGNDOM.COM

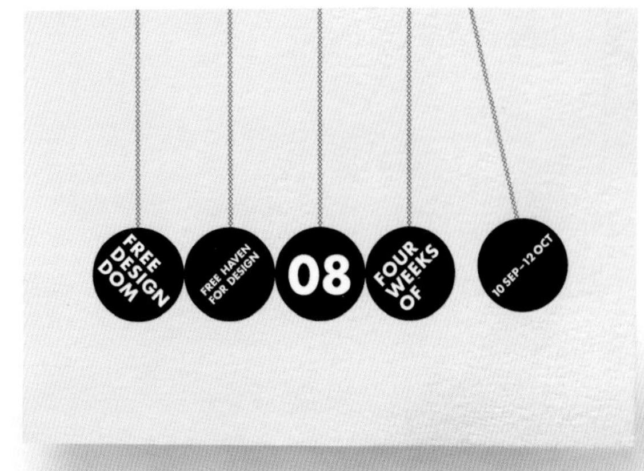

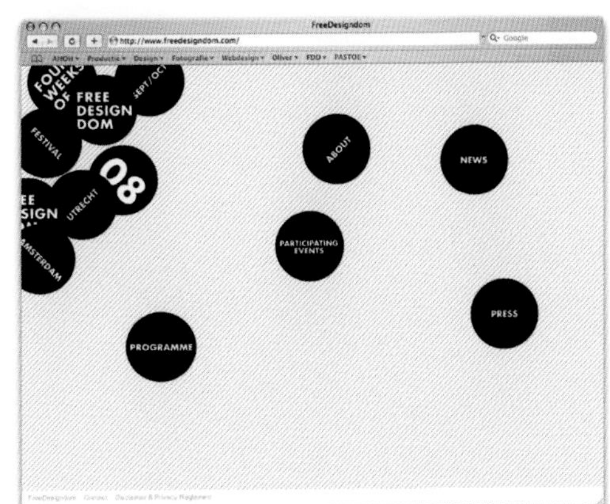

GOLD
COMPANY IMPLEMENTATION

TITLE
Messkunst
COMPANY
Fuenfwerken Design AG
CLIENT
Messkunst
URL
www.messkunst.com
COUNTRY
Germany

97,667 mm
85,883 mm **messkunst** 67,48 pt

An arresting identity. A few numbers and some words. A principle of arrangement. The curious viewer will quickly decipher the proposed code. Measuring. The logo is systematically presented with its vertical and horizontal coordinates on the page, and its own dimension is expressed in point size. A formidably effective system which, once understood by those who take the trouble to discover it, enables you to identity the company and its activity. A very simple idea with near-infinite potential; an invitation to dream up all its possible applications. This execution reflects a growing tendency in contemporary visual design: to invent a visual code based on a minimalist but highly modular register, rather than confining an identity in an extremely rigid system that ends up getting old and needing ever more fastidious supervision.

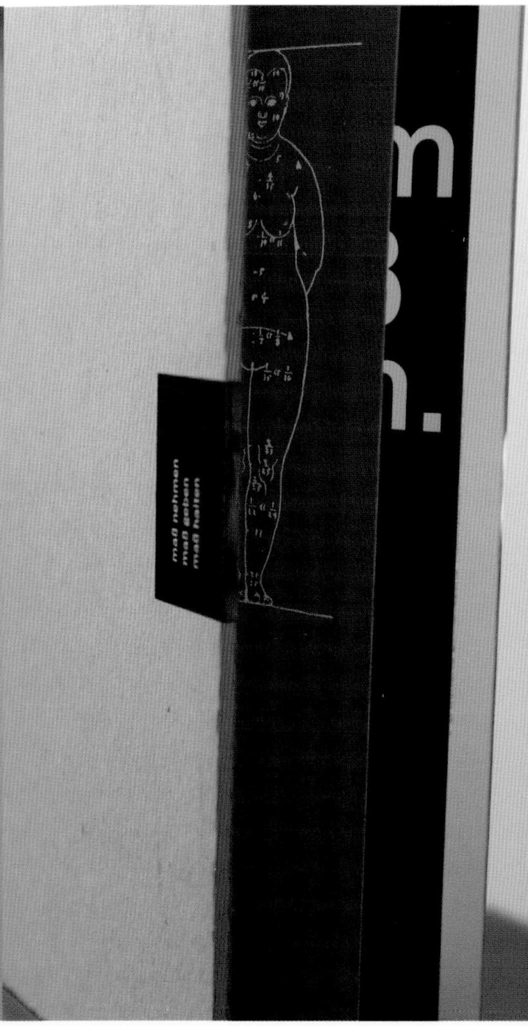

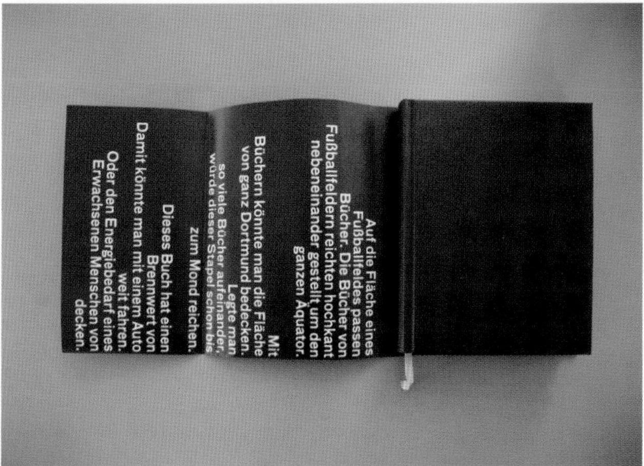
Auf die Fläche eines
Fußballfeldes passen
Bücher. Die Bücher von
Fußballfeldern reichten hochkant
nebeneinander gestellt um den
ganzen Äquator.
Mit
Büchern könnte man die Fläche
von ganz Dortmund bedecken.
Legte man
so viele Bücher aufeinander,
würde dieser Stapel schon bis
zum Mond reichen.
Dieses Buch hat einen
Brennwert von
Damit könnte man mit einem Auto
weit fahren.
Oder den Energiebedarf eines
Erwachsenen Menschen von
decken.

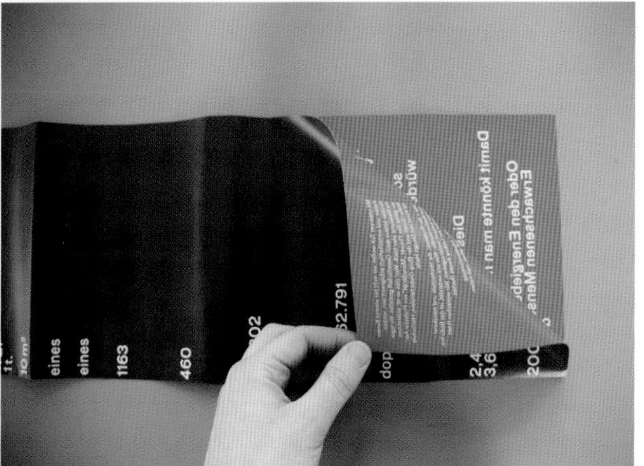
eines
eines
1163
460

GOLD
COMPANY IMPLEMENTATION

TITLE
Carrerotondes
COMPANY
a | part
CLIENT
Carrerotondes
URL
www.carrerotondes.lu
COUNTRY
Luxembourg

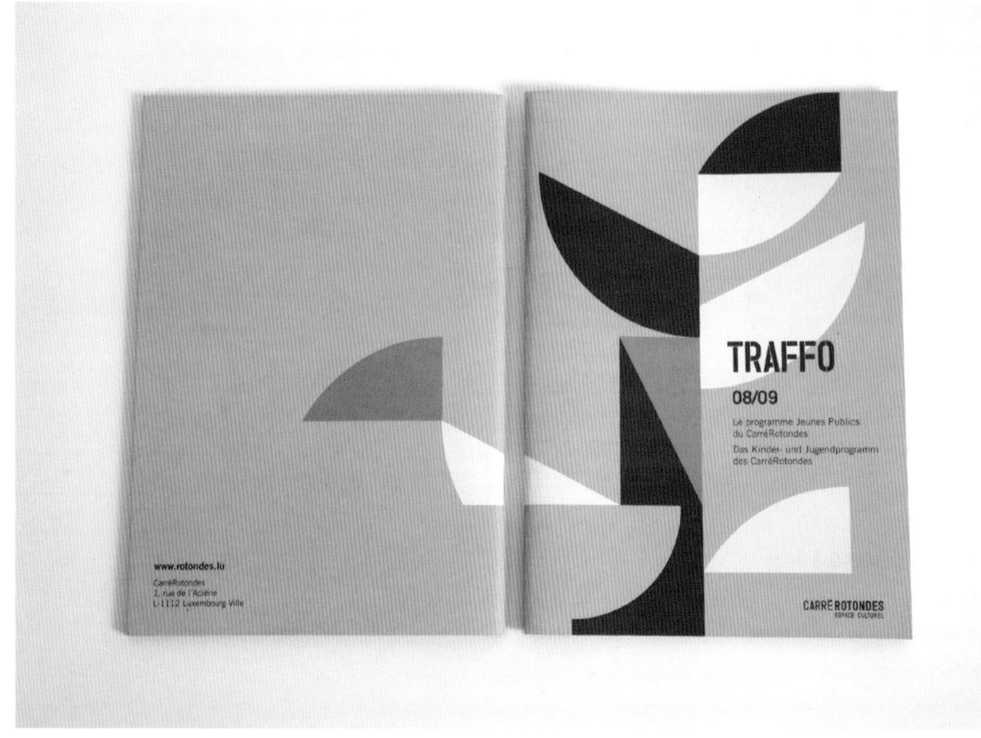

CARRĒ ROTONDES
ESPACE CULTUREL

CARRĒ ROTONDES
ESPACE CULTUREL

CARRĒ ROTONDES
ESPACE CULTUREL

CARRĒ ROTONDES
ESPACE CULTUREL

CARRĒ ROTONDES
ESPACE CULTUREL

CARRĒ ROTONDES
ESPACE CULTUREL

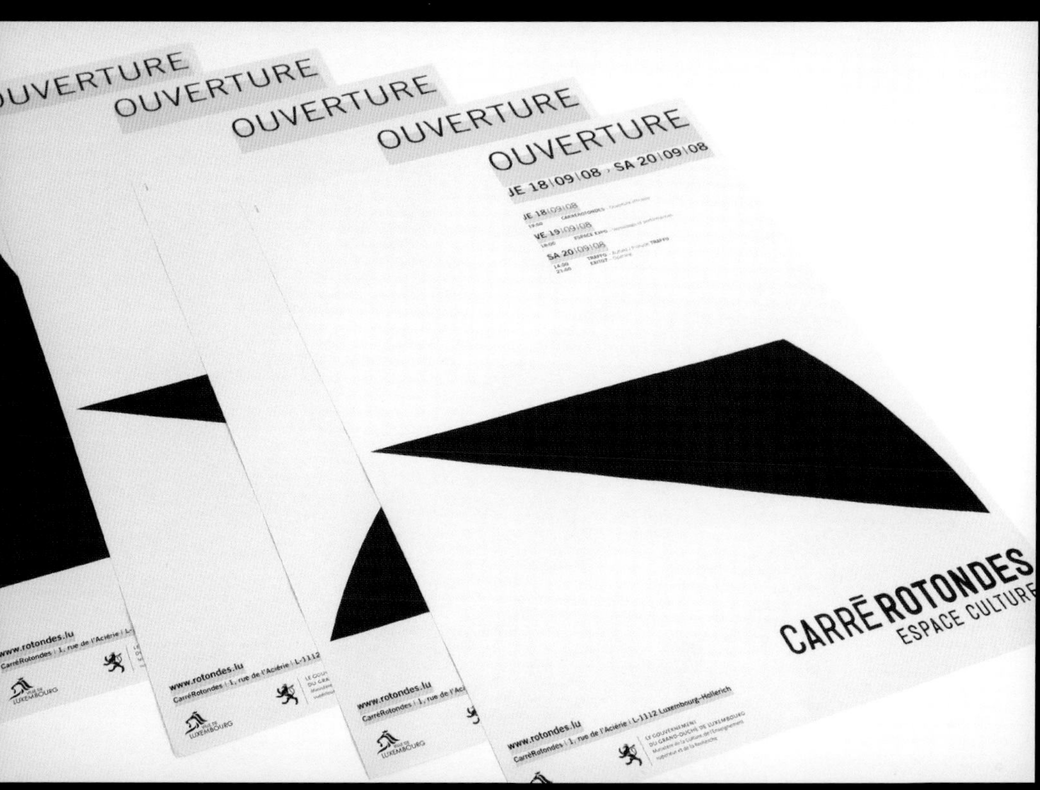

Carrérotondes is a cultural venue with more of a youth-audience focus. This identity, based on simple geometric forms, is inspired by the Chinese game of tangram. The identity thus acquires a playful dimension, and become multiform. This choice allows vast creative scope that is easy to memorise. Another open system which, despite its apparent simplicity, turns out to be rich and endlessly renewed, able to switch from abstraction to more narrative figures.

SILVER
COMPANY IMPLEMENTATION

TITLE
Getronics visual identity
COMPANY
Koeweiden Postma
CLIENT
Getronics
DESIGNERS
Menno van Waardhuizen
Jorn Dal
Peter van Deursen
Wendy Grootscholten
CREATIVE DIRECTOR
Jacques Koeweiden
DESIGN DIRECTOR
Menno van Waardhuizen
ILLUSTRATOR
Onno van Braam
Tim van der Wiel
INTERACTION DESIGNER
Tim van der Wiel
URL
www.getronics.com
COUNTRY
Netherlands

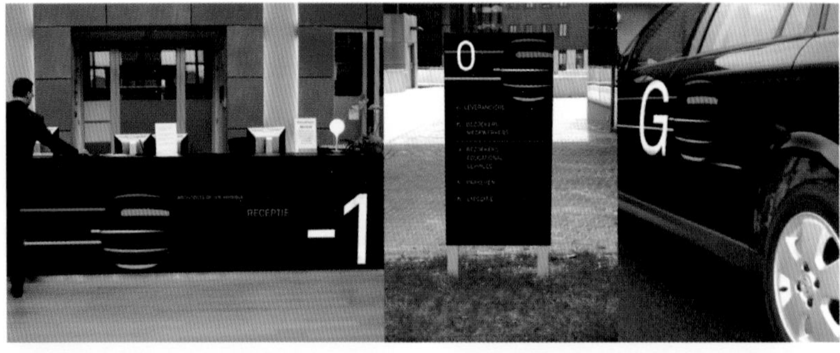

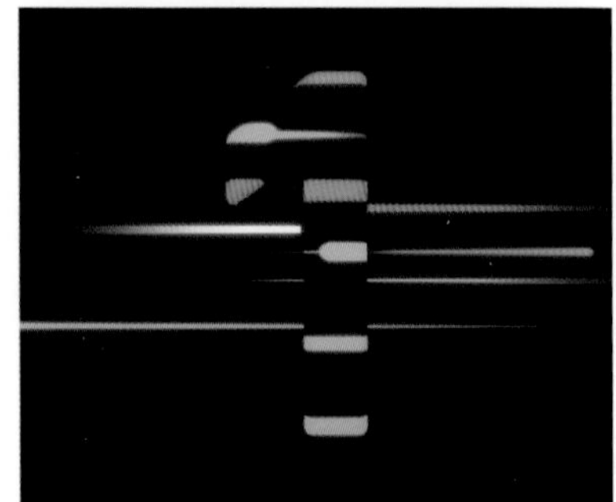

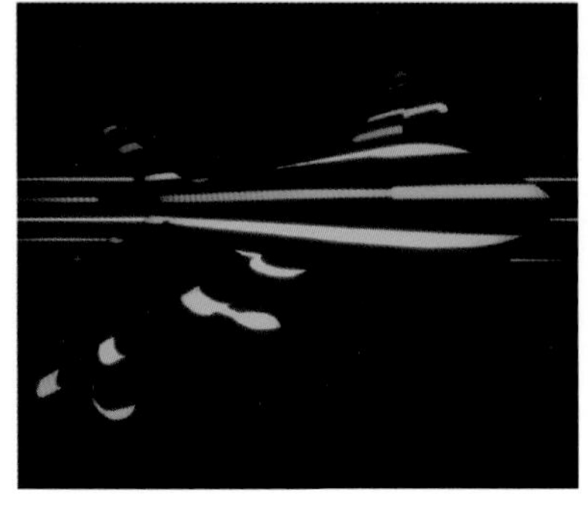

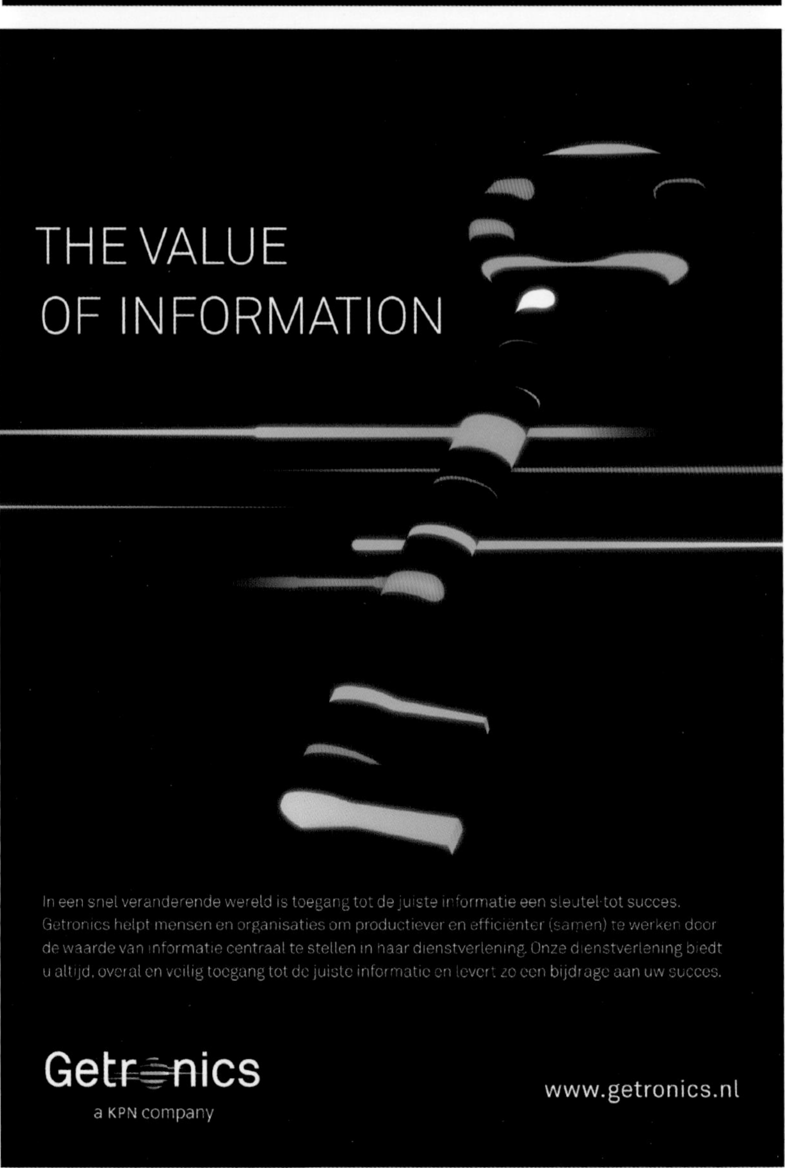

SILVER
COMPANY IMPLEMENTATION

TITLE
Coos!
COMPANY
Trapped in suburbia
CLIENT
Coos!
DESIGNERS
Cuby Gerards
Karin Langeveld
ART DIRECTORS
Cuby Gerards
Karin Langeveld
COUNTRY
Netherlands

COOS!

PUBLIC RELATIONS SPONSORING EVENEMENTEN COMMUNICATIE

BRONZE
COMPANY IMPLEMENTATION

TITLE
Patient Diagnostics
COMPANY
Mixer
CLIENT
Patient Diagnostics AG
URL
www.patientdiagnostics.ch
COUNTRY
Switzerland

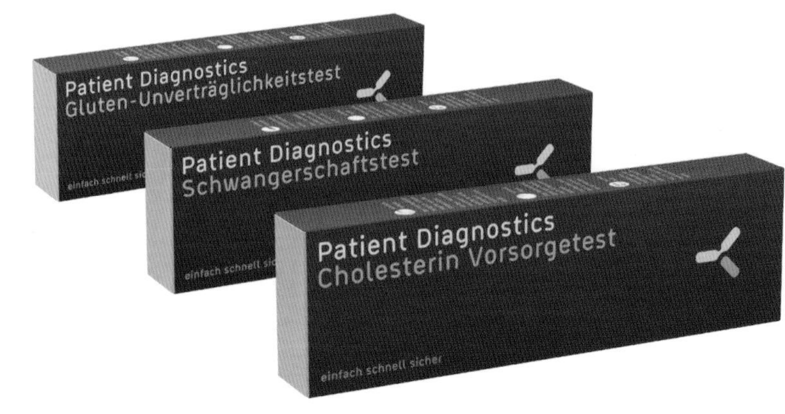

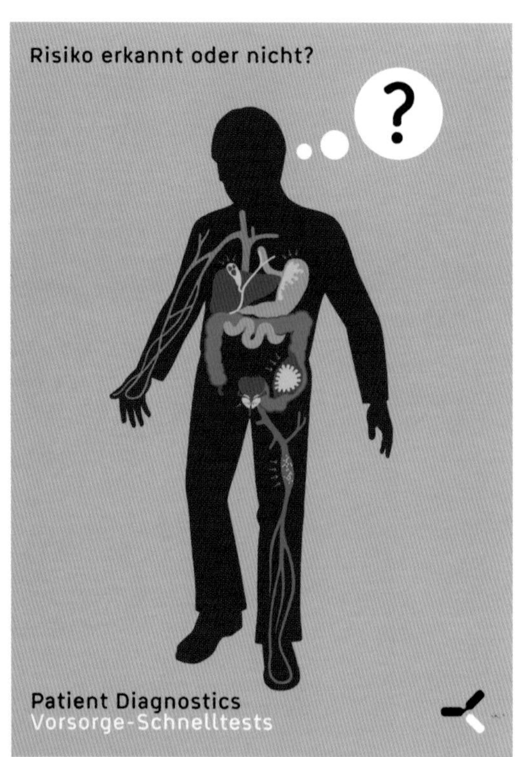

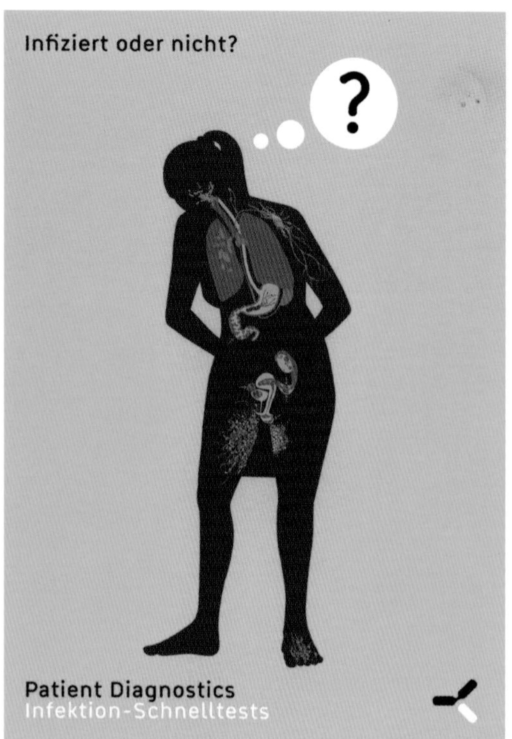

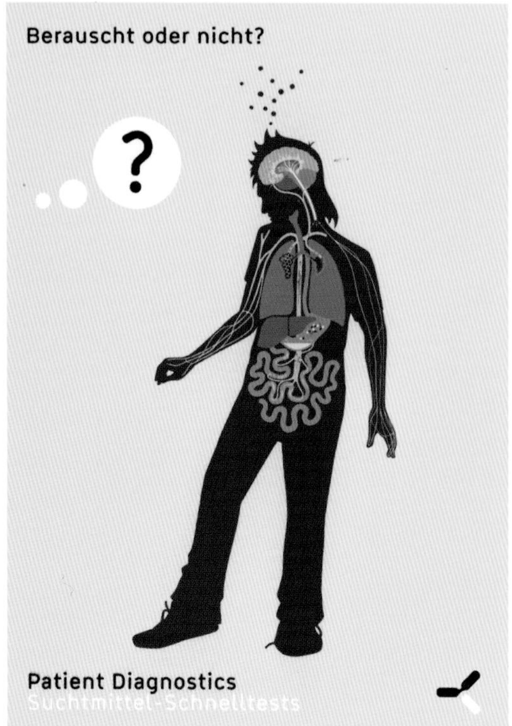

BRONZE
COMPANY IMPLEMENTATION

TITLE
ASVZ
COMPANY
Koeweiden Postma
CLIENT
ASVZ
URL
www.asvz.nl
COUNTRY
Netherlands

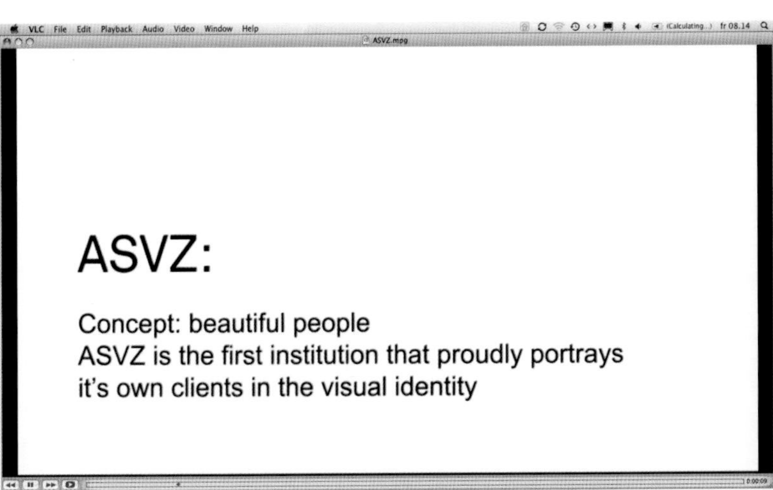

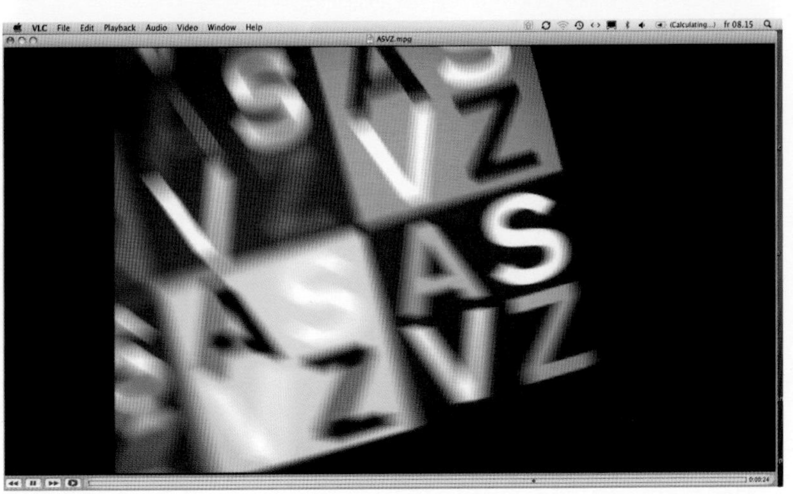

BRONZE
COMPANY IMPLEMENTATION

TITLE
Wide Photography
COMPANY
Vidale-Gloesener Sarl
CLIENT
Wide Photography
COUNTRY
Luxembourg

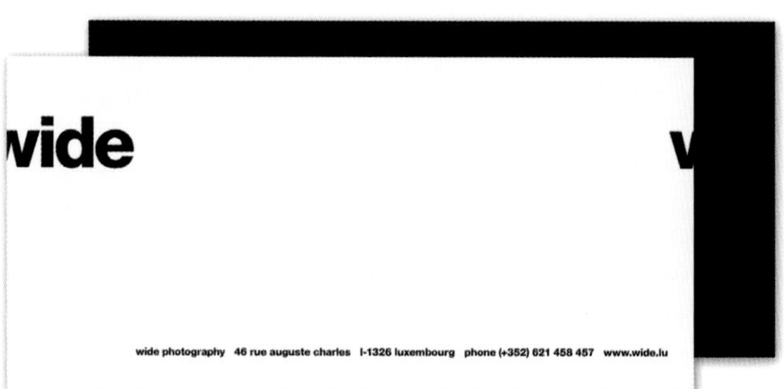

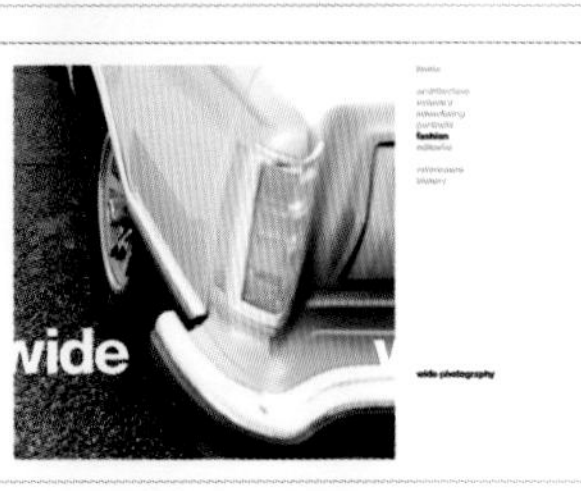

BRONZE
COMPANY IMPLEMENTATION

TITLE
DWP / Digital Water Pavillion
COMPANY
studio FM milano srl
CLIENT
Ayuntamiento de Zaragoza
URL
www.digitalwaterpavilion.com
COUNTRY
Italy

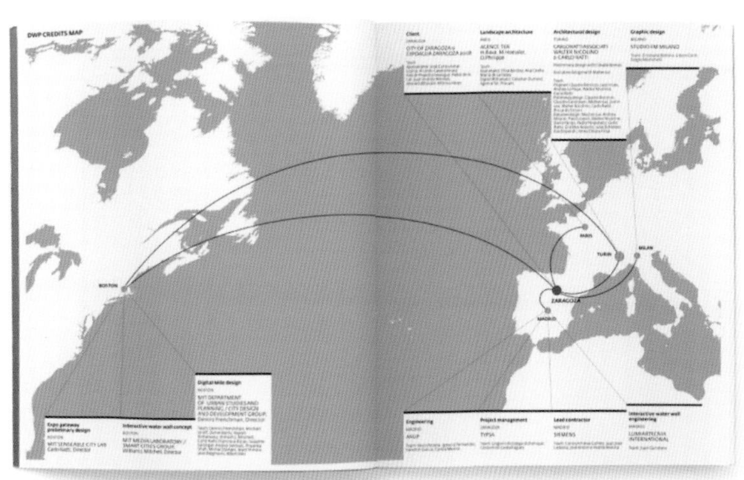

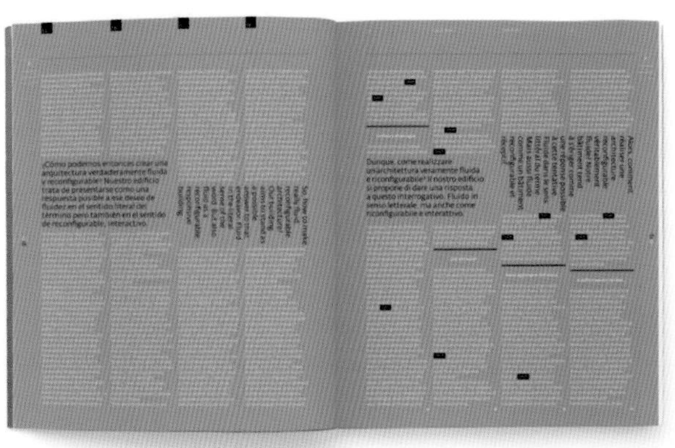

dshare

ving Brands

dshare

ted Kingdom

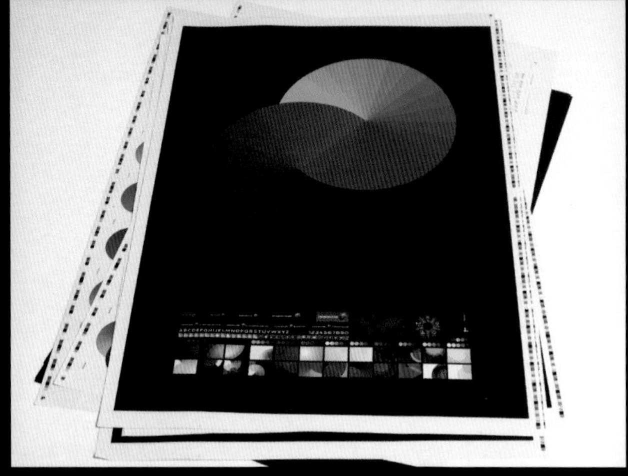

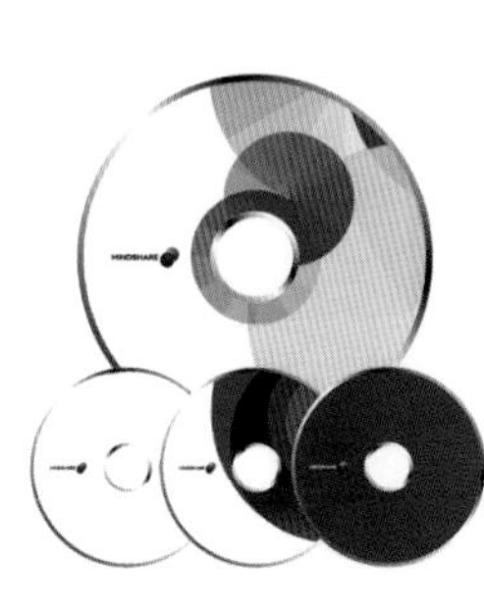

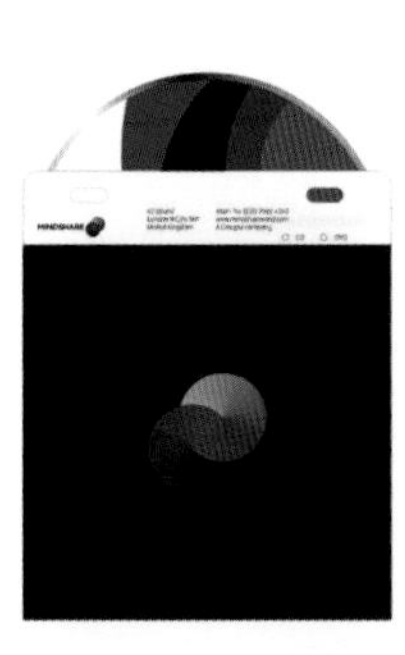

BRONZE
COMPANY IMPLEMENTATION

TITLE
Swisscom
COMPANY
Moving Brands
CLIENT
Swisscom
COUNTRY
United Kingdom

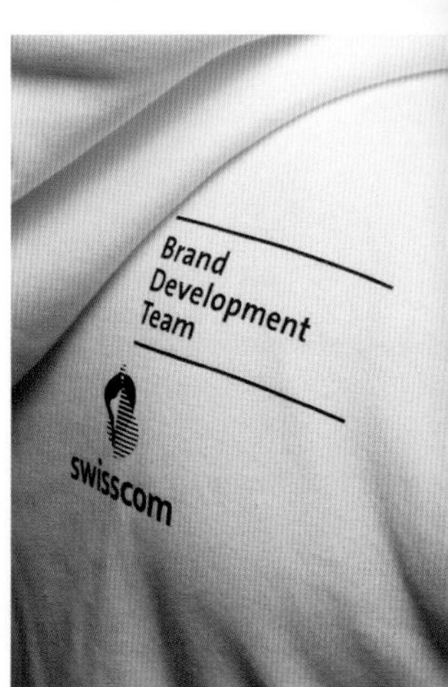

BRONZE
COMPANY IMPLEMENTATION

TITLE
Geozug Ingenieure
COMPANY
Hotz & Hotz
CLIENT
Geozug Ingenieure
COUNTRY
Switzerland

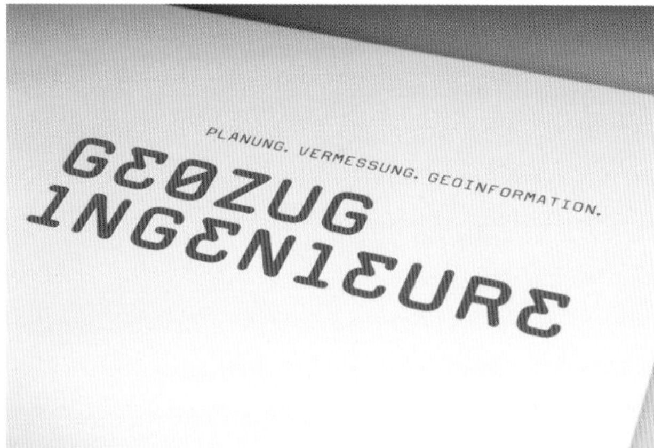

N47°11.5370'
GEØZUG
INGENIEURE
PLANUNG. VERMESSUNG. GEOINFORMATION.
WWW.GEOZUG.CH

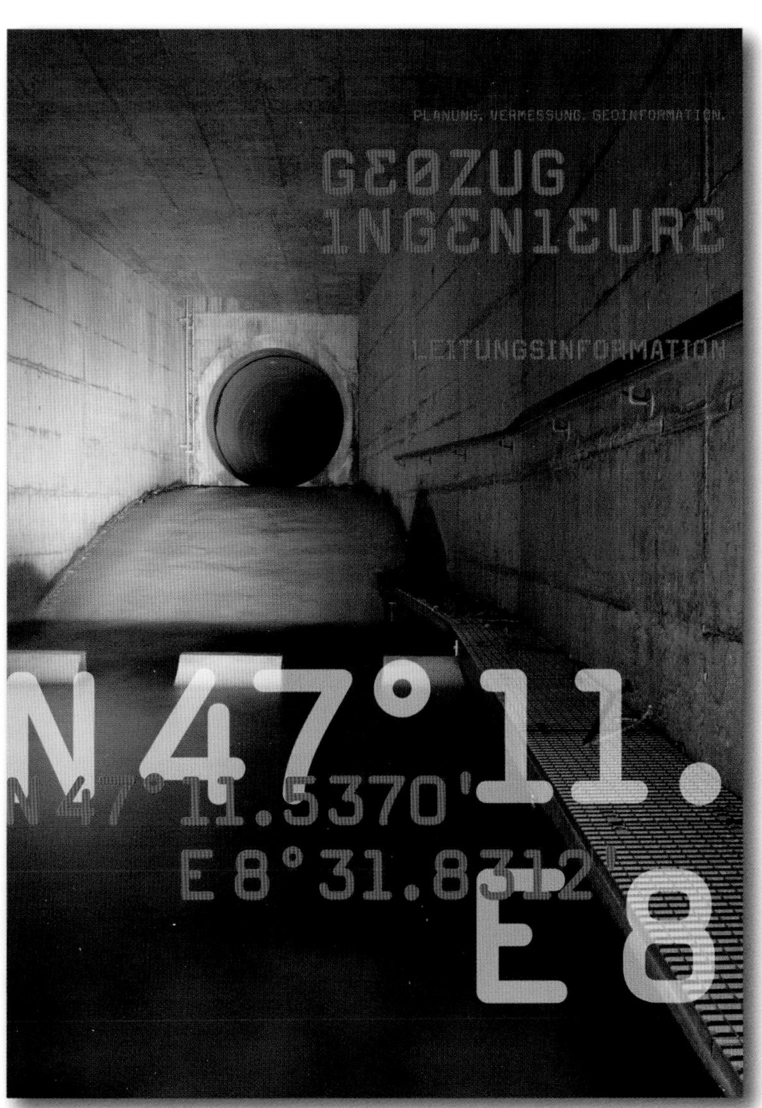
PLANUNG. VERMESSUNG. GEOINFORMATION.
GEØZUG
INGENIEURE
LEITUNGSINFORMATION
N47°11.
N47°11.5370'
E8°31.8312'
E8

PLANUNG. VERMESSUNG. GEOINFORMATION.
GEØZUG
INGENIEURE
PLANUNG. UMWELT
N47°11.
N47°11.5370'
E8°31.8312'
E8

PUBLICATIONS

GOLD
ANNUAL REPORT

TITLE
The way things are
COMPANY
Dietwee
CLIENT
Insingerde Beaufort N.V.
DESIGNERS
Jami Mitchel
Sybren Kuiper
ART DIRECTOR
Tirso Frances
CREATIVE DIRECTOR
Tirso Frances
DESIGNER DIRECTOR
Sybren Kuiper
ILLUSTRATOR
Gonda Poelman
PHOTOGRAPHER
Neil Massey
EDITOR
Aquarium writers
WRITER
Aquarium writers
COUNTRY
Netherlands

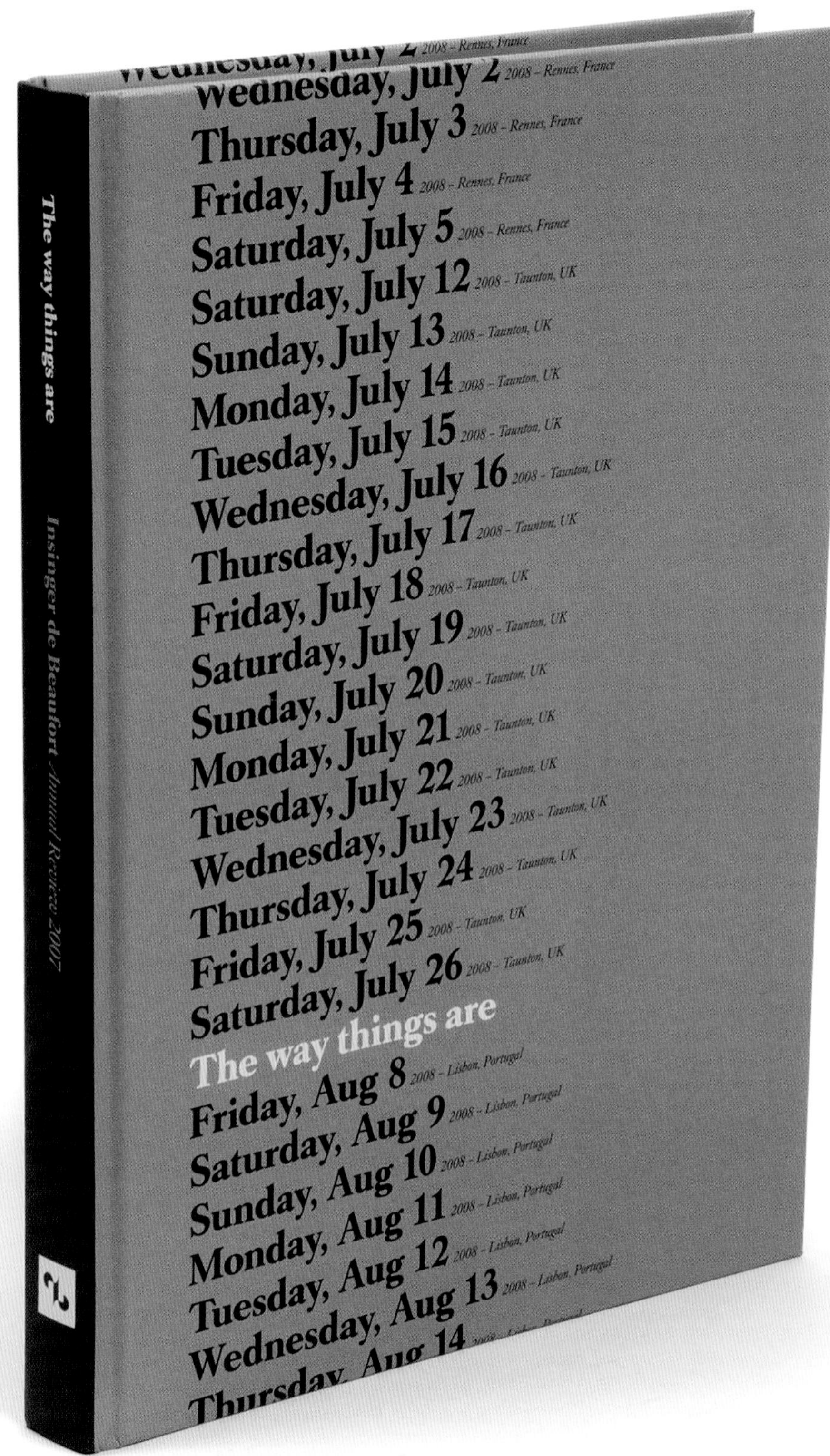

There were many contenders in this section, and plenty had a claim to victory. The jury reached its decision after lengthy discussion, with Dietwee's work getting the nod. Uncertainties: a fine theme for the annual report of a financial institution that is not skirting the global economic realities taking shape before our eyes. The jury was receptive to the relevance and realism of this original approach. The report comprises five booklets, each of which highlights a facet of the chosen message. The overall work benefits from total mastery of typography and of the visual organisation of the information.

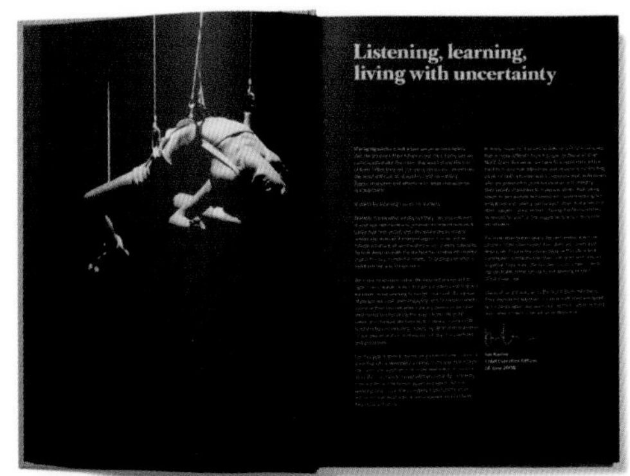

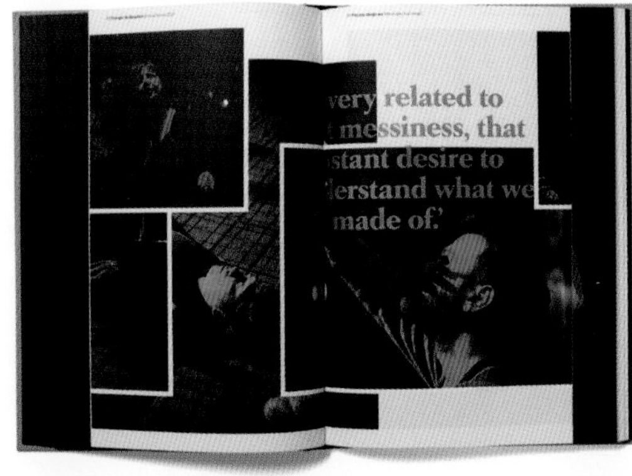

Consolidated Balance Sheet

as at 31 December before result appropriation

Consolidated Profit & Loss Account

for the year ended 31 December 2007

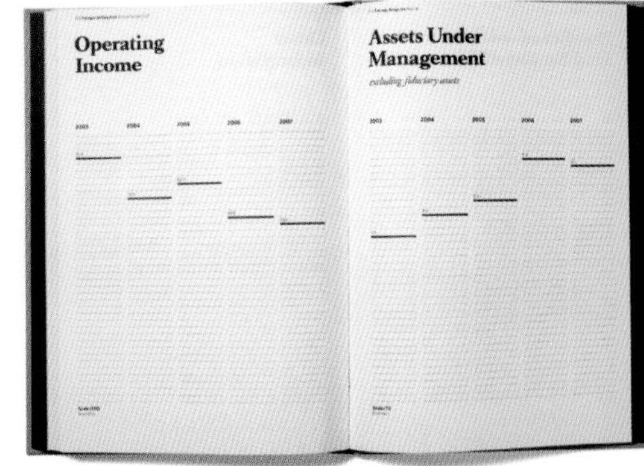

SILVER
ANNUAL REPORT

TITLE
Look/Book 2008
COMPANY
Rosebud, Inc.
CLIENTS
departure
wirtschaft
kunst und kultur gmbh
DESIGNER
Daniel Hammer
ART DIRECTOR
Raphael Drechsel
CREATIVE DIRECTOR
Ralph Herms
PHOTOGRAPHER
Martin Stöbich
EDITORS
Heinz Wolf
Dorothea Köb
COUNTRY
Germany

NINA
PETER
Fast wie eine Couture-Arbeit
Almost like doing couture

ANNA
AICHINGER
Liebeszeichen für Alphafrauen
Love signs for alpha women

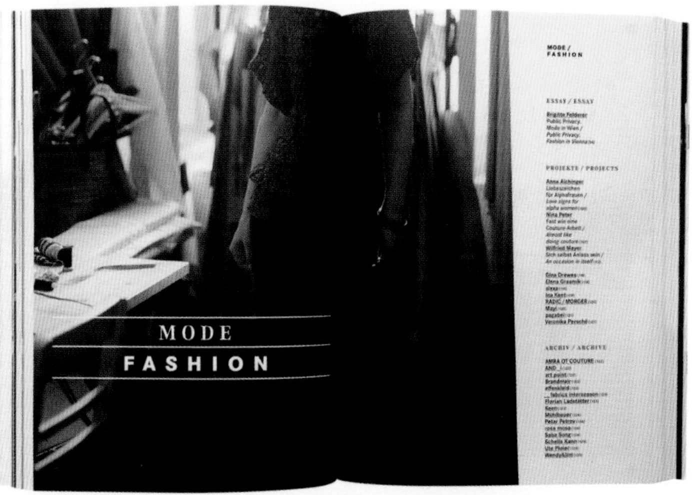
MODE
FASHION

DEPARTURE
FASHION NIGHT
8 FESTIVAL

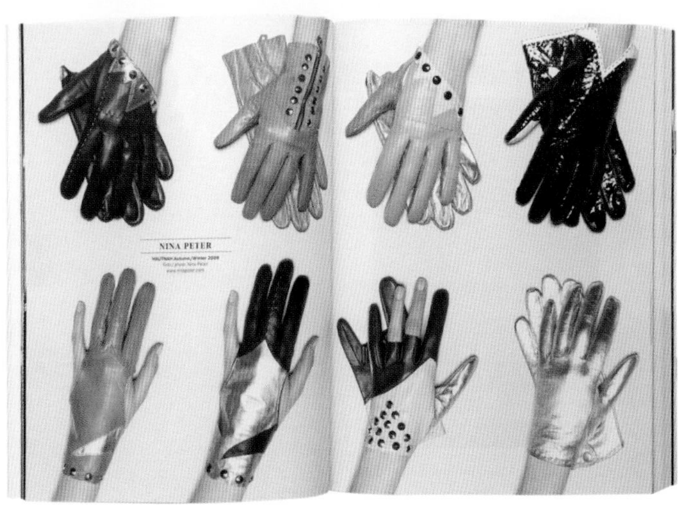
NINA PETER

INHALT
CONTENTS
EINLEITUNG
PREFACE
PRODUCT PLACEMENT
ARCHITEKTUR
ARCHITECTURE
MODE
FASHION

SILVER
ANNUAL REPORT

TITLE
Auf Hemd reimt sich fremd
COMPANY
Kochan & Partner
CLIENT
Studiosus Reisen Muenchen
CREATIVE DIRECTOR
Martin Summ
PHOTOGRAPHER
Dominik Parzinger
WRITERS
Sandra Hachmann
Ullrich Müller
Martin Rasper
Zehra Spindler
Gabriele Werner
OTHERS
Katja Knahn
Robert Iwen
Daniela Gattinger
COUNTRY
Germany

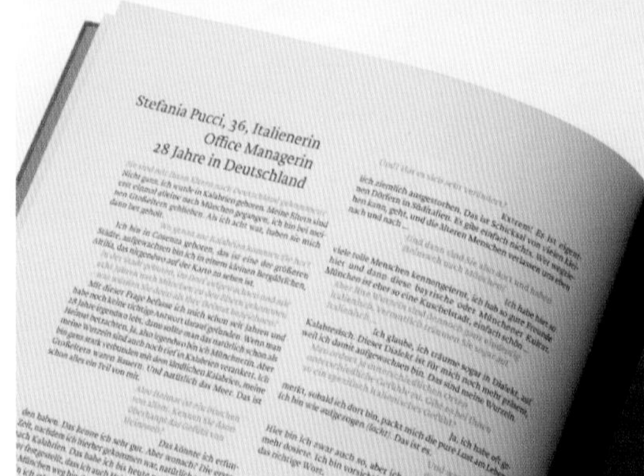

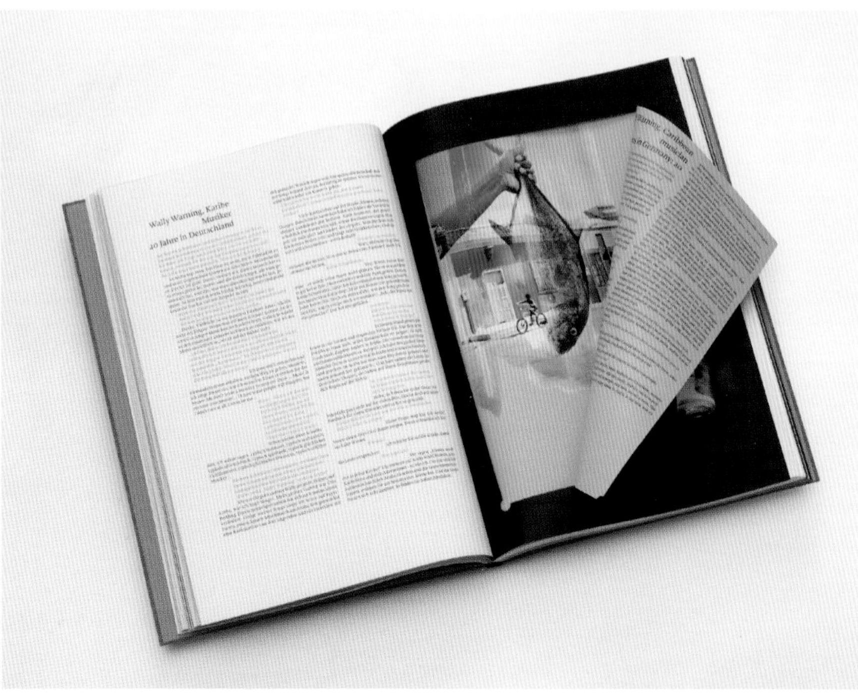

Wally Warning, Karibe
Musiker
20 Jahre in Deutschland

Gästezahlen 2008

Number of participants

Unternehmensgruppe Studiosus

Studiosus Group

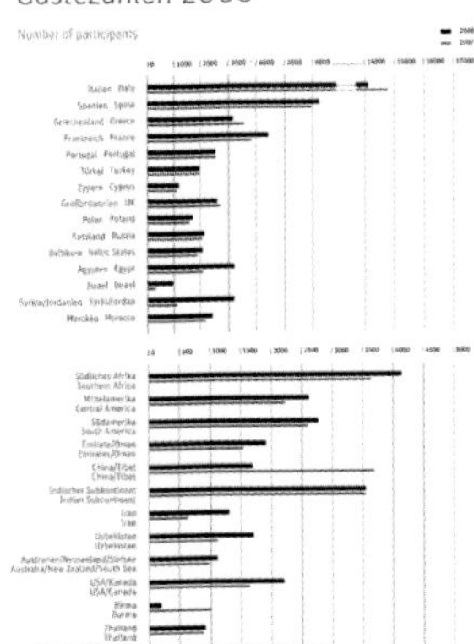

Stefania Pucci, 36, Italienerin
Office Managerin
28 Jahre in Deutschland

Lilli (10) und Lea (7) Kang
Chinesinnen, Schülerinnen
zehn und sieben Jahre in Deutschland

Das Studiosus-Unternehmensleitbild

Im Unternehmensleitbild von Studiosus sind die Richtlinien für das Handeln nach außen und innen festgeschrieben. Diese »inneren Werte« des Unternehmens besitzen für die Mitarbeiterinnen und Mitarbeiter eine hohe Verbindlichkeit.
Im Folgenden haben wir Auszüge aus dem Leitbild zu unserer Unternehmensvision, den Unternehmenszielen, der Unternehmenspolitik und den Unternehmensstrategien zusammengestellt.

Unternehmensvision

Die Unternehmensziele

SILVER
ANNUAL REPORT

TITLE
We're travelling...
COMPANY
Studio Kluif
CLIENT
Nedap
DESIGNERS
Paul Roeters
Christina Casnellie
ART DIRECTOR
Paul Roeters
DESIGN DIRECTOR
Sander Tielen
ILLUSTRATION
Christina Casnellie
WRITERS
Christina Casnellie
Paul Roeters
COUNTRY
Netherlands

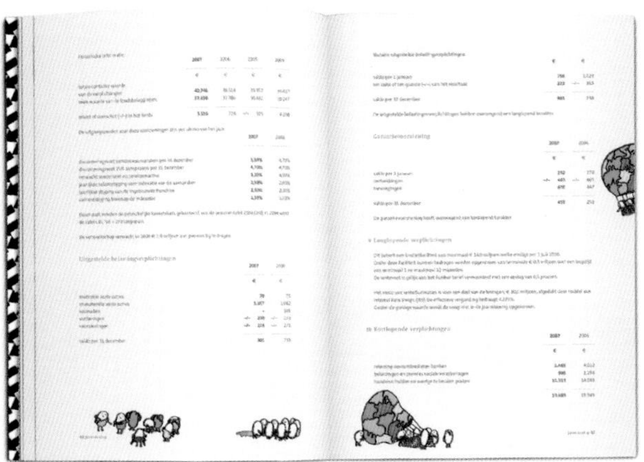

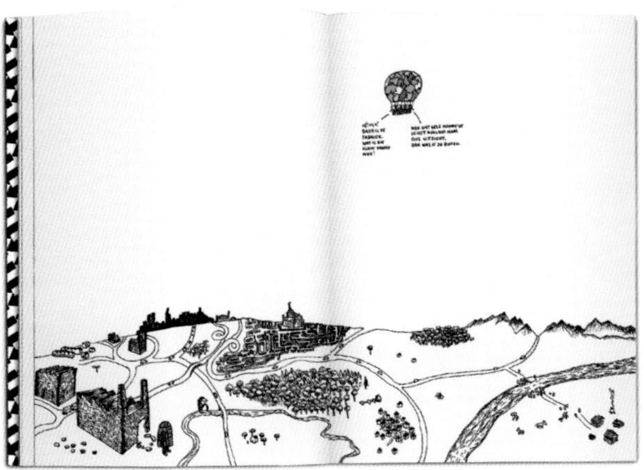

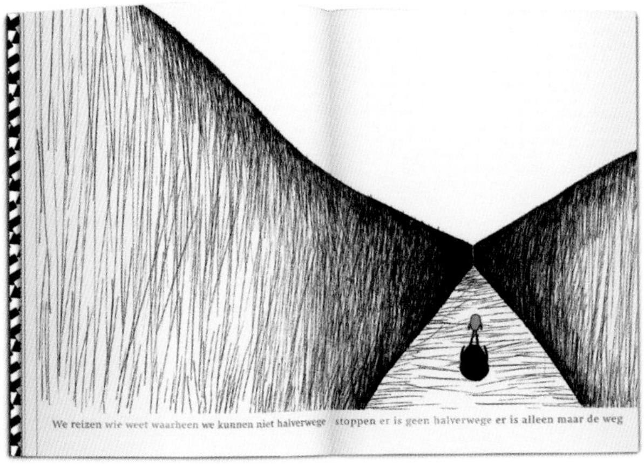
We reizen wie weet waarheen we kunnen niet halverwege stoppen er is geen halverwege er is alleen maar de weg

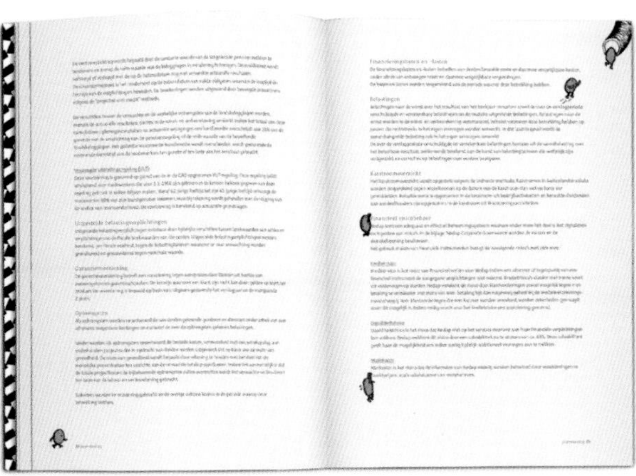

WERKEN!
WERKEN!
WERKEN!
WERKEN!
WERKEN!
WERKEN!
WERKEN!
WERKEN!
WERKEN!
AAN HET WERK

SILVER
ANNUAL REPORT

TITLE
Aids Fonds Jaarverslag 2007
COMPANY
Dietwee
CLIENT
Aids Fund
DESIGNERS
Penny Lee
Stijn van de Ven
ART DIRECTOR
Ron Faas
CREATIVE DIRECTOR
Ron Faas
DESIGN DIRECTOR
Penny Lee
ILLUSTRATOR
David Boon
PHOTOGRAPHERS
Jan van Breda
Adriaan Backer
Lodewijk van Duijvensteijn
Giorgos Gripeos
Jan Hooiveld
Raymond van Jaarsveld
Harmen de Jong
Geert van Kesteren
Ilse van de Reep
JanCarel Warffemius
EDITOR
Aids Fonds
WRITER
Aids Fonds
COUNTRY
Netherlands

Aids F
onds – jaar
verslag 200
7,

Het jaar
tweeduizend-
zeven
Ondersteuning
van mensen
met hiv

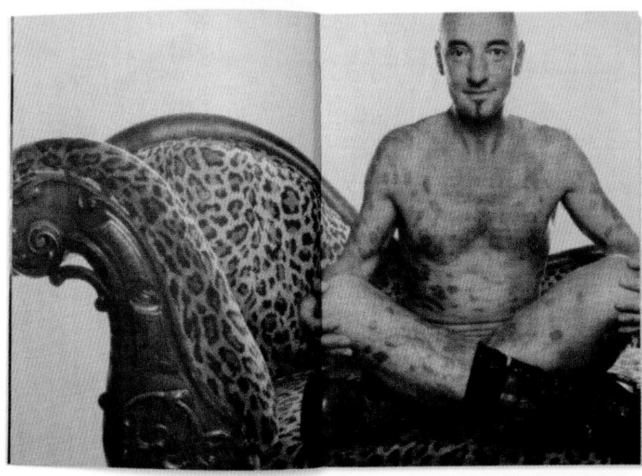

AIDSFONDS
COLLECT

"Condooms be
spreekbaar ma
ken, is in A
een grotere uitda
ging dan om h
t continent va
condooms t
rzien"

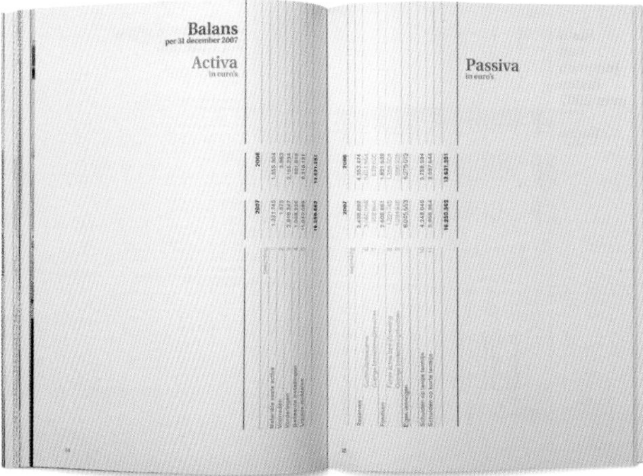
Balans
per 31 december 2007
Activa
In euro's
Passiva
In euro's

BRONZE
ANNUAL REPORT

TITLE
365 / 21246
COMPANY
TRIDVAJEDAN market communication Ltd.
CLIENT
Ericsson Nikola Tesla
COUNTRY
Croatia

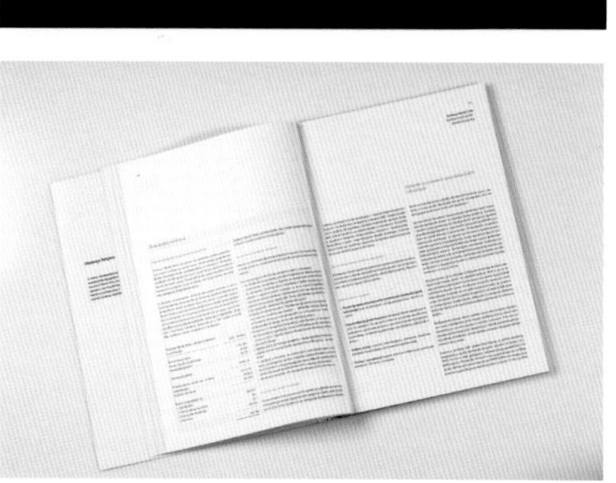

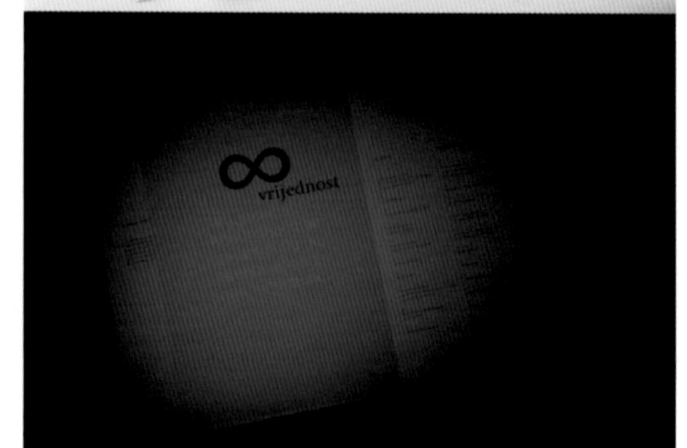

BRONZE
ANNUAL REPORT

TNT Annual Report 2007

Fabrique Communicatie en Design

TNT

Netherlands

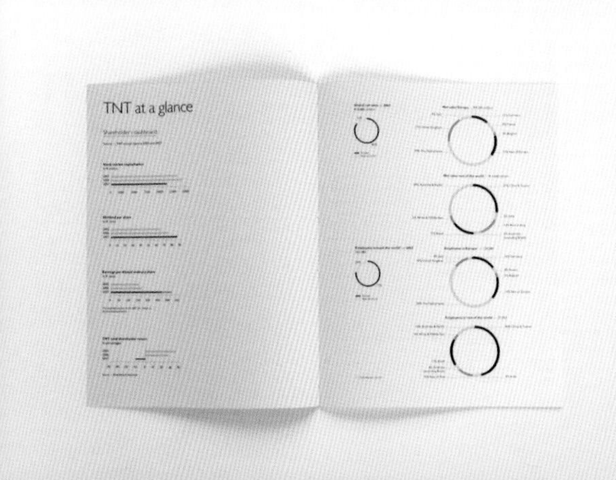

BRONZE
ANNUAL REPORT

TITLE
Internationalisation

COMPANY
Simon & Goetz Design GmbH & Co. KG

CLIENT
Sal. Oppenheim jr. & Cie.

COUNTRY
Germany

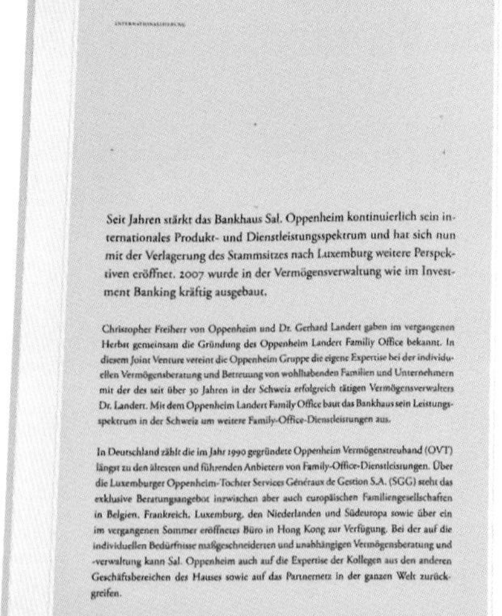

Seit Jahren stärkt das Bankhaus Sal. Oppenheim kontinuierlich sein internationales Produkt- und Dienstleistungsspektrum und hat sich nun mit der Verlagerung des Stammsitzes nach Luxemburg weitere Perspektiven eröffnet. 2007 wurde in der Vermögensverwaltung wie im Investment Banking kräftig ausgebaut.

Christopher Freiherr von Oppenheim und Dr. Gerhard Landert gaben im vergangenen Herbst gemeinsam die Gründung des Oppenheim Landert Familiy Office bekannt. In diesem Joint Venture vereint die Oppenheim Gruppe die eigene Expertise bei der individuellen Vermögensberatung und Betreuung von wohlhabenden Familien und Unternehmern mit der des seit über 30 Jahren in der Schweiz erfolgreich tätigen Vermögensverwalters Dr. Landert. Mit dem Oppenheim Landert Family Office baut das Bankhaus sein Leistungsspektrum in der Schweiz um weitere Family-Office-Dienstleistungen aus.

In Deutschland zählt die im Jahr 1990 gegründete Oppenheim Vermögenstreuhand (OVT) längst zu den ältesten und führenden Anbietern von Family-Office-Dienstleistungen. Über die Luxemburger Oppenheim-Tochter Services Généraux de Gestion S.A. (SGG) steht das exklusive Beratungsangebot inzwischen aber auch europäischen Familiengesellschaften in Belgien, Frankreich, Luxemburg, den Niederlanden und Südeuropa sowie über ein im vergangenen Sommer eröffnetes Büro in Hong Kong zur Verfügung. Bei der auf die individuellen Bedürfnisse maßgeschneiderten und unabhängigen Vermögensberatung und -verwaltung kann Sal. Oppenheim auch auf die Expertise der Kollegen aus den anderen Geschäftsbereichen des Hauses sowie auf das Partnernetz in der ganzen Welt zurückgreifen.

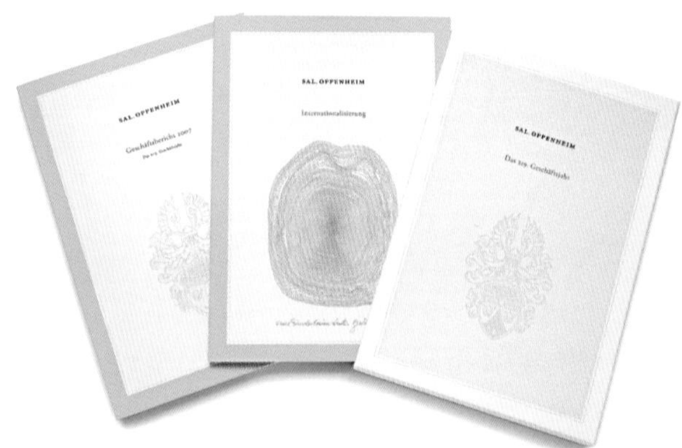

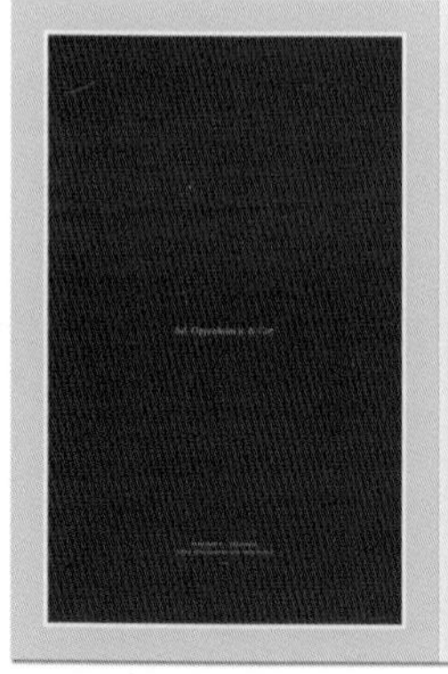

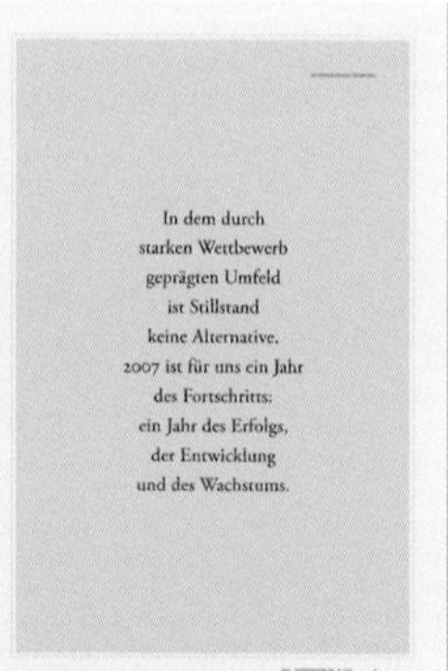

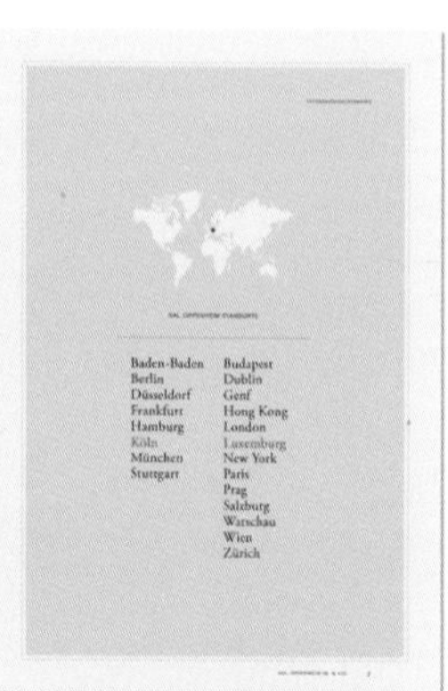

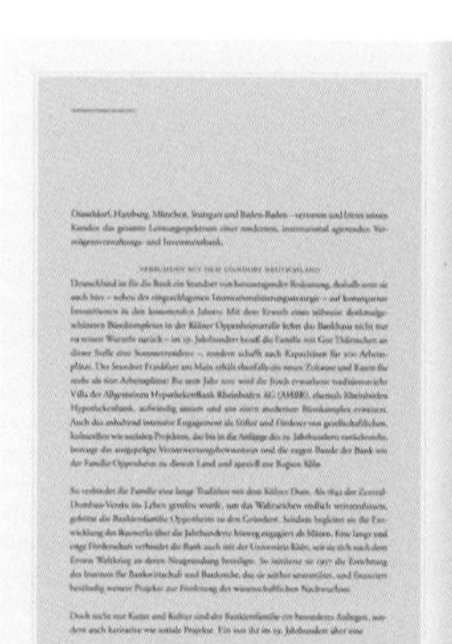

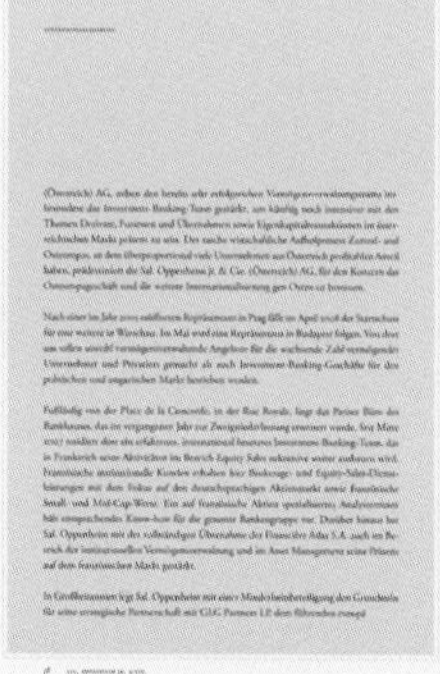

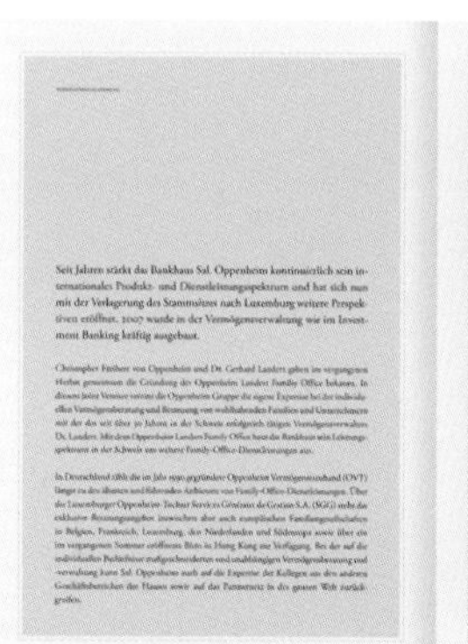

BRONZE
ANNUAL REPORT

TITLE
Haag Wonen
COMPANY
Studio 't Brandt Weer
CLIENTS
housing corporation
Haag Wonen
COUNTRY
Netherlands

BRONZE
ANNUAL REPORT

TITLE
SSB
COMPANY
fasett
CLIENT
Sandnes Sparebank
COUNTRY
Norway

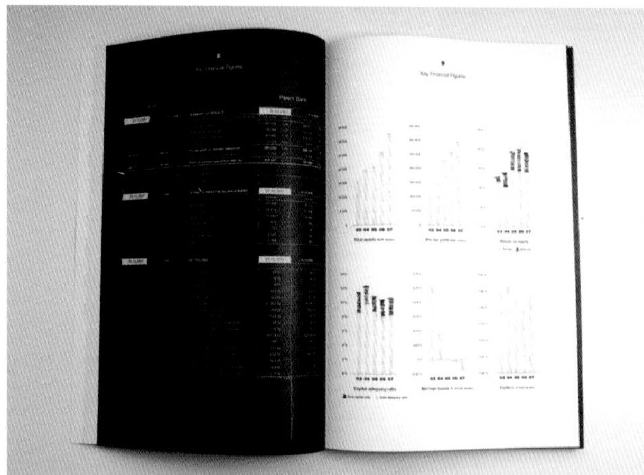

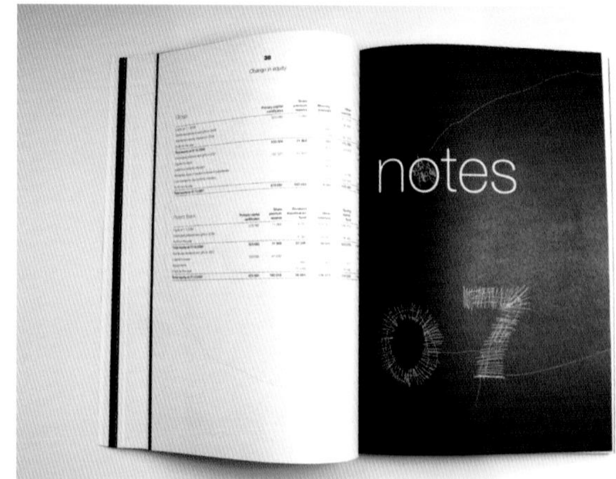

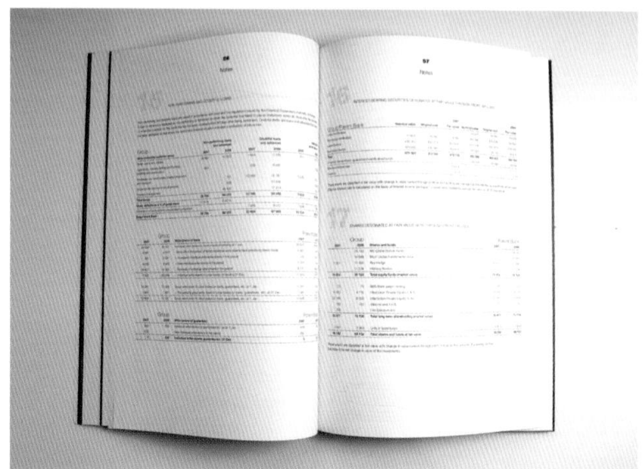

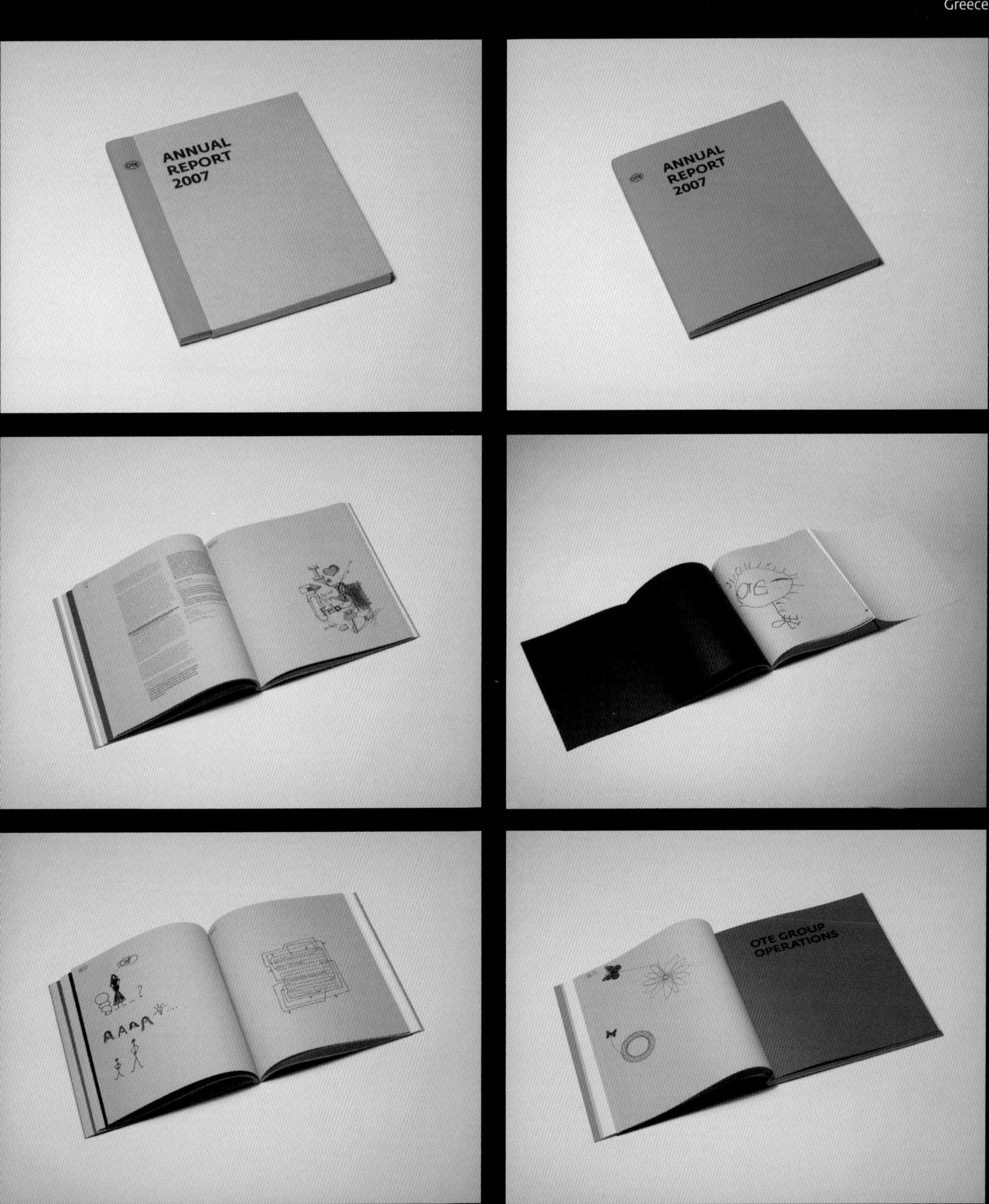
ANNUAL
REPORT
2007
ANNUAL
REPORT
2007
OTE GROUP
OPERATIONS

GOLD
BOOK COVER

TITLE
Kafka
COMPANY
Vier für Texas
CLIENT
S. Fischer Verlag
DESIGNERS
Philipp Erlach
Sven Kils
Sonja Weber
COUNTRY
Germany

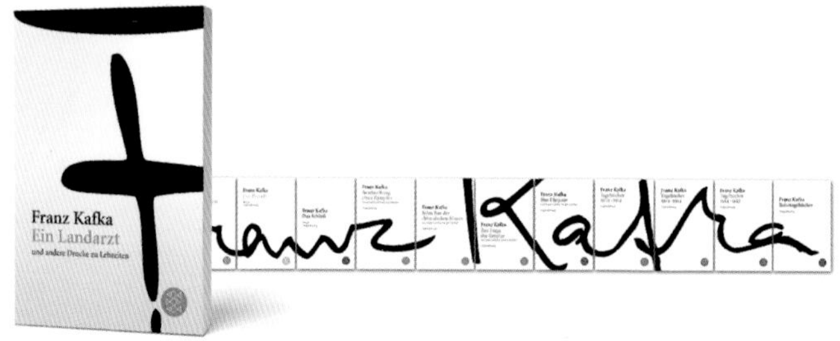

A book cover is comparable to the facing of any supermarket product. It aims first to catch the eye, then to display its singularity, and lastly to make you want to find out more by reading it. For this award, we were receptive to the coherence of this series of covers which gathers disparate works by Kafka. This is a brave and remarkable exercise: pocket collections often opt for more standardised modalities. Each impeccable cover beckons you to discover the others so that one can enter the full expanse of the œuvre; the signature creates a sensitive, personal link with the author. A good example of synergy between style and substance.

SILVER
BOOK COVER

TITLE
Sketchbook uncensored
COMPANY
Fuenfwerken Design AG
CLIENT
Werte Erleben e. V. and
Deichtorhallen Hamburg
COUNTRY
Germany

BRONZE
BOOK COVER

TITLE
Eat Love
COMPANY
Studio Kluif
CLIENT
Bis Publishers
COUNTRY
Netherlands

BRONZE
BOOK COVER

TITLE
HMKV
Hartware MedienKunstVerein
1996-2008
COMPANY
labor b designbüro
CLIENT
HMKV
Hartware MedienKunstVerein
COUNTRY
Germany

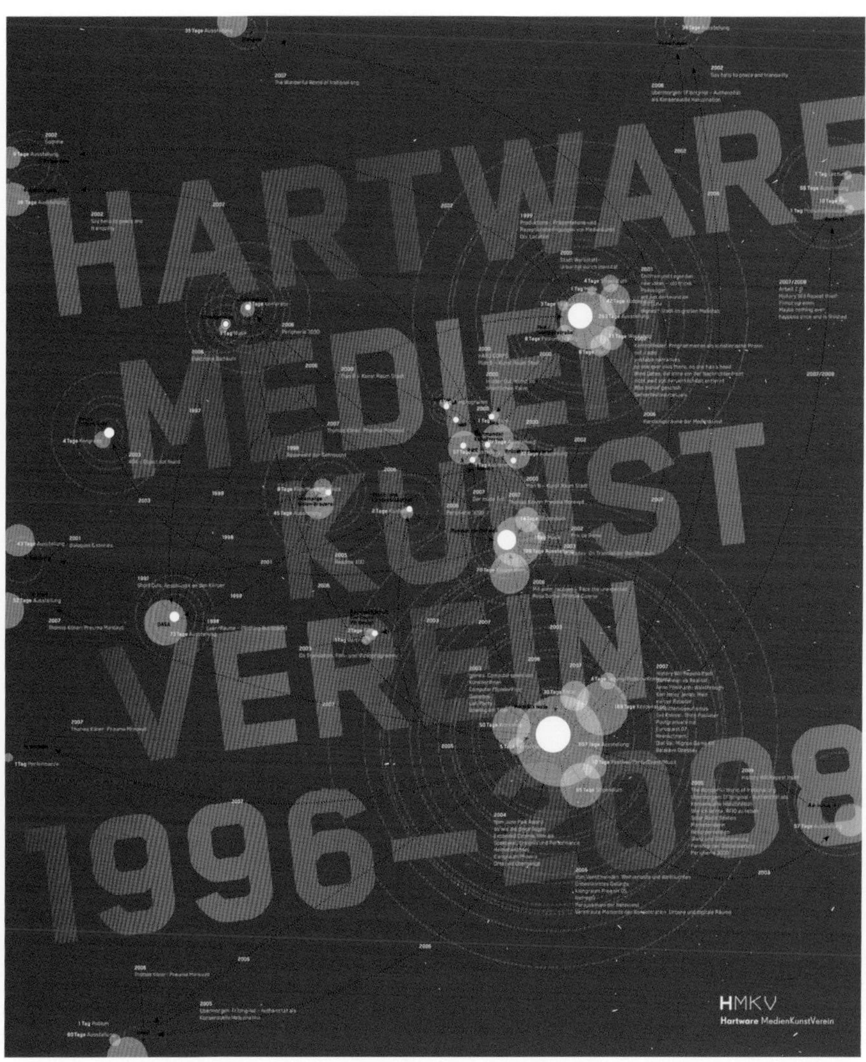

Des Wahnsinns Fette Beute

weehsel - Frederik Linke

Die Neue Sammlung München

Switzerland

the fat Booty of madness

des Wahnsinns fette Beute

Arnoldsche Art Publishers

ART ARNOLDSCHE PUBLISHERS

FETTE BEUTE

ISBN 978-3-89790-281-7

9 783897 902817

FINALIST
BOOK COVER

01.
TITLE
Radio Kootwijk Frequency
COMPANY
En publique
CLIENT
Belvedere Foundation
COUNTRY
Netherlands

02.
TITLE
Narrativa Galaxia Gutenberg
COMPANY
Josep Bagà Associats
CLIENT
Círculo de Lectores
COUNTRY
Spain

Vasili Grossman
Vida y destino

Saul Bellow
Mueren más por desamor

GOLD
BOOK LAYOUT

TITLE
projekt 68/89 (series of 4 book-journals)
COMPANY
formdusche
CLIENT
Zentrum für zeithistorische Forschung, Potsdam
DESIGNERS
Svenja von Döhlen,
Tim Finke
Timo Hummel
Steffen Wierer
ART DIRECTORS
Svenja von Döhlen
Tim Finke
Timo Hummel
Steffen Wierer
CREATIVE DIRECTORS
Svenja von Döhlen
Tim Finke
Timo Hummel
Steffen Wierer
DESIGN DIRECTORS
Svenja von Döhlen
Tim Finke
Timo Hummel
Steffen Wierer
EDITORS
Jürgen Danyel
Jennifer Schevardo
Stephan Kruhl
ASSISTANCE DESIGNERS
Frederic Groß
Sebastian Vollmar
COUNTRY
Germany

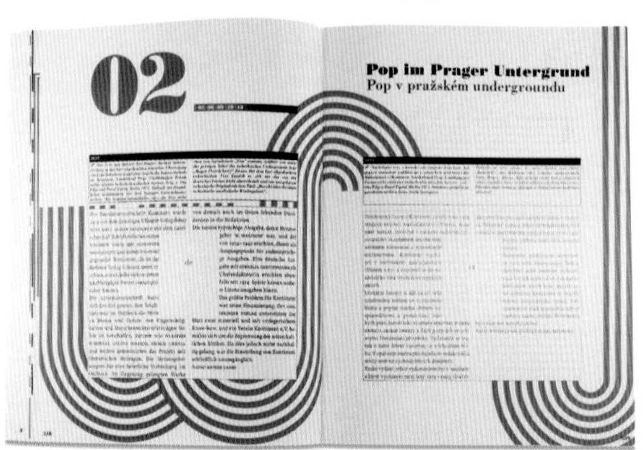

The boundaries between books, magazines and brochures grow ever hazier, as the fight with other media for our attention becomes increasingly fierce. Hybridisation is yielding new bookazine concepts – and nothing could be more suitable for a book celebrating the 40th anniversary of the '68-'89 period of the student revolution in Germany. This period's complexity and richness are masterfully evoked in this series of four booklets, each of which has its own graphic style inspired by the visual movements of the era; they are revived here in a remarkable, pastiche-free and highly contemporary reinterpretation with no dud notes.

MISUNDERSTANDING 68/89
MIS
UNDER
STAN
DING 68/89

CHANGE
ISOLATI
IMPOSS
MIS
UNDER
STAN
DING 68/89

CROSSING 68/89
CROSS
ING 68/
/89
X

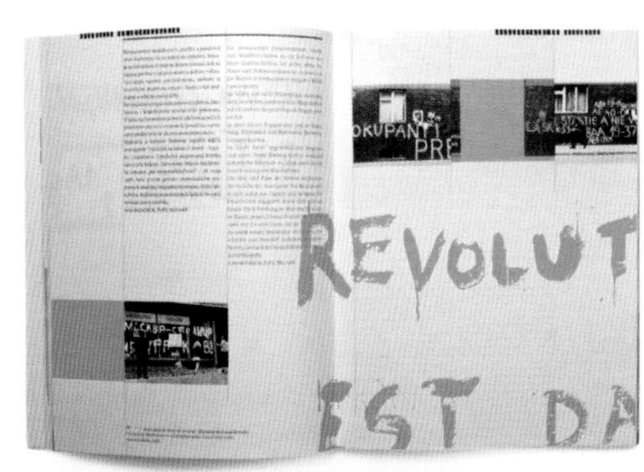
REVOLUT
EST DA

WE WANT
LD AND W
NOW.
CROSSING 68/89

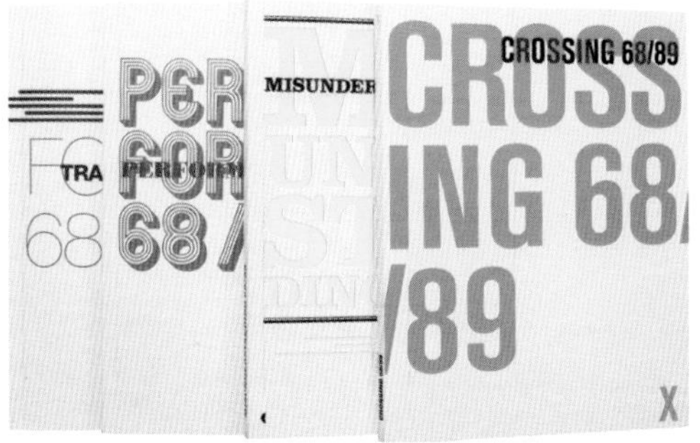
CROSSING 68/89
MISUNDER
CROSS
ING 68/
/89
X

SILVER
BOOK LAYOUT

TITLE
Master Chefs for Home Chefs 2
COMPANY
Studio Dumbar
CLIENT
TNT Post
DESIGNER
Studio Dumbar
PHOTOGRAPHERS
Thomas Pelgrom
Gerold Febis
COUNTRY
Netherlands

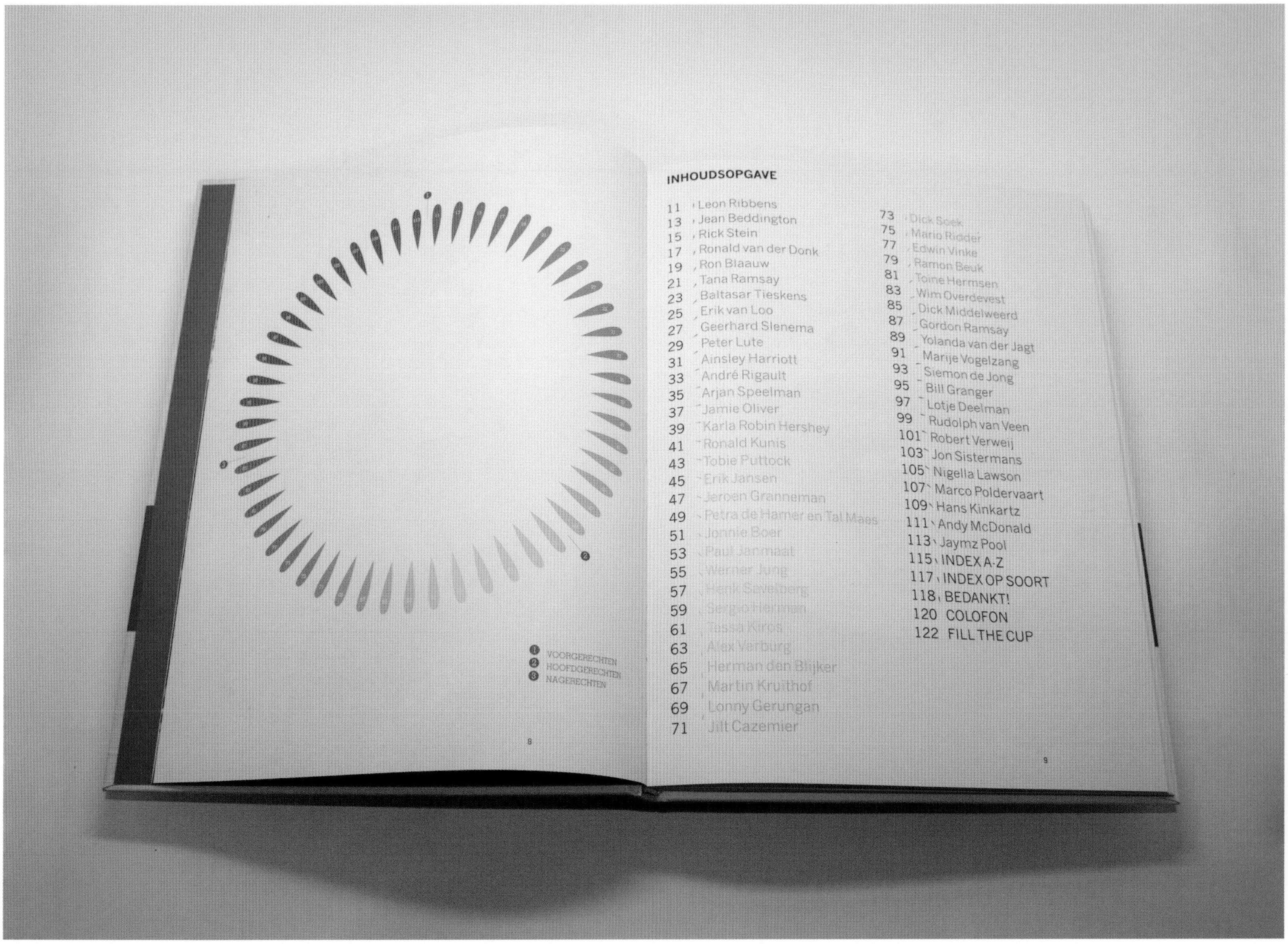

INHOUDSOPGAVE
11 Leon Ribbens
13 Jean Beddington
15 Rick Stein
17 Ronald van der Donk
19 Ron Blaauw
21 Tana Ramsay
23 Baltasar Tieskens
25 Erik van Loo
27 Geerhard Slenema
29 Peter Lute
31 Ainsley Harriott
33 André Rigault
35 Arjan Speelman
37 Jamie Oliver
39 Karla Robin Hershey
41 Ronald Kunis
43 Tobie Puttock
45 Erik Jansen
47 Jeroen Granneman
49 Petra de Hamer en Tal Maes
51 Jonnie Boer
53 Paul Janmaat
55 Werner Jung
57 Henk Savelberg
59 Sergio Herman
61 Tessa Kiros
63 Alex Verburg
65 Herman den Blijker
67 Martin Kruithof
69 Lonny Gerungan
71 Jilt Cazemier
73 Dick Soek
75 Mario Ridder
77 Edwin Vinke
79 Ramon Beuk
81 Toine Hermsen
83 Wim Overdevest
85 Dick Middelweerd
87 Gordon Ramsay
89 Yolanda van der Jagt
91 Marije Vogelzang
93 Siemon de Jong
95 Bill Granger
97 Lotje Deelman
99 Rudolph van Veen
101 Robert Verweij
103 Jon Sistermans
105 Nigella Lawson
107 Marco Poldervaart
109 Hans Kinkartz
111 Andy McDonald
113 Jaymz Pool
115 INDEX A-Z
117 INDEX OP SOORT
118 BEDANKT!
120 COLOFON
122 FILL THE CUP
VOORGERECHTEN
HOOFDGERECHTEN
NAGERECHTEN

SILVER
BOOK LAYOUT

TITLE
The Best German Book Design 2007
COMPANY
L2M3 Kommunikations design GmbH
CLIENT
Stiftung Buchkunst
DESIGNERS
Ina Bauer
Frank Geiger
Sascha Lobe
Thorsten Steidle
CREATIVE DIRECTOR
Sascha Lobe
COUNTRY
Germany

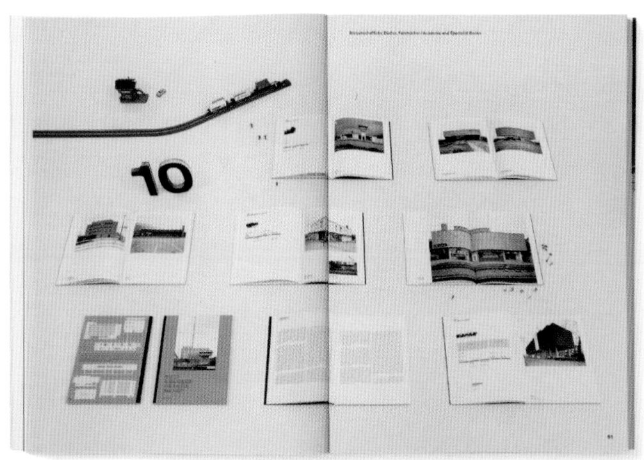
10

11

10

11

gemeine
Literatur
General
Literature

Kunstbücher,
Fotobücher,
Ausstellungs-
kataloge
Art and Photo-
graphy, Exhibi-
tion Catalogues
5

SILVER
BOOK LAYOUT

TITLE
Orientation & Identity
COMPANY
STRUKTIV & bauer
CLIENT
Springer-Verlag GmbH
DESIGNERS
Erwin K. Bauer (bauer)
Dieter Mayer (STRUKTIV)
PHOTOGRAPHER
Dieter Mayer (STRUKTIV)
WRITER
Erwin K. Bauer (bauer)
URL
www.signaletik.at
COUNTRY
Austria

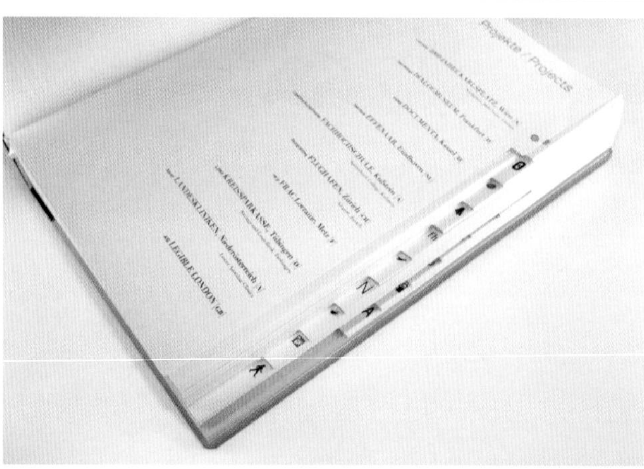

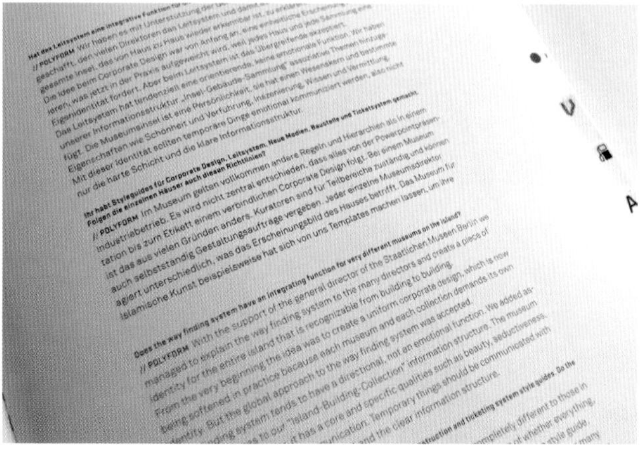

toilettes
salle de conférence

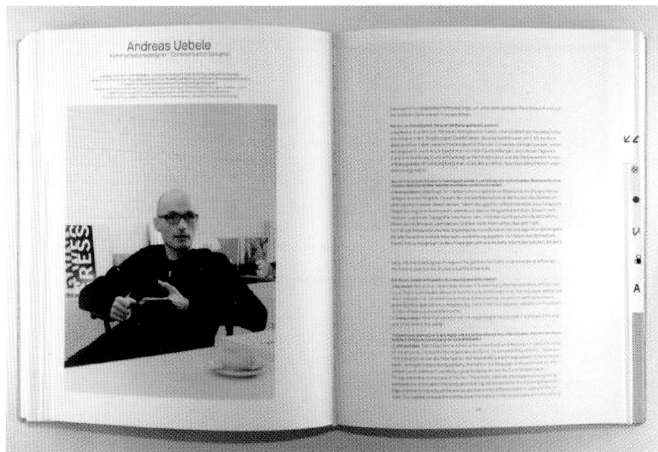

Andreas Uebele

Schoorl 5
Alkmaar 13

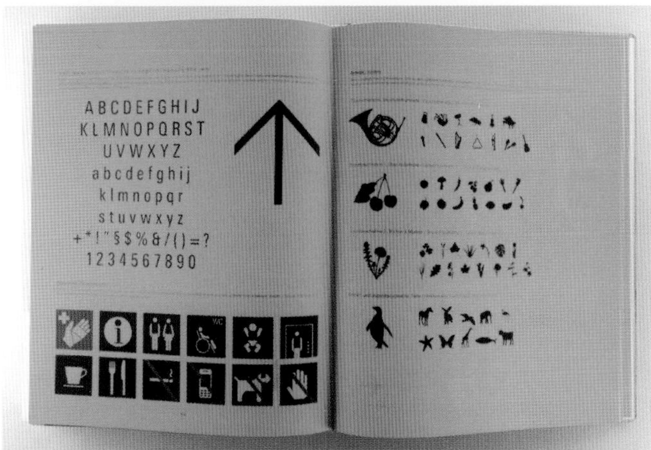

ABCDEFGHIJ
KLMNOPQRST
UVWXYZ
abcdefghij
klmnopqr
stuvwxyz
1234567890

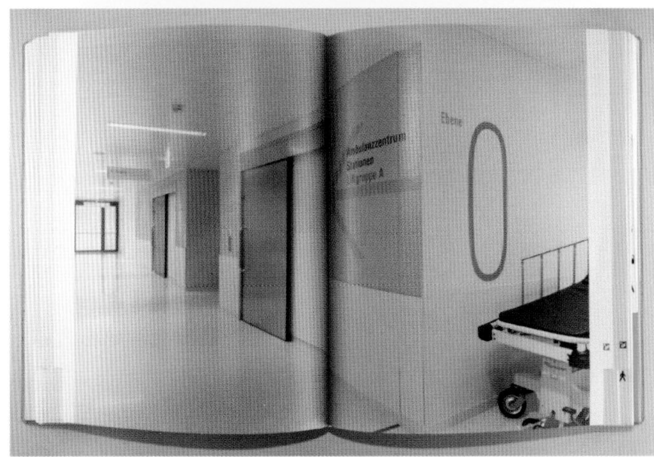

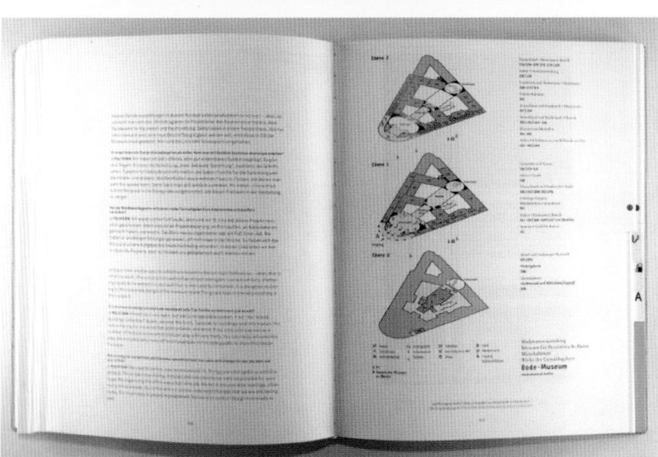

INFOS

SILVER
BOOK LAYOUT

TITLE
Helvetica Forever.
Geschichte einer Schrift
COMPANY
Lars Müller Publishers
DESIGNERS
Integral Lars Müller
Séverine Mailler
EDITORS
Victor Malsy
Lars Müller
WRITERS
Axel Langer
Indra Kupferschmid
CONCEPT
Victor Malsy
Lars Müller
COUNTRY
Switzerland

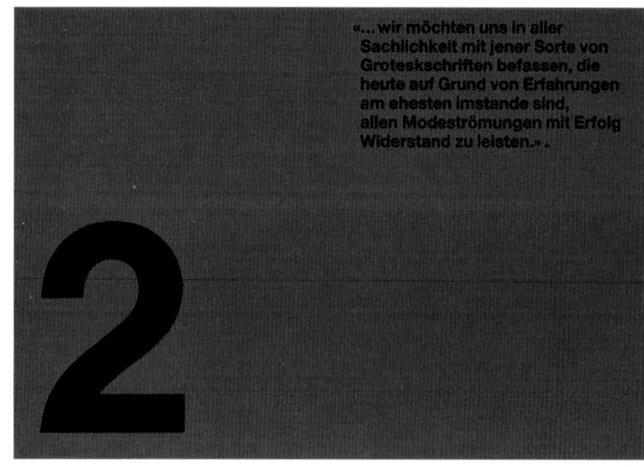

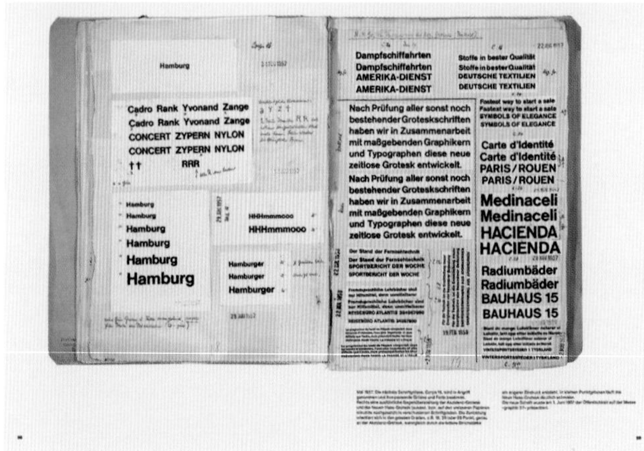

my lord archbishop
your excellencies
your graces
my lords
ladies and
gentlemen
men and
women
children
embryos if any
spermatozoa reclining
at the
edge
of your
chairs
all living cells
bacteria
viruses
molecules of air and
dust and
water,

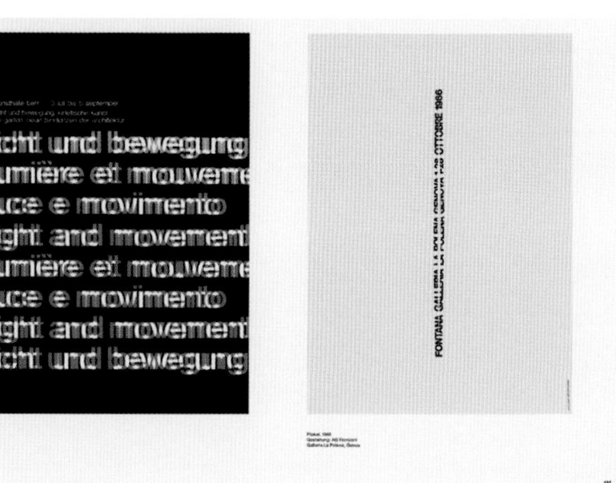

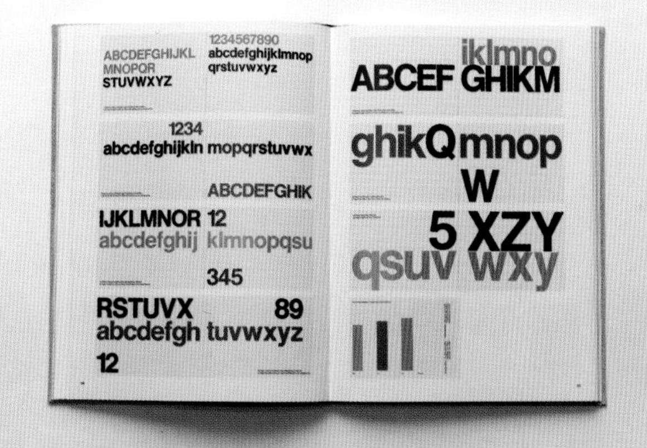
1234567890
ABCDEFGHIJKL
MNOPQR
STUVWXYZ
abcdefghijklmnop
qrstuvwxyz
1234
abcdefghijkln mopqrstuvwx
ABCDEFGHIK
IJKLMNOR 12
abcdefghij klmnopqsu
345
RSTUVX 89
abcdefgh tuvwxyz
12
iklmno
ABCEF GHIKM
ghikQmnop
W
5 XZY
qsuv wxy

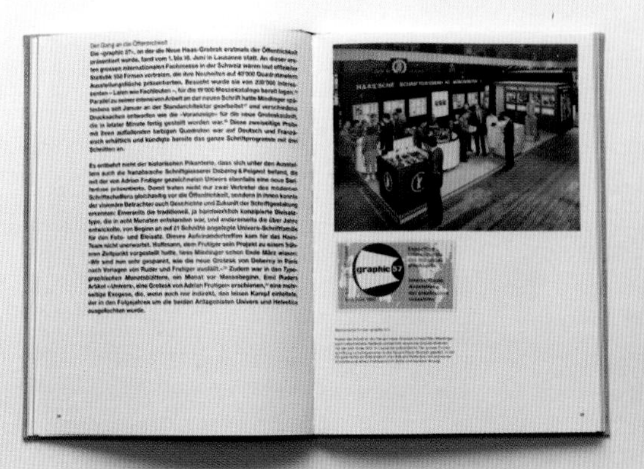

Die Neue
Haas
Grotesk

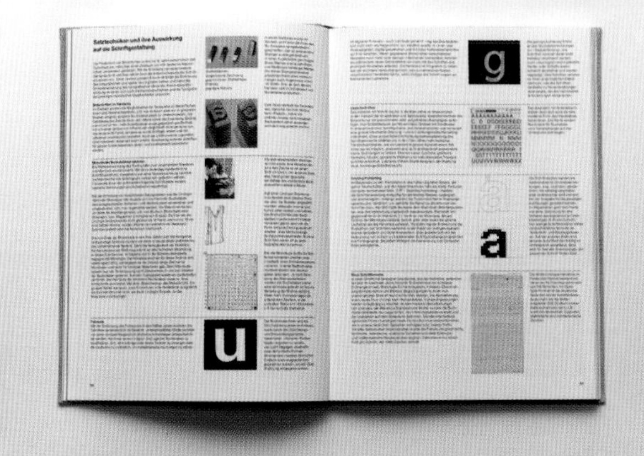
g
a
u

aktGQR1
aktGQR1
aftGQ1R
agtGKQR

Piccolo Teatro
di Milano
Piccolo Teatro
di Milano
CAPRIOLEN

Naturfreunde Kinderheim
Homberg Minigolf Olten Linde
Reinhard Steiner Quinten jung
Johann Pfund Trogen Rekord
SIMON KLING TOMLISHORN

SILVER
BOOK LAYOUT

TITLE
Trener prawniczy book series
COMPANY
Parastudio
CLIENT
"Park" publishing house
DESIGNERS
Jan Krzysztofiak
Grzegorz Podsiadlik
EDITOR
Ewa Galczak
COUNTRY
Poland

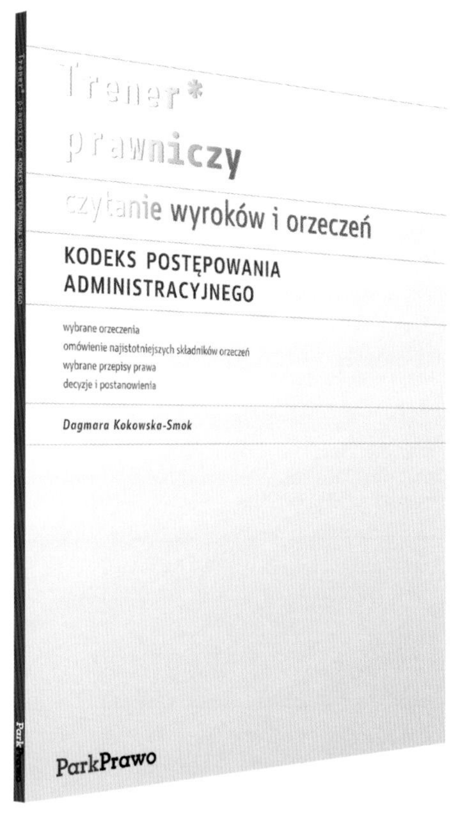

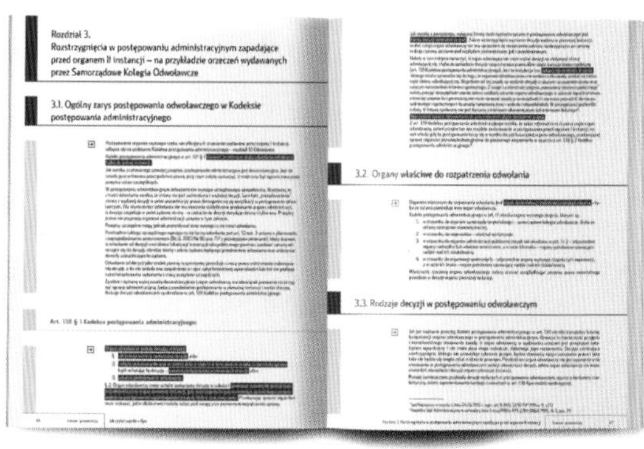

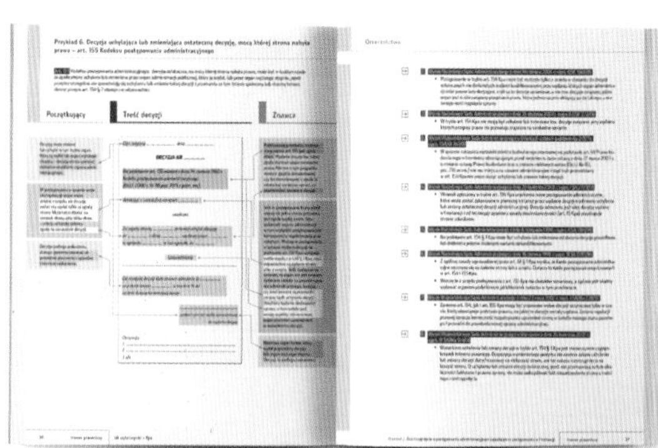

Trener* prawniczy
jak czytać wyroki
KODEKS KARNY
przykłady wyroków i ich omówienie
ważne przepisy
najczęściej zadawane pytania
Maciej Czajka
ParkEdukacja

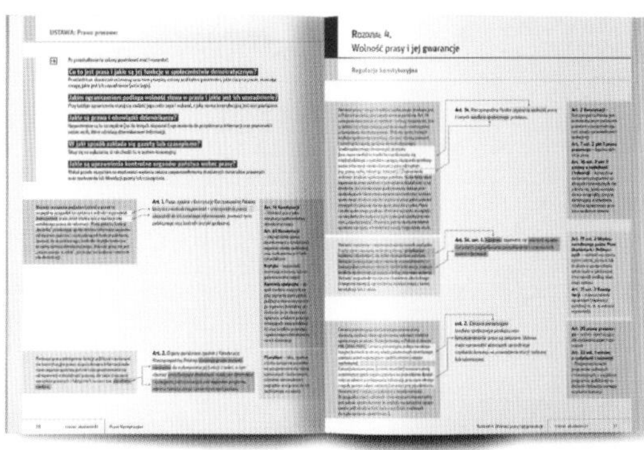

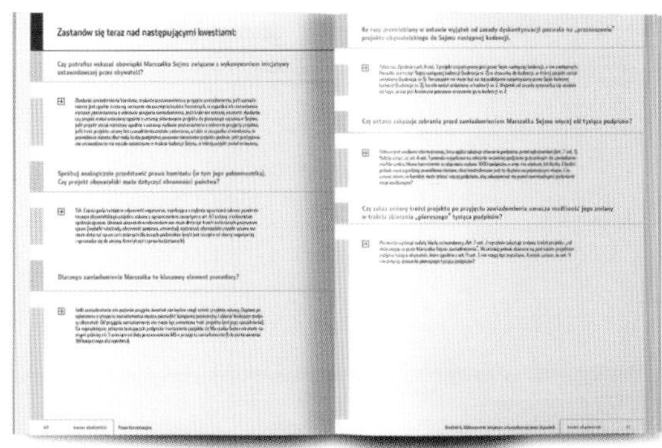

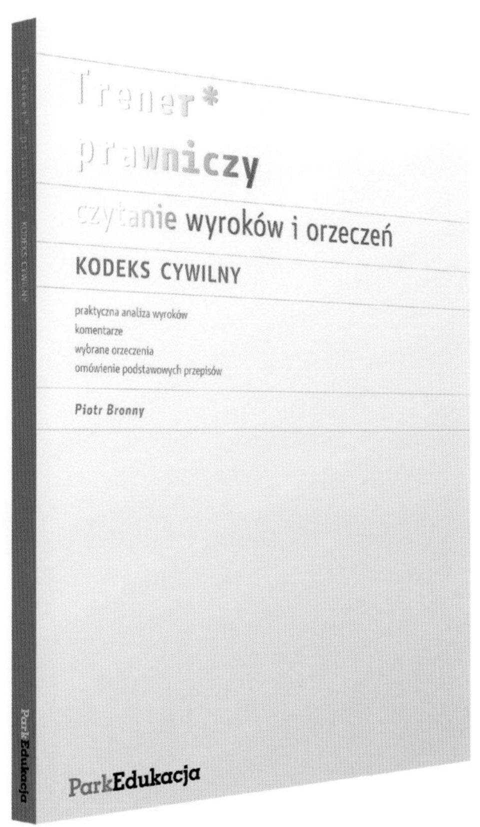
Trener* prawniczy
czytanie wyroków i orzeczeń
KODEKS CYWILNY
praktyczna analiza wyroków
komentarze
wybrane orzeczenia
omówienie podstawowych przepisów
Piotr Bronny
ParkEdukacja

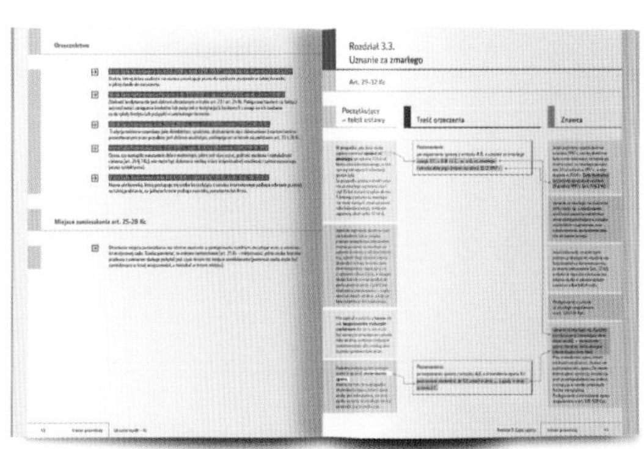

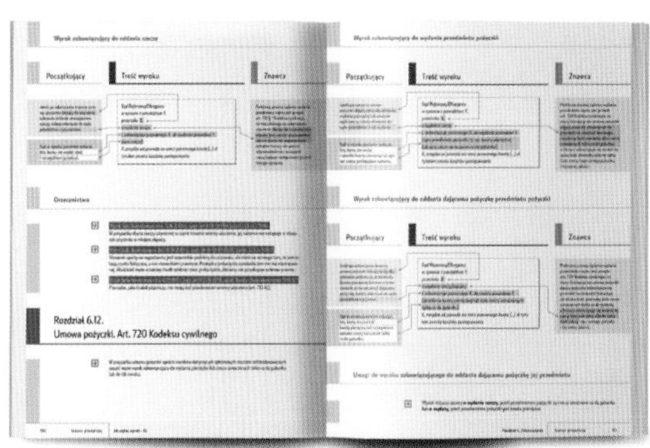

BRONZE
BOOK LAYOUT

TITLE
HQ high quality
COMPANY
A/Heine/Lenz
Zizka Projekte GmbH
CLIENT
Edition Braus
COUNTRY
Germany

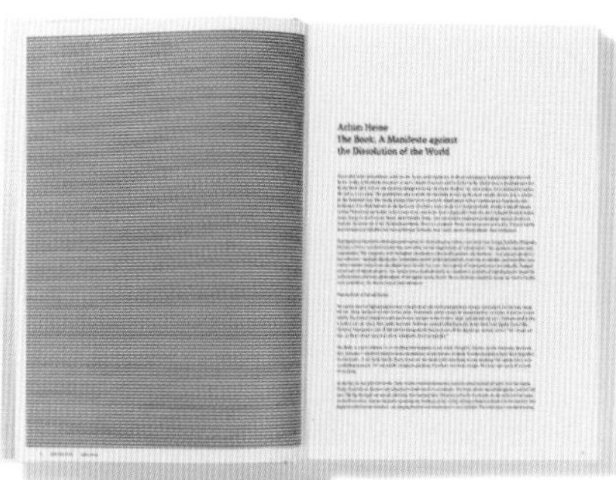

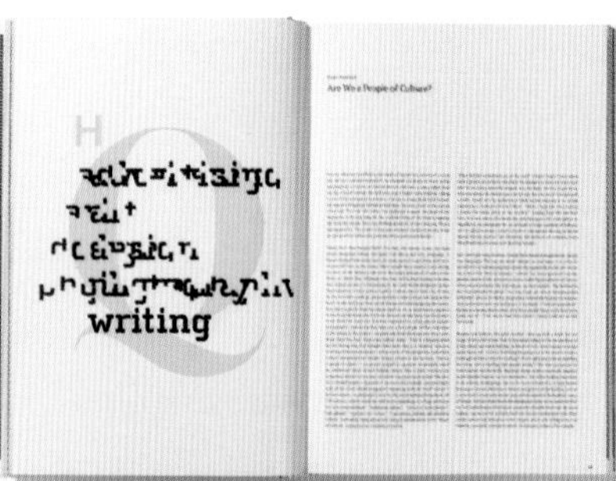

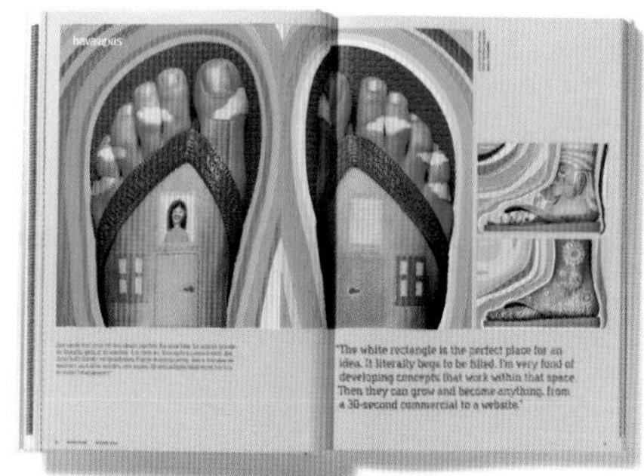

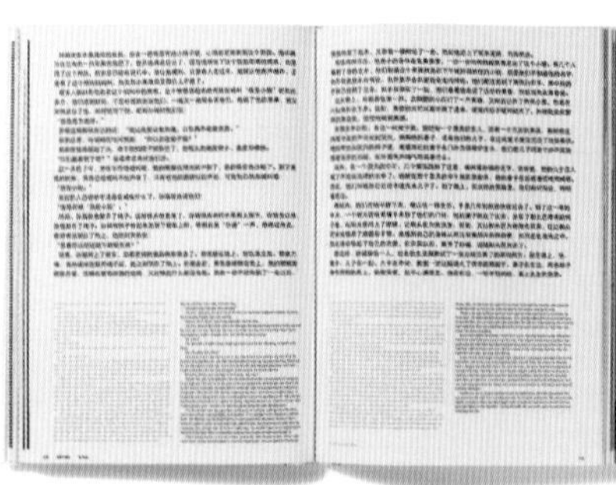

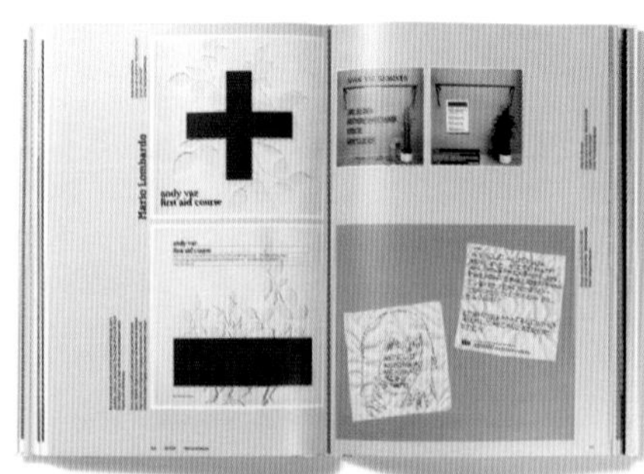

"More than gold, lead has changed the world, and more than the lead in muskets, it was that in the letter cases of the printers."

BRONZE
BOOK LAYOUT

TITLE
Lt. Eugeniusz Lokajski „Brok"
COMPANY
Muzeum Powstania Warszawskiego
CLIENT
Warsaw Rising Museum
COUNTRY
Poland

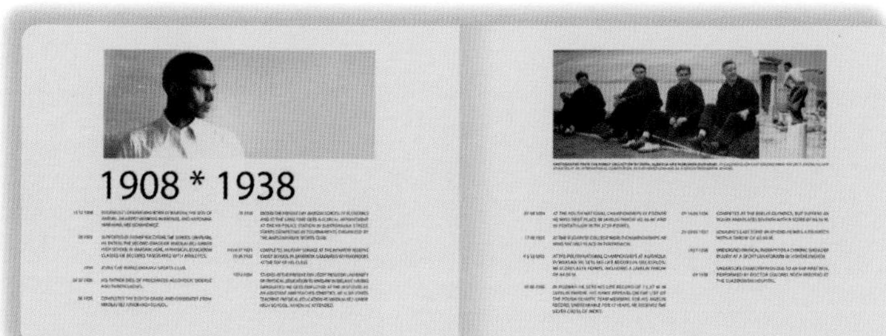

BRONZE
BOOK LAYOUT

TITLE
Von B und C / Of B and C
COMPANY
Hahn und Zimmermann
CLIENT
Christoph Merian Verlag
COUNTRY
Switzerland

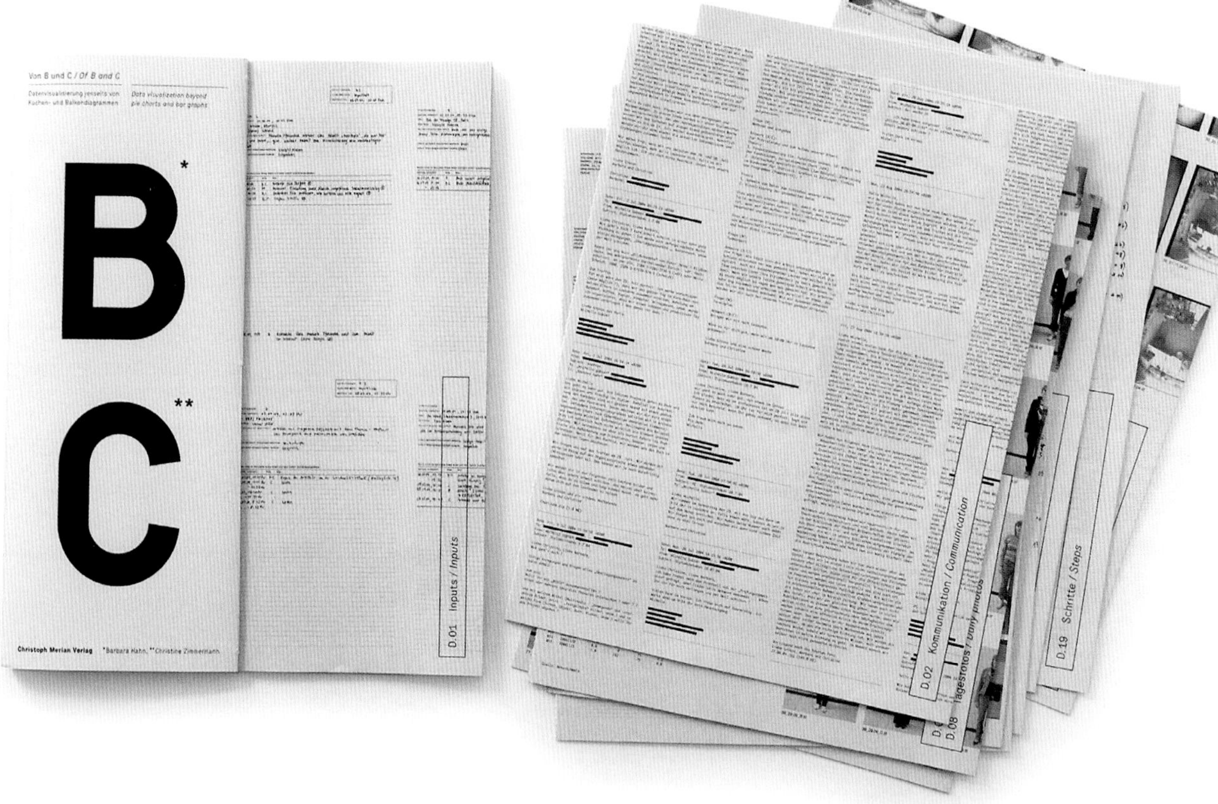

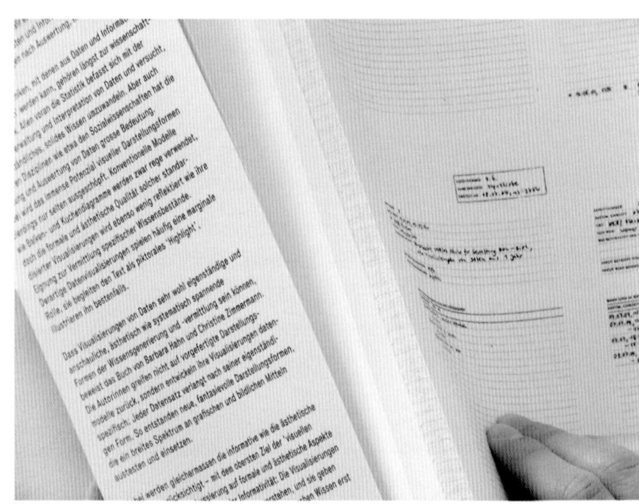

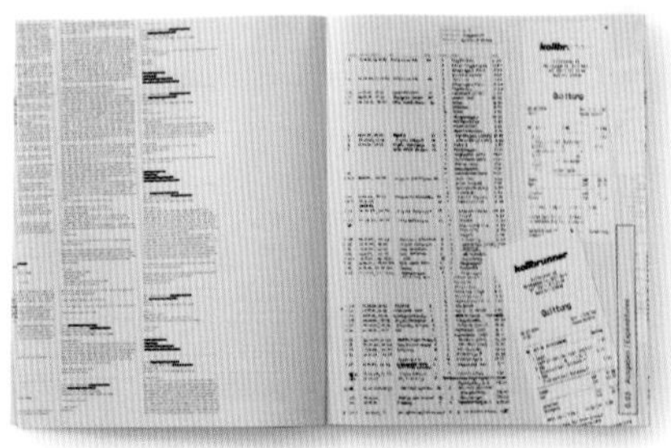

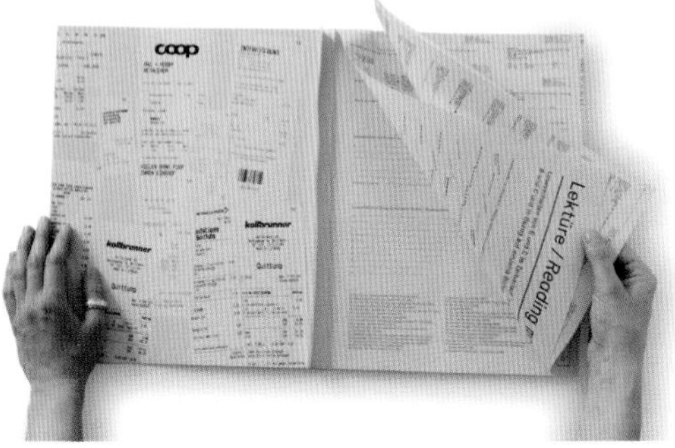

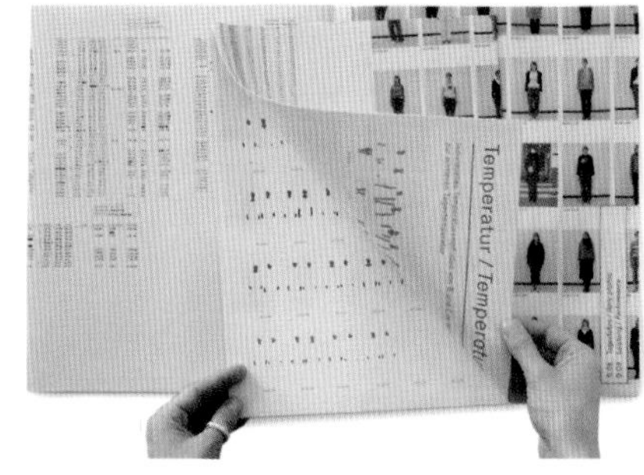

BRONZE
BOOK LAYOUT

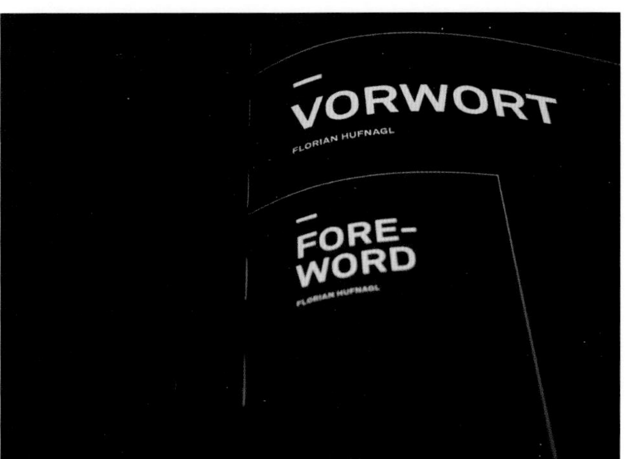

TITLE
Des Wahnsinns Fette Beute
COMPANY
weehsel - Frederik Linke
CLIENT
Die Neue Sammlung München
COUNTRY
Switzerland

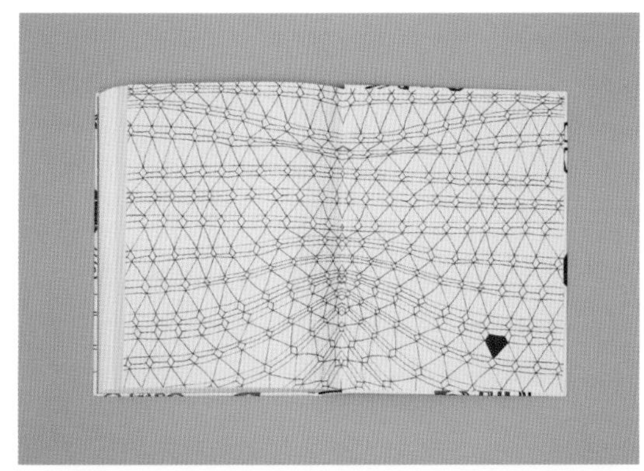

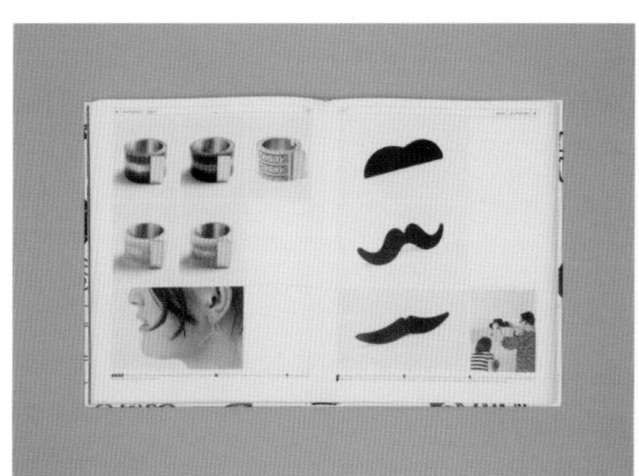

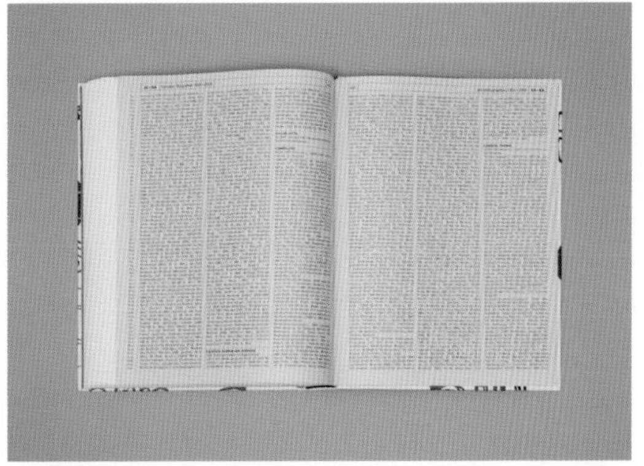

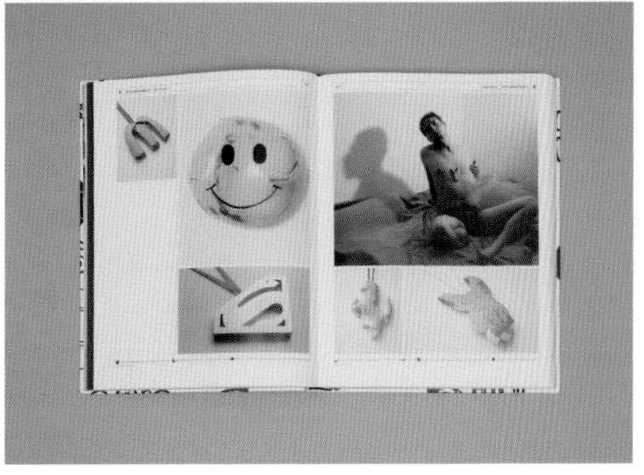

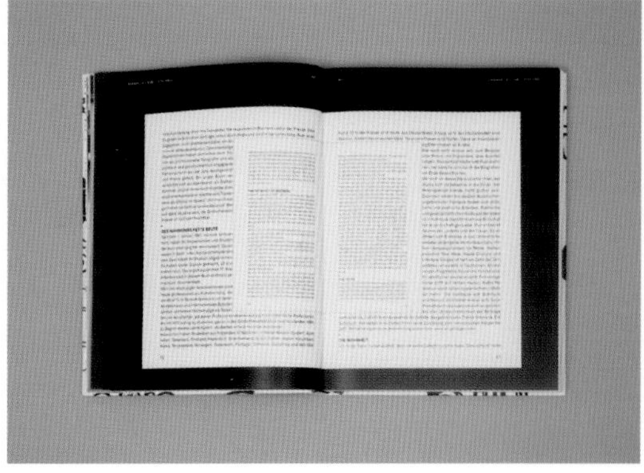

BRONZE
BOOK LAYOUT

TITLE
Marte.Marte Architects

COMPANY
Atelier Reinhard Gassner

CLIENT
Marte.Marte Architects

COUNTRY
Austria

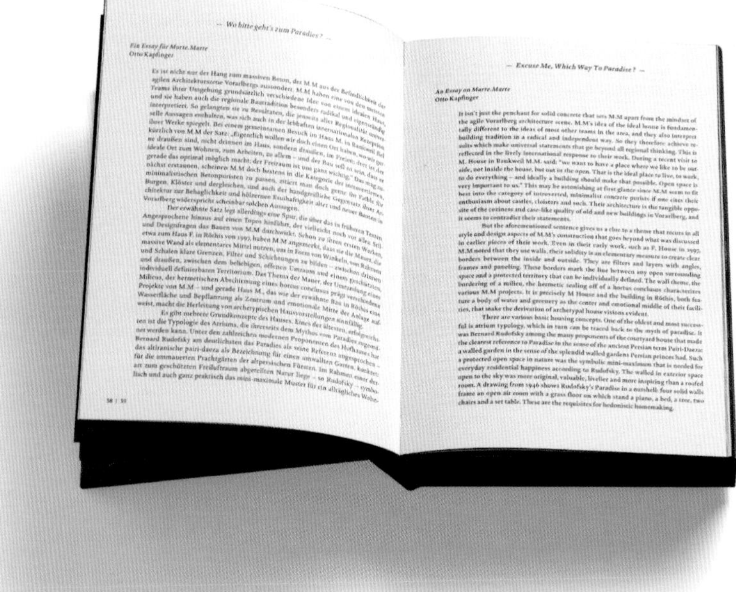

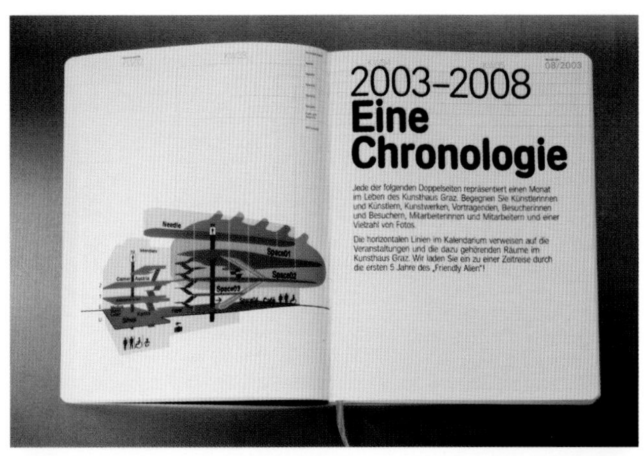

BRONZE
BOOK LAYOUT

TITLE
2003-2008 Kunsthaus Graz

COMPANY
Lichtwitz – Büro für visuelle Kommunikation

CLIENT
Kunsthaus Graz am Landesmuseum Joanneum

COUNTRY
Austria

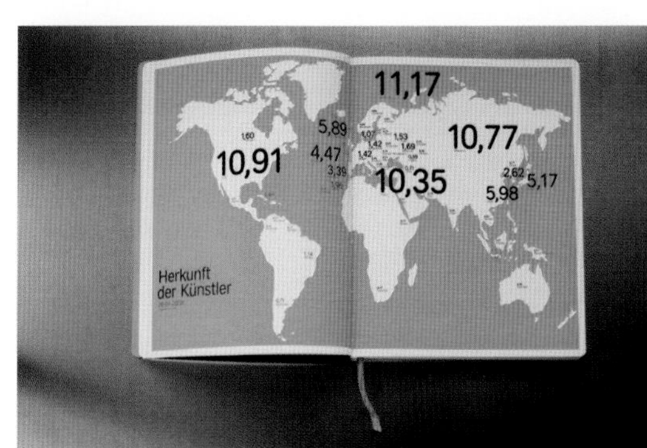

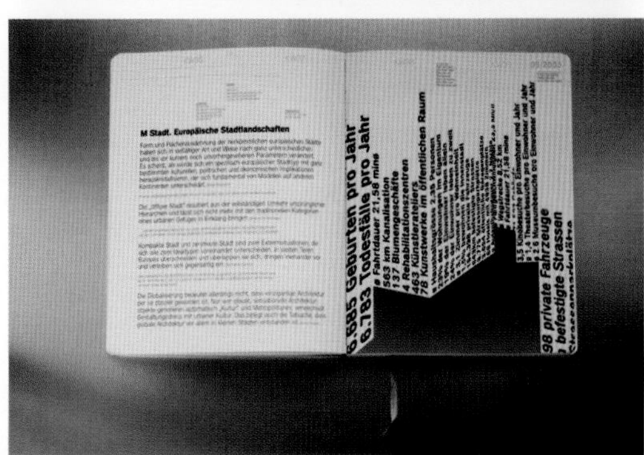

BRONZE
BOOK LAYOUT

TITLE
Designlehren.
Wege deutscher
Gestaltungsausbildung
COMPANY
Office for Design
CLIENTS
Hochschule Darmstadt
Fachbereich Gestaltung
COUNTRY
Switzerland

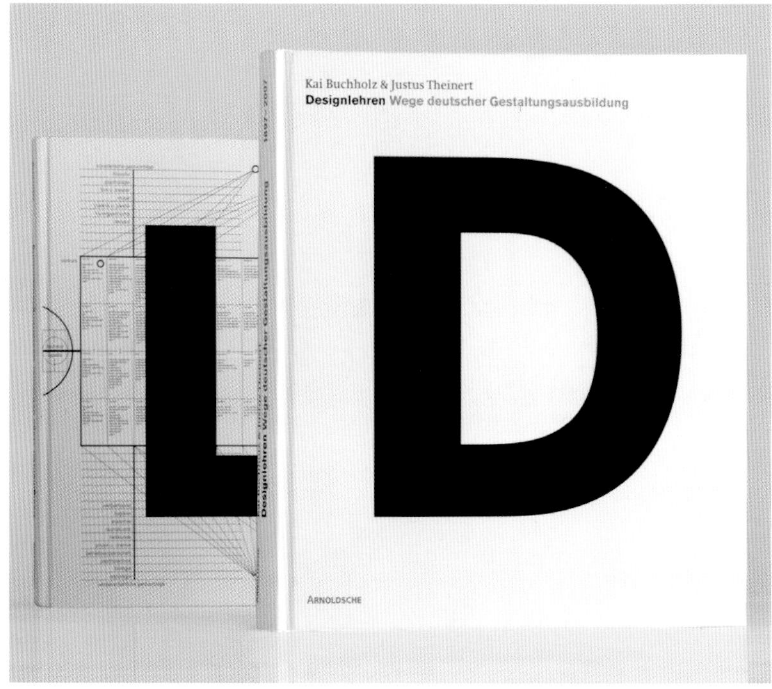

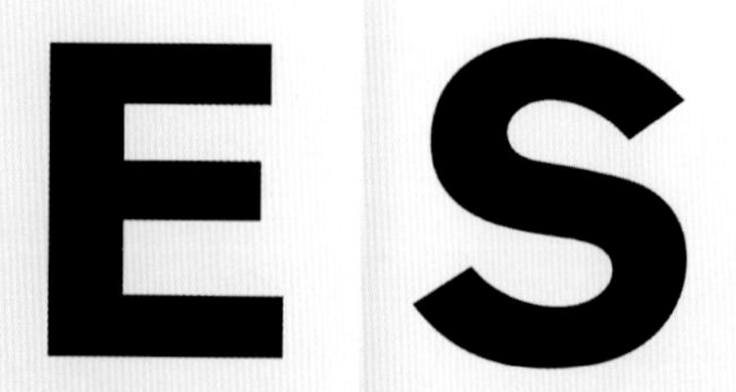
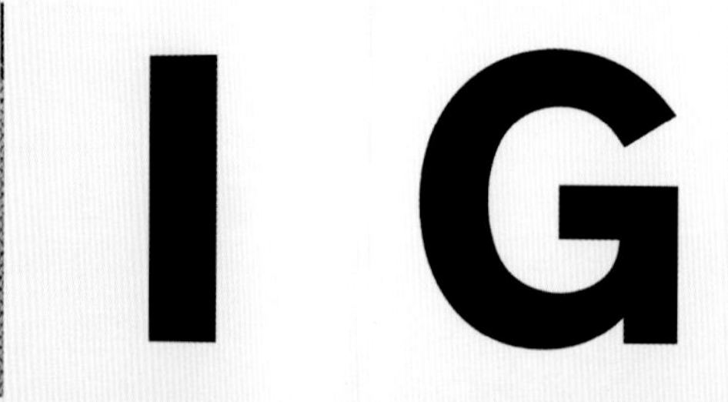

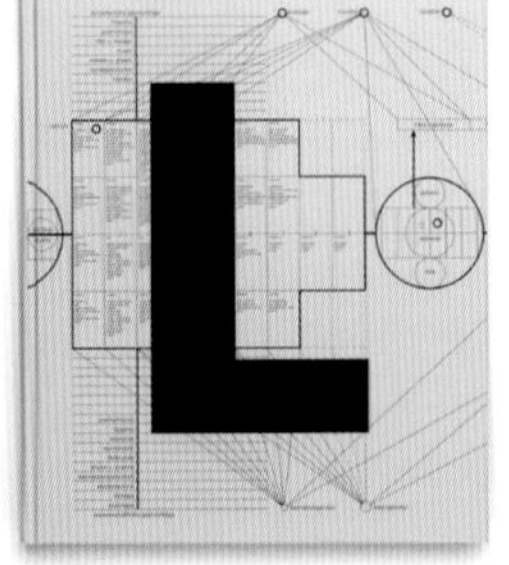
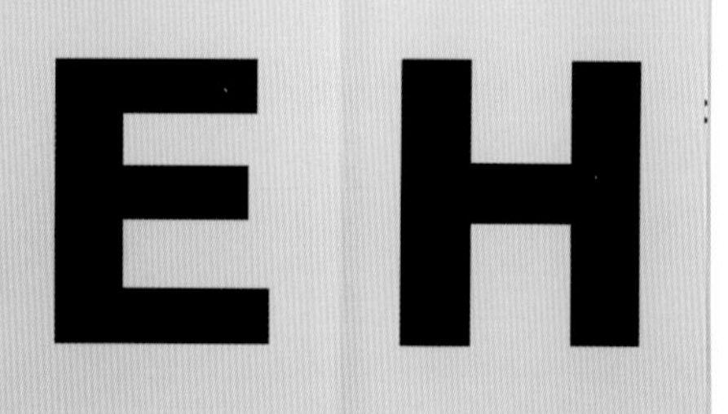

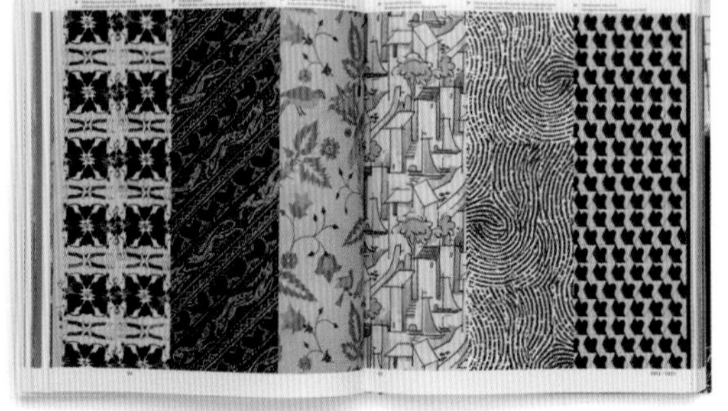

BRONZE
BOOK LAYOUT

TITLE
Hochachtend Heiter

COMPANY
TGG Hafen Senn Stieger

CLIENT
VGS Verlagsgemeinschaft

COUNTRY
Switzerland

GOLD
BROCHURE

TITLE
No sales, just good advice
COMPANY
Jäger & Jäger
CLIENT
Nils Holger Moormann GmbH
DESIGNER
Jäger & Jäger
ART DIRECTORS
Olaf Jäger
Regina Jäger
TRAINEES
Nicola Nolle
Georg Plass
COUNTRY
Germany

At 26, on is usually in the full bloom of youth. But for a business it is already a very decent age, offering proof of continuity and the capacity to endure in ever-changing conditions. The catalogue's designers have given this anniversary book a strongly festive flavour. The illustrations are meticulously chosen and combine to tell a story which, from page to page, is very meaningful. It is also an object-book in which the reader comes across a host of inserts, which reinforces its festive side.

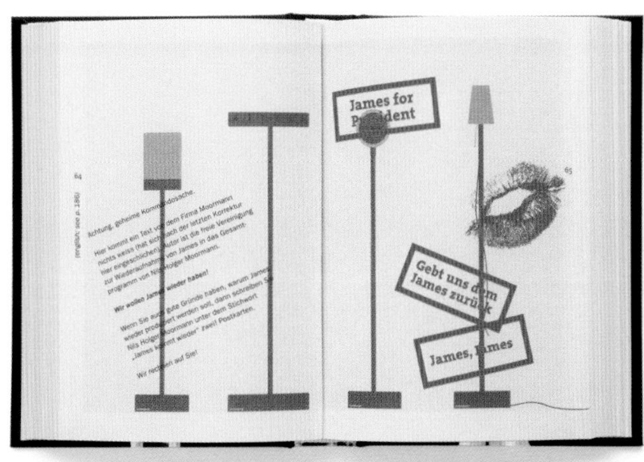
James for
Gebt uns

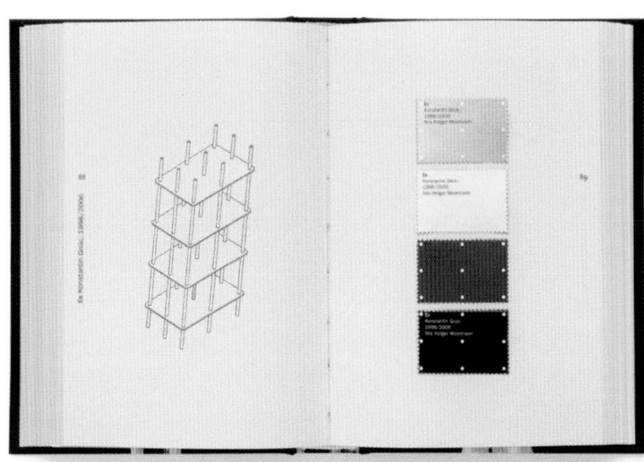

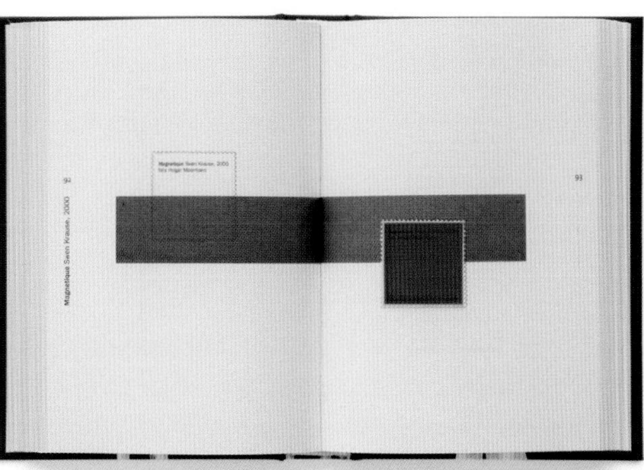

Holocaust - Naftali Fürst

Sigi Ramoser Sägenvier DesignKommunikation

erinnern.at Nationalsozialismus und Holocaust

Silvia Keckeis

Sigi Ramoser

Sigi Ramoser

Sigi Ramoser

erinnern.at - Joachim Wiesner

Joachim Wiesner

Austria

#1

Kindheit – Familie – Bratislava

Die glücklichen Tage unserer Kindheit dauerten nicht sehr lange.

1918 1930 1932

Zwei Namen

Die Familie Blum

Die Familie Fürst

Eine typisch jüdische Familie der Zeit

Wirtschaftliche Prosperität

Petržalka

Der Slowakische Nationalaufstand

Die Juden in der Slowakei vor 1945

Die Hlinka-Garde

Unsere frühe Kindheit war glücklich und sorgenfrei.

Sie vertreiben mich aus meinem Haus

#2.1

Der Holocaust

Komme, was wolle, wir müssen überleben!

1945 1946 1947 1948 194

Überlebenskampf im ersten KZ

Nur den Deportationen entkommen

Wir hofften, dass irgendein Wunder geschehen würde...

Seht ihr die Flammen? Dahin werdet ihr bald gehen.

#3

Neuanfang und Leben in Israel

Alles, was in meiner Kindheit existiert hatte, hatte sich in Luft aufgelöst

1944 1949 1955 1986 20

Wieder Schule

Geschichte Israels

Atmosphäre der Auflösung

Wir sind Überlebende, Kohlestücke, die in den Flammen des Schreckens nicht völlig verbrannt sind.

Die Befreiung

Rückkehr nach Bratislava

Zurück ins Leben

Aufbruch nach Eretz Israel

#4

Informationen für Lehrende

1. Geschichte des Buchenwald-Fotos
2. Pädagogisches Konzept von Yad Vashem
3. Anmerkungen für den Einsatz im Unterricht
4. Fußnoten, Bildnachweis
5. Das Projekt und seine Entstehung

1. Geschichte des Buchenwald-Fotos

2. Gedanken zur pädagogischen Vermittlung des Themas Holocaust im Unterricht

2.1 Die Welt des jüdischen Opfers

2.2 Täter, Zuschauer, Retter

SILVER
BROCHURE

TITLE
National Theatre of Greece
COMPANY
MNP
CLIENT
Play Publications Series of National Theatre of Greece
DESIGNER
MNP
ART DIRECTORS
Vasilis Marmatakis
Katerina Papanagiotou
Ifigenia Vasiliou
ILLUSTRATOR
Christina Christoforou
PHOTOGRAPHERS
Tasia Voytiropoulou
Mihalis Klokinas
Evi Filahtou
Marilena Stafilidou
COUNTRY
Greece

BRONZE
BROCHURE

01.
TITLE
Mister Beaver
COMPANY
xhoch4 design feat. Ben Wittner
CLIENT
Biber GmbH & Co. KG
URL
www.mister-beaver.de
COUNTRY
Germany

02.
TITLE
Choros profile
COMPANY
Colibri
CLIENT
Choros Constructions
COUNTRY
Greece

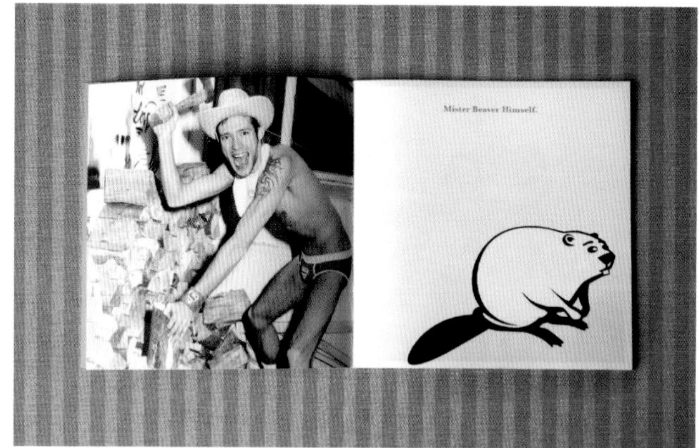

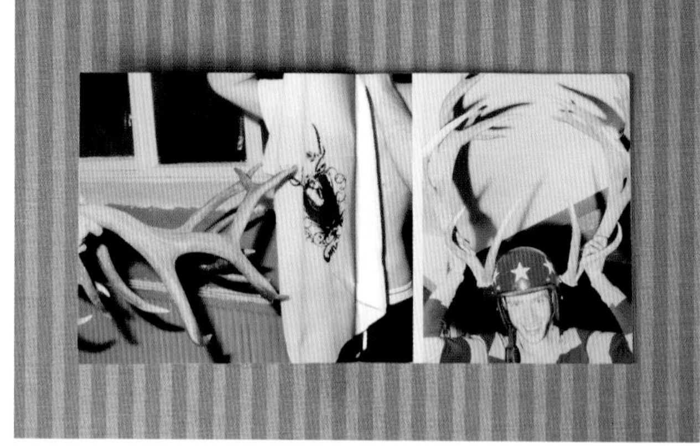

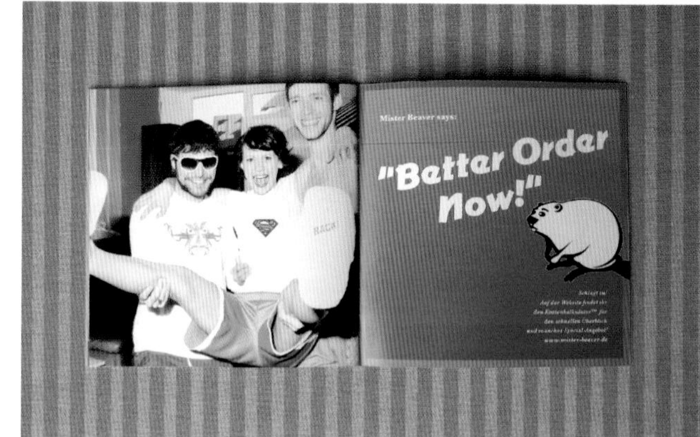

BRONZE
BROCHURE

03.
TITLE
The New Shoppingbag
COMPANY
Studio Beige
CLIENT
Susan Bijl
COUNTRY
Netherlands

04.
TITLE
The Slade School of Fine Art
COMPANY
Paarpiloten
CLIENT
The Slade School of Fine Art
COUNTRY
Germany

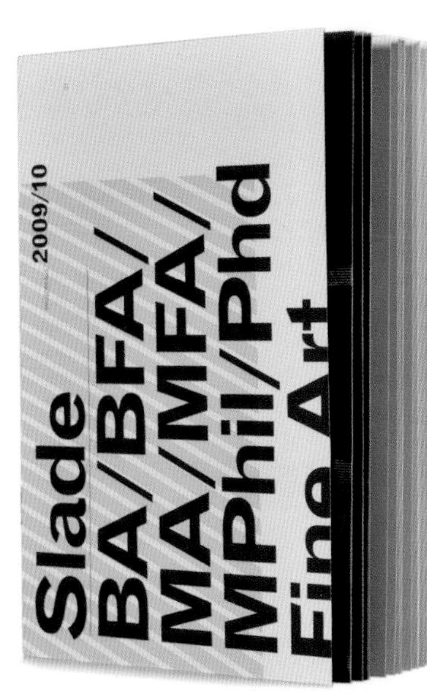

GOLD
PRODUCT CATALOGUE

TITLE
The Colour Envelope
COMPANY
Studio Laucke
CLIENT
Akzo Nobel Decorative Coatings
DESIGNER
Studio Laucke
ART DIRECTOR
Dirk Laucke
CREATIVE DIRECTORS
Dirk Laucke
Marc Karpstein
DESIGN DIRECTORS
Dirk Laucke
Marc Karpstein
STYLING & PRODUCTION
PHOTOGRAPHY
Kamer 465
EDITOR
Anne van der Zwaag
WRITER
Gert Staal
COUNTRY
Netherlands

A piece in praise of colour, somewhere between seriousness and humour – thus could we summarise this brochure, which consists of several elements. Derridaean destructurings and dismantlings seem to be an underlying trend strongly present in several award entries. The intelligence of the presentation, as well as the display of the product's actual appearance, unanimously convinced the jury. The sophisticated execution is definitely a standard-setter. Numerous caustic visuals punctuate the booklets, which retain a highly-controlled elegance and sobriety.

Sharing

Interpon F

Interpon F
Interpon F
The Colour
Envelope #08
Unlimited

SILVER
PRODUCT CATALOGUE

TITLE
Ingolstadt Theatre, theatre programme 2008#2009
COMPANY
xhoch4
CLIENT
Ingolstadt Theatre
DESIGNERS
B. Schmelter
R. Arbeithuber
C. Bolza
C. Mescher
ART DIRECTORS
Boris Schmelter
René Arbeithuber
PHOTOGRAPHER
xhoch4
Theater Ingolstadt
EDITOR
Theater Ingolstadt
URL
www.theater.ingolstadt.de
COUNTRY
Germany

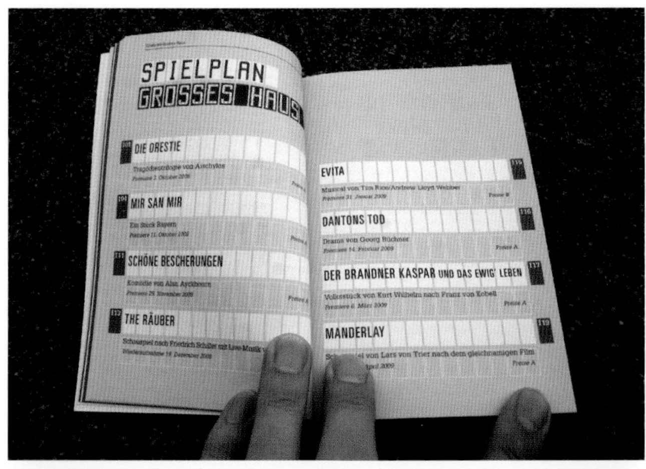
SPIELPLAN
GROSSES HAUS
DIE ORESTIE
MIR SAN MIR
SCHÖNE BESCHERUNGEN
THE RÄUBER
EVITA
DANTONS TOD
DER BRANDNER KASPAR UND DAS EWIG' LEBEN
MANDERLAY

SUSANNE
ENGELHARDT

DIE
ORESTIE
Tragödientrilogie von Aischylos

NOTIZEN
ZUR
DEMOKRATIE

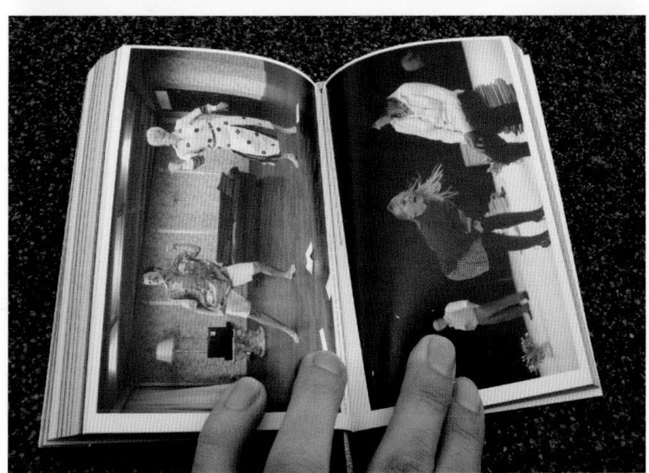

SAALPLAN
GROSSES HAUS

BEFREIT
DIE
BOTSCHAFT
STRÖER
deutsche städte medien

DEMOKRATIE
EIN FÜR
ALLE MAL?
von William Pfaff (2005)

SILVER
PRODUCT CATALOGUE

TITLE
Hering Berlin: Purism and Poetry
COMPANY
Edenspiekermann
CLIENT
Hering Berlin: Purism and Poetry
DESIGNERS
Eva Schekorr
Christian Hanke
CREATIVE DIRECTOR
Ralf Weissmantel
PHOTOGRAPHERS
Mathias Schormann
Andreas Deffner
Attila Hartwig
COUNTRY
Netherlands

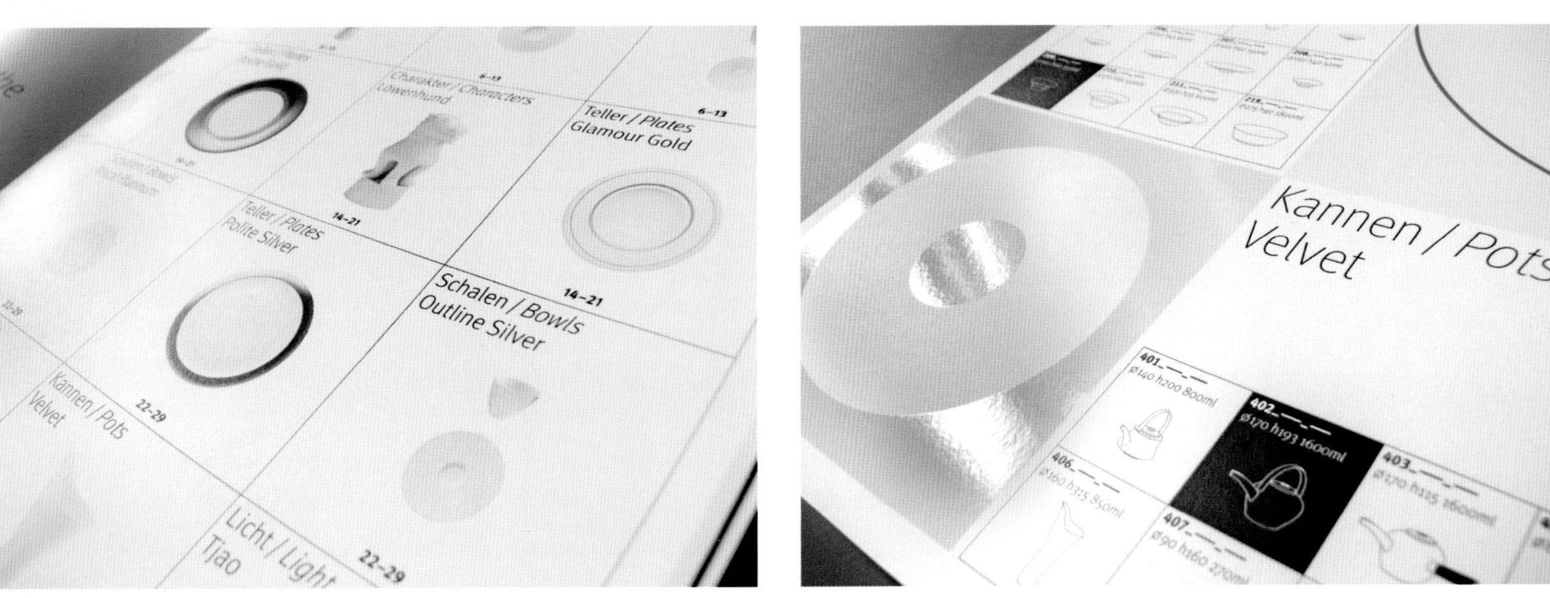
Teller / Plates
Glamour Gold
Teller / Plates
Polite Silver
Schalen / Bowls
Outline Silver
Kannen / Pots
Velvet
Licht / Light
Tjao
Kannen / Pots
Velvet
401.
ø140 h200 800ml
402.
ø170 h193 1600ml
403.
ø170 h125 1600ml
406.
ø160 h315 850ml
407.
ø90 h160 270ml

BRONZE
PRODUCT CATALOGUE

TITLE
Zen Mascaro
COMPANY
beetroot design group
CLIENT
E&K Fashion Group
COUNTRY
Greece

BRONZE
PRODUCT CATALOGUE

Work by

Form Us
With Love

Work by

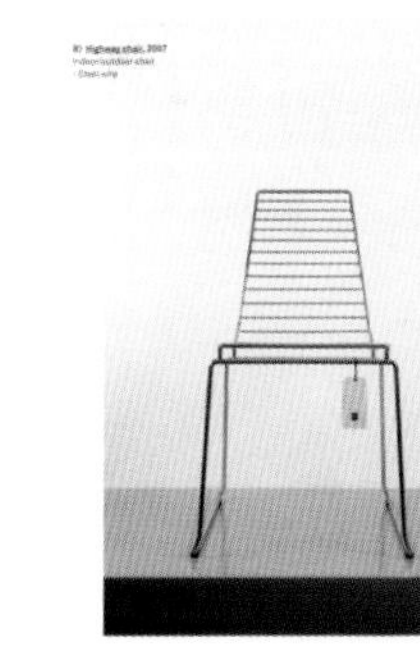

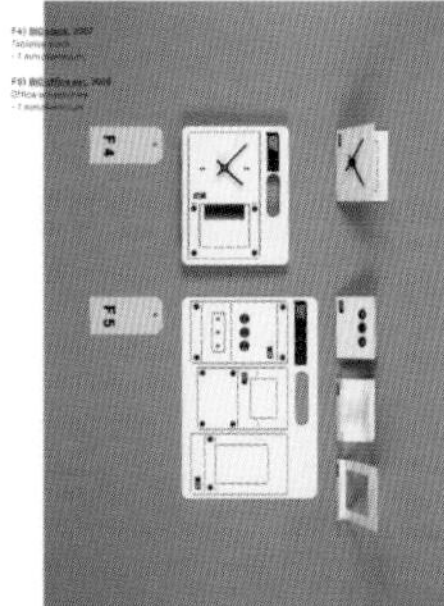

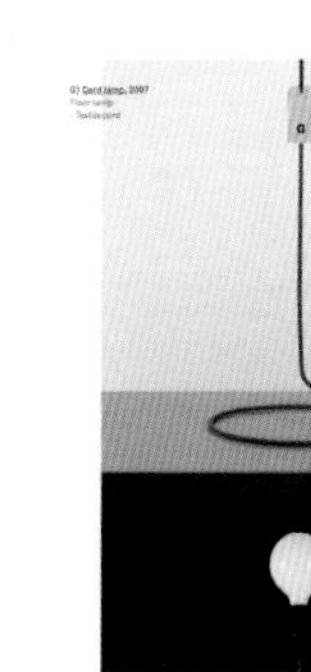

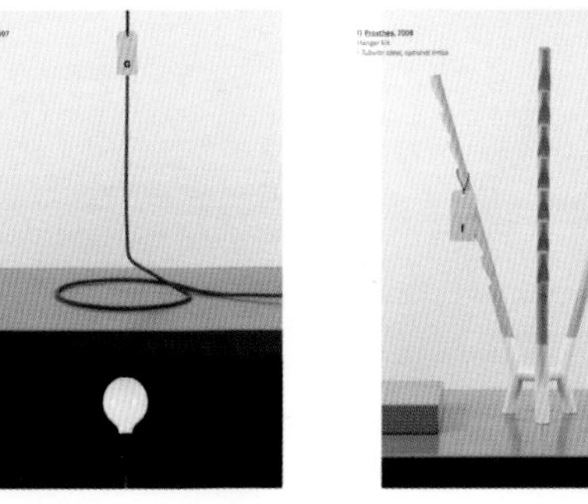

TITLE
Work by Form Us With Love
COMPANY
Daquar
CLIENT
Form Us With Love
COUNTRY
Sweden

TITLE
Wistoba
COMPANY
Heine Warnecke Design GmbH
CLIENT
Wistoba Pinselfabrik Wilhelm Stollberg GmbH & Co.
URL
www.wistoba.de
COUNTRY
Germany

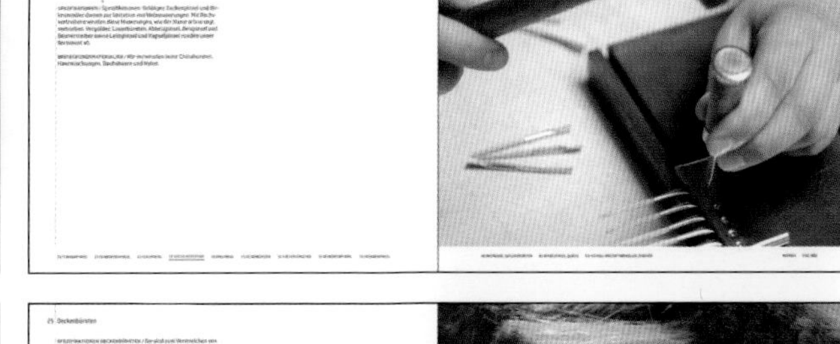

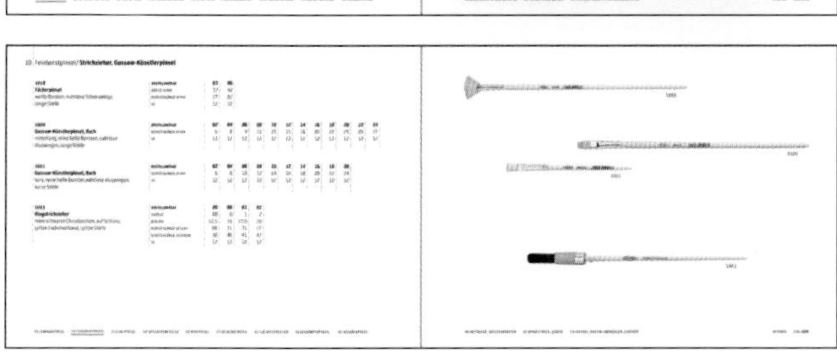

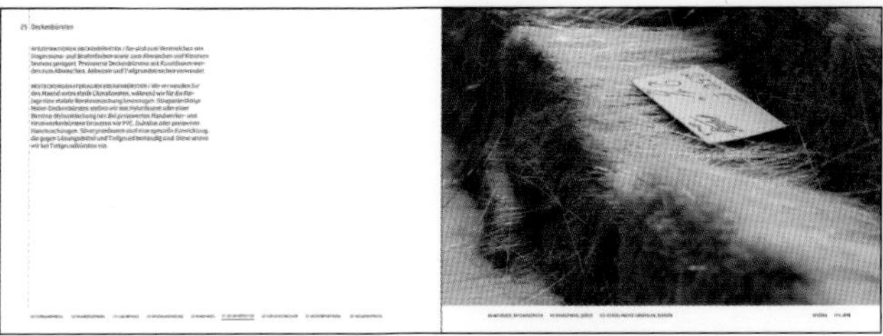

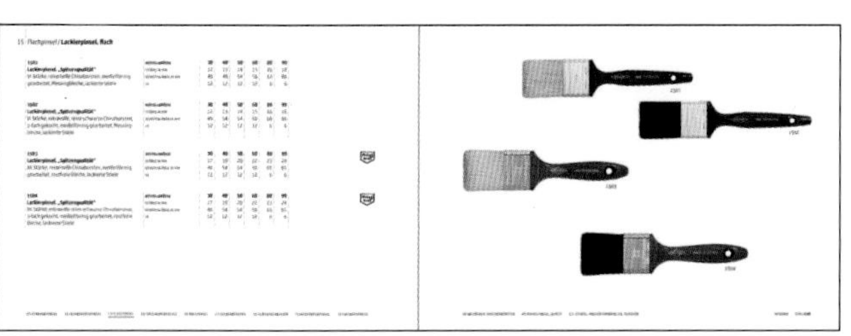

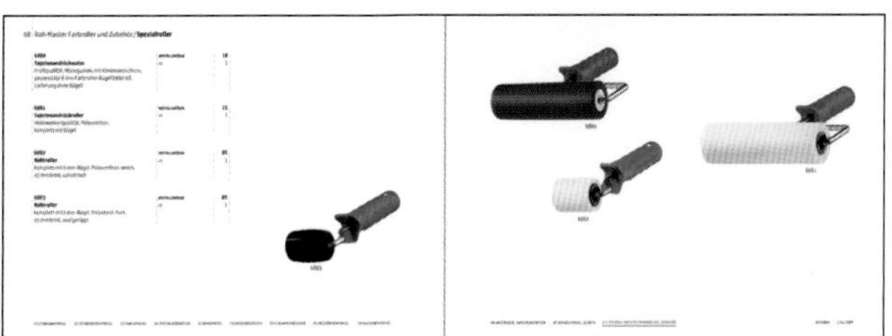

GOLD
ARTISTIC CATALOGUE

TITLE
The LAB 40 Exhibitions
COMPANY
Creative Inc
CLIENTS
The LAB
Dublin City Council
DESIGNER
Ciara Cantwell
CREATIVE DIRECTOR
Mel O'Rourke
DESIGN DIRECTOR
Ciara Cantwell
EDITOR
Gemma Tipton
PRINTER
Booxs, The Netherlands
COUNTRY
Ireland

This section is always tricky to judge: one must separate designer from artist. The same paradigm applies to the designer, who must showcase while avoiding the easy option of absence or cold distance or the excess of an obtrusive mise en scène. The match must be just right, and each intention measured. The Lab pulled off this difficult balancing-act, which is why the jury picked its catalogue – which, moreover, is flawlessly executed, with no overload of production effects.

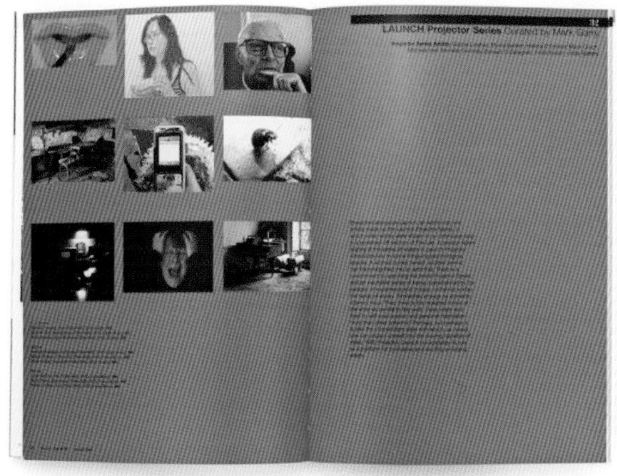

SILVER
ARTISTIC CATALOGUE

TITLE
Ten Images for Ithaca 2009
COMPANY
the design shop
CLIENT
Municipality of Ithaca
DESIGNER
Maria Kefala
ART DIRECTOR
Dionysis Livanis
PROJECT MANAGER
Olympia Aivazi
COUNTRY
Greece

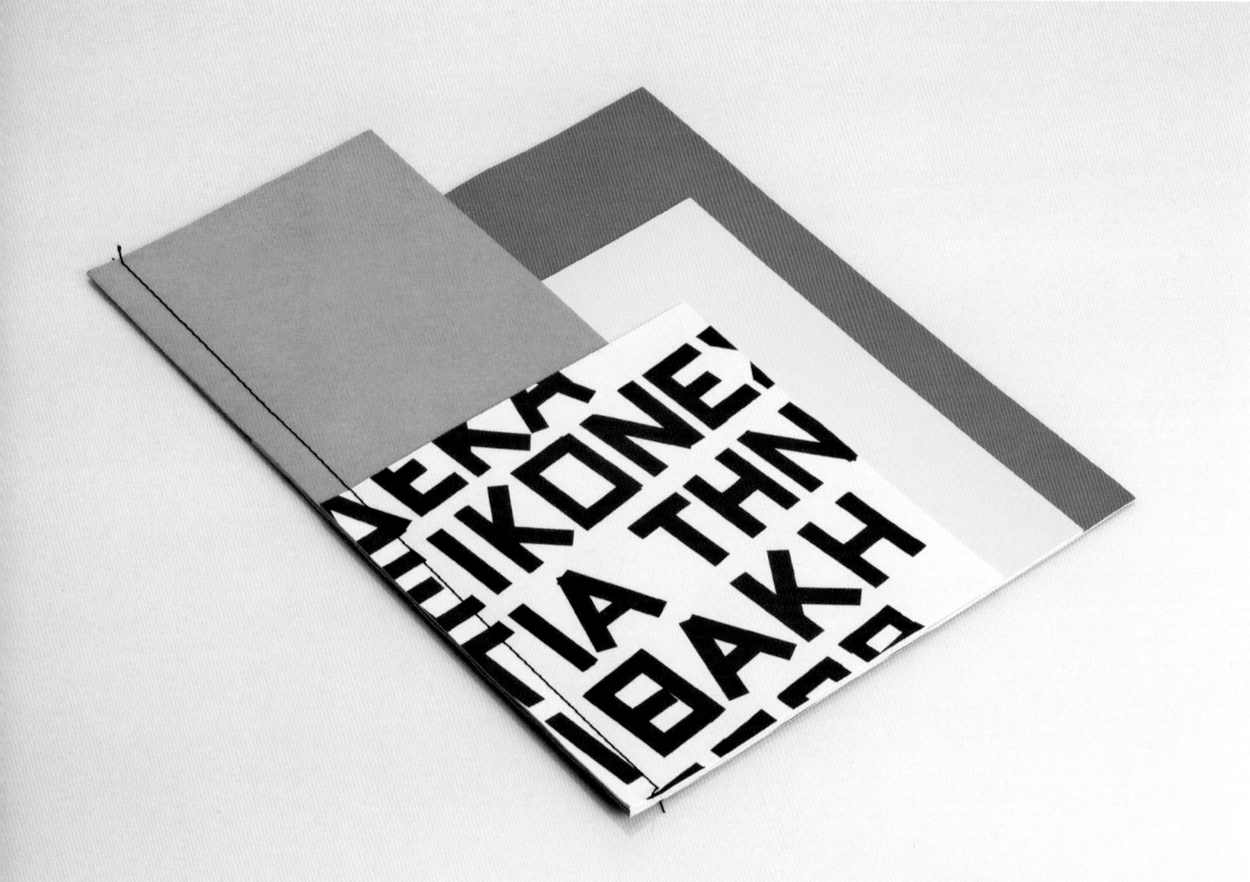

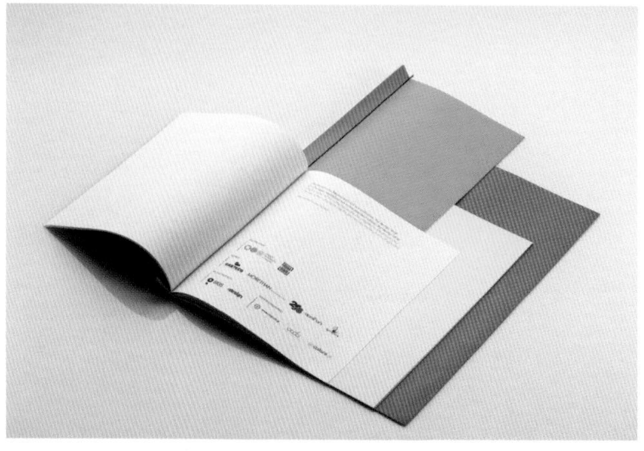

Ralf Ziervogel:
Every Adidas Got Its Story

20FIRST

Südhausbau
Ralf Ziervogel

Helder Suffenplan
Ralf Ziervogel

Helder Suffenplan

Dominikus Müller

Björn Streeck
Elena Hinterpohl

Germany

BRONZE
ARTISTIC CATALOGUE

01.

TITLE
Waves -The Art of
the Electromagnetic Society
COMPANY
labor b designbüro
CLIENT
HMKV
Hartware MedienKunstVerein
COUNTRY
Germany

02.

TITLE
Enter
COMPANY
Designbolaget
CLIENT
Brandts
COUNTRY
Denmark

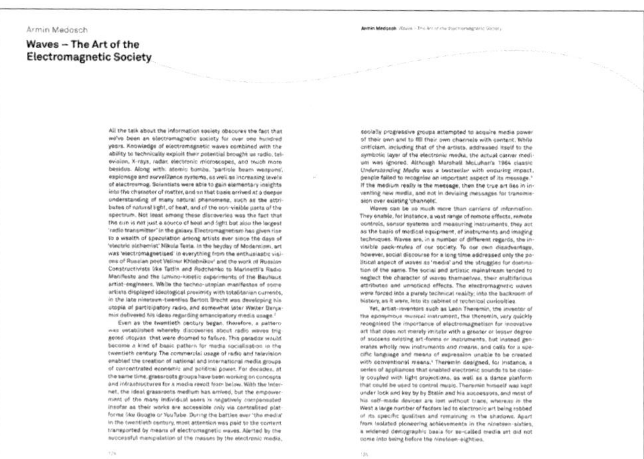
Armin Medosch
Waves – The Art of the Electromagnetic Society

Zweitägiger GPS-Workshop mit Evamaria Trischak
Two day GPS Workshop with Evamaria Trischak
5107: Dortmunder Stadtexpeditionen entlang der GPS-Matrix

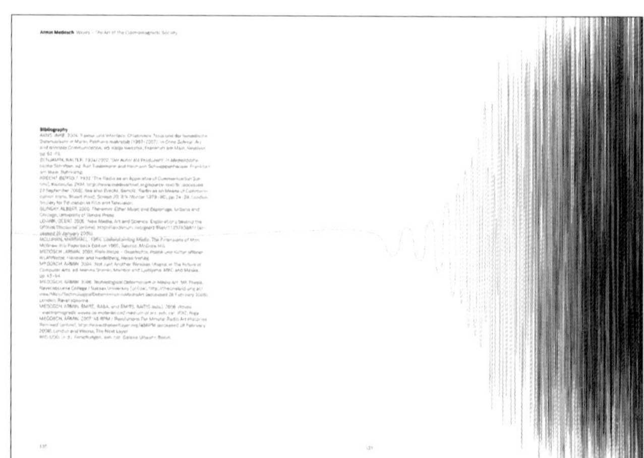

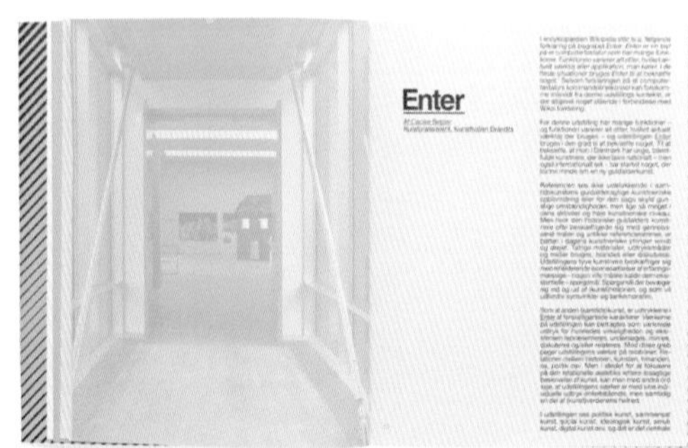

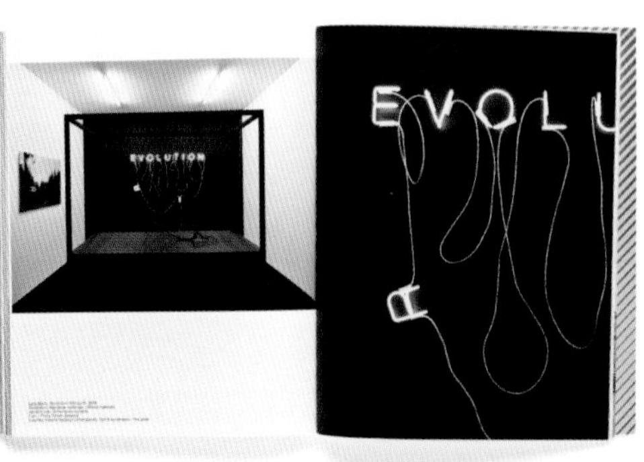

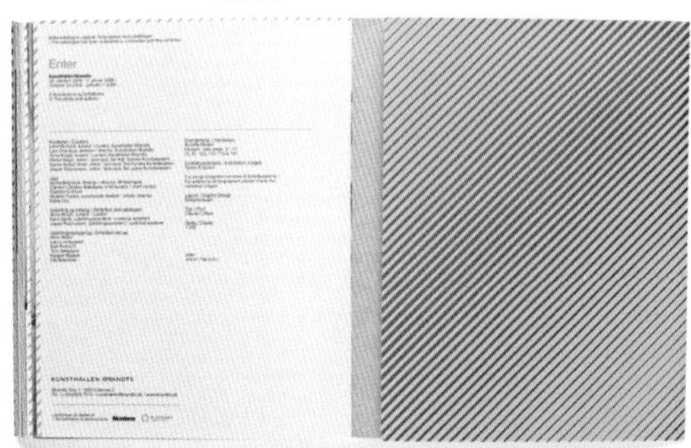

BRONZE
ARTISTIC CATALOGUE

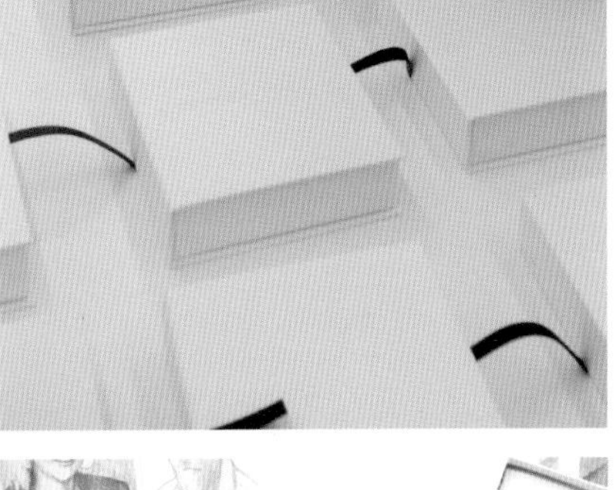

03.
TITLE
Individual Utopias
COMPANY
Laboratorium
CLIENT
Lala Rascic
COUNTRY
Croatia

04.
TITLE
Solid Coded
COMPANY
KW Neun Grafikagentur
CLIENT
FH Augsburg
COUNTRY
Germany

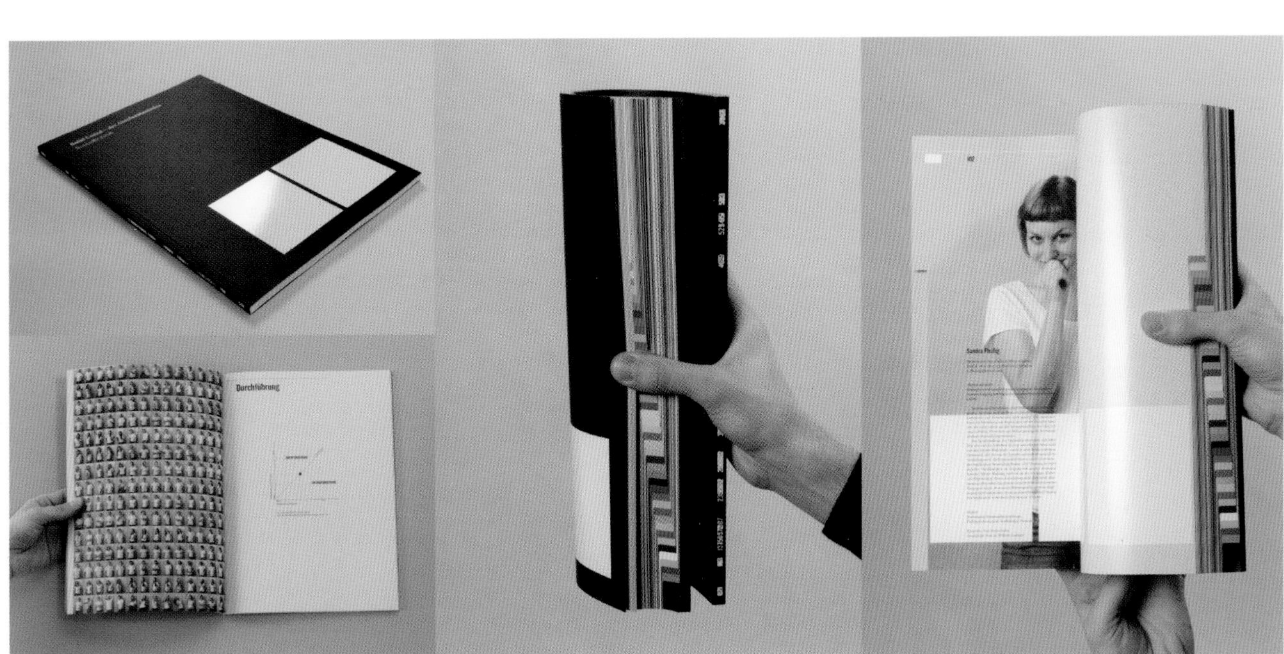
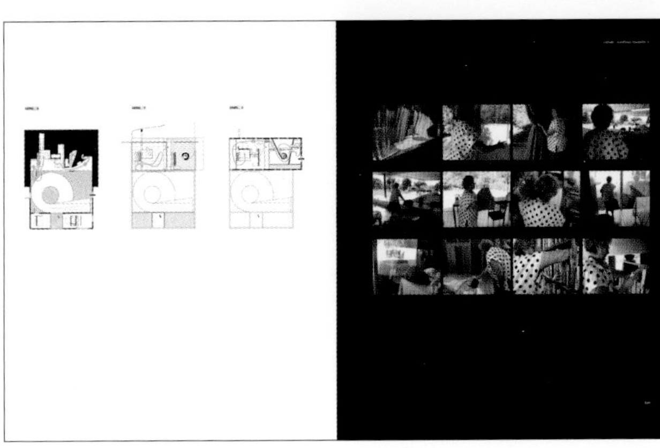
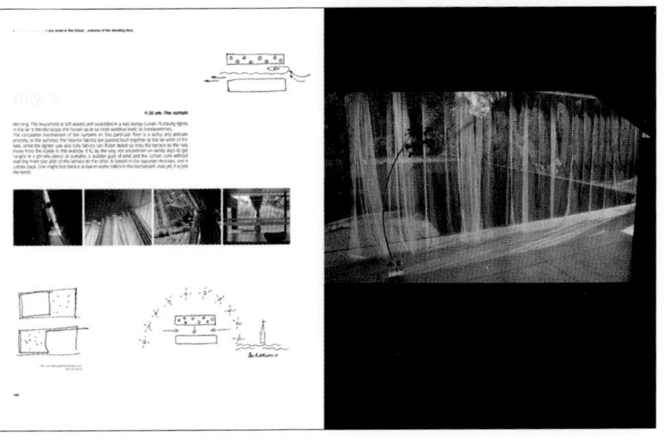

BRONZE
ARTISTIC CATALOGUE

05.
TITLE
Reflektor 1
COMPANY
Design Department of the University of Applied Sciences and Arts in Dortmund
CLIENT
Fachhochschule Dortmund
COUNTRY
Germany

06.
TITLE
Mutation II
COMPANY
a | part
CLIENT
Mois Européen de la Photographie (Café-Crème)
COUNTRY
Luxembourg

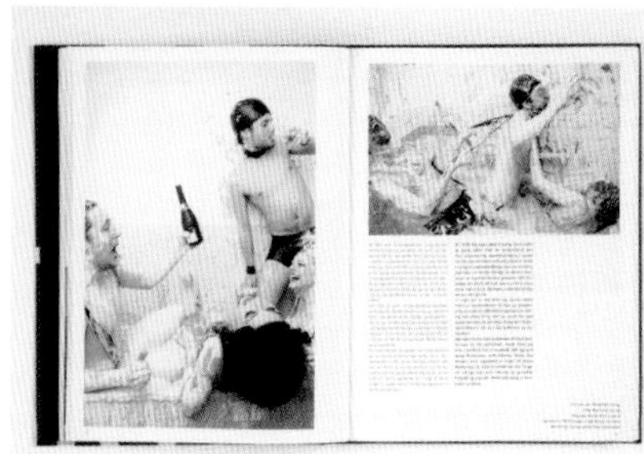

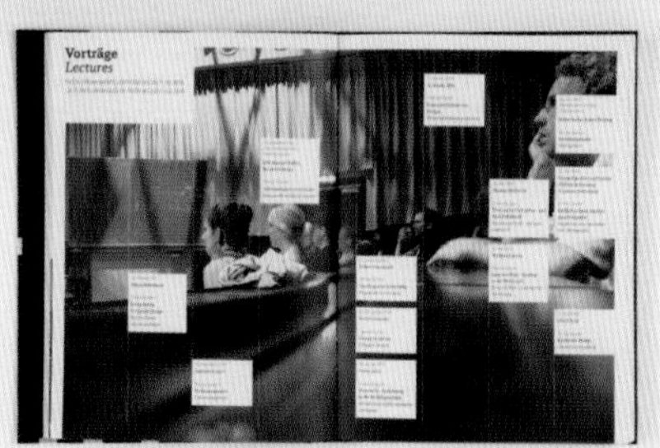

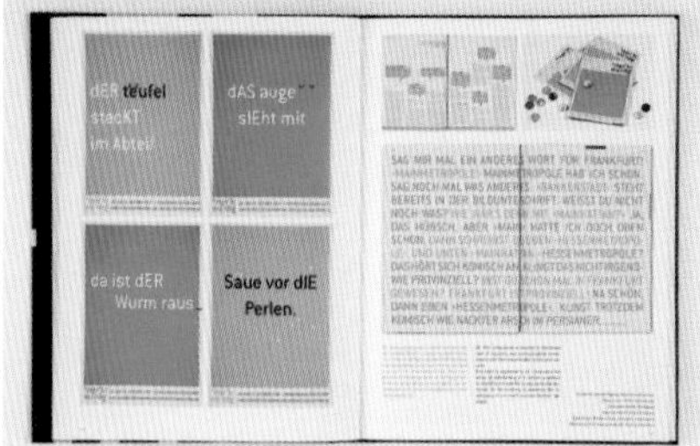

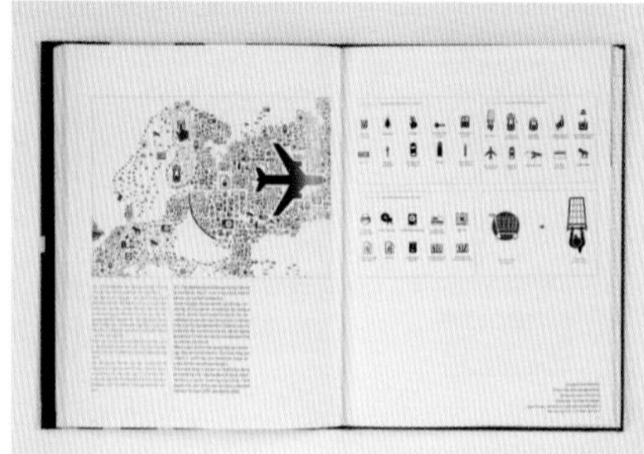

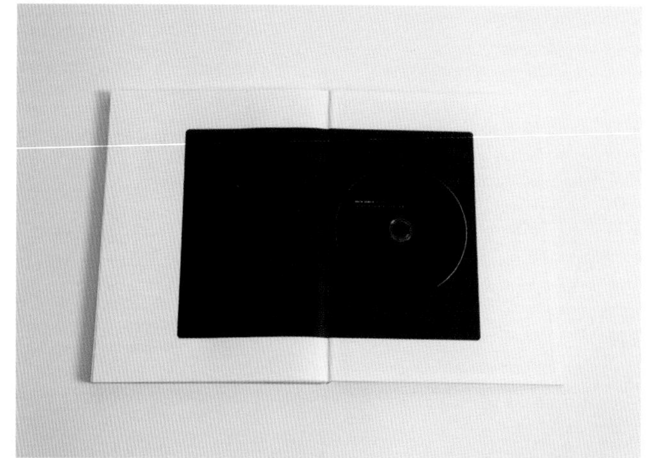

BRONZE
ARTISTIC CATALOGUE

07.

TITLE
WYSIWYG*
COMPANY
a | part
CLIENT
CNA - Centre National de l'Audiovisuel
COUNTRY
Luxembourg

08.

TITLE
Banks Violette
COMPANY
Linie 3 - Design- & Werbeagentur GmbH
CLIENT
Galerie Thaddaeus Ropac
COUNTRY
Austria

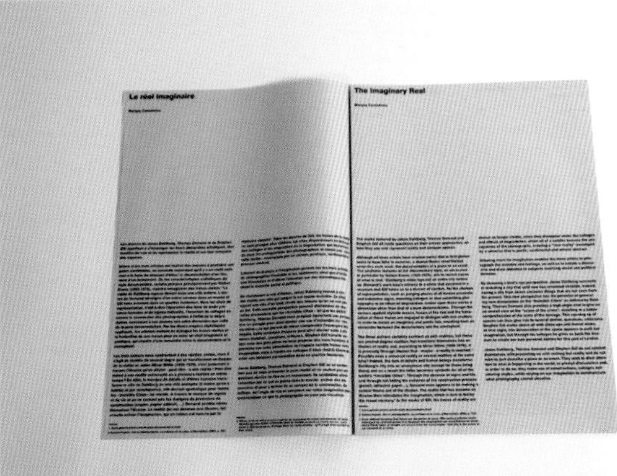

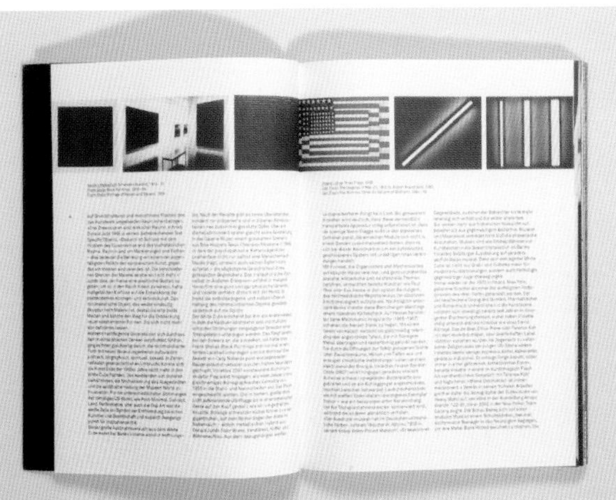

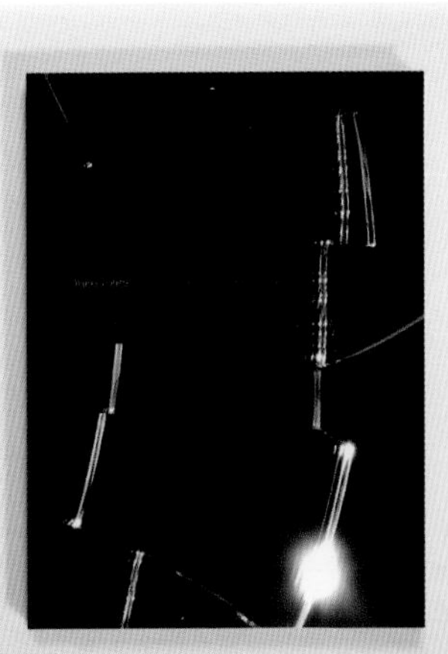

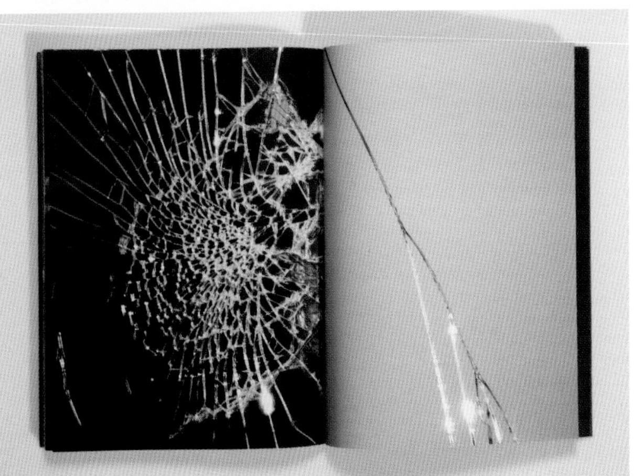

BRONZE
ARTISTIC CATALOGUE

09.
TITLE
Antony Gormley, Between You and Me
COMPANY
Linie 3 - Design- & Werbeagentur GmbH
CLIENT
Antony Gormley
COUNTRY
Austria

10.
TITLE
koolhaas houselife
COMPANY
Bruno Morello design
CLIENT
Bekafilms
COUNTRY
Italy

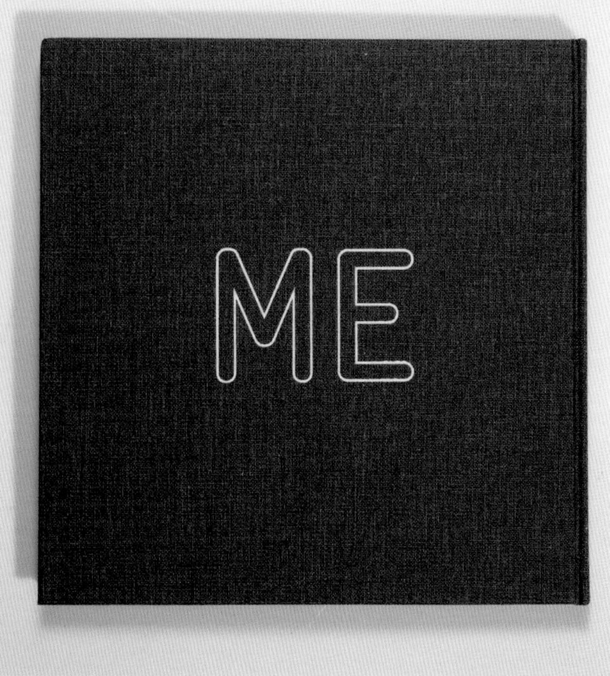

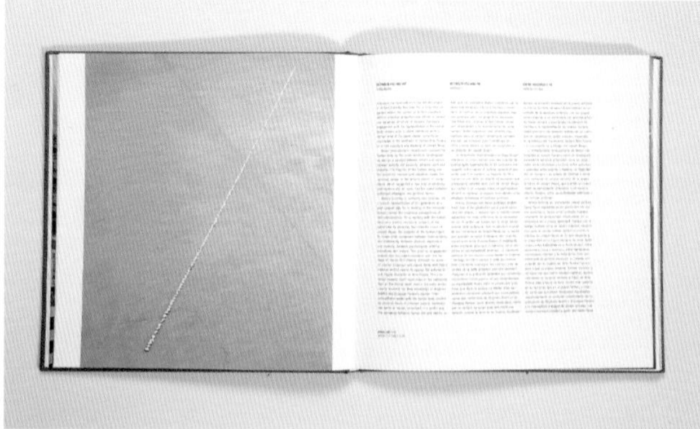

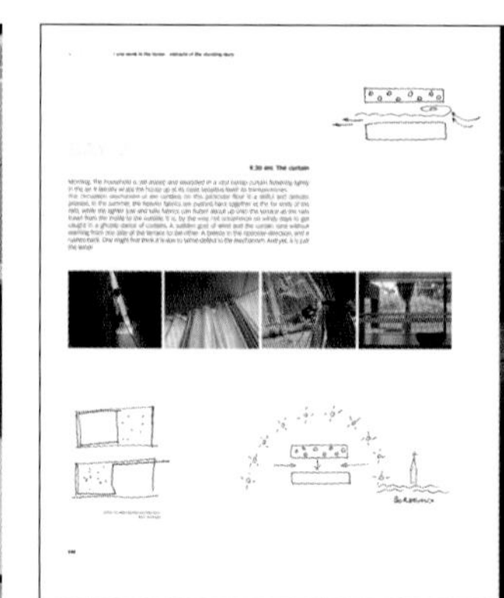

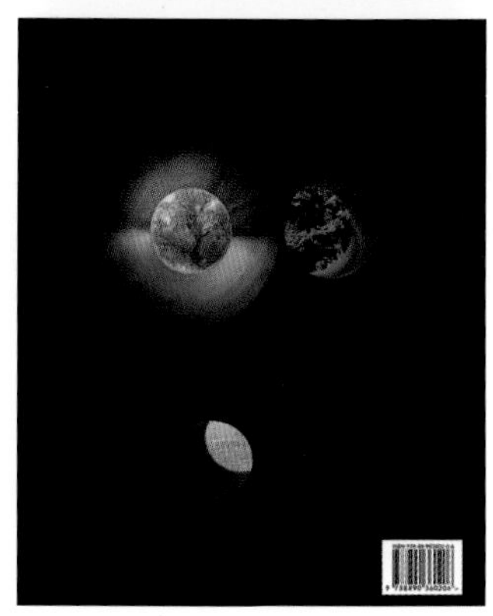

FINALIST
ARTISTIC CATALOGUE

01.
TITLE
Park X, exhibition catalogue
COMPANY
SE IDEA AB
CLIENT
Janne Björkman
COUNTRY
Sweden

02.
TITLE
Porous Borders
COMPANY
beetroot design group
CLIENT
Cyprus Architect Association
COUNTRY
Greece

GOLD
MAGAZINE

TITLE
IL - Intelligence in Lifestyle
COMPANY
Sole 24 ore Spa
CLIENT
Il Sole 24 ORE
DESIGNERS
Francesco Franchi
Luca Pitoni
Ilaria Tomat
ART DIRECTOR
Francesco Franchi
CREATIVE DIRECTOR
Luca Pitoni
EDITOR
Walter Mariotti
Paolo Martini
Guido Furbesco
WRITERS
Sara Deganello
Saverio Fossati
PHOTO EDITOR
Raffaele Vertaldi
COUNTRY
Italy

The magazine is a tough exercise for visual designers: an industrial product subject to many constraints. Made by a host of participants, it is truly the work of a team, with all the hitches that this entails. Another constraint is topicality: a magazine must always be in the zeitgeist but without every losing sight of the reader, whose satisfaction will dictate its success and therefore its survival.Il magazine, which draws inspiration from the visual quality of '70s style without every lapsing into vulgar pastiche, is a perfect example of a well-performed score. The covers are especially accomplished, and could account for the magazine's success on their own.

Ammirate le strisce colorate fuori dal finestrino.

GLOBAL REPORT

Debutto nero

Gelli, il barone e la Gelmini

Più veloce dell'aereo

Chloë Sevigny

CAPELLI BIONDI, OCCHI AZZURRI E UNA VERA PIOGGIA DI DOLLARI.

MA ALLORA CHE COSA LE MANCA?

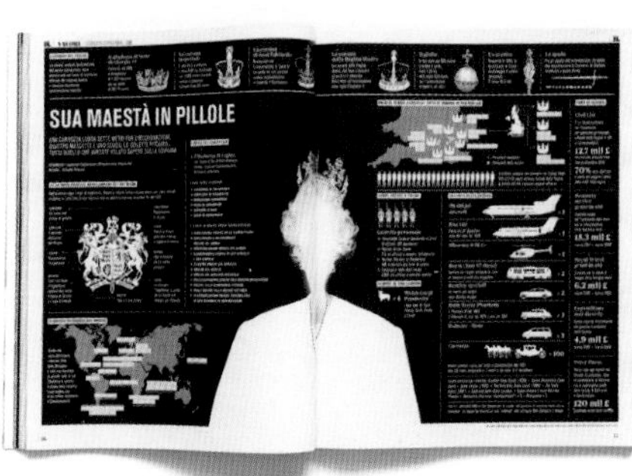
SUA MAESTÀ IN PILLOLE

OGGI 19 SETTEMBRE 2008 È TORNATO

DOISNEAU

RON, IL SEGUGIO DELLE STAR

NEW YORK

APPUNTAMENTO AL TOP

IN VASCA CON IL SILURO

SILVER
MAGAZINE

TITLE
Silver Magazine
COMPANY
wortwerk
CLIENT
Silver Server
DESIGNER
Verena Panholzer
ART DIRECTOR
Verena Panholzer
PHOTOGRAPHERS
Irina Gavrich
Michael Winkelmann
EDITOR
Andreas Kump
WRITER
Andreas Kump
OTHER
Bert Estl
URL
www.sil.at
COUNTRY
Austria

06Z036727 M
P.b.b. Verlagspostamt 1160 Wien

SILVER

DAS NETZ.KULTUR-MAGAZIN VON SILVER SERVER // NR.16 // 2008 // WWW.SIL.AT

WIR SIND DA *FLEXIBEL.*

Ein Heft zum Thema *Arbeit.*

SILVER
MAGAZINE

TITLE
Quart Heft für Kultur Tirol
COMPANY
Circus. Büro für Kommunikation und Gestaltung
CLIENT
Land Tirol/Austria
DESIGNER
Klasse Fons Hickmann (Universität d. Künste Berlin)
ART DIRECTOR
Circus. Büro für Kommunikation ung Gestaltung
CREATIVE DIRECTORS
Heidi Hackl
Andreas Schett
DESIGN DIRECTORS
Klaus Mayr
Peter Neurauter
Michaela Wurzer
EDITORS
Heidi Hackl
Andreas Schett
COUNTRY
Austria

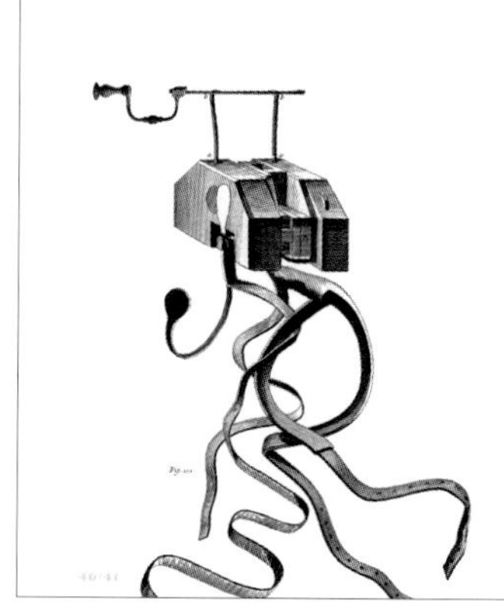

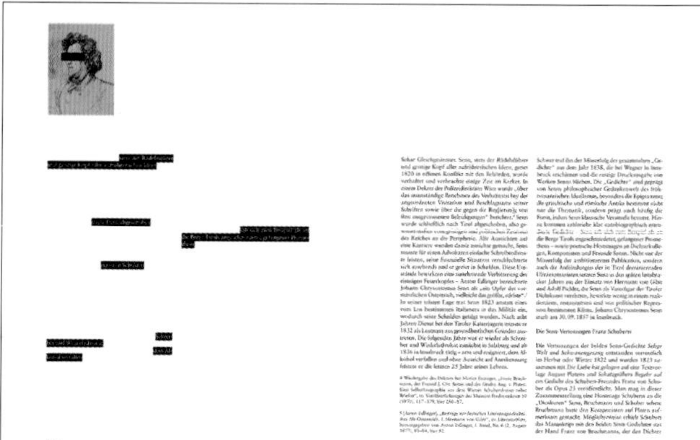

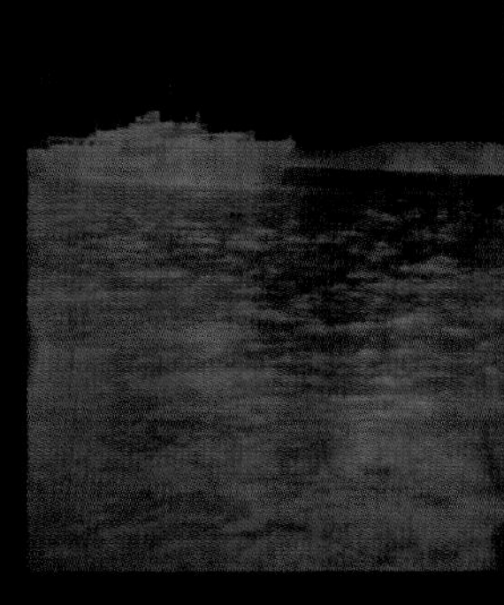

Sounding Lead

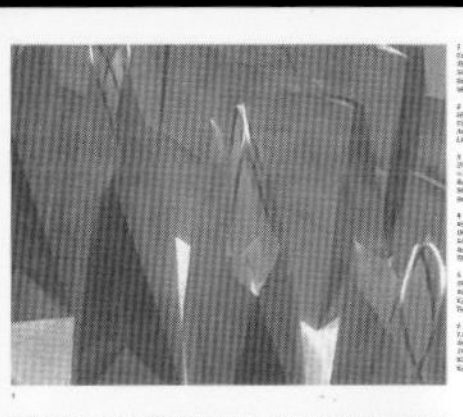

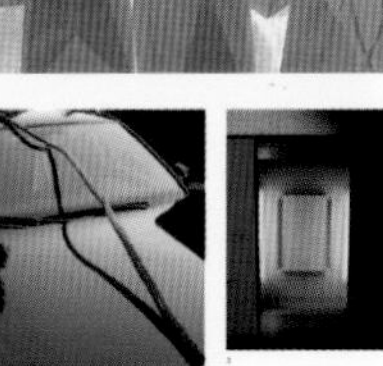

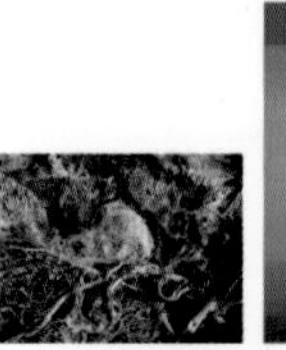

Inhalt

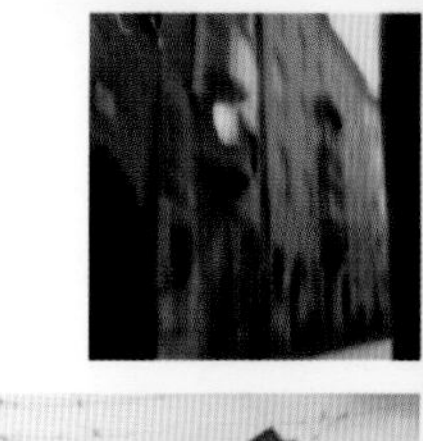

„Man muss froh sein, dass es das gibt.“

„Man muss froh sein, dass es das gibt.“

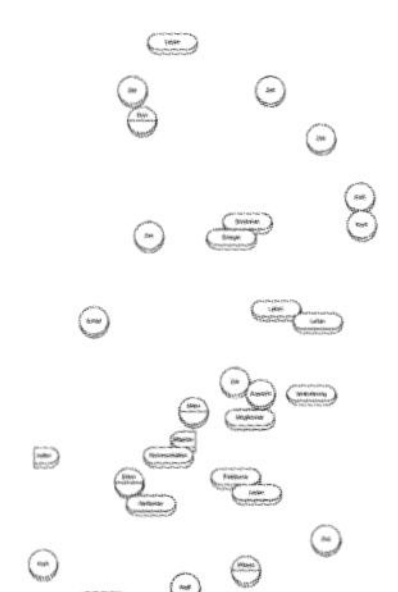

Die Möglichkeit, dem Stumpfsinn zu begegnen

BRONZE
MAGAZINE

TITLE
komma
DESIGNER
komma editorial department
CLIENT
Fakultaet fuer Gestaltung
COUNTRY
Germany

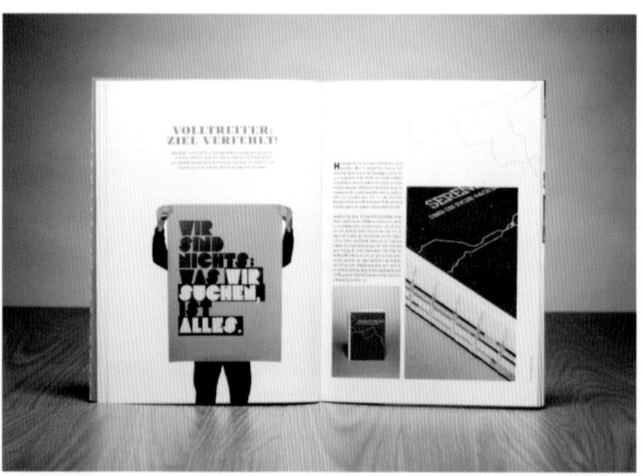

BRONZE
MAGAZINE

Komfort mag

Radek Sidun

Olga Benesova

DIY

Czech Republic

DIGITAL

GOLD
PROMOTIONAL SITE

TITLE
Roostein Hopkins Foundation promotional site
COMPANY
Moving Brands
CLIENT
Roostein Hopkins Foundation
DESIGNER
Arthur Nurse
DESIGN DIRECTOR
Mat Heinl
ART DIRECTOR
Samo Smon
CREATIVE DIRECTOR
James Bull
OTHER
Ying Miller
URL
www.rhfoundation.org.uk
COUNTRY
United Kingdom

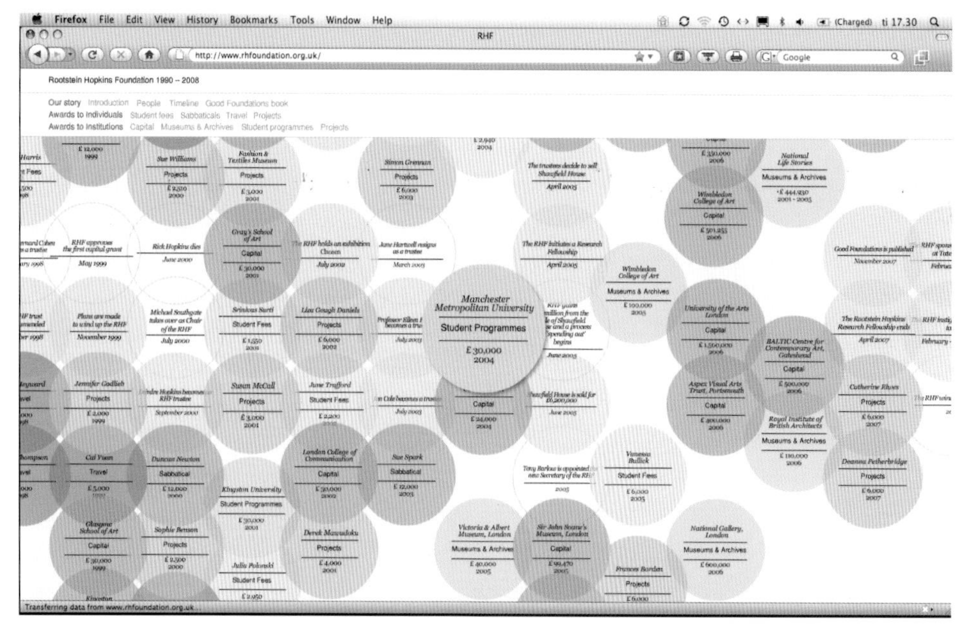

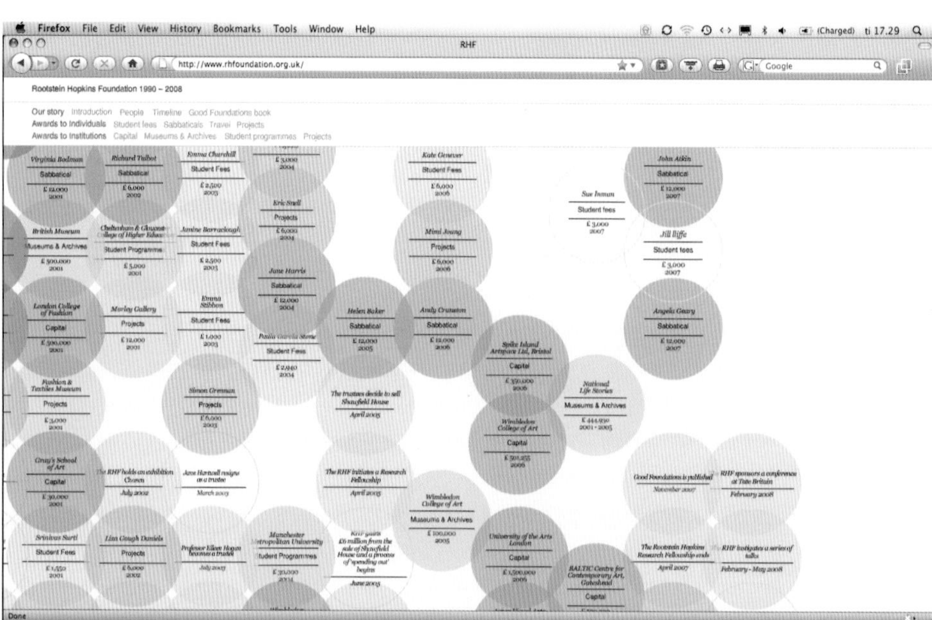

Visual design is increasingly expressing its power and inventiveness in the world of the web. Not only has it become a discipline in its own right, with specific métiers and knowledge; it is also a realm of experimentation where graphic design in the literal sense of the term spans its entire spectrum, because it involves interacting with visual content where notions of functional ergonomics and interaction are more important than anywhere in the print sector. This execution, among finalists of a very high standard, finally won through. It shows simply how access to and navigation in a mass of information can be at once straightforward, intuitive, innovative and aesthetic.

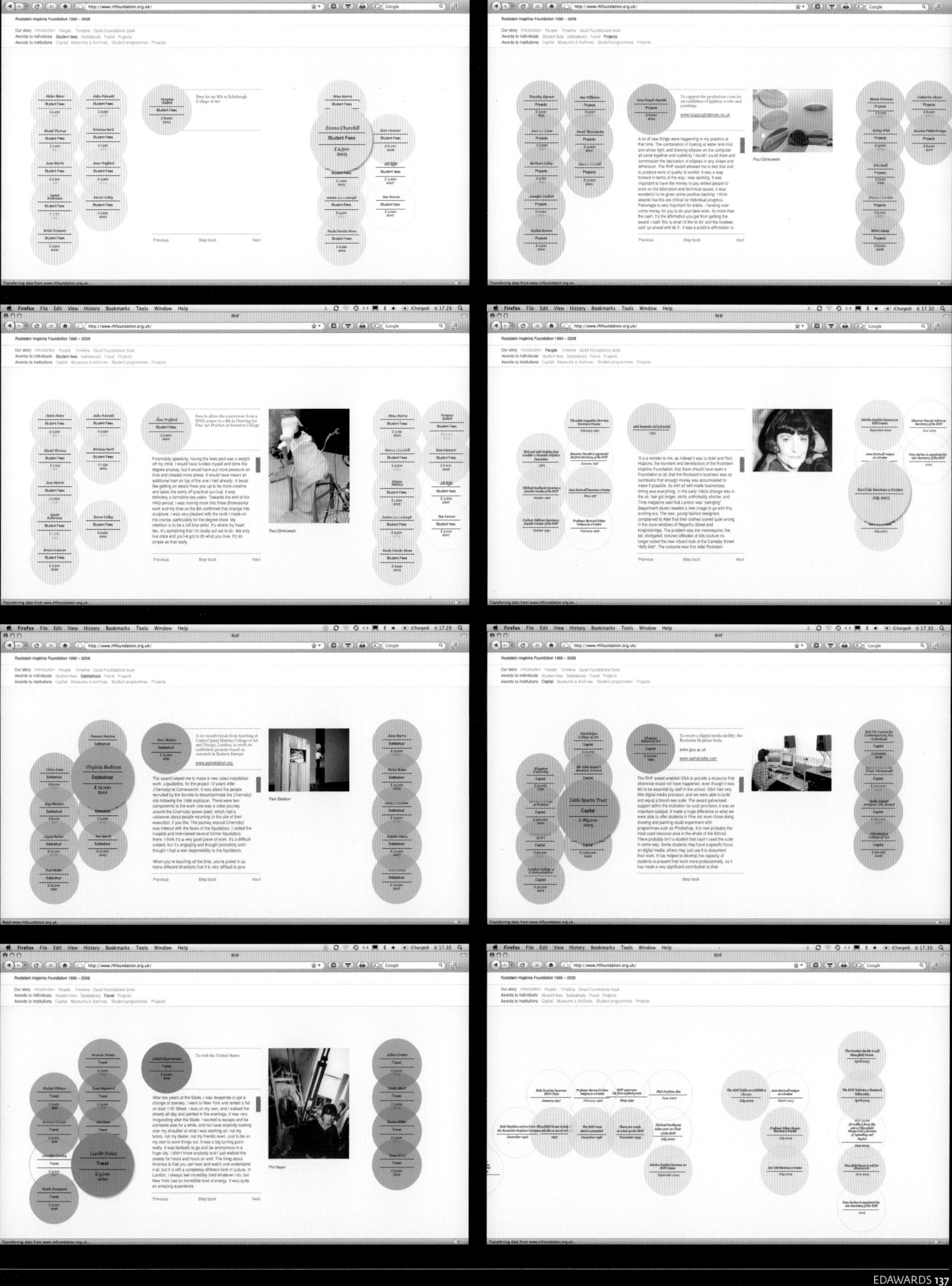

BRONZE
PROMOTIONAL SITE

TITLE
IAmsterdam
COMPANY
Fabrique Communicatie en Design
CLIENT
Gemeente Amsterdam
URL
www.iamsterdam.com
COUNTRY
Netherlands

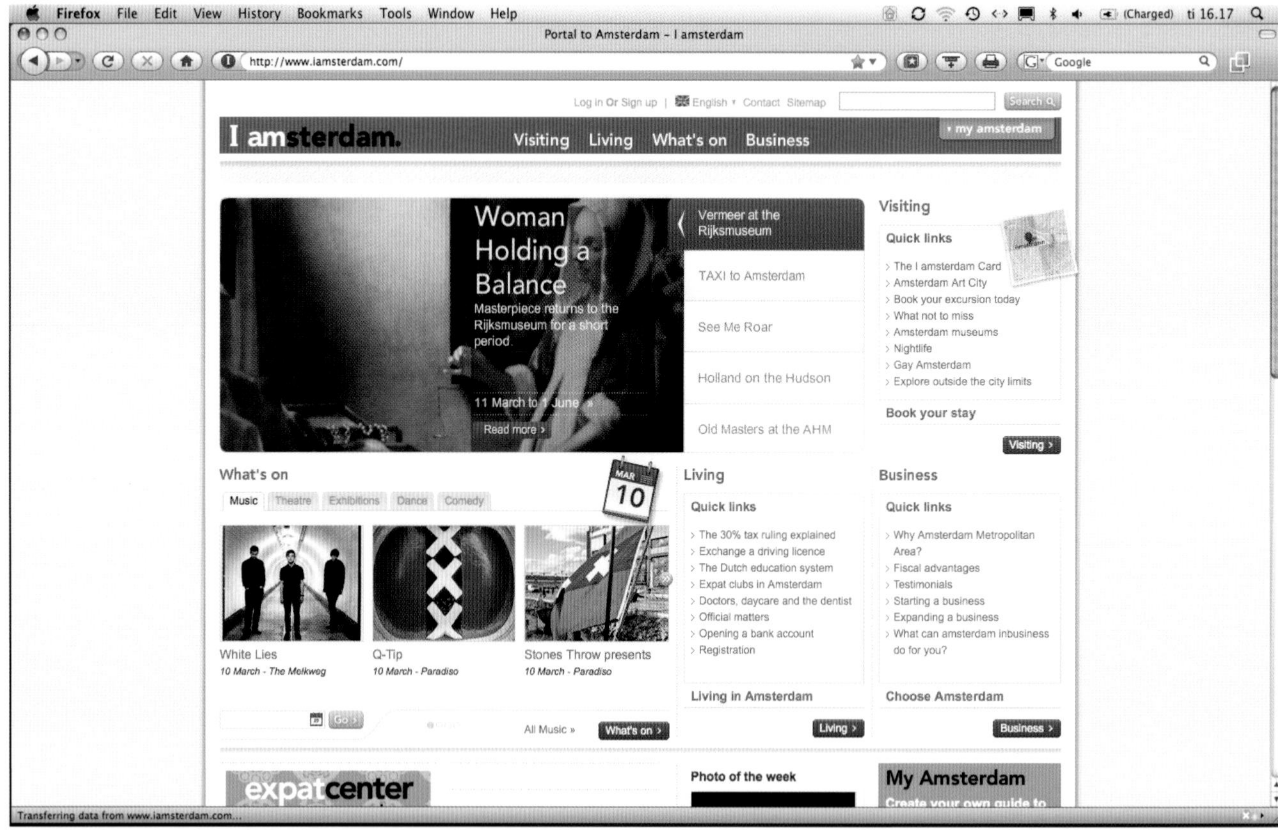

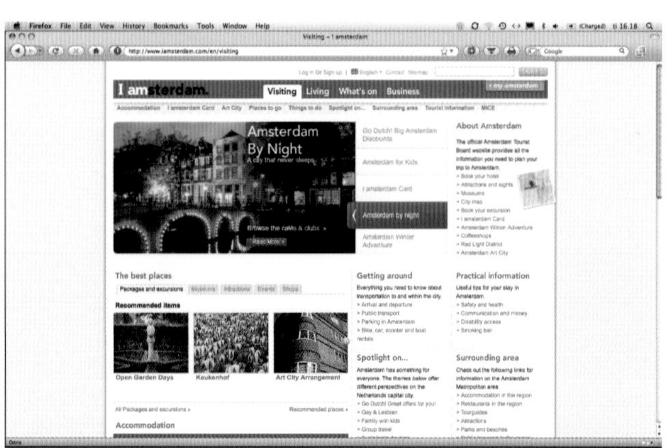

BRONZE
PROMOTIONAL SITE

TITLE
Help The Honey Bees
COMPANY
unit9
CLIENT
Haagen Dazs
URL
www.helpthehoneybees.com
COUNTRY
United Kingdom

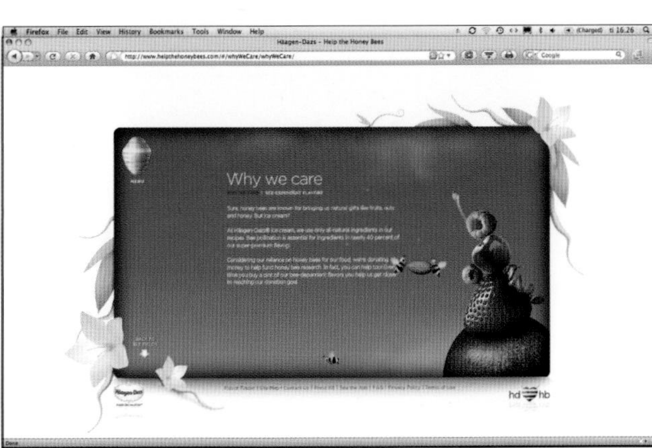

BRONZE
PROMOTIONAL SITE

TITLE
Samsung 8 series
COMPANY
Projector
CLIENT
Samsung
URL
www.designthatperforms.com
COUNTRY
Sweden

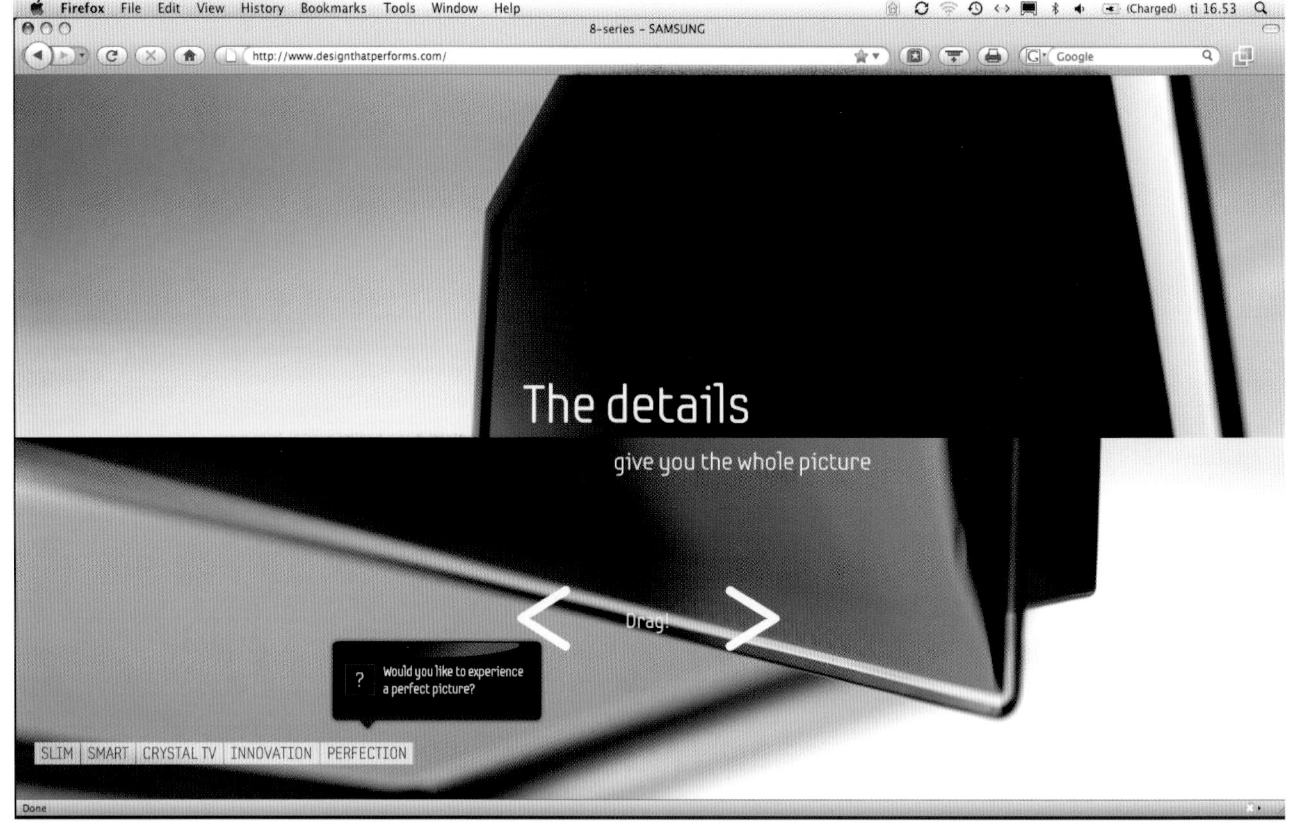

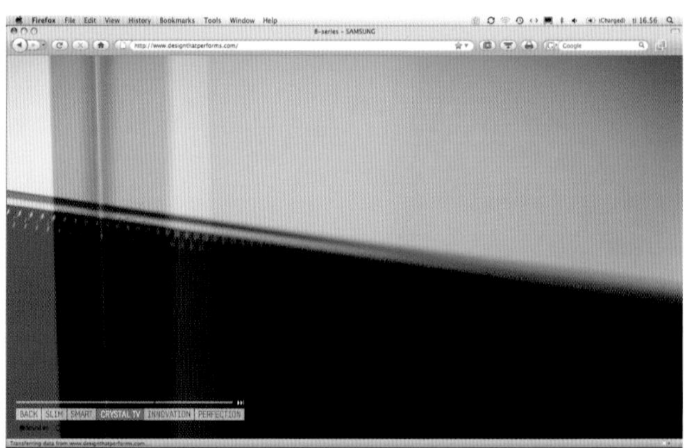

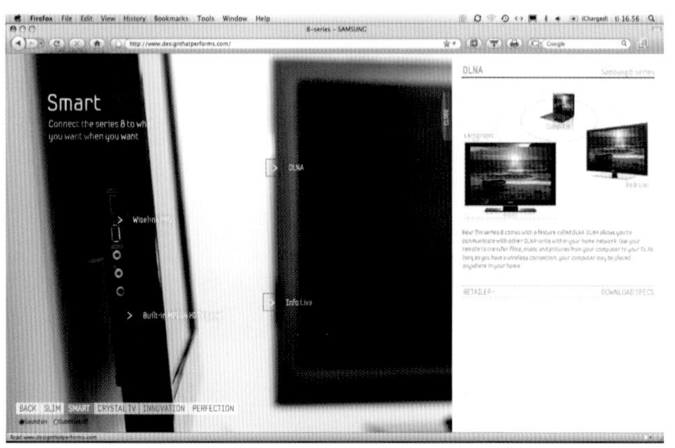

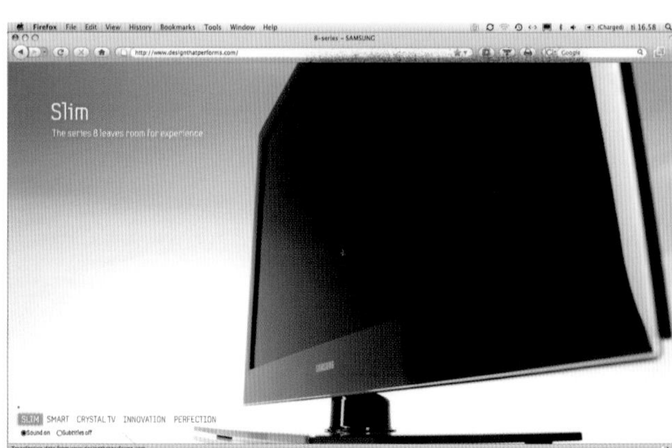

BRONZE
PROMOTIONAL SITE

TITLE
Henry M. Lion - Moments of Excellence
COMPANY
Newton 21
CLIENT
Vierke Corporate Fashion + Concepts
URL
www.henrym-lion.com
COUNTRY
Germany

BRONZE
PROMOTIONAL SITE

TITLE
Rick Mather Architects
COMPANY
KentLyons
CLIENT
Rick Mather Architects
URL
www.rickmather.com
COUNTRY
United Kingdom

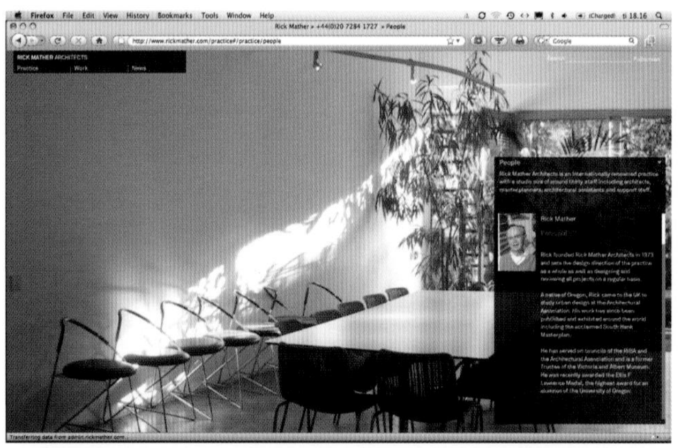

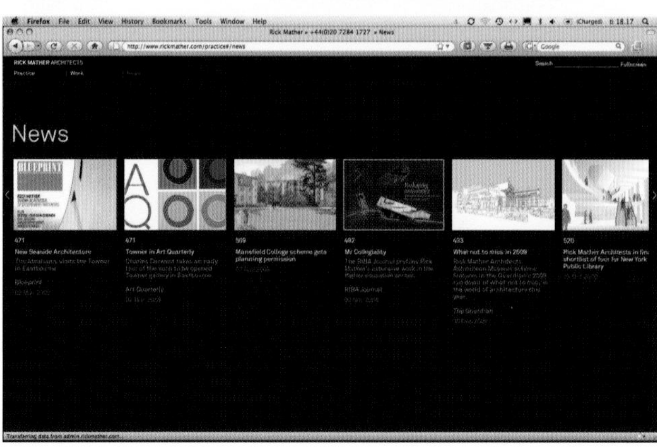

BRONZE
PROMOTIONAL SITE

TITLE
Snøhetta
COMPANY
Bleed
CLIENT
Snøhetta Architects
URL
www.snohetta.com
COUNTRY
Norway

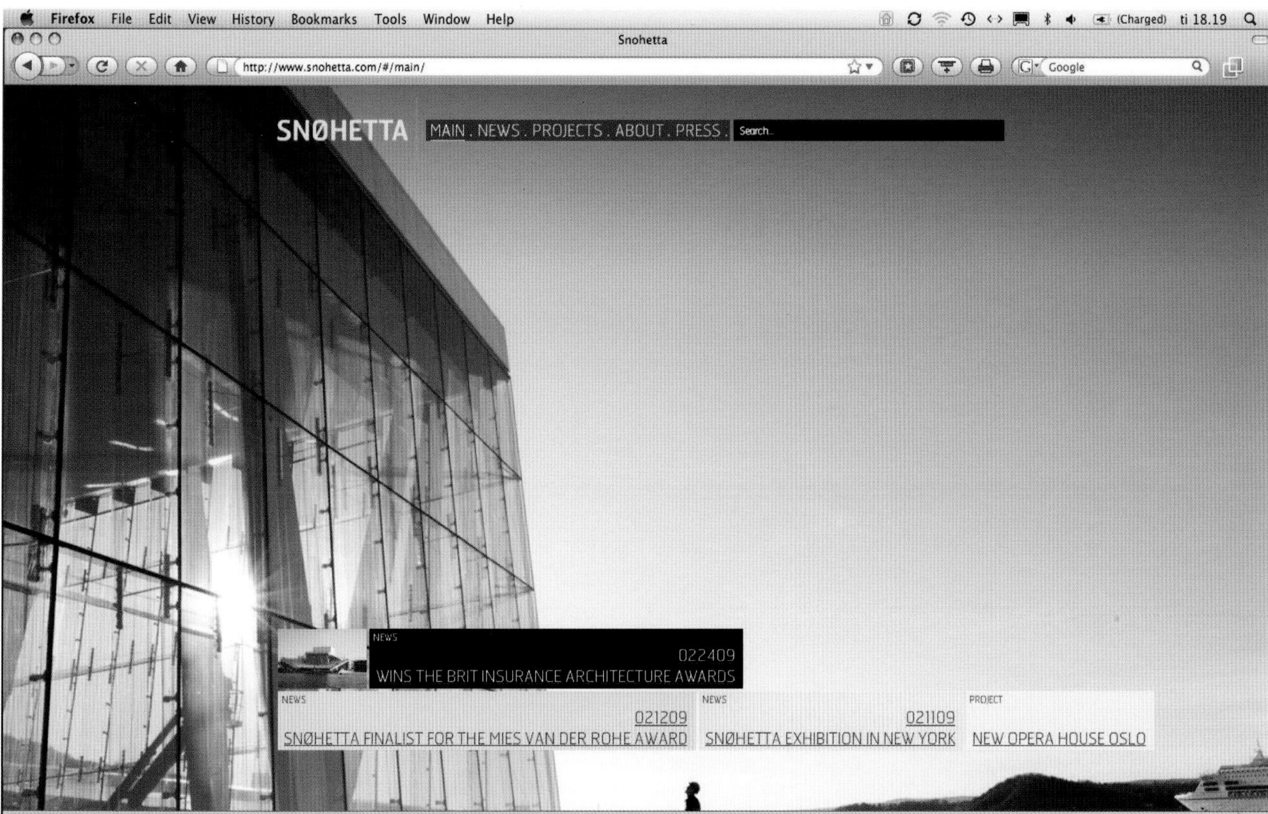

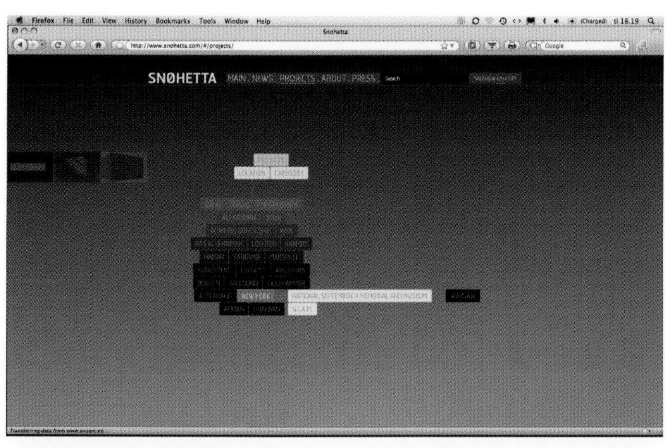

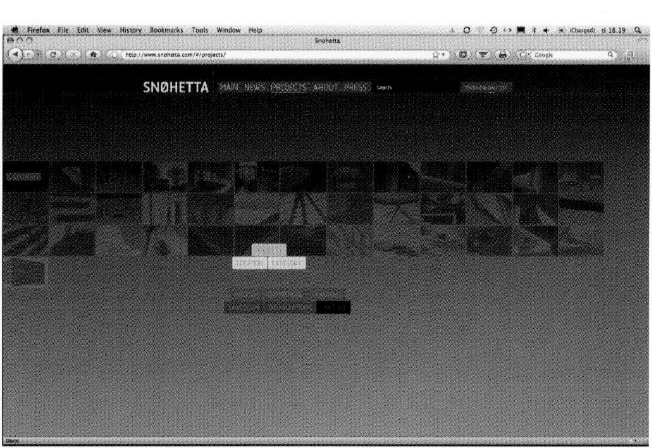

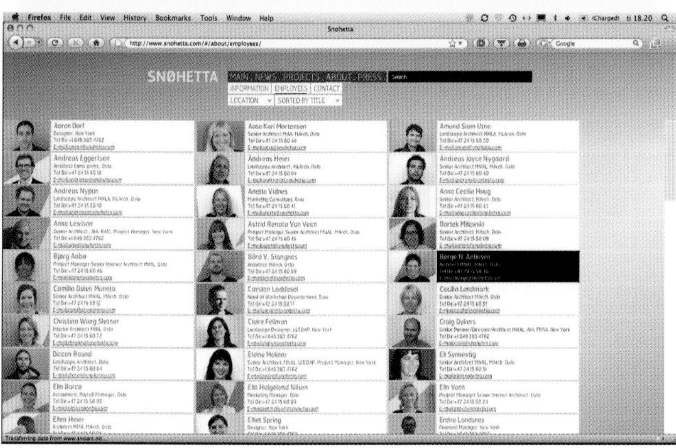

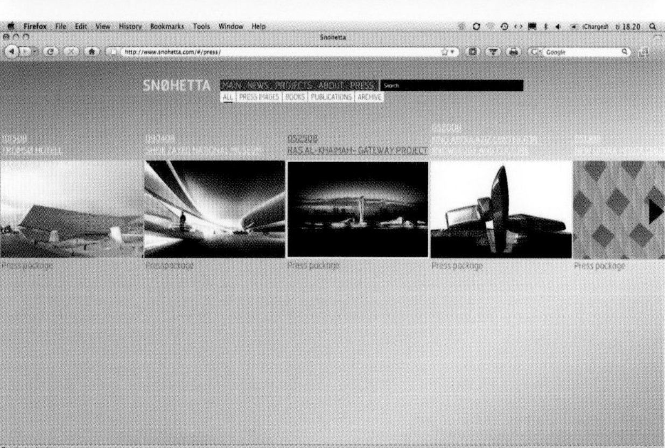

BRONZE
PROMOTIONAL SITE

TITLE
Mediations Biennale
COMPANY
Huncwot
CLIENT
Mediations Biennale
URL
www.mediations.pl/2008
COUNTRY
Poland

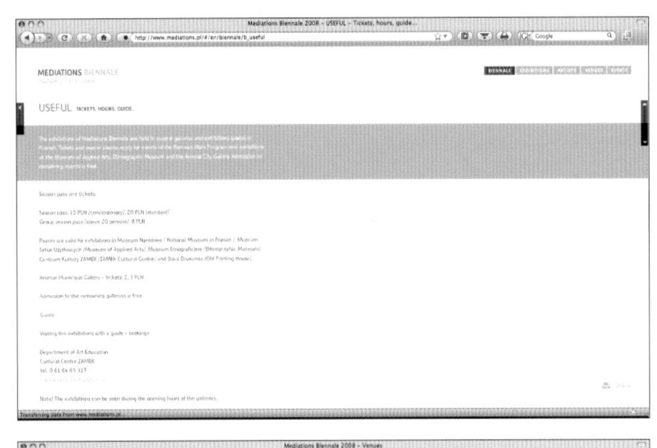

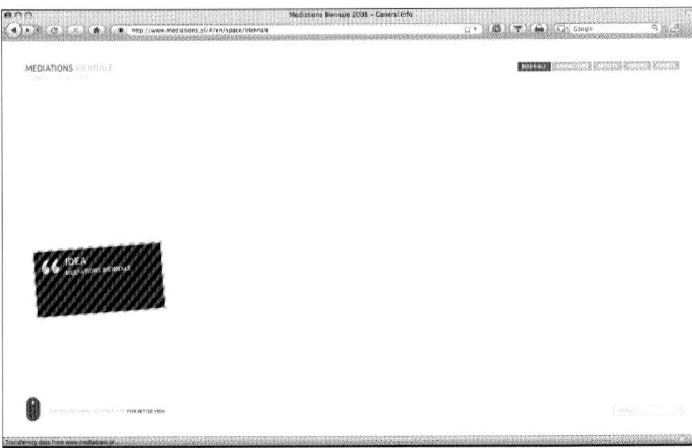

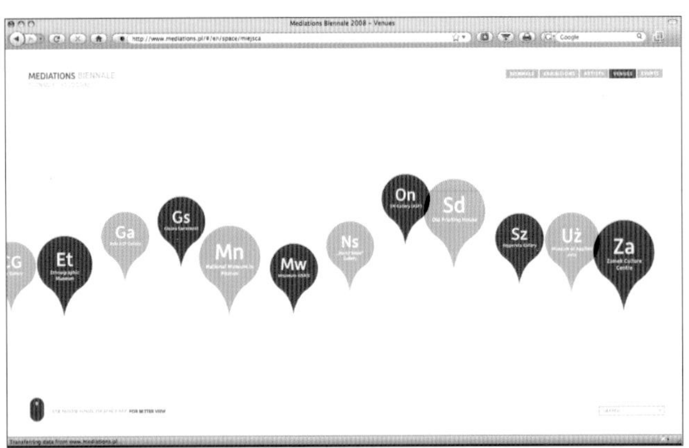

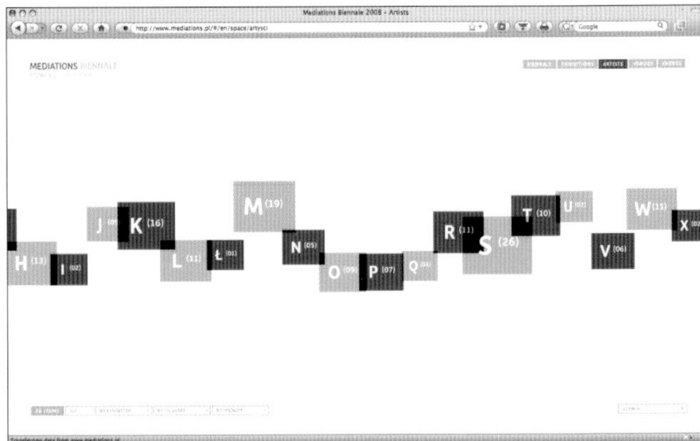

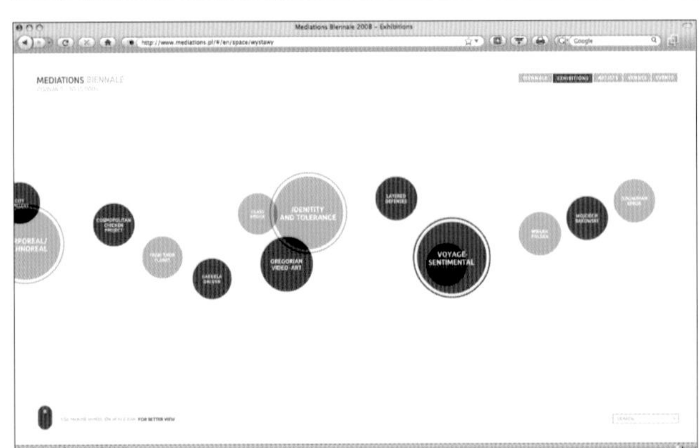

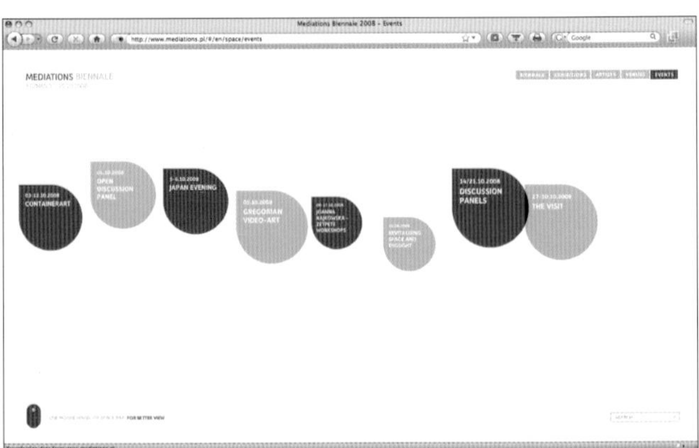

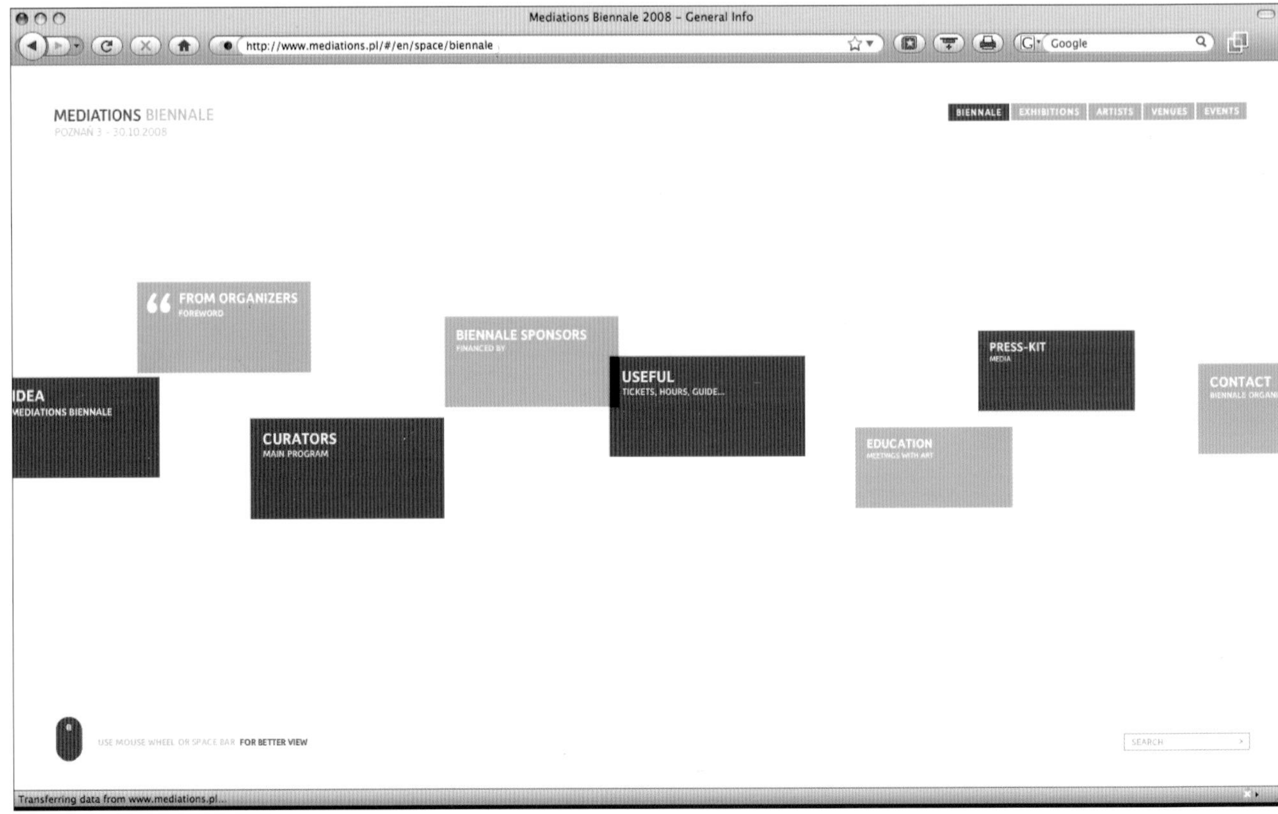

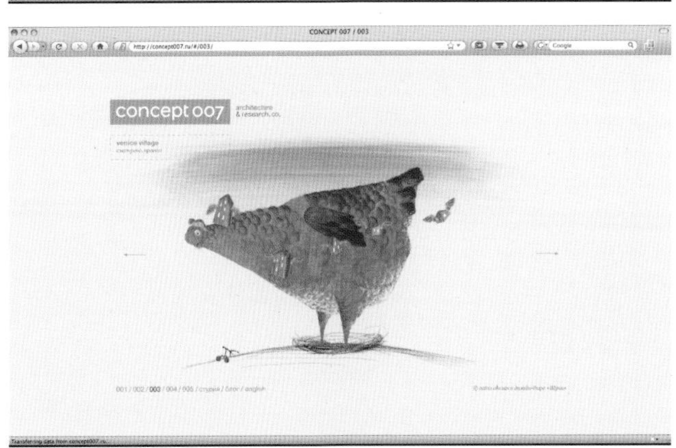

BRONZE
PROMOTIONAL SITE

TITLE
Concept 007
COMPANY
Shuka
CLIENT
architecture bureau
Concept 007
URL
concept007.ru
COUNTRY
Russia

BRONZE
PROMOTIONAL SITE

TITLE
Dreispitzhalle
COMPANY
Hauser
Schwarz GmbH
CLIENT
Christoph Merian Stiftung
Basel
URL
www.dreispitzhalle.ch
COUNTRY
Switzerland

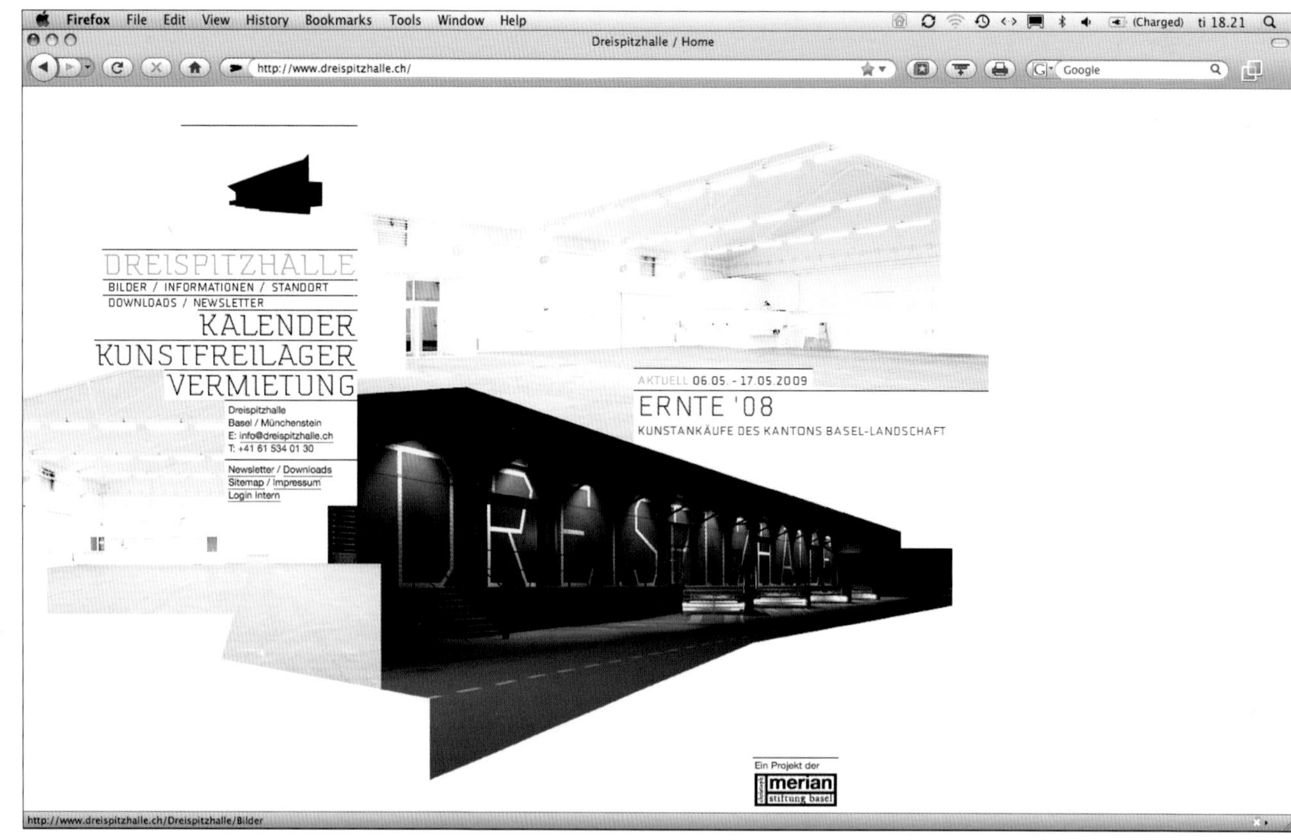

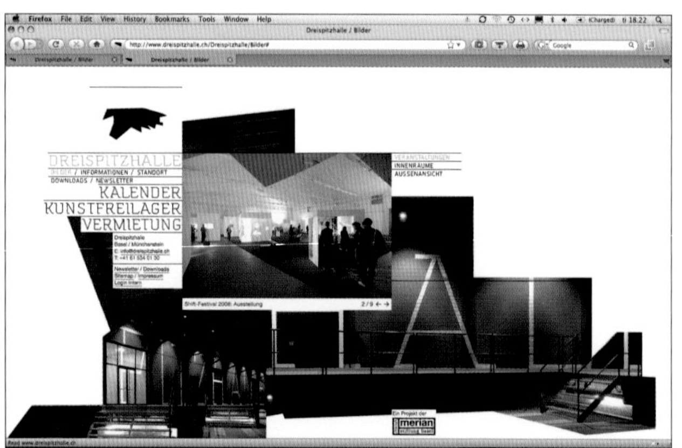

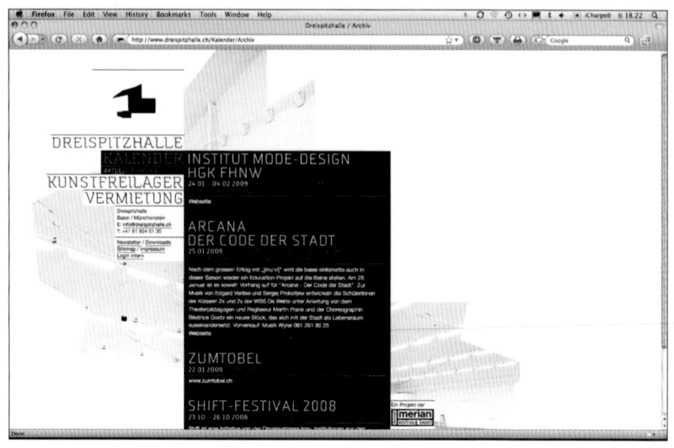

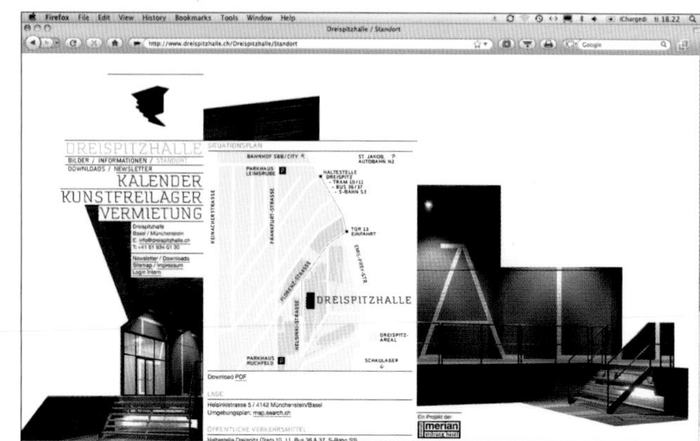

FINALIST
PROMOTIONAL SITE

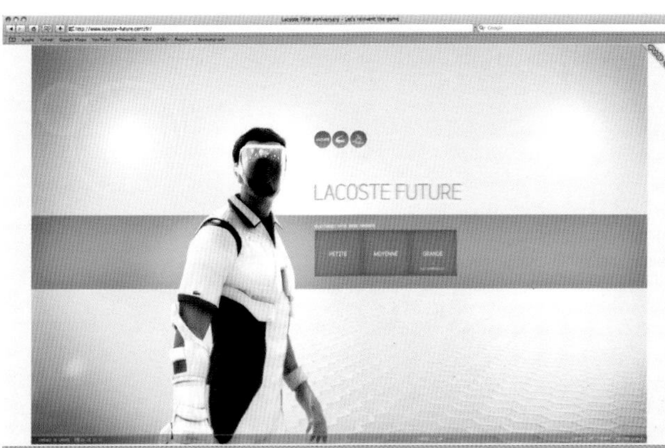

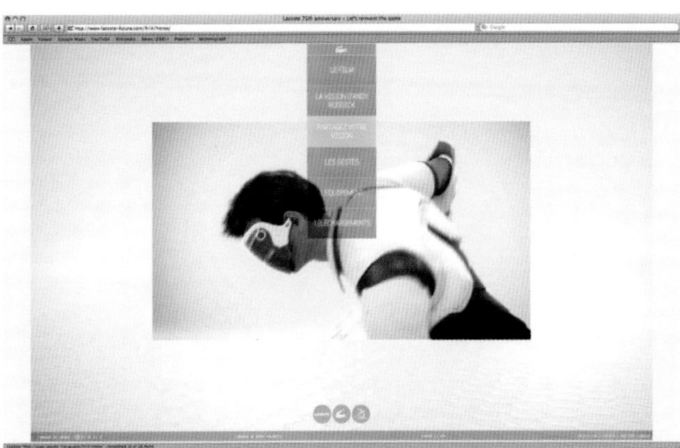

01.
TITLE
Lacoste Future
COMPANY
Megalo(s)
CLIENT
Lacoste
URL
www.megalos.net/lacoste/awards/index_4.html
COUNTRY
France

02.
TITLE
Diesel Genes of Sweden
COMPANY
AD&D
CLIENT
Diesel
URL
www.dieselgenes.se
COUNTRY
Sweden

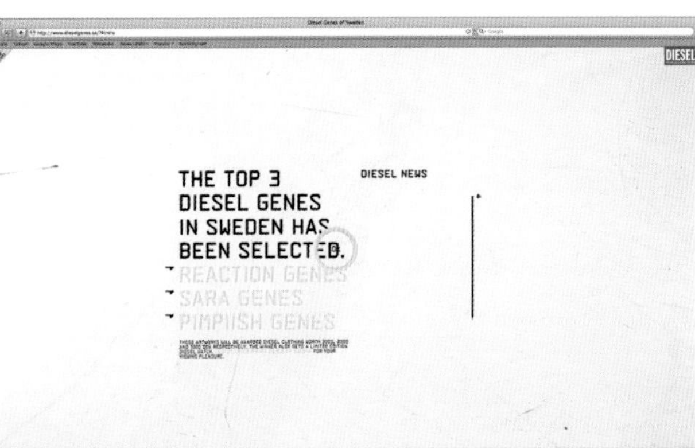

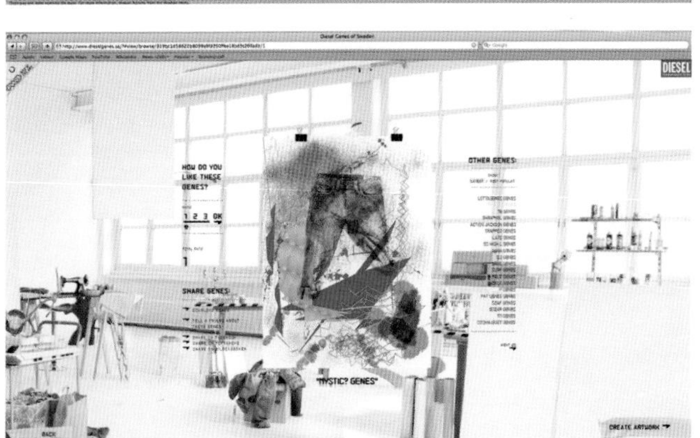

SILVER
INFORMATION SITE

TITLE
Formex magazine
COMPANY
Ottoboni Group
CLIENT
Formex
DESIGNER
Christian Egnell
ART DIRECTOR
Anna Johansson
CREATIVE DIRECTOR
Magnus Liljegren
DESIGN DIRECTOR
Ulrika Grönérus
WRITER
Linda Johansson
URL
www.formexmagazine.se
COUNTRY
Sweden

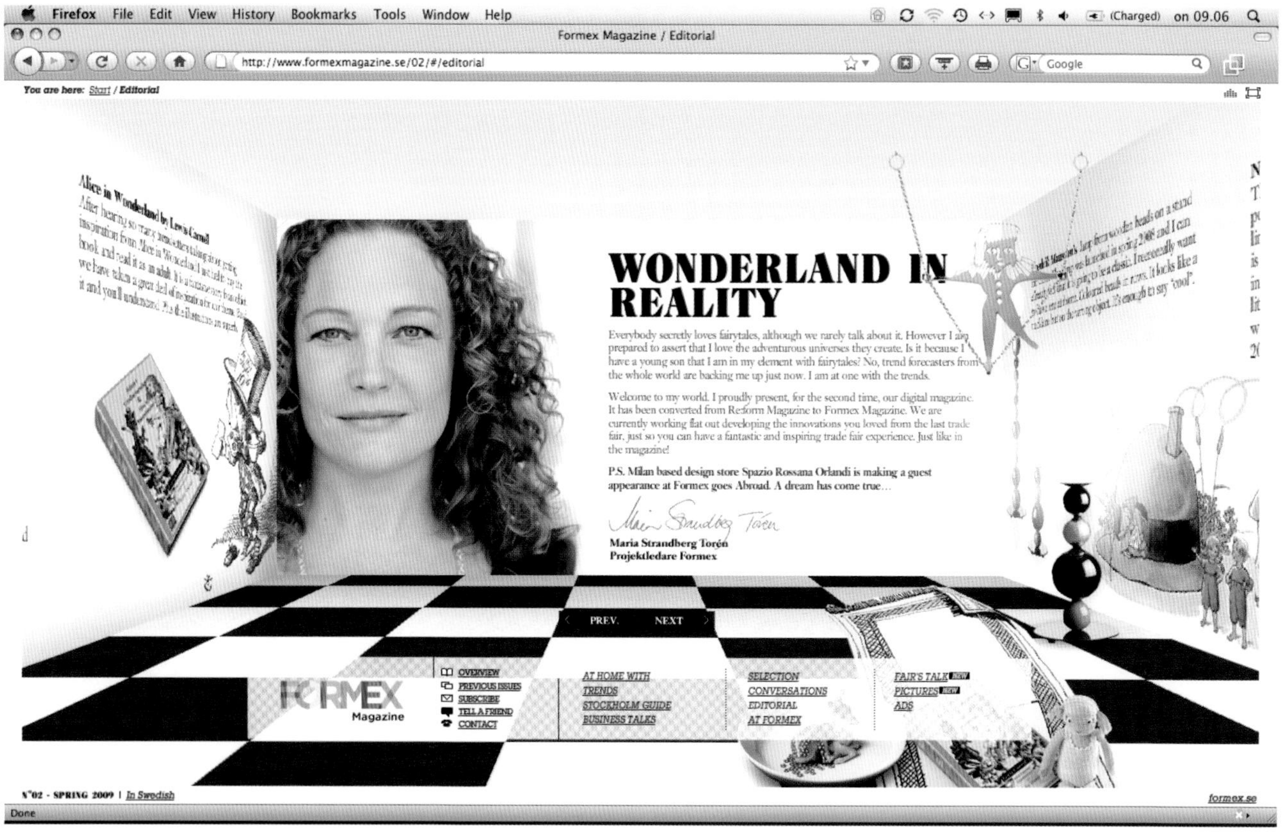

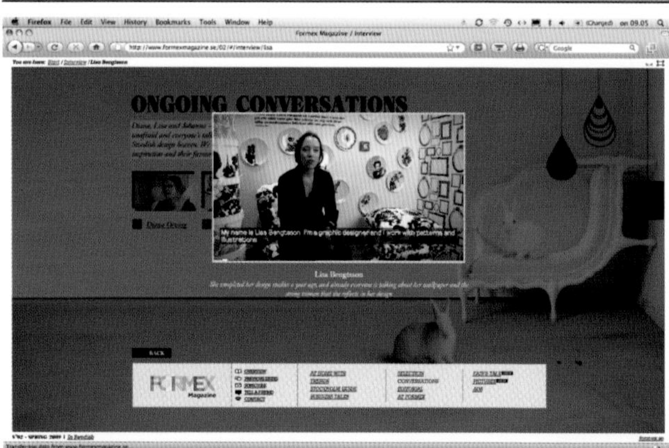

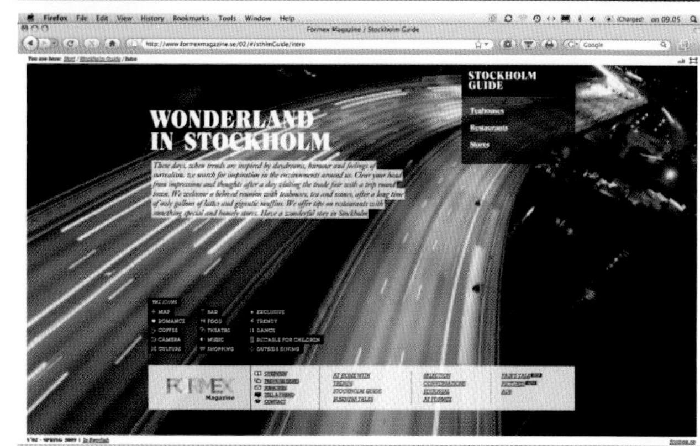

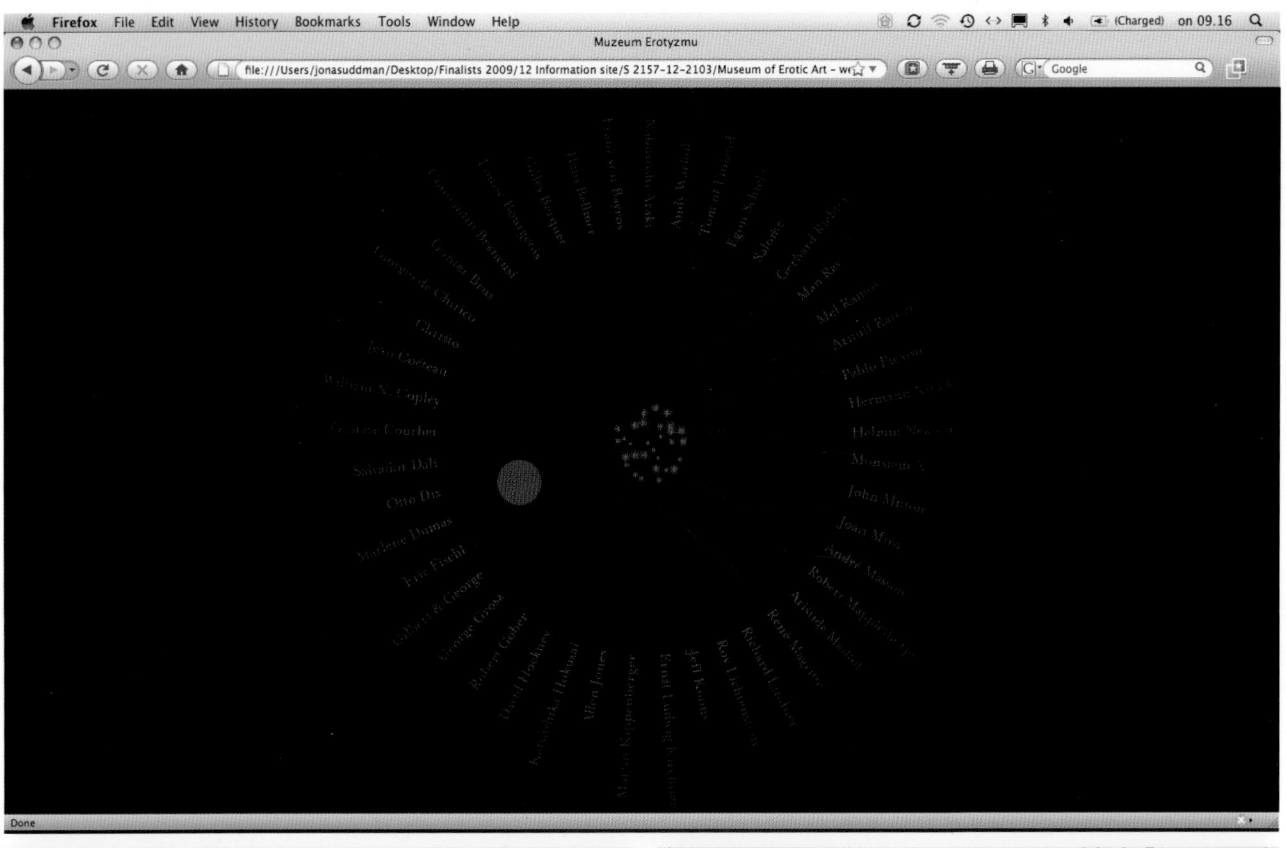

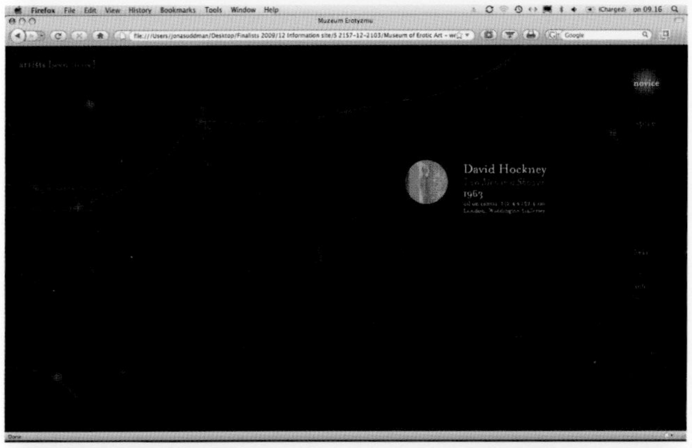

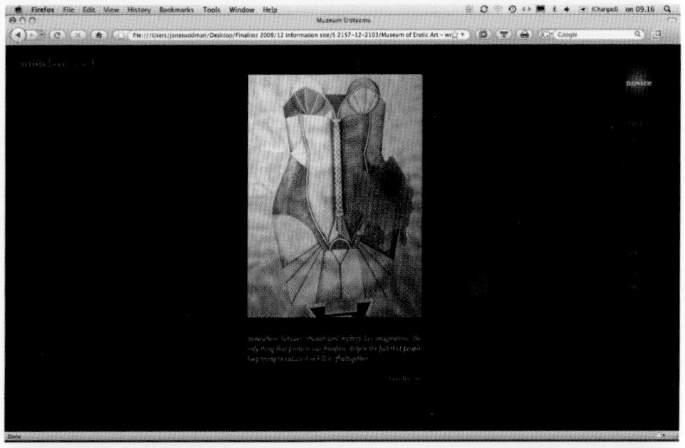

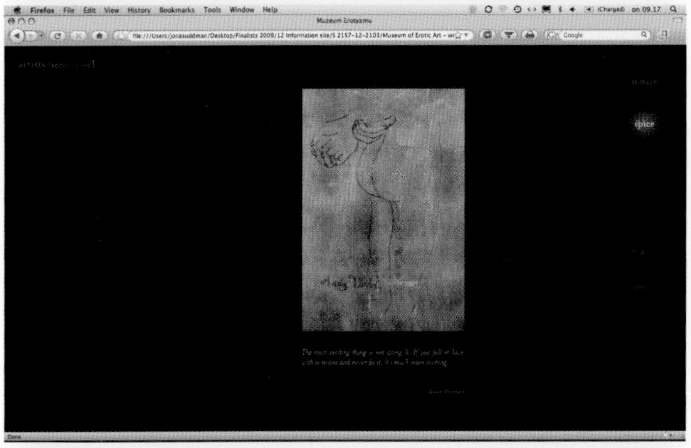

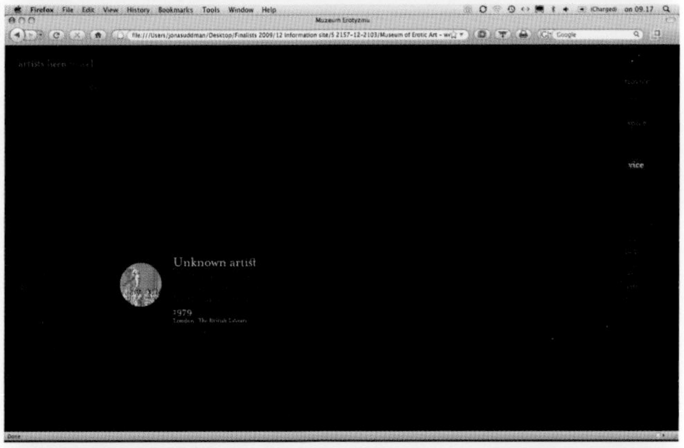

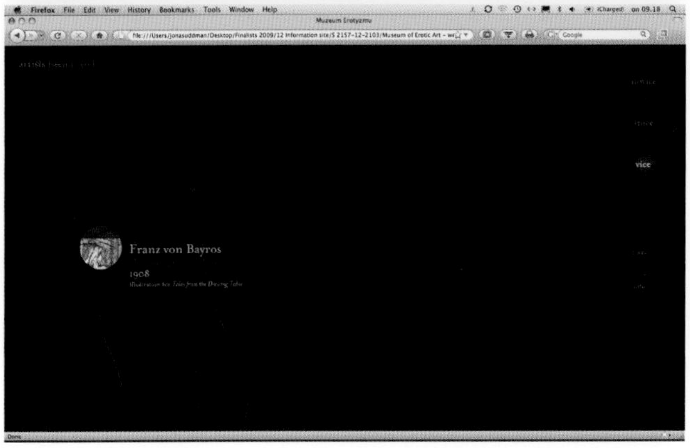

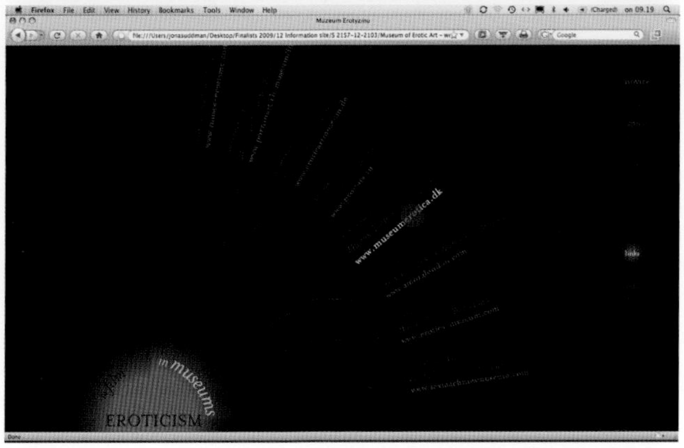

SILVER
INFORMATION SITE

TITLE
Virtual Museum of Erotic Art
CLIENT
Muzeum Sztuki Erotycznej
(Museum of Erotic Art)
DESIGNER
Aleksandra Toborowicz
EDITOR
Michal Palasz
MUSIC
Michal Palasz
PROGRAMMER
Grzegorz Bolek
URL
muzeumerotyzmu.pl
COUNTRY
Poland

BRONZE
INFORMATION SITE

TITLE
TechTower - the virtual research station
COMPANY
Lekkerwerken
CLIENT
VDI Technologiezentrum GmbH
URL
www.techtower.de
COUNTRY
Germany

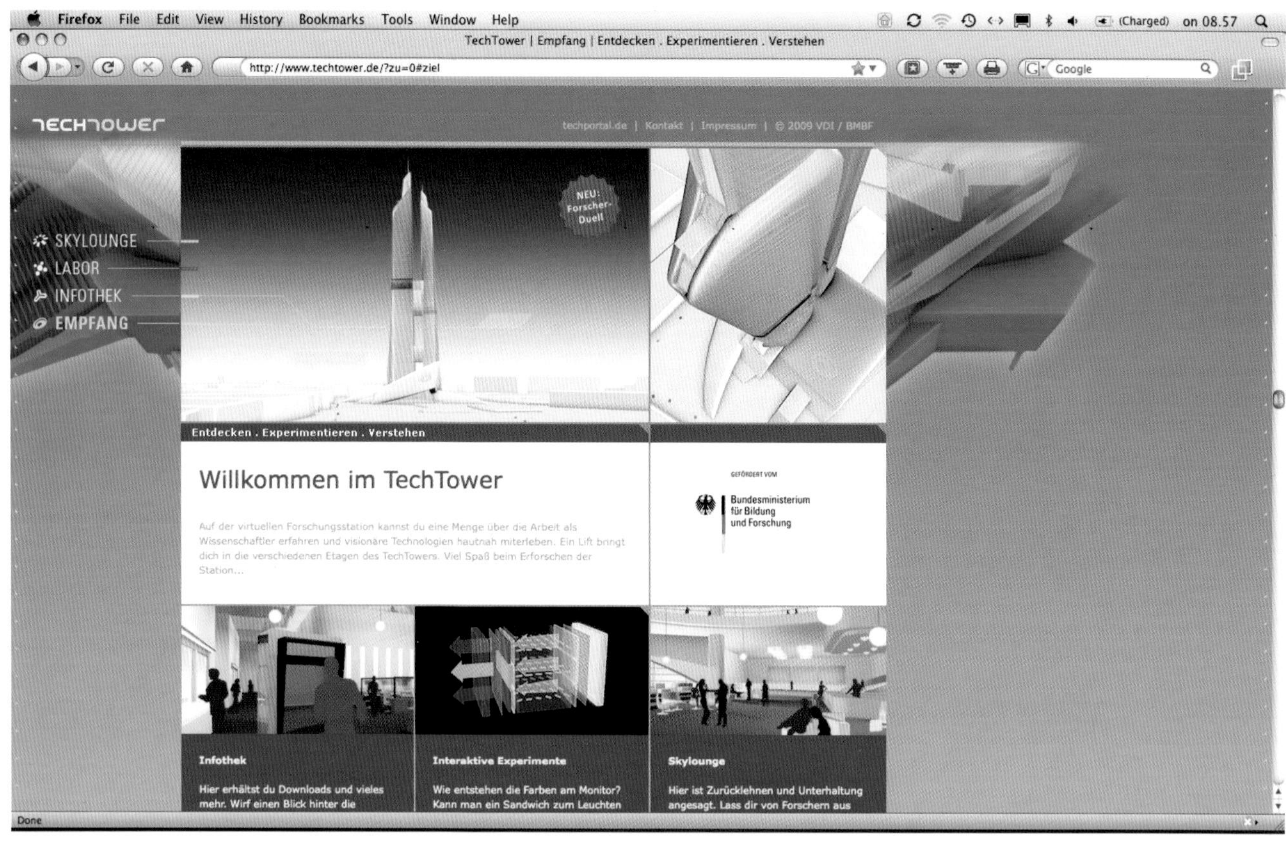

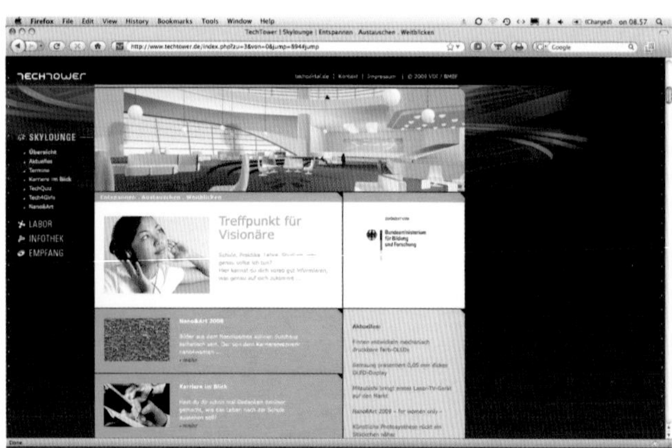

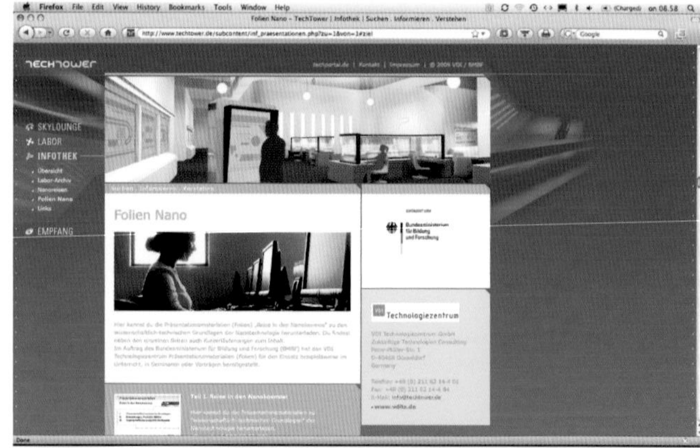

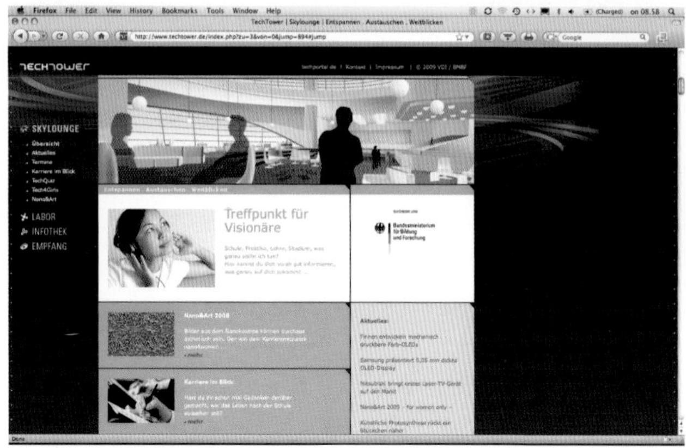

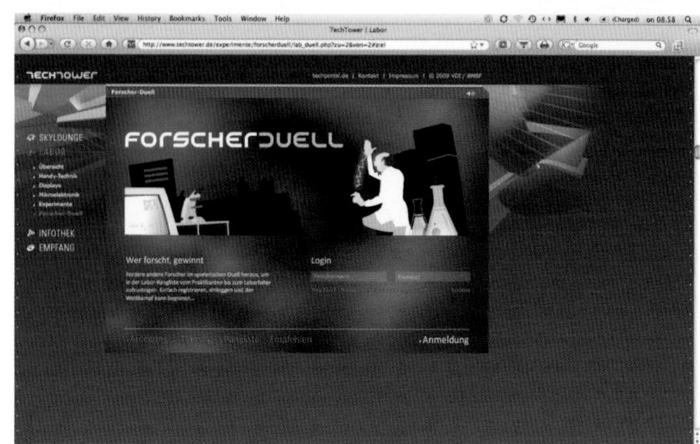

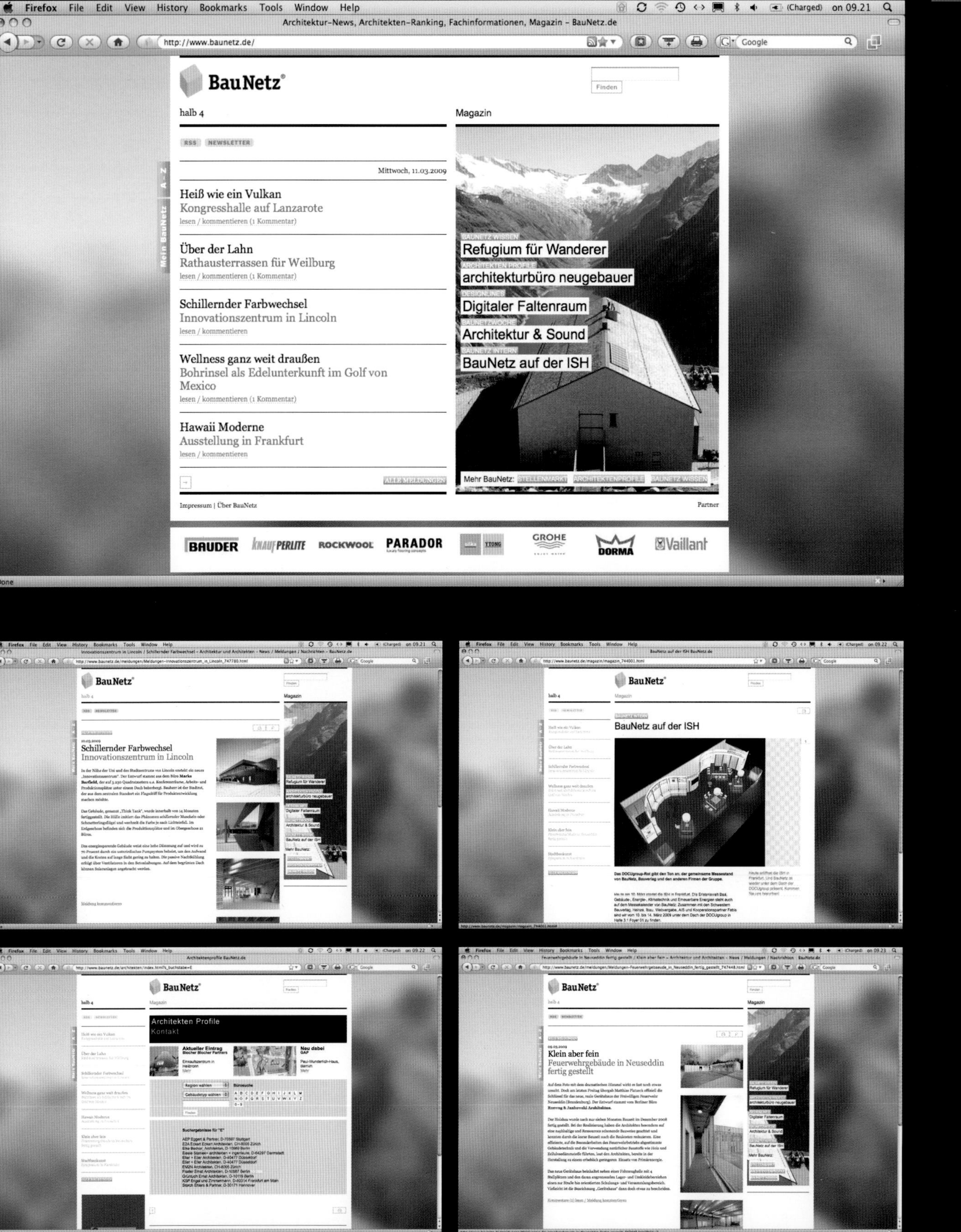

BauNetz Relaunch

Projektbuero Henkel.Hiedl

BauNetz Online-Dienst GmbH & Co. KG

www.baunetz.de

Germany

BRONZE
INFORMATION SITE

TITLE
Prova Magazine
COMPANY
Ottoboni Group
CLIENT
V&S/Pernod Ricard
URL
www.provamagazine.se
COUNTRY
Sweden

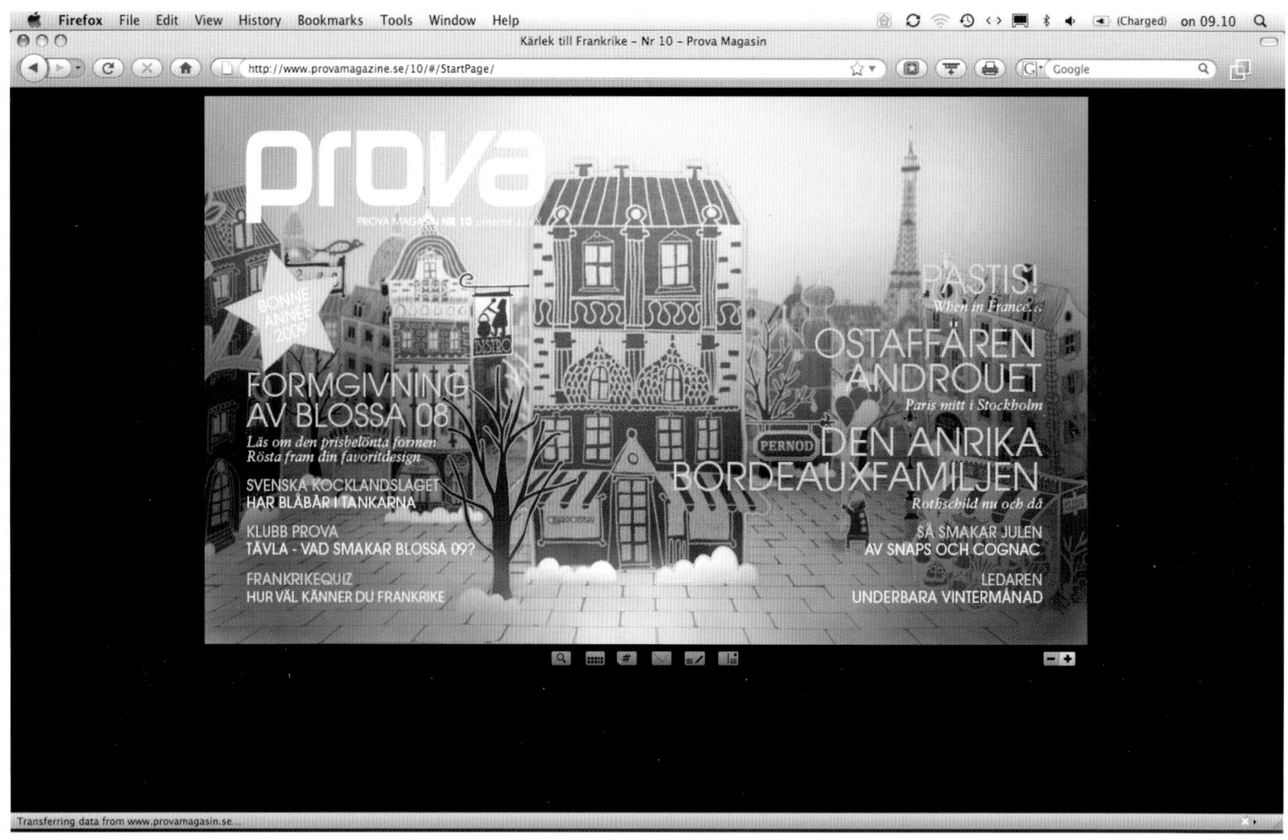

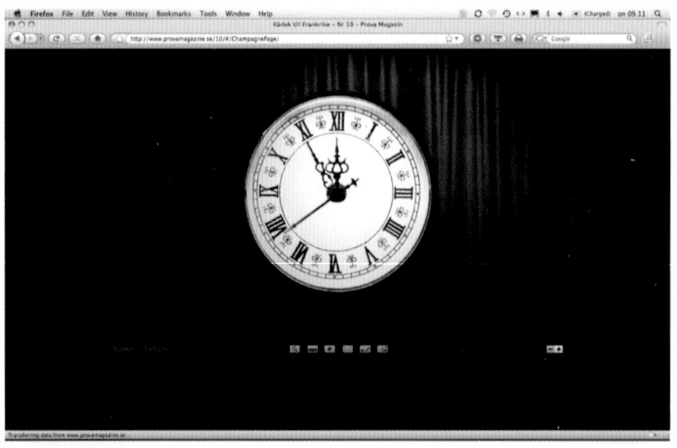

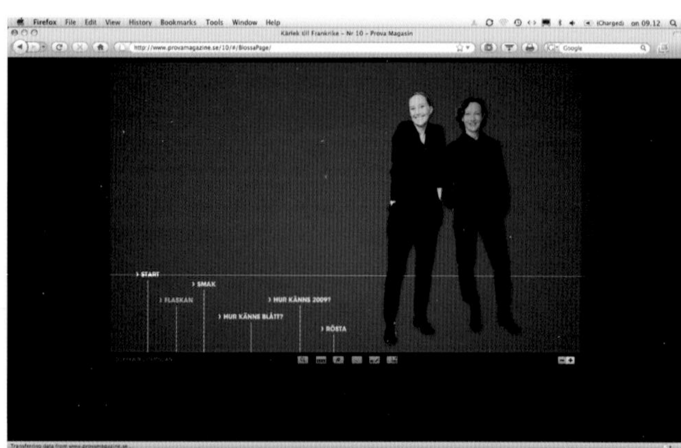

TITLE
iPoint
COMPANY
Ekidna Design Bureau
CLIENT
AiEP
URL
www.innetproject.net/ipoint
COUNTRY
Italy

BRONZE
INFORMATION SITE

TITLE
Unga Aktiesparare
COMPANY
Oakwood Creative AB
CLIENT
Unga Aktiesparare
URL
www.ungaaktiesparare.se
COUNTRY
Sweden

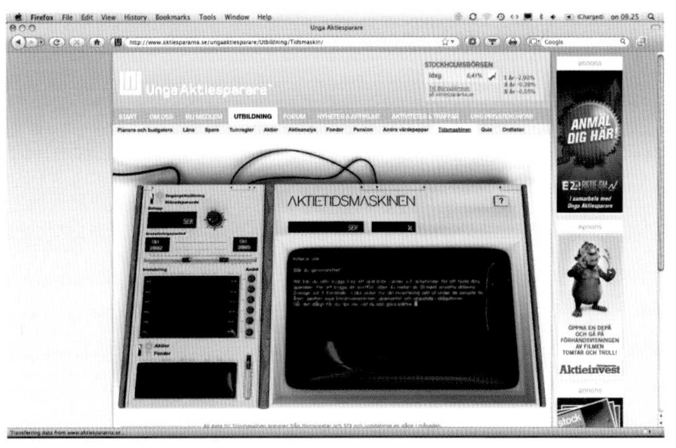

01.

Skruf.se

River Cresco AB

Skruf Snus AB

www.skruf.se

Sweden

02.

visitnorway.com

Making Waves

Innovasjon Norge

www.visitnorway.com

Norway

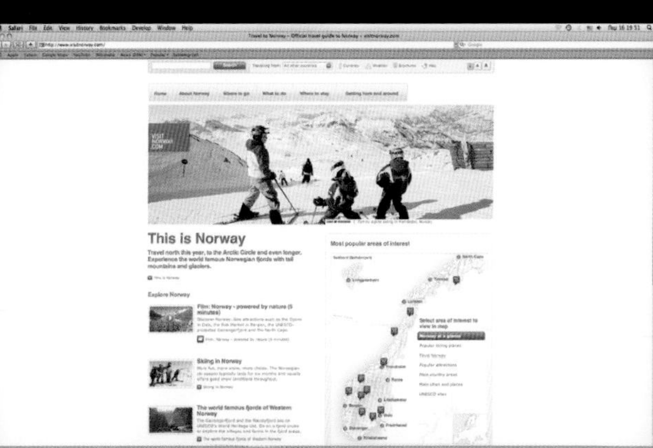

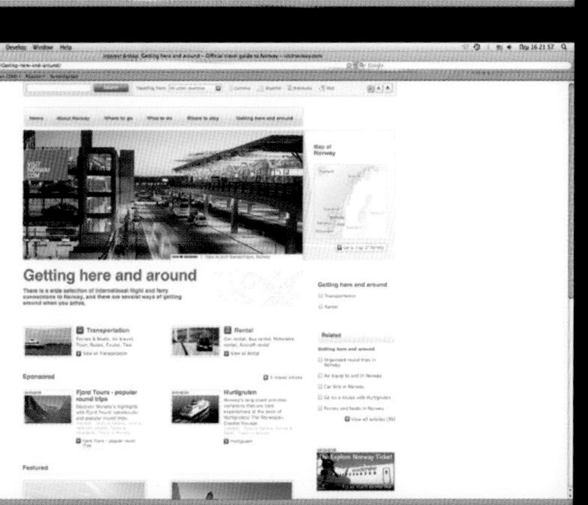

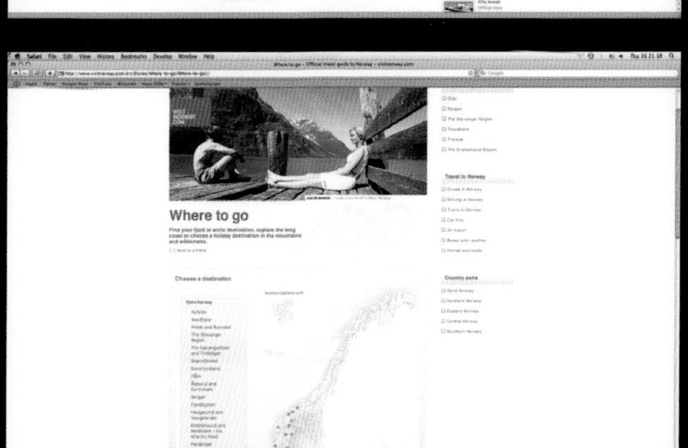

GOLD
MOTION GRAPHICS

TITLE
E4-Merry Critters With Hot Wax On Their Nipples
COMPANY
Nomint Motion Design
CLIENT
E4/Channel 4
CONCEPT/CREATIVE DIRECTION
Christos Lefakis
Yannis Konstantinidis
Georgios Xanthos
DIRECTION
Christos Lefakis
Yannis Konstantinidis
SENIOR DESIGNER
Georgios Xanthos
DESIGN/COMPOSITING TEAM
Christos Lefakis
Yannis Konstantinidis
Stamatis Arapakis
Haris Martis
3D MODELING/ANIMATION
Nikos Spathis
Haris Martis
Simos Magliveras
Dimitris Papadimitriou
Kostas Diamantis
SOUND DESIGN
Christos Lefakis
Haris Martis
PRODUCTION ASSISTANT
Pelina Makri
ILLUSTRATOR
Georgios Xanthos
COUNTRY
Greece

Along with the web, motion graphics is the most stimulating discipline in the field of visual design. This is no longer just image-making or visual language, but the melding of techniques of narration, sound, direction, editing, etc. Criteria for judging and appraising the work are becoming more instinctive, with more emotional values. This is why the jury members instantly and unanimously selected Nomint's carte blanche commission for Channel 4. The result is a series of short, non-narrative sequences laced with dark humour and poetry, which engage every viewer's perception, history and emotion. One could not fail to be seduced.

SILVER
MOTION GRAPHICS

TITLE
The Magnificent Town of Vilnius
COMPANY
PetPunk
CLIENT
PE "Vilnius European Capital of Culture 2009"
DESIGNER
PetPunk
ART DIRECTOR
Gediminas Šiaulys
CREATIVE DIRECTOR
Andrius Kirvela
DESIGN DIRECTOR
PetPunk
EXTRA 3D
Mantas Skrupskelis
URL
www.petpunk.com/vilnius
COUNTRY
Lithuania

CREATiVENESS

TITLE
WDCS Whale Saver
COMPANY
OPIUM effect GmbH
CLIENT
WDCS
DESIGNER
Joerg Zuber
ART DIRECTOR
Joerg Zuber
CREATIVE DIRECTOR
Joerg Zuber
DESIGN DIRECTOR
Joerg Zuber
OTHER
Klaus Schaefer
COUNTRY
Germany

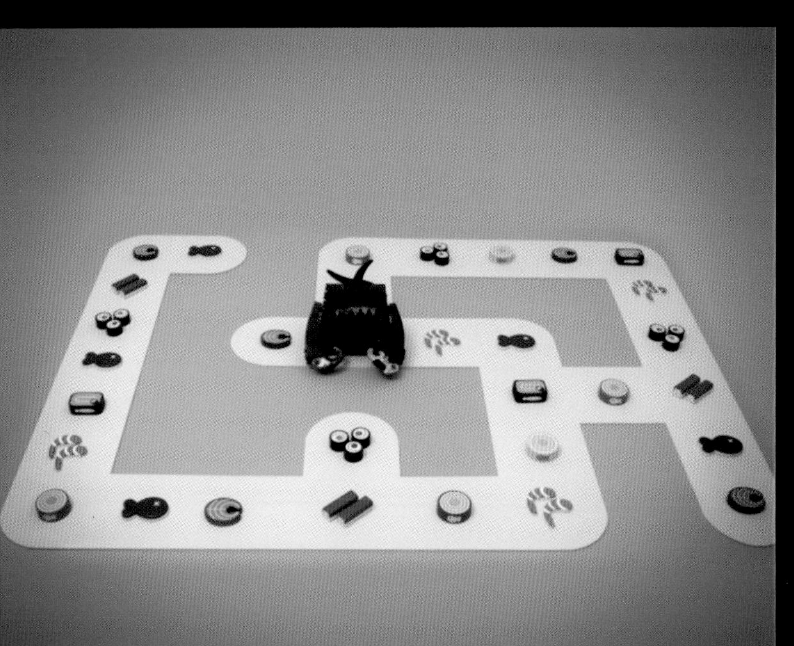

500

insert coin
www.wale.org
WDCS

BRONZE
MOTION GRAPHICS

TITLE
you
COMPANY
o.pudov
CLIENT
sony
COUNTRY
Russia

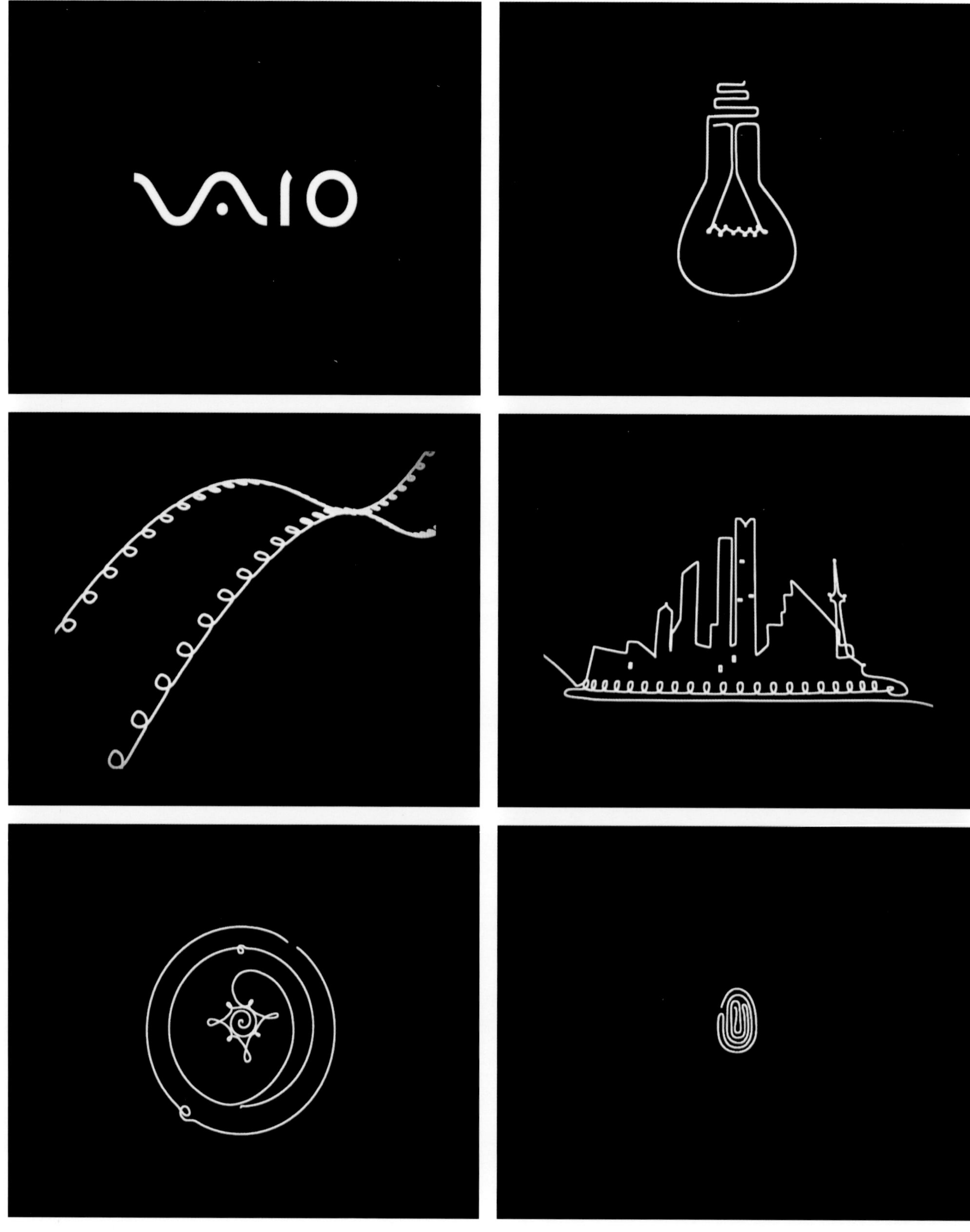

BRONZE
MOTION GRAPHICS

TITLE
MDR TV - Unser Sommer (Our Summer)
COMPANY
MDR Mitteldeutscher Rundfunk
CLIENT
MDR Fernsehen (MDR TV); D/Leipzig
COUNTRY
Germany

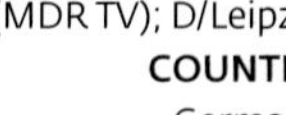

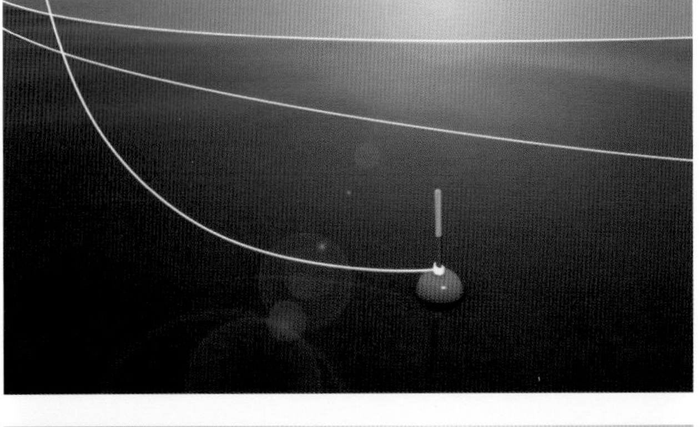

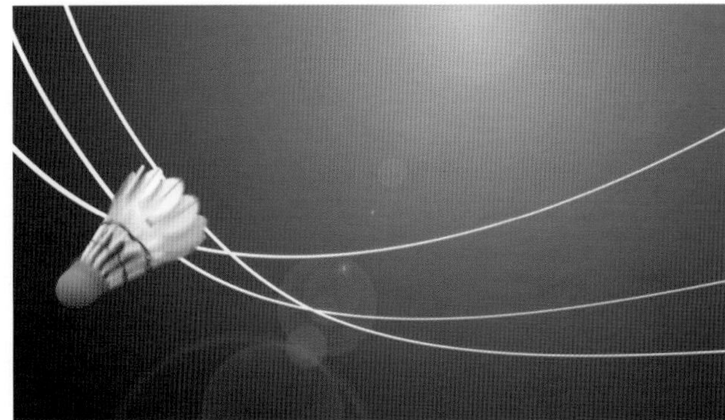

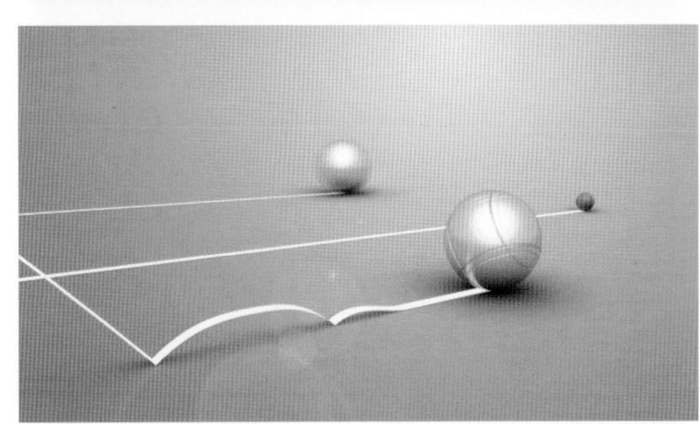

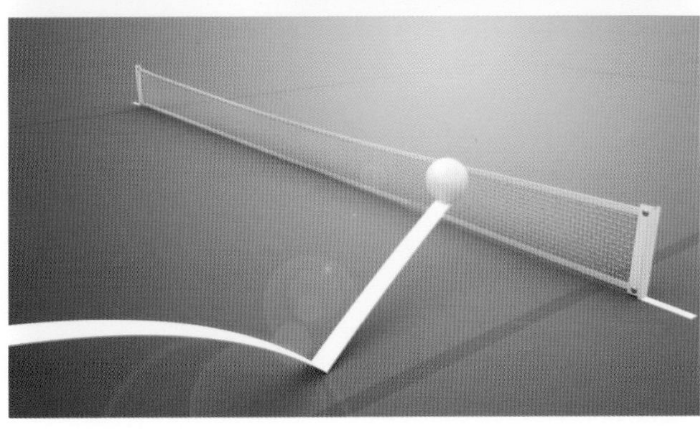

Replace

Nomint Motion Design

Carteco

Greece

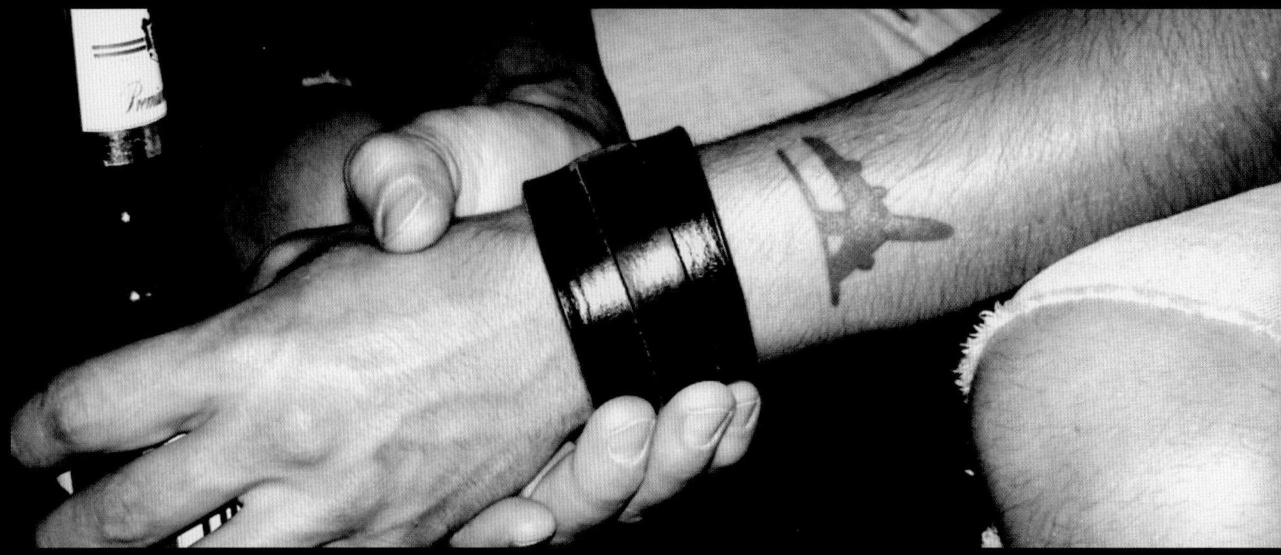

BRONZE
MOTION GRAPHICS

TITLE
Anecdotari.historias singulars
COMPANY
WeMake
CLIENT
TVE
URL
www.rtve.es/tve/b
/anecdotari/index.htm
COUNTRY
Spain

BRONZE
MOTION GRAPHICS

TITLE
Ermis Awards 2008
DESIGNER
Christos Magganas
CLIENT
Top Cut + Modiano for Edee
COUNTRY
Greece

FINALIST
MOTION GRAPHICS

TITLE
Stalad video installation
COMPANY
HollandCentraal
CLIENT
Stalad
COUNTRY
Netherlands

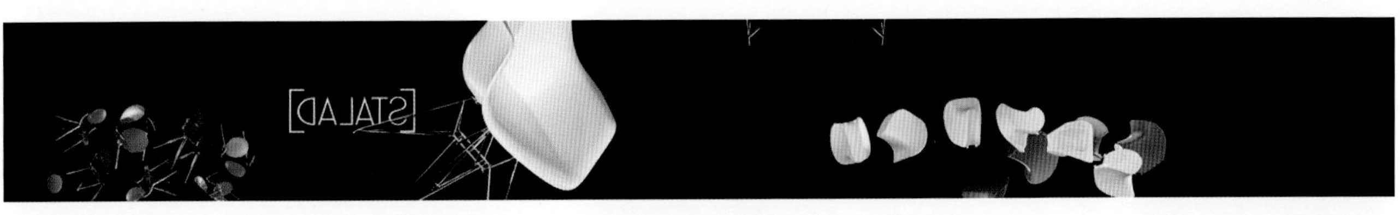

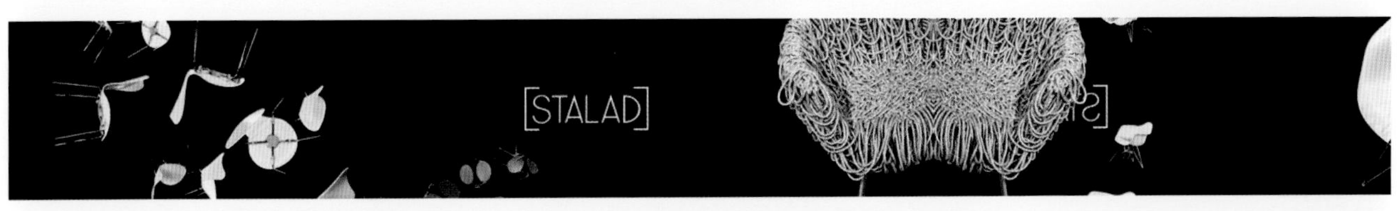

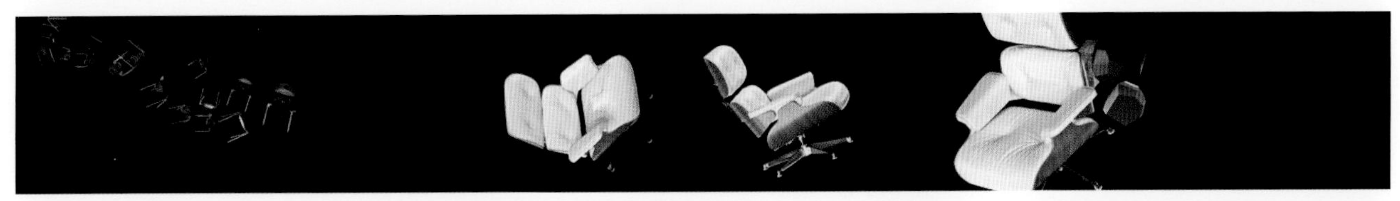

GOLD
MISCELLANEOUS
DIGITAL MEDIA

TITLE
WATT Systems monitor
COMPANY
Punchcard
CLIENT
WATT Rotterdam
DESIGNERS
Richard Vijgen
Thomas Kopperschläge
ART DIRECTOR
Richard Vijgen
CREATIVE DIRECTOR
Thomas Kopperschläger
PROGRAMMING
Ralf Brandenstein
Richard Vijgen
COUNTRY
Netherlands

We know we are heading for a major eco-disaster. Yet it is hard to understand and feel the impact of our tiny personal activities on the environment; they seem so small, set against the gigantic metrics of our eco-system. Basic everyday gestures and constant carefulness may postpone the deadline, but how can our awareness be raised at every single moment? The Watt, a dance club in Rotterdam, ventured an answer by trying to reduce its CO2 impact by a third. Punchard's installation displays the impact of the dancers' activity, and raises their awareness to it in real time. By awarding this initiative a prize, the jury hopes to encourage its development.

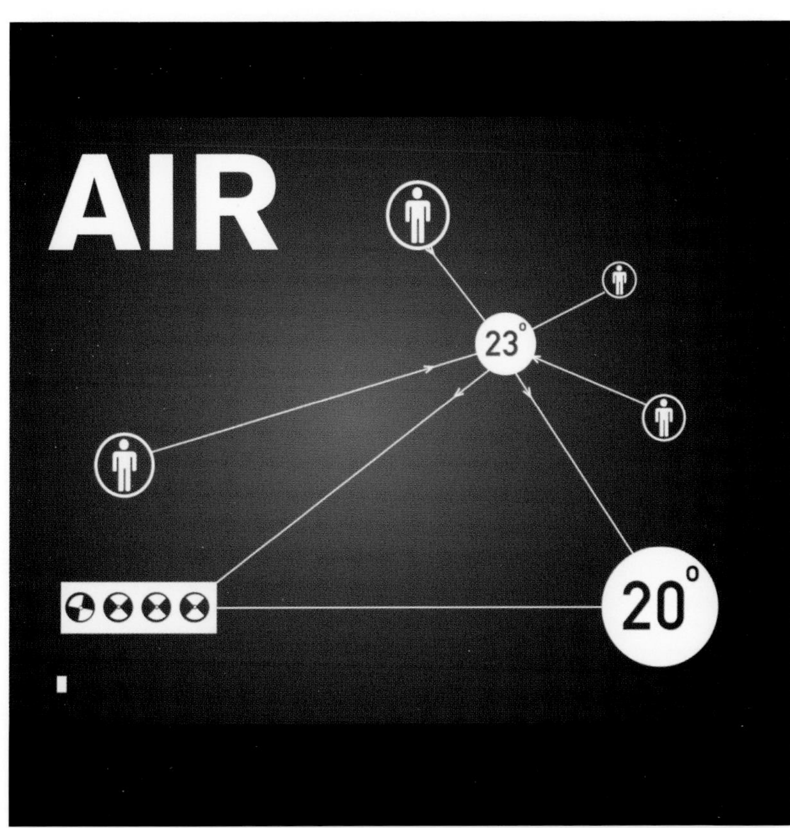
AIR
23°
20°

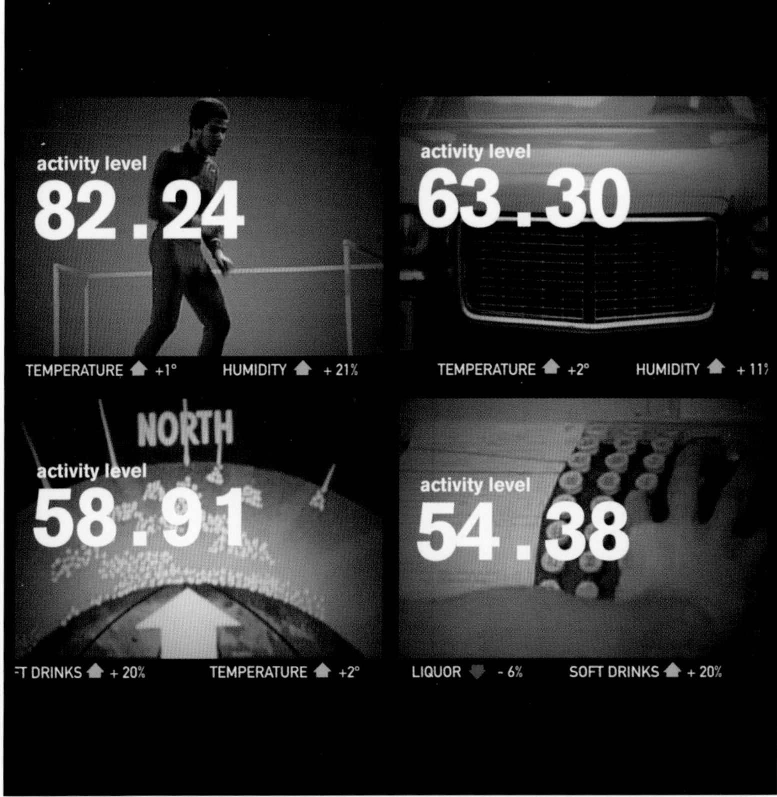
activity level
82.24
TEMPERATURE +1° HUMIDITY + 21%
activity level
63.30
TEMPERATURE +2° HUMIDITY + 11%
NORTH
activity level
58.91
activity level
54.38
LIQUOR - 6% SOFT DRINKS + 20%

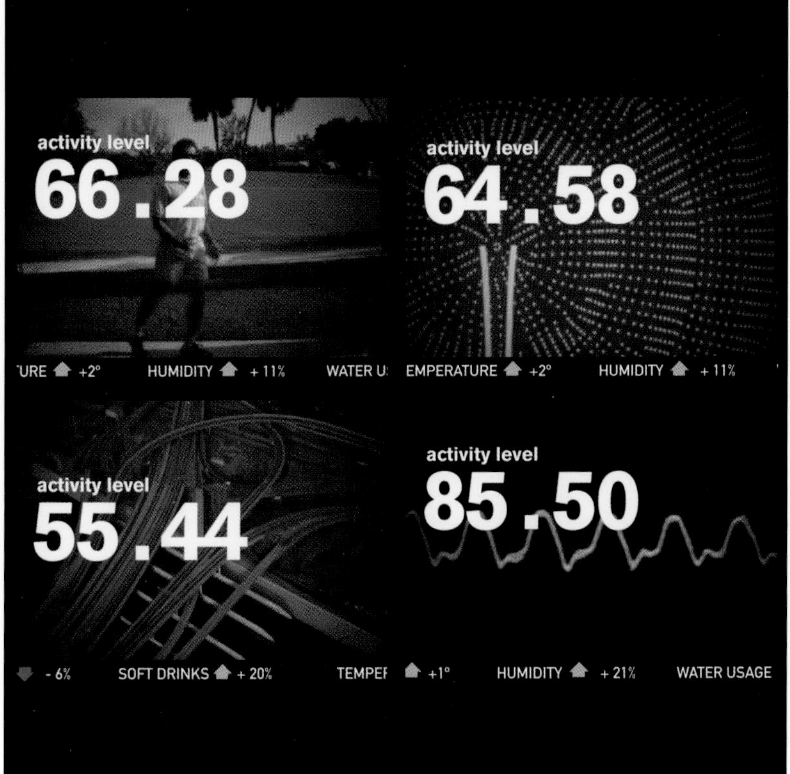
activity level
66.28
HUMIDITY + 11%
activity level
64.58
HUMIDITY + 11%
activity level
55.44
SOFT DRINKS + 20%
activity level
85.50
HUMIDITY + 21%
WATER USAGE

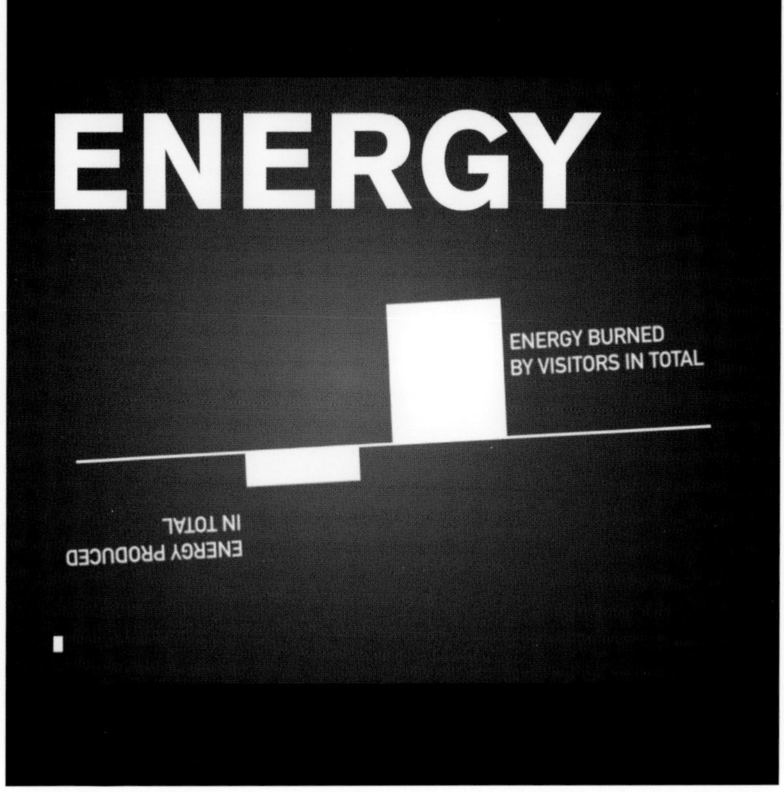
ENERGY
ENERGY BURNED
BY VISITORS IN TOTAL
ENERGY PRODUCED
IN TOTAL

GOLD
MISCELLANEOUS
DIGITAL MEDIA

TITLE
The Turn by Fredo Viola
COMPANY
Aer visual studio
CLIENT
Fredo Viola and Because Music
DESIGNERS
Fredo Viola
Aer visual studio
Guille Lopez
CONCEPT
Fredo Viola
Steph Thirion
PROGRAMMER
Guille Lopez
URL
www.theturn.tv
COUNTRY
Spain

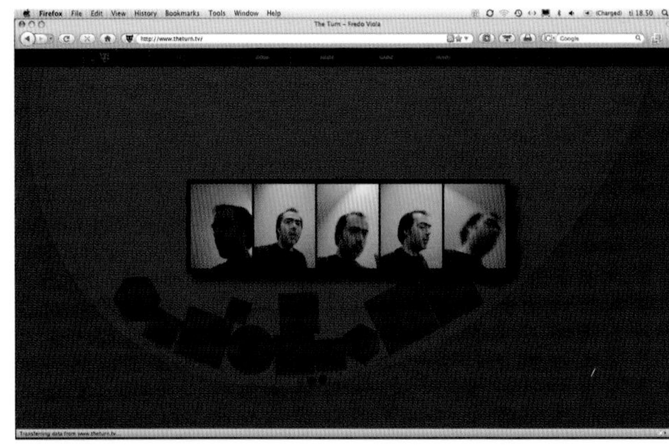
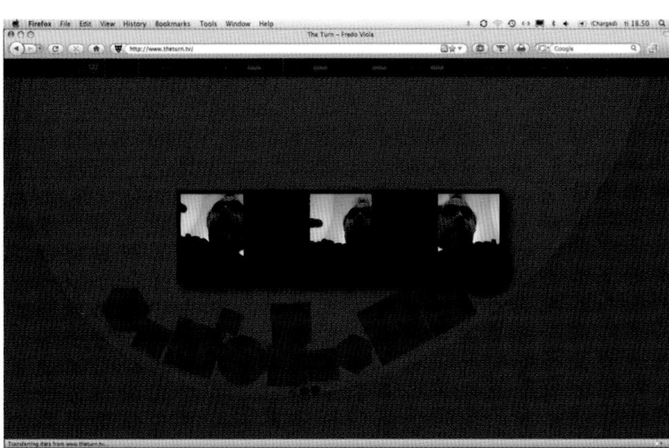
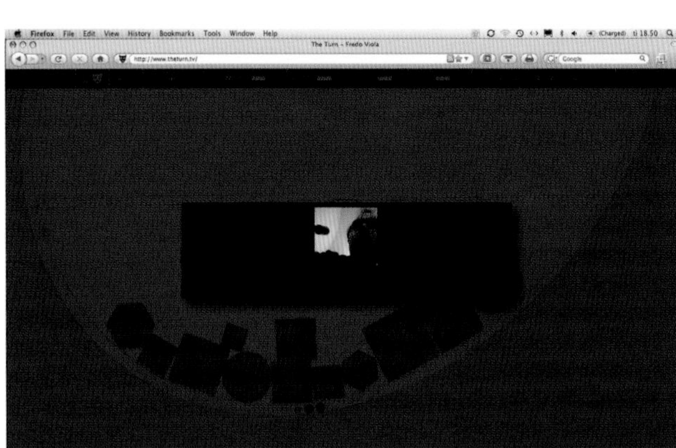
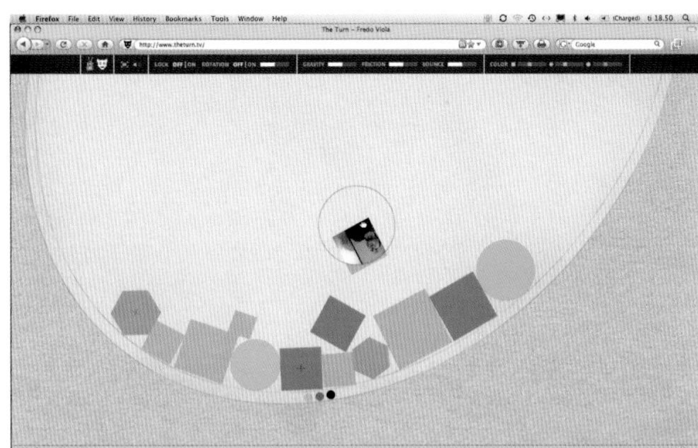
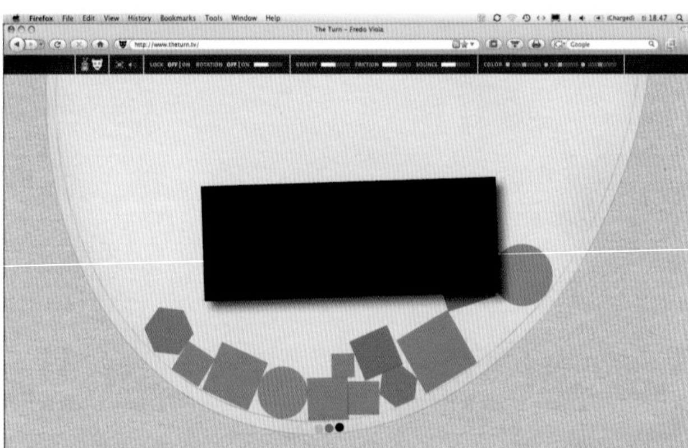

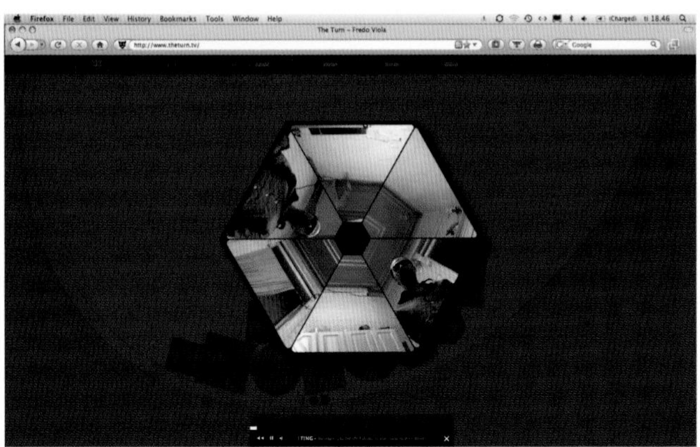

Fredo Viola, to whom we owe a fabulous reworking of John Lennon's "Being for the Benefit of Mr Kite!", is a hybrid artist of the new generation. Both a musician and video artist, he has developed an extremely personal style that is attracting an ever-expanding following. He is often the sole writer-performer of his generally choral songs, in which he blends voice and instruments on multiple tracks. The idea of playing with his own avatar quickly emerged in his first clips, with a micro-video for each recording track. This multi-play is also to be found on his website, where interaction lets each visitor create their own musical mood, in agreeable harmony with the artist's style.

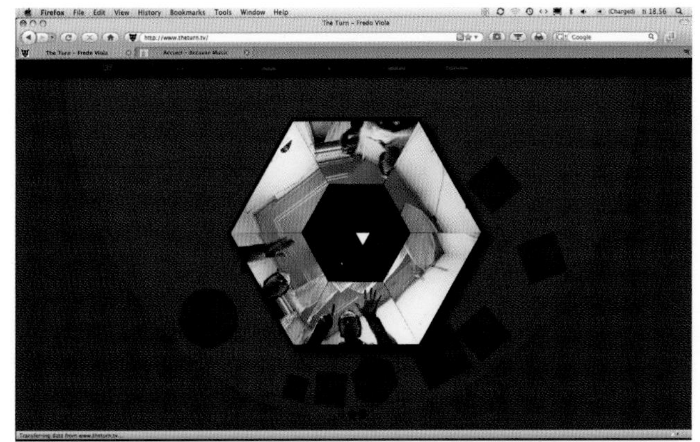

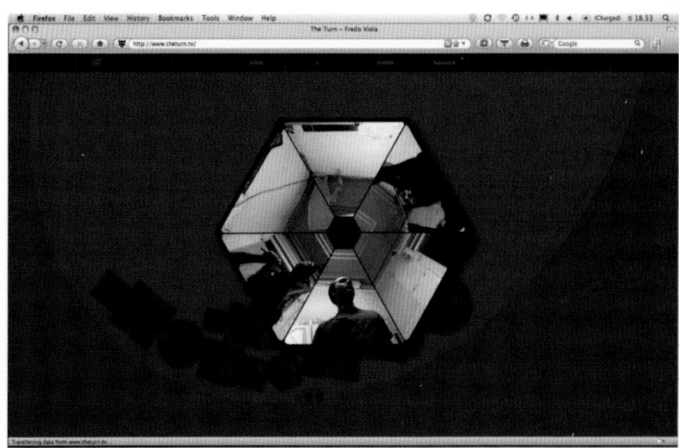

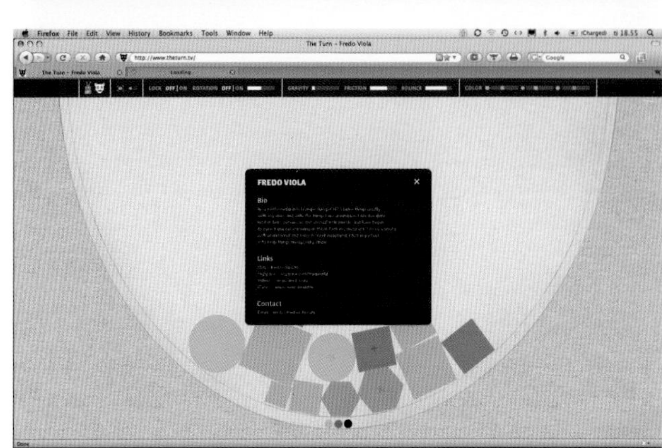
FREDO VIOLA

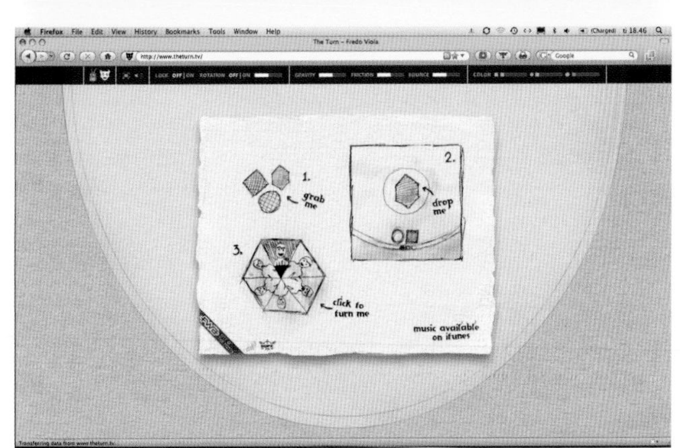
1.
grab me
2.
drop me
3.
click to turn me
music available on itunes

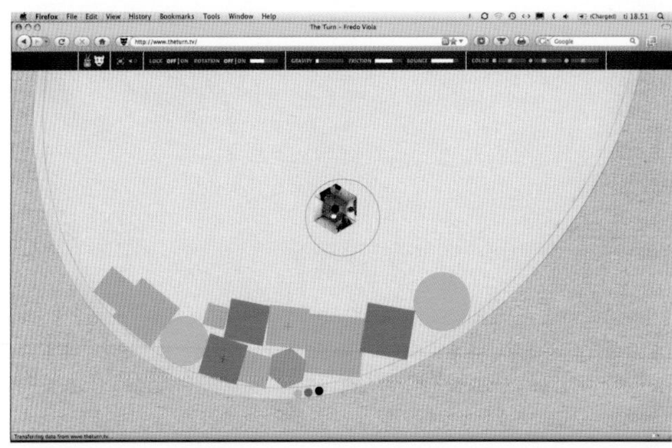

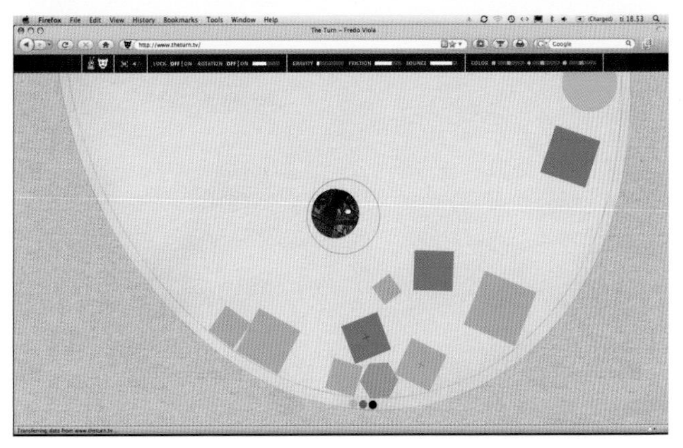

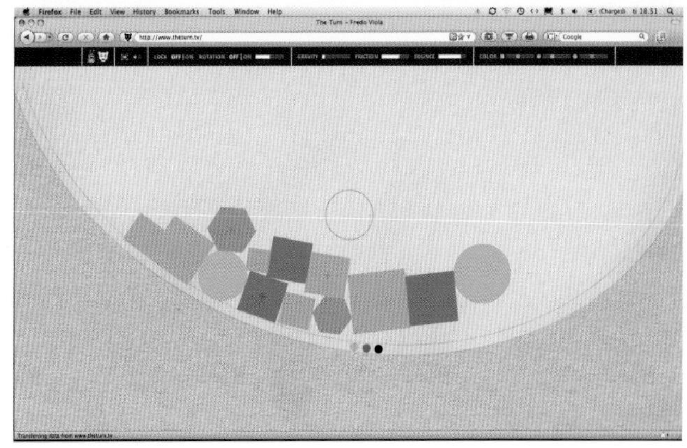

SILVER
MISCELLANEOUS
DIGITAL MEDIA

TITLE
Rijkswaterstaat Futurecenter
COMPANY
Punchcard
CLIENT
Rijkswaterstaat
DESIGNERS
Richard Vijgen
Thomas Kopperschläger
ART DIRECTOR
Richard Vijgen
CREATIVE DIRECTOR
Thomas Kopperschläger
PROGRAMMING
Ralf Brandenstein
Richard Vijgen

COUNTRY
Netherlands

Hoeveel kilometer reis je per jaar?
Hoe hoog woon je?

BRONZE
MISCELLANEOUS
DIGITAL MEDIA

LCF Graduate Exhibition

Moving Brands

London College of Fashion

vimeo.com/1393556

United Kingdom

BRONZE
MISCELLANEOUS
DIGITAL MEDIA

TITLE
Civimatic
DESIGNER
Andreas Gysin
CLIENT
Repubblica e Canton
Ticino - Cancelleria dello St
COUNTRY
Switzerland

Design is the man's imprint

ESIETE

Ddi, spanish association to promote design & innov

www.eldiseñoeslahuella
delhombre.com

Spain

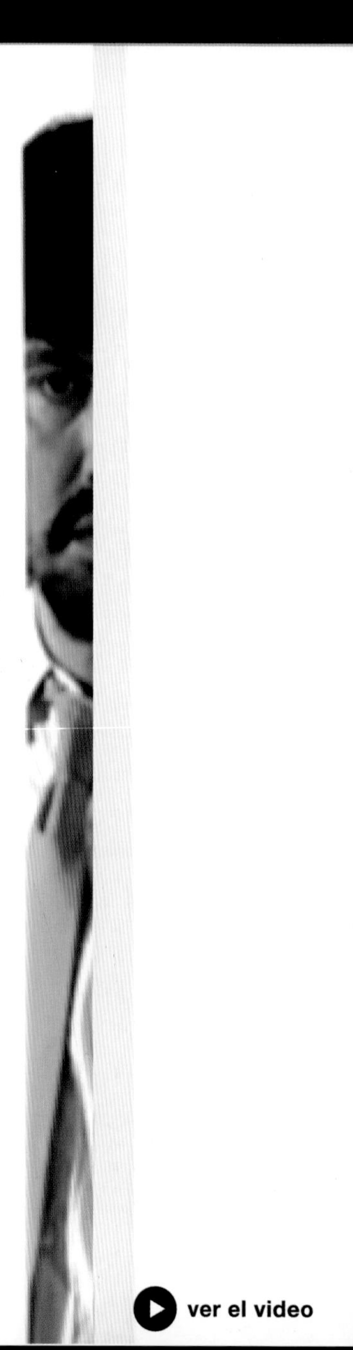

Estreno 7 de Noviembre 2008

ver el video

BRONZE
MISCELLANEOUS
DIGITAL MEDIA

TITLE
The Mataró model Touchscreen application
COMPANY
Fier Concept & Design
CLIENT
Maritiem Museum Rotterdam
URL
www.maritiemmuseum.nl/pix/tentoon/mataro/online/mataro.html
COUNTRY
Netherlands

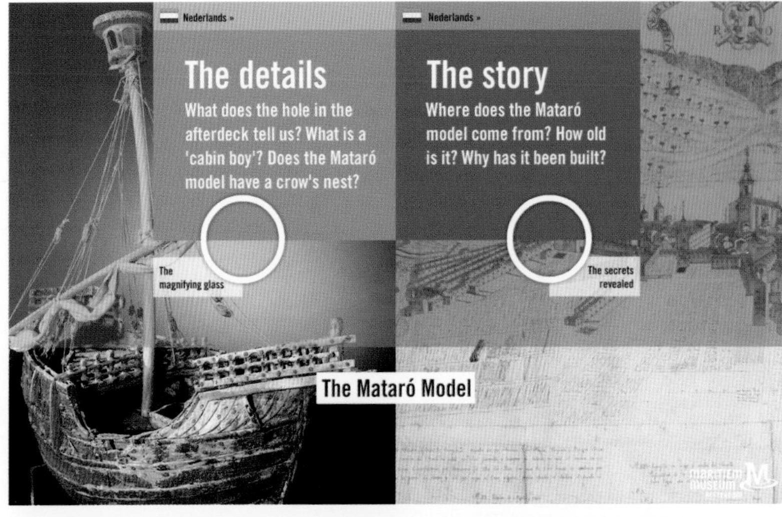

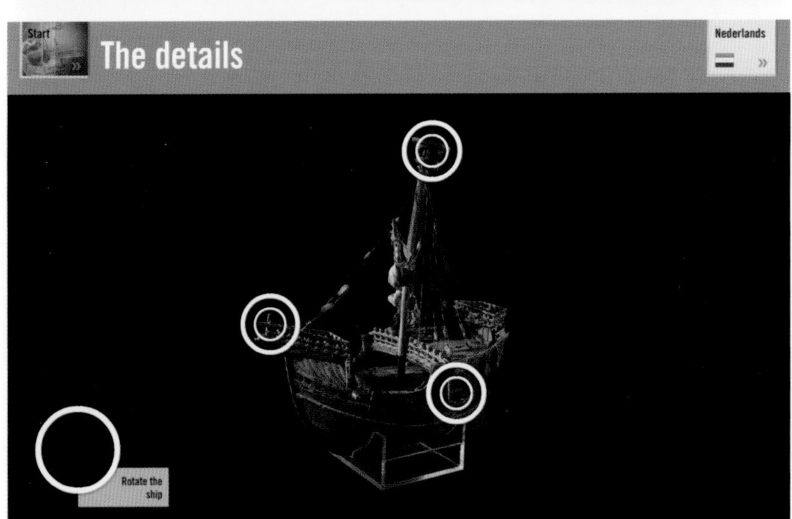

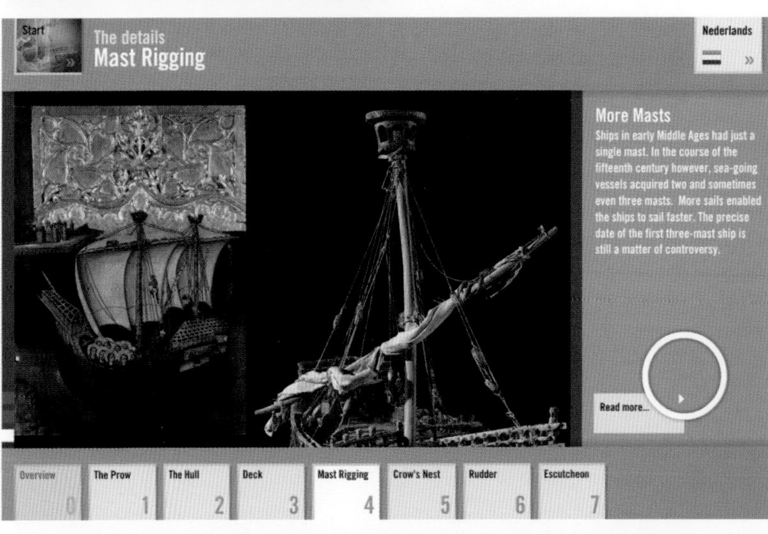

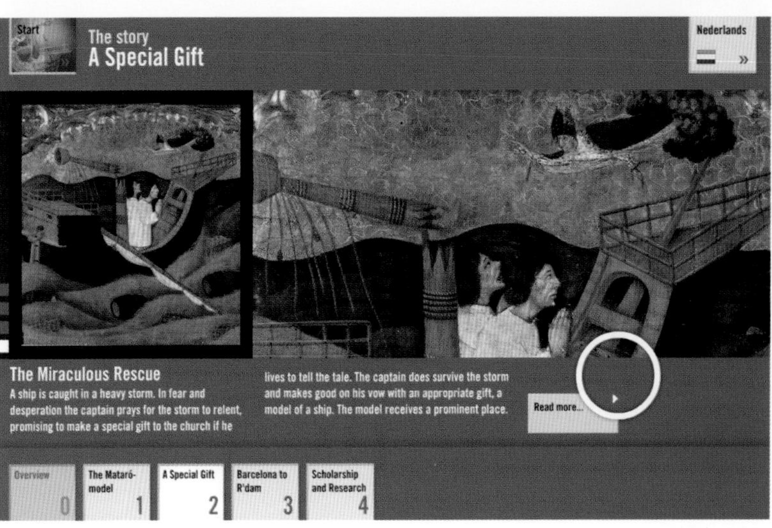

PACKAGING

SILVER
PACKAGING
ALCOHOLIC DRINKS

TITLE
Schnapps / Linz 2009
COMPANY
Buchegger, Denoth, Feichtner / Haslinger, Keck
CLIENT
Linz 2009 European Capital of Culture
ART DIRECTOR
Michael Denoth
CREATIVE DIRECTORS
Michael Denoth
Bernhard Buchegger
ILLUSTRATOR
Florian Knogler
WRITER
Patsy Koeppel-Haslinger
COUNTRY
Austria

SILVER
PACKAGING
ALCOHOLIC DRINKS

TITLE
Assemblage
CLIENT
Stéphane Gros
DESIGNER
Elsa Degirmenciler
ART DIRECTOR
Arts-Appliqués de Genève
DIRECTOR
Guy Mérat
ENSEIGNANTE
Esther Schenkel
PHOTOGRAPHER
Elsa Degirmenciler
WRITER
Elsa Degirmenciler
PRINTER
Gern étiquette Neuchâtel
COUNTRY
Switzerland

BRONZE
PACKAGING
ALCOHOLIC DRINKS

TITLE
Wine labels for Miradero
COMPANY
Valladares, diseño y comunicacion
CLIENT
Bodegas Insulares de Tenerife
COUNTRY
Spain

BRONZE
PACKAGING
ALCOHOLIC DRINKS

TITLE
don't drink and drive
COMPANY
Mousegraphics
CLIENT
biotos
COUNTRY
Greece

BRONZE
PACKAGING
ALCOHOLIC DRINKS

TITLE
Le Tourment Vert Absinthe Francaise 2008
COMPANY
Turner Duckworth: London & San Francisco
CLIENT
Distillery Vinet EGE
COUNTRY
United Kingdom

BRONZE
PACKAGING
ALCOHOLIC DRINKS

Design system for seasonal beer variations

gysimarketing Kreation & Strategie

Bier Paul

Switzerland

BRONZE
PACKAGING
ALCOHOLIC DRINKS

TITLE
Silver Bottle
COMPANY
Ideenwerk Werbeagentur GmbH
CLIENT
Brauerei Schloss Eggenberg
COUNTRY
Austria

BRONZE
PACKAGING
ALCOHOLIC DRINKS

TITLE
Türk Wine
COMPANY
bauer konzept
& gestaltung gmbh
CLIENT
Wine-Growing Estate Türk
COUNTRY
Austria

BRONZE
PACKAGING
ALCOHOLIC DRINKS

TITLE
Incanto
COMPANY
Bruketa&Zinic OM
CLIENT
Fructus
COUNTRY
Croatia

FINALIST
PACKAGING
ALCOHOLIC DRINKS

TITLE
Wine / Linz 2009
COMPANY
Buchegger, Denoth, Feichtner / Haslinger, Keck
CLIENT
Linz 2009 European Capital of Culture
COUNTRY
Austria

GOLD
PACKAGING
FOOD & BEVERAGES

TITLE
Andreas Caminada Packaging Design
COMPANY
graphic design
CLIENT
Andreas Caminada
DESIGNER
Remo Caminada
ART DIRECTOR
Remo Caminada
CREATIVE DIRECTOR
Remo Caminada
DESIGN DIRECTOR
Remo Caminada
ILLUSTRATORS
Remo Caminada
Donat Caduff
Michael Häne
WRITERS
GM Cavelty
A Camenisch
M Jemmy
M & A Decurtins
R Arpagaus
COUNTRY
Switzerland

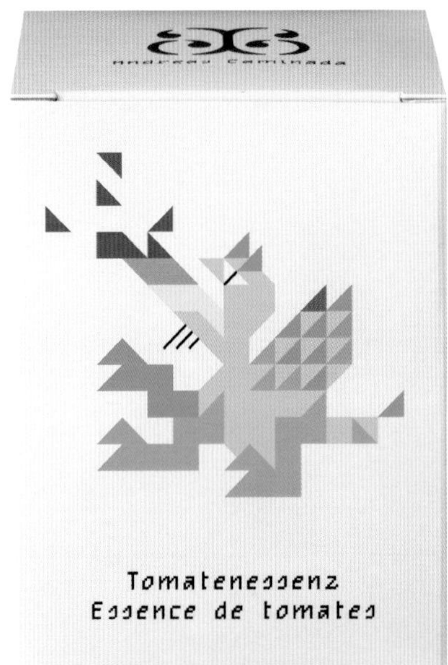

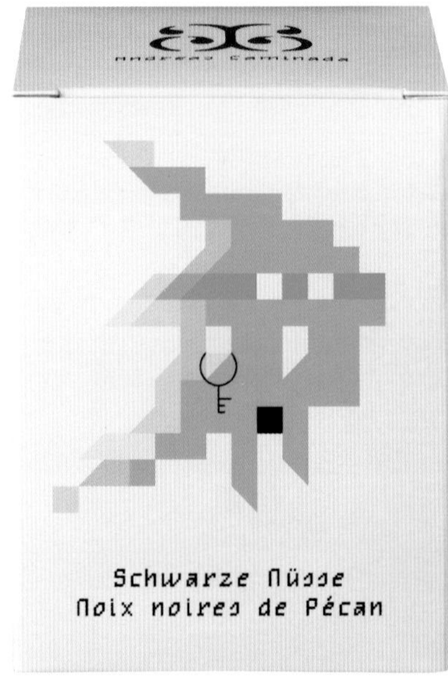

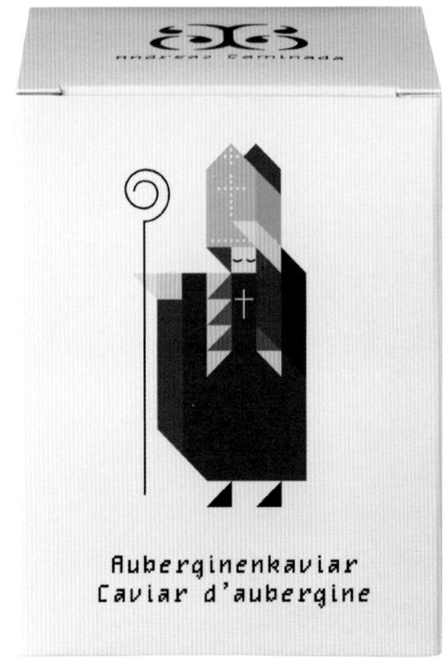

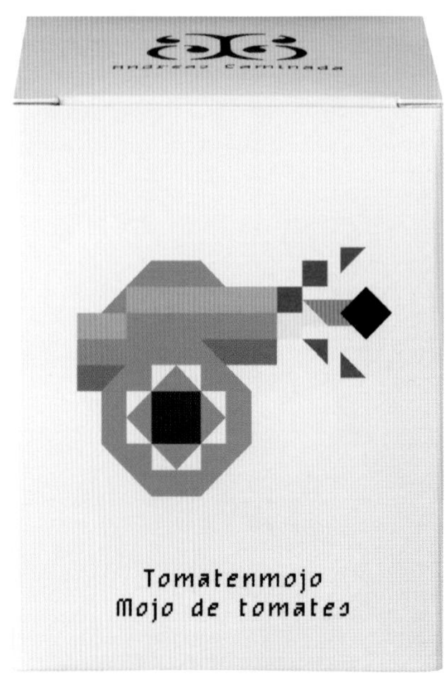

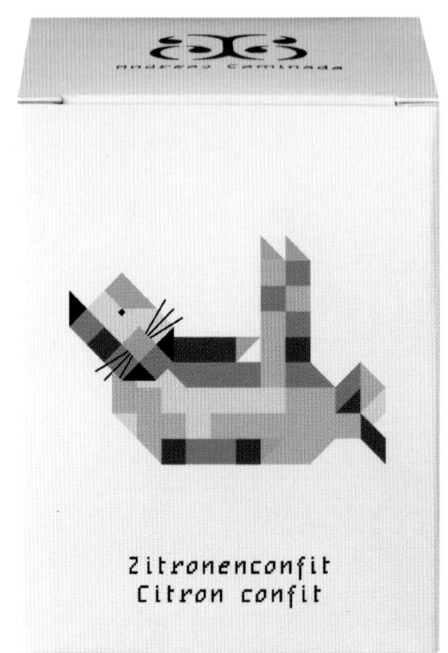

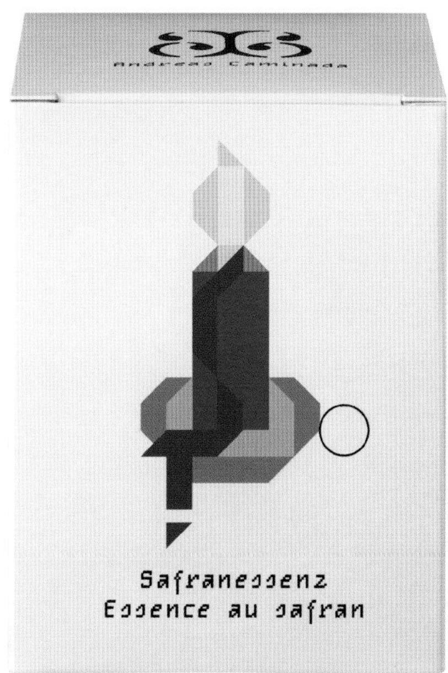

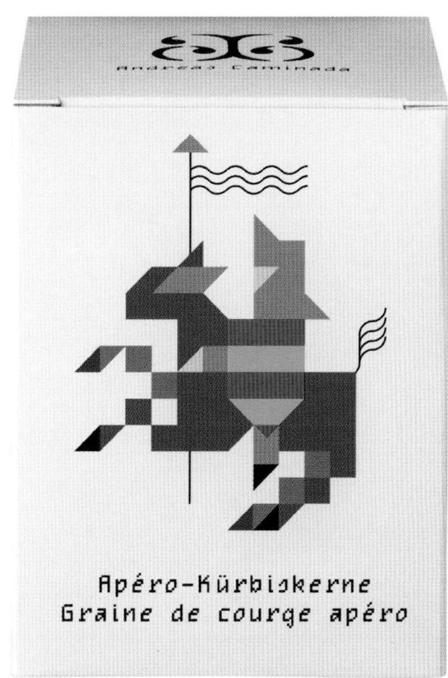

When a top chef launches a product range, the first pitfall is the clichés, such as the photo-portrait on every pack or a look of dime-a-dozen luxury that is sometimes outrageously at odds with the contents. The exercise is thus a delicate one, producing the best and the worst. For this collection by chef Andréas Carminada, we particularly liked the touch of humour supplied by the pixellated illustrations; the risk taken in choosing a strong identity and an original concept; the contemporary edge of the typography; and lastly, the spirit of the system, which in no way restricts the potential for range extensions.

GOLD
PACKAGING
FOOD & BEVERAGES

TITLE
TCHO
COMPANY
Edenspiekermann
CLIENT
TCHO
DESIGNERS
Tobias Trost
Francesca Bolognini
Thomas Waltz
CREATIVE DIRECTOR
Erik Spiekermann
DESIGN DIRECTOR
Susanna Dulkinys
OTHER
Gordon Protz
URL
www.tcho.com
COUNTRY
Netherlands

For a long time, chocolate was a little treat for regular consumption. But in recent years, master-chocolatiers have refined tastes and raised the pedigree of flavours. Their chocolates have fast become sophisticated luxury items, with vintages and increasingly distinct terroirs. The rare pleasure of an exceptional tasting experience demands a package of equal ambition. This is the idea behind Tcho. Marrying style with modernity, it revisits the commonplaces of the luxury sphere with a series of very pared-down geometric motifs in guillochage, and redefines luxury in a contemporary idiom. Well-behaved and conscientious, the jury did not succumb to the temptation of sampling the chocolates before reaching its verdict. But afterwards...

DARK
CHOCOLATE
"CHOCOLATEY"
Ghana
70% Cacao
60g (2.12oz)

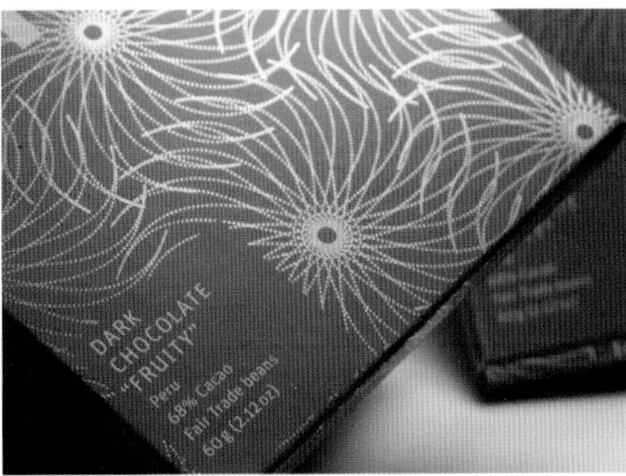
DARK
CHOCOLATE
"FRUITY"
Peru
68% Cacao
Fair Trade beans
60g (2.12oz)

TCHO

TCHO

TCHO

TCHO

TCHO

TCHO
TCHO
DARK
CHOCOLATE
"FRUITY"
Peru
68% Cacao
Fair Trade beans
60g (2.12oz)
"CITRUS"
"CITRUS"
"EARTHY"
"EARTHY"
"FRUITY"
"FRUITY"
"NUTTY"
"NUTTY"

SILVER
PACKAGING
FOOD & BEVERAGES

TITLE
Soft drinks / Linz 2009
COMPANY
Buchegger, Denoth, Feichtner / Haslinger, Keck
CLIENT
Linz 2009 European Capital of Culture
ART DIRECTOR
Michael Denoth
CREATIVE DIRECTORS
Michael Denoth
Bernhard Buchegger
ILLUSTRATOR
Florian Knogler
WRITER
Patsy Koeppel-Haslinger
COUNTRY
Austria

SILVER
PACKAGING
FOOD & BEVERAGES

TITLE
Jytte flour
COMPANY
M8 design
CLIENT
Holmen Crisp as
DESIGNERS
Arild Kristiansen
Phen Hunter
ART DIRECTOR
Arild Kristiansen
COUNTRY
Norway

BRONZE
PACKAGING
FOOD & BEVERAGES

TITLE
Waitrose Fresh Herbs
COMPANY
Lewis Moberly
CLIENT
Waitrose
COUNTRY
United Kingdom

BRONZE
PACKAGING
FOOD & BEVERAGES

TITLE
Soso Salt
COMPANY
Dfraile
CLIENT
SosoFactory
COUNTRY
Spain

BRONZE
PACKAGING
FOOD & BEVERAGES

TITLE
Frank´s Energizers
COMPANY
Ansichts.sache Designkollektiv
CLIENT
MCP Holding GmbH
COUNTRY
Germany

BRONZE
PACKAGING
FOOD & BEVERAGES

TITLE
Regent's Park
COMPANY
Bug
CLIENT
Fresh Food Village
COUNTRY
France

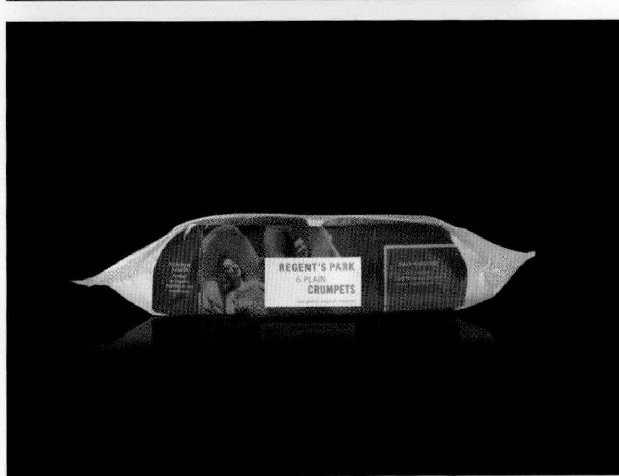

BRONZE
PACKAGING
FOOD & BEVERAGES

TITLE
Packaging design
for organic honey
COMPANY
mërz punkt
CLIENT
Bienenhof Pausch (small
organic honey manufacture)
COUNTRY
Germany

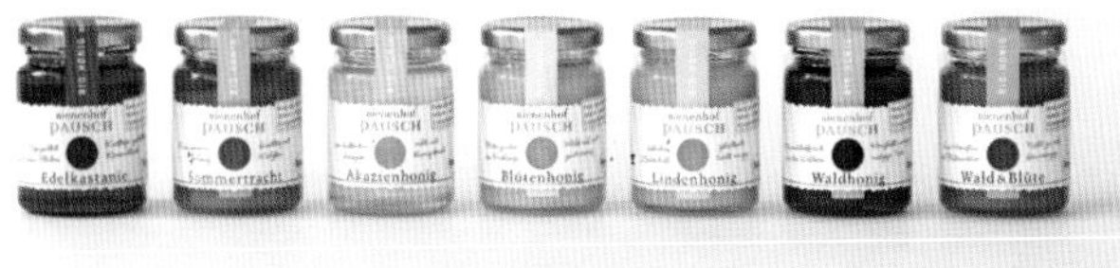

BRONZE
PACKAGING
FOOD & BEVERAGES

TITLE
Saltå Kvarn
COMPANY
himlaform
CLIENT
Saltå Kvarn AB
COUNTRY
Sweden

GOLD
PACKAGING
MISCELLANIOUS

TITLE
moshi moshi mind
COMPANY
Designbolaget
CLIENT
moshi moshi
DESIGNER
Henriette Kruse Jørgensen
ART DIRECTOR
Claus Due
CREATIVE DIRECTOR
Claus Due
DESIGN DIRECTOR
Claus Due
COUNTRY
Denmark

Should a food package be a showcase or informative. How far can the content-metaphor go? Many paths have been travelled in the history of modern packaging. Should the product be shown, or rather its allegorical image? Its origin or principal quality? In the wellness-product category, all of these questions must be rigorously posed, and the response must convince the consumer. The jury especially appreciated the restful and serene look of the solution for the Moshi Moshi brand, though it certainly does not lack character.

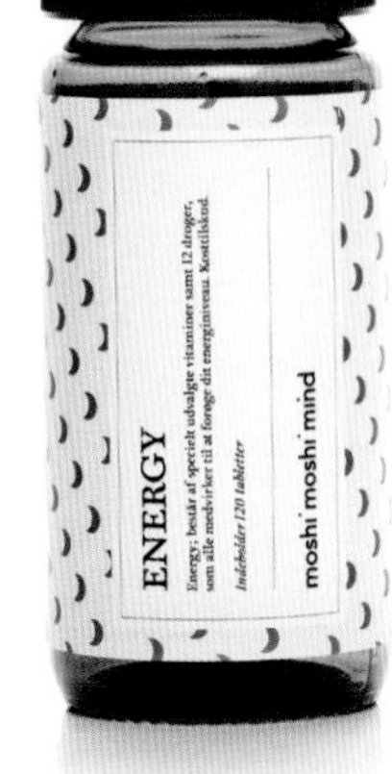

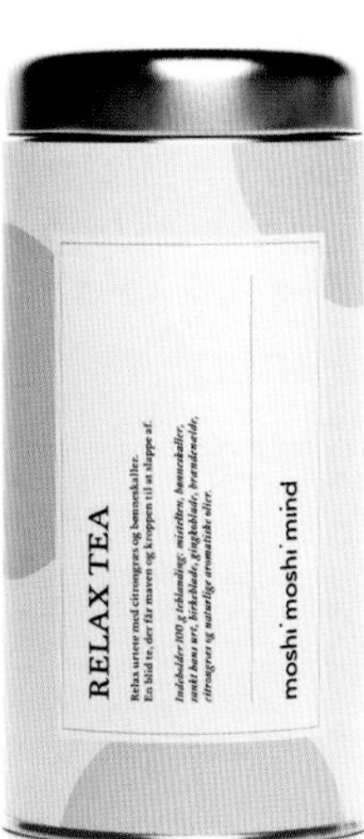
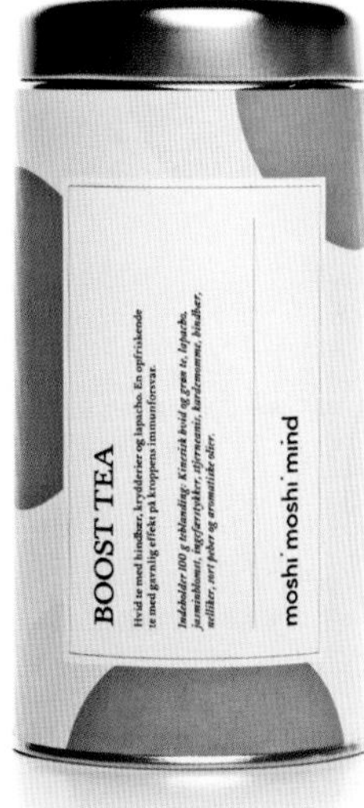

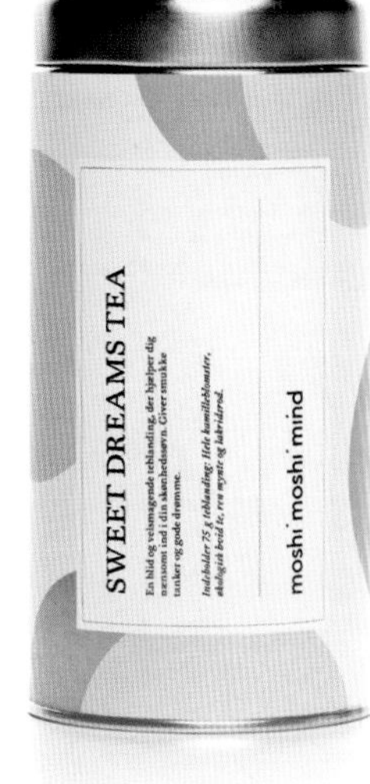

SILVER
PACKAGING
MISCELLANIOUS

TITLE
Emulsion paints
COMPANY
K2DESIGN
CLIENT
Cosmos colours
ART DIRECTOR
Alexis Marinis
CREATIVE DIRECTOR
Yiannis Kouroudis
PHOTOGRAPHER
Tassos Vrettos
COUNTRY
Greece

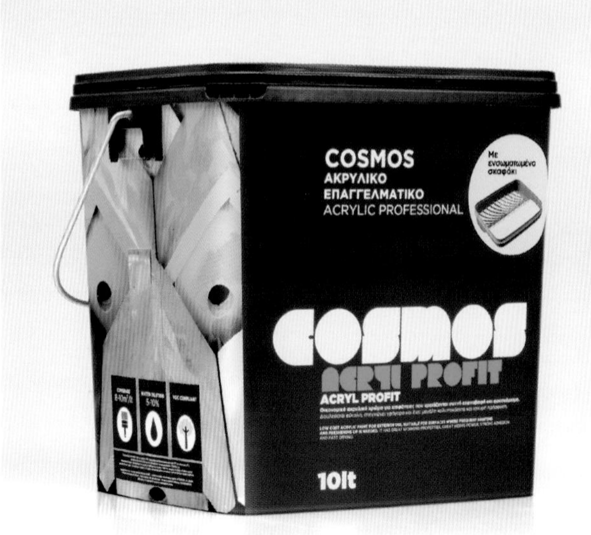

SILVER
PACKAGING
MISCELLANIOUS

TITLE
Traidcraft Tissue Range
COMPANY
Studio Blackburn
CLIENT
Traidcraft
CREATIVE DIRECTOR
Susie Blackburn
ILLUSTRATOR
Andrew Dyer
WRITER
Nick Rootes
COUNTRY
United Kingdom

SILVER
PACKAGING
MISCELLANIOUS

TITLE
Viktor&Rolf StrongBox
COMPANY
R'Pure Studio (Raison Pure Design Group)
CLIENT
Viktor&Rolf
DESIGNER
R'Pure Studio
ART DIRECTOR
Sébastien Servaire
COUNTRY
France

Waks Nature

the design shop

Hellenic Candle Company

Greece

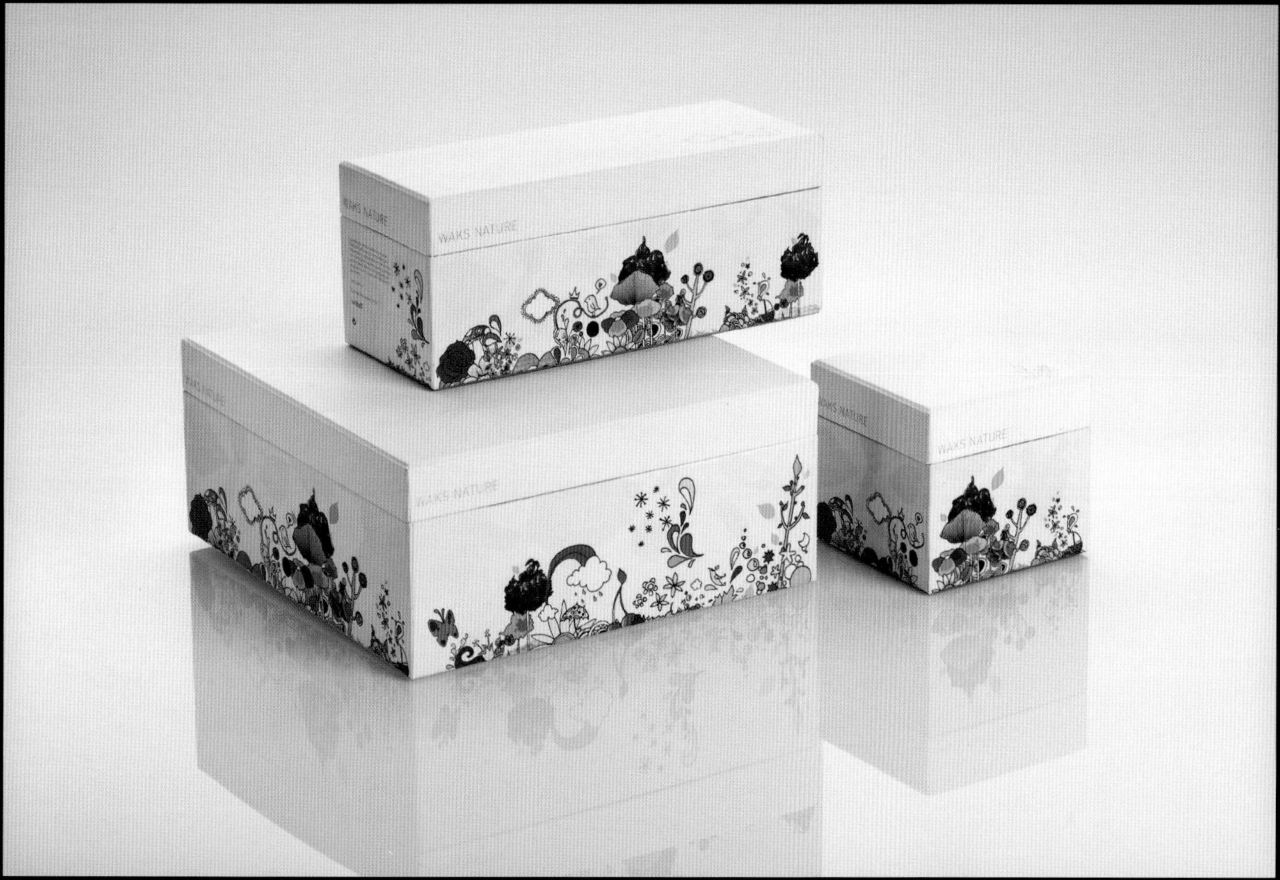

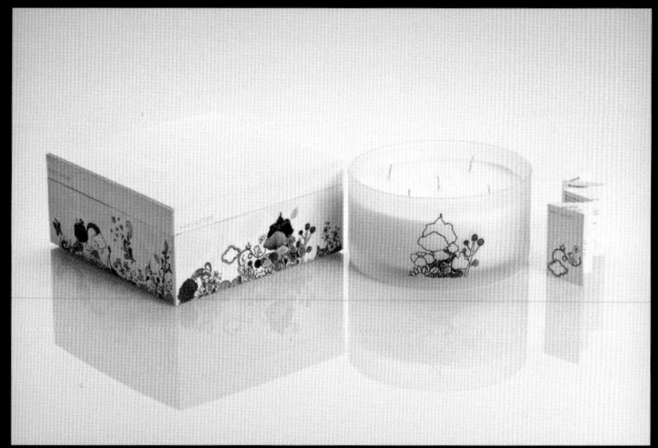

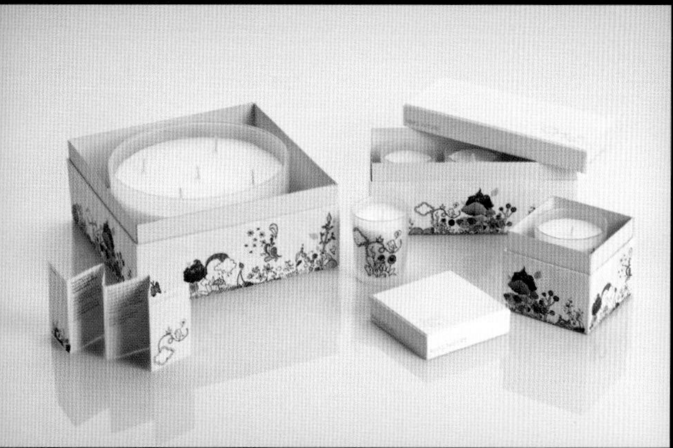

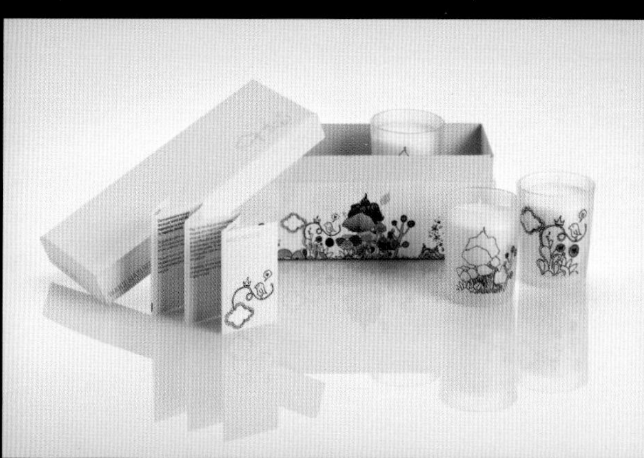

BRONZE
PACKAGING
MISCELLANIOUS

TITLE
Books and more
COMPANY
designersunited.gr
CLIENT
Papasotitiriou Book Stores
COUNTRY
Greece

Coasters

ChrisTrivizas | Design

Paperkingdom

Greece

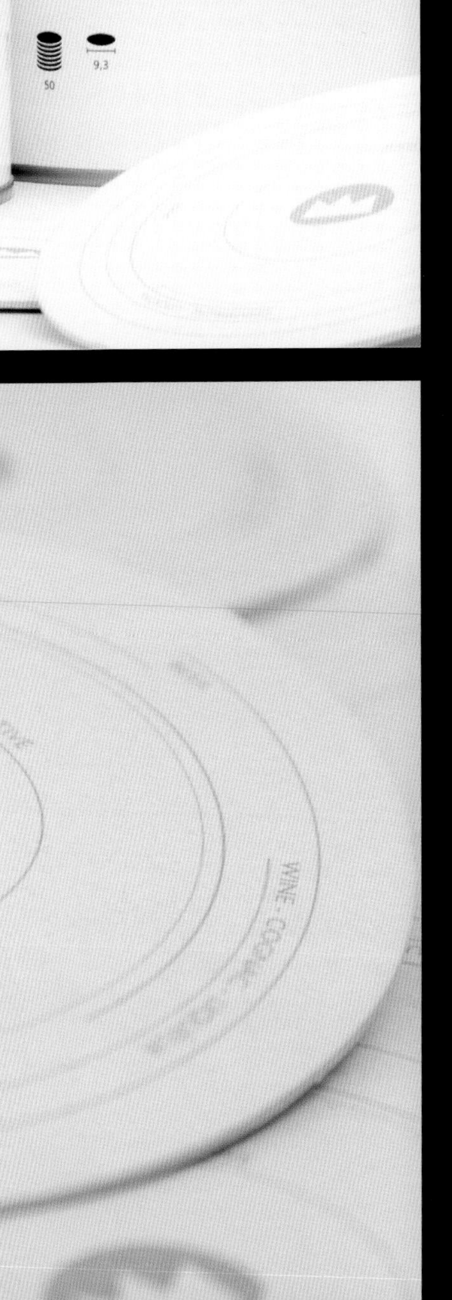

SILVER
CD/DVD COVER

TITLE
Binova Eurocucina 2008
COMPANY
zup associati srl
CLIENT
Binova SpA
DESIGNERS
Andrea Medri
Lucia Roscini
Marco Fagioli
COUNTRY
Italy

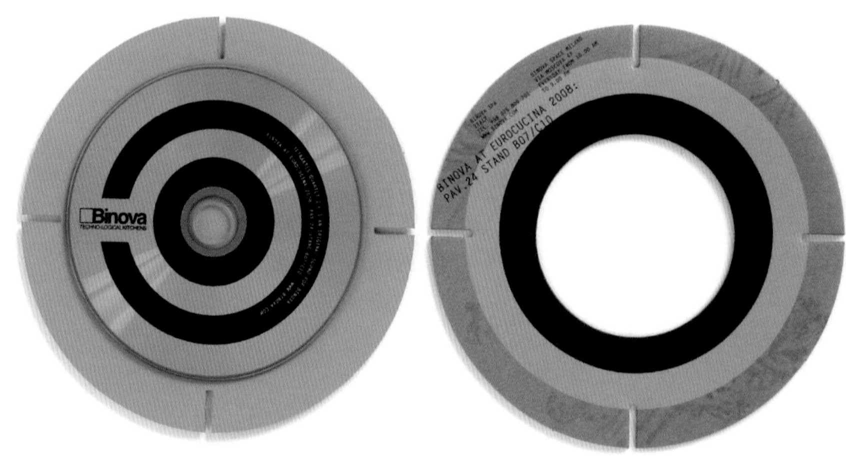

SILVER
CD/DVD COVER

Super 8

Poor Records

Olivier Weber

Pascal Greco
Olivier Weber

Pascal Greco
Olivier Weber

Pascal Greco

Nicolas Ducret

www.super-8.tv

Switzerland

BRONZE
CD/DVD COVER

TITLE
tris stigmes / three moments
COMPANY
kapanigraphix
CLIENT
the Prefabricated Quartet (tPQ)
COUNTRY
Greece

BRONZE
CD/DVD COVER

TITLE
Helmut Lachenmann – NUN
COMPANY
Jäger & Jäger
CLIENT
Ensemble Modern
COUNTRY
Germany

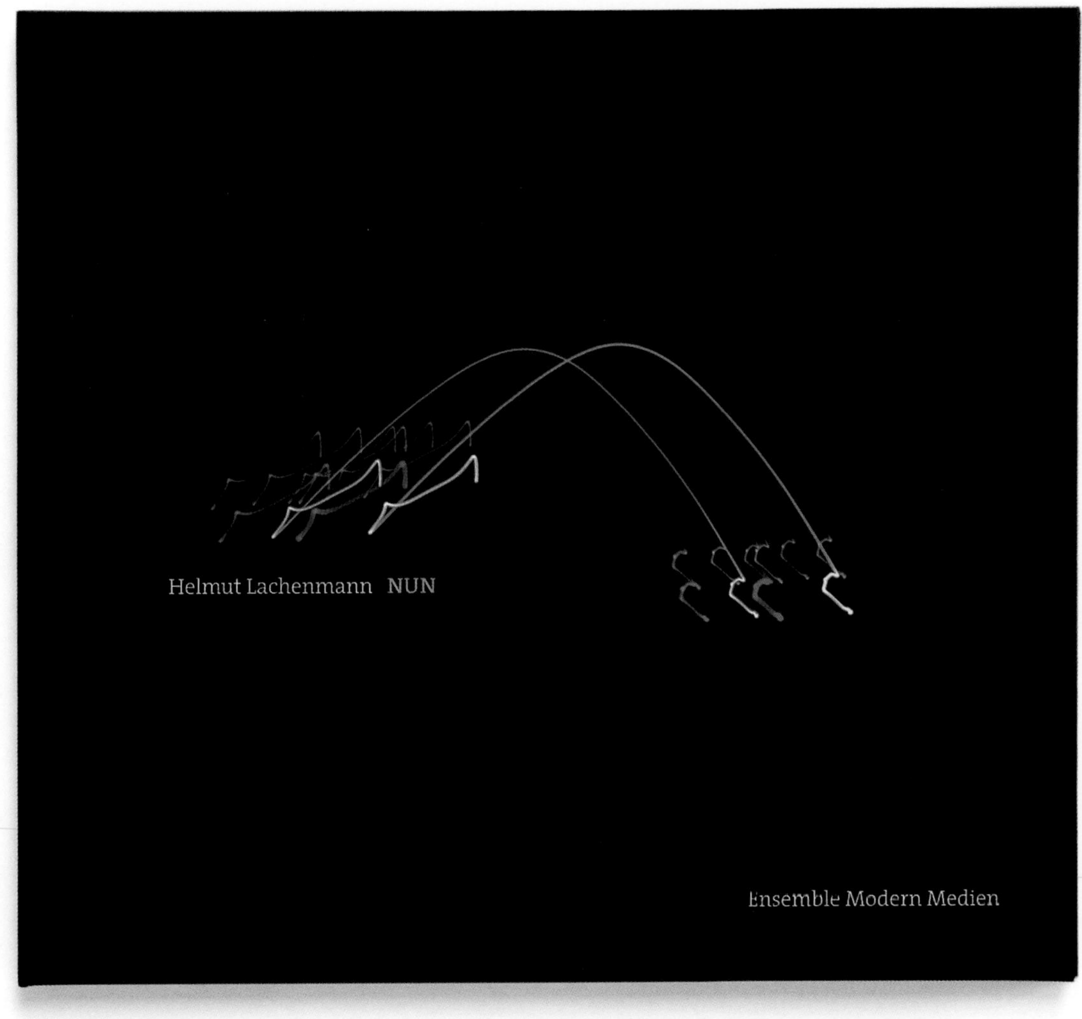

BRONZE
CD/DVD COVER

TITLE
Death Magnetic
COMPANY
Turner Duckworth:
London & San Francisco
CLIENT
Metallica
COUNTRY
United Kingdom

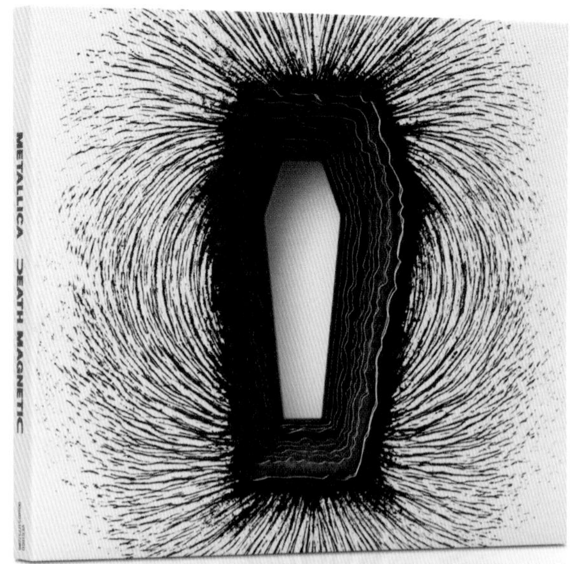

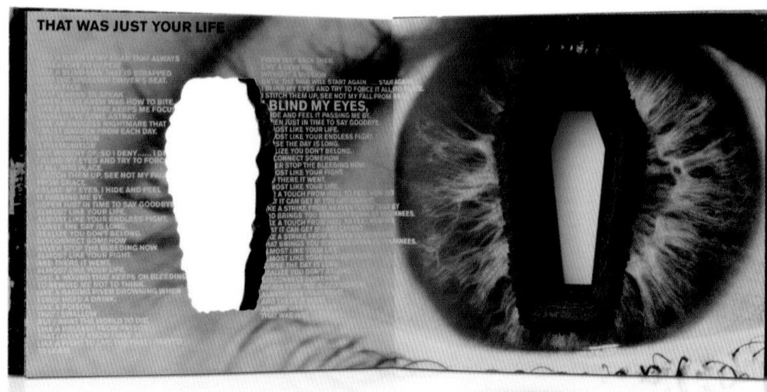

BRONZE
CD/DVD COVER

TITLE
Black Cargoes - Glass
DESIGNER
Iwan Negro
CLIENT
Black Cargoes
COUNTRY
Switzerland

BRONZE
CD/DVD COVER

TITLE
Necessarily Two
COMPANY
Vladan Srdic / Studio 360
CLIENT
Peter Wegele, Annedore Wienert
COUNTRY
Slovenia

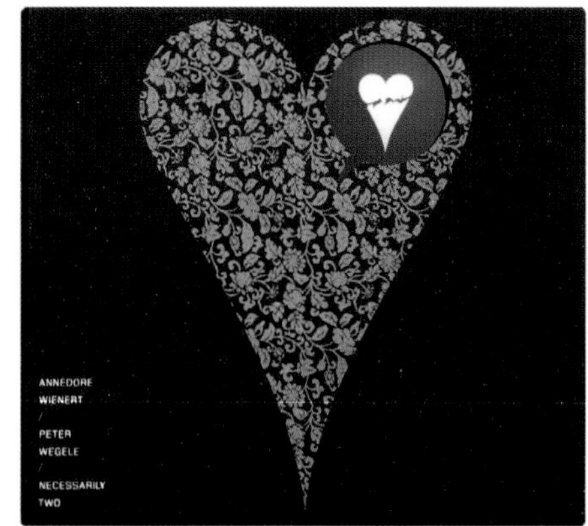

Marcheaux/Ghost

mnp

Undo Records

Greece

ILLUSTRATIONS

SILVER
BOOK & EDITORIAL ILLUSTRATION

TITLE
First money
COMPANY
Roel Venderbosch
CLIENT
nrc.next
ILLUSTRATOR
Roel Venderbosch
OTHER
Annelies Kuiper
COUNTRY
Netherlands

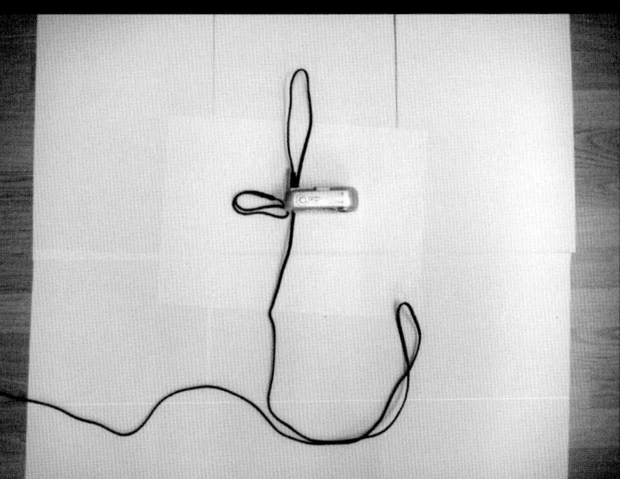

NRC Next Pre. One

Autobahn

NRC Next

Autobahn

Autobahn

Jordi Huisman

Netherlands

BRONZE
BOOK & EDITORIAL ILLUSTRATION

TITLE
Phonetic Alphabet
COMPANY
Dfraile
CLIENT
Julio Telio
COUNTRY
Spain

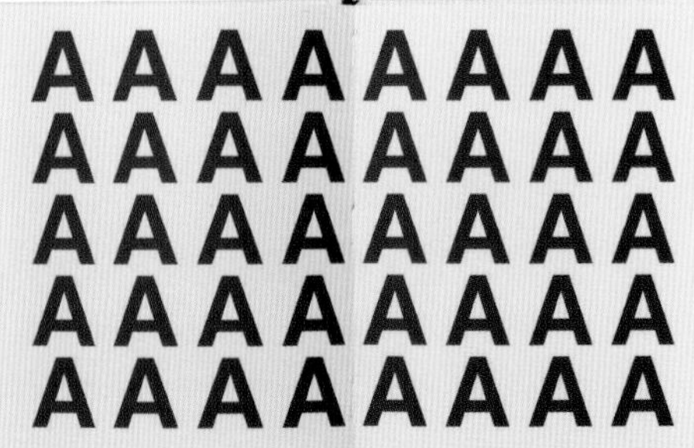

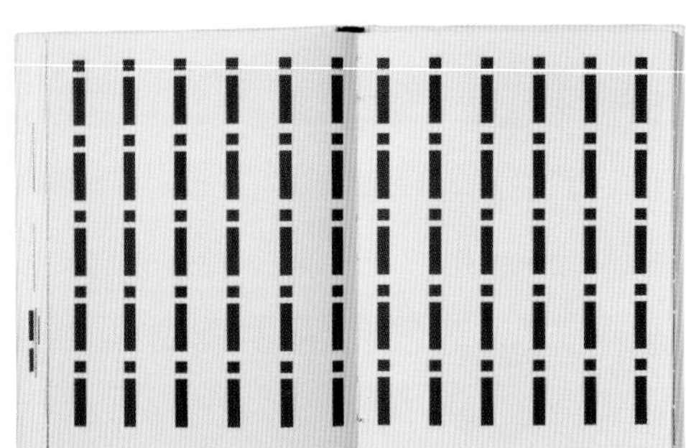

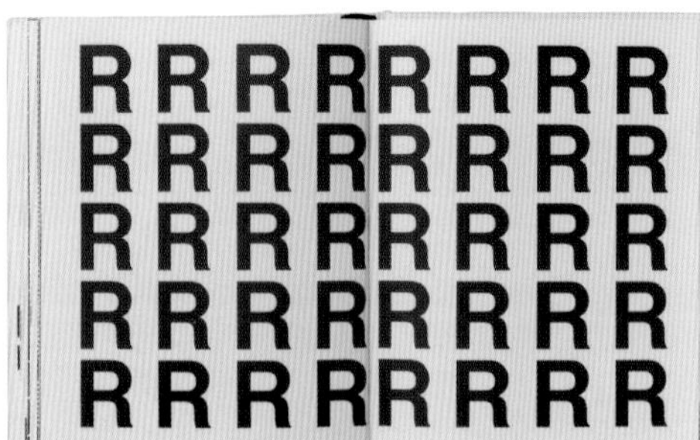

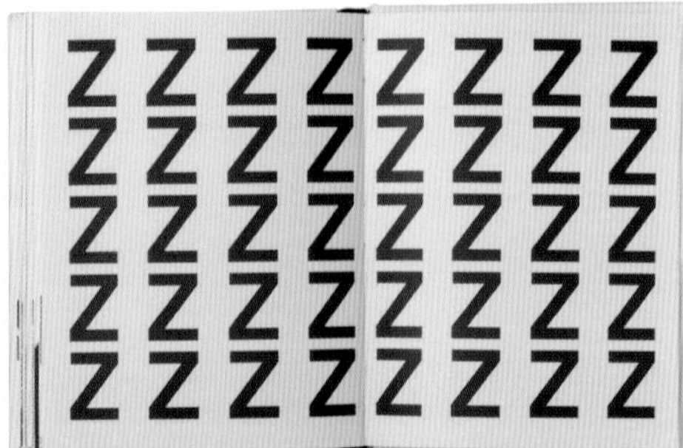

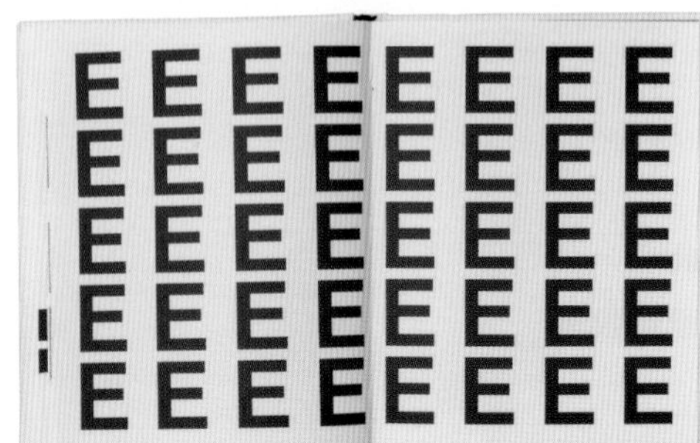

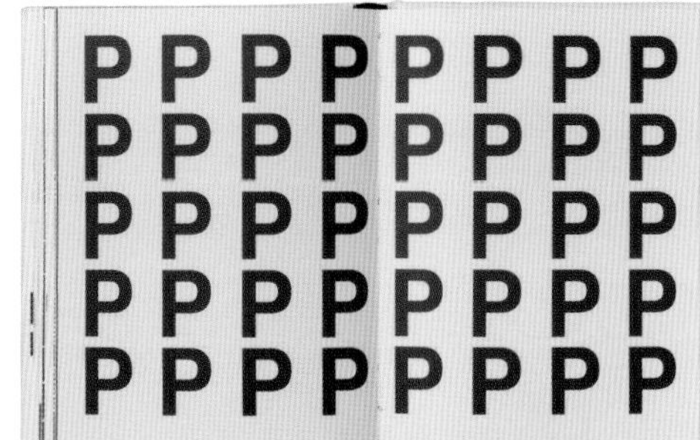

BRONZE
BOOK & EDITORIAL ILLUSTRATION

AR Illustration

P-06 atelier, ambientes e comunicação, lda

Portuguese Assembly of the Republic

Portugal

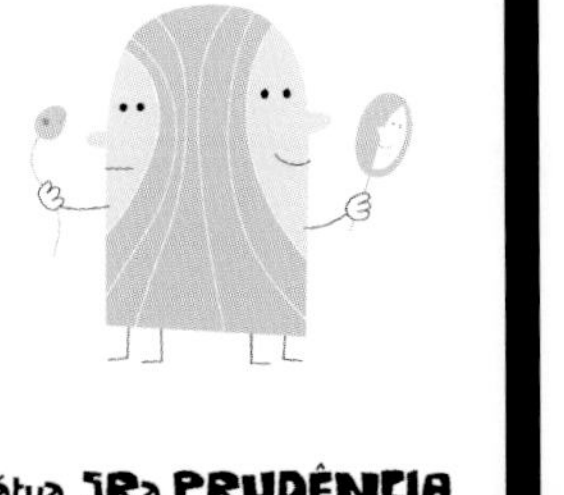

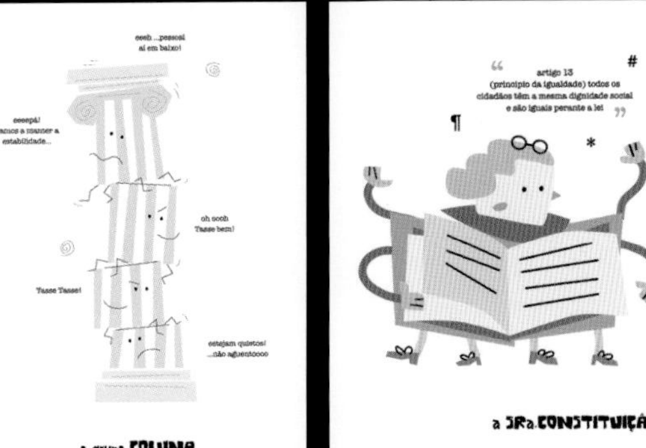

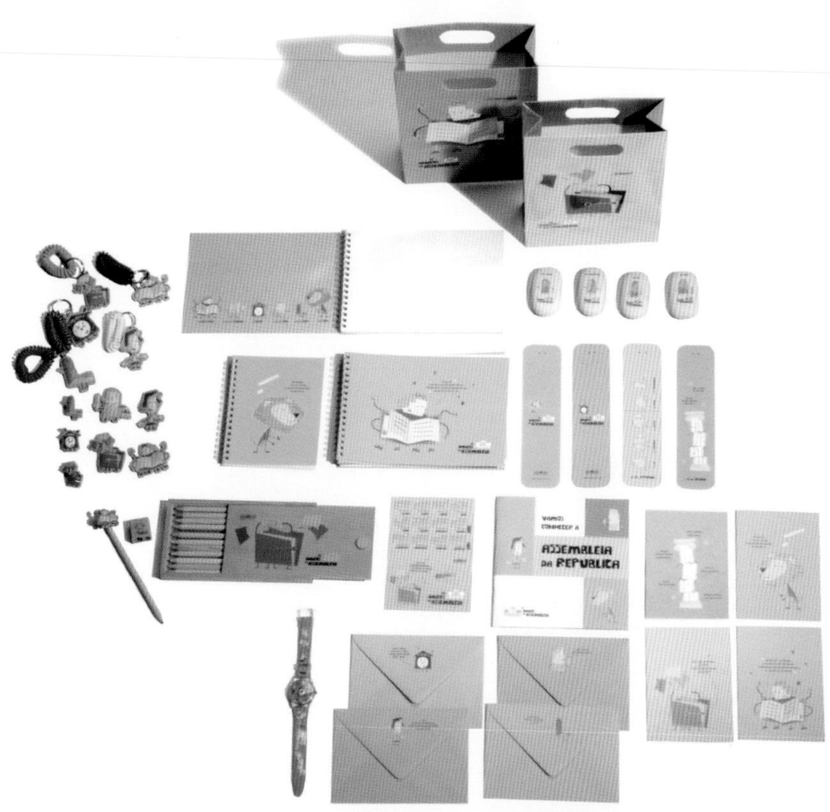

SILVER
CORPORATE ILLUSTRATION

TITLE
Untitled
(X-Ray Vector Smart Object)
COMPANY
Bodin
CLIENT
smart/Daimler AG
DESIGNER
Halvor Bodin
ART DIRECTOR
Halvor Bodin
ILLUSTRATOR
Halvor Bodin
COUNTRY
Norway

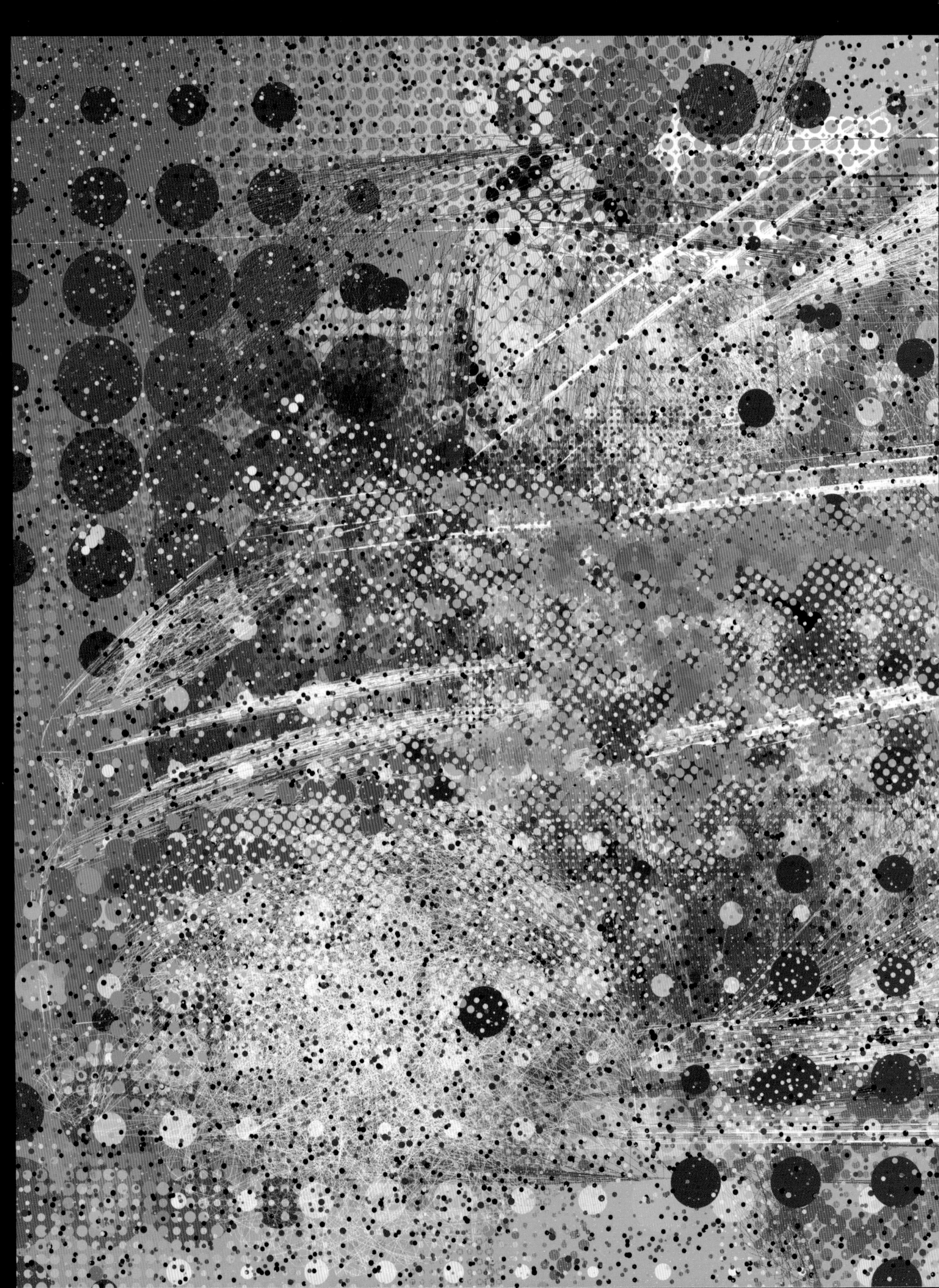

SILVER
CORPORATE ILLUSTRATION

Blank Handbook

Publicis Yorum

Publicis Yorum

Örgüt Çaylı

Örgüt Çaylı

Cevdet Kizilay

Örgüt Çaylı

Örgüt Çaylı

Turkey

Buralarda banka var mı?

PROGRAM 8
Bırakın doğru ayarları ütünüz düşünsün!

GÜZELLİK

BRONZE
CORPORATE ILLUSTRATION

TITLE
Ekies animals
COMPANY
beetroot design group
CLIENT
Ekies all senses resort
COUNTRY
Greece

BRONZE
CORPORATE ILLUSTRATION

TITLE
Design Cagematch
COMPANY
Vier für Texas
CLIENT
30elm (Matt Meyers, Chris Conley)
URL
www.30elm.com/battles
COUNTRY
Germany

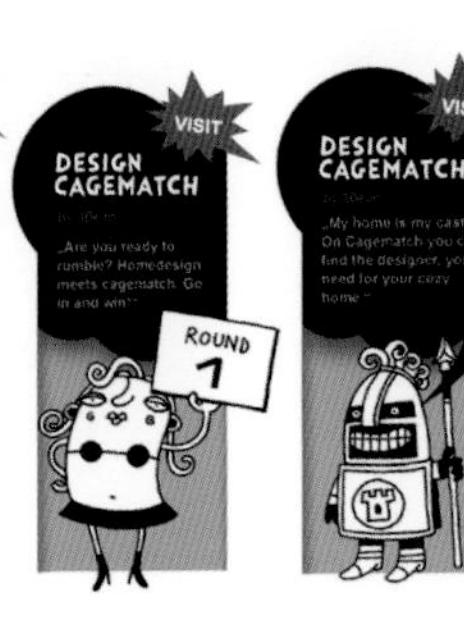

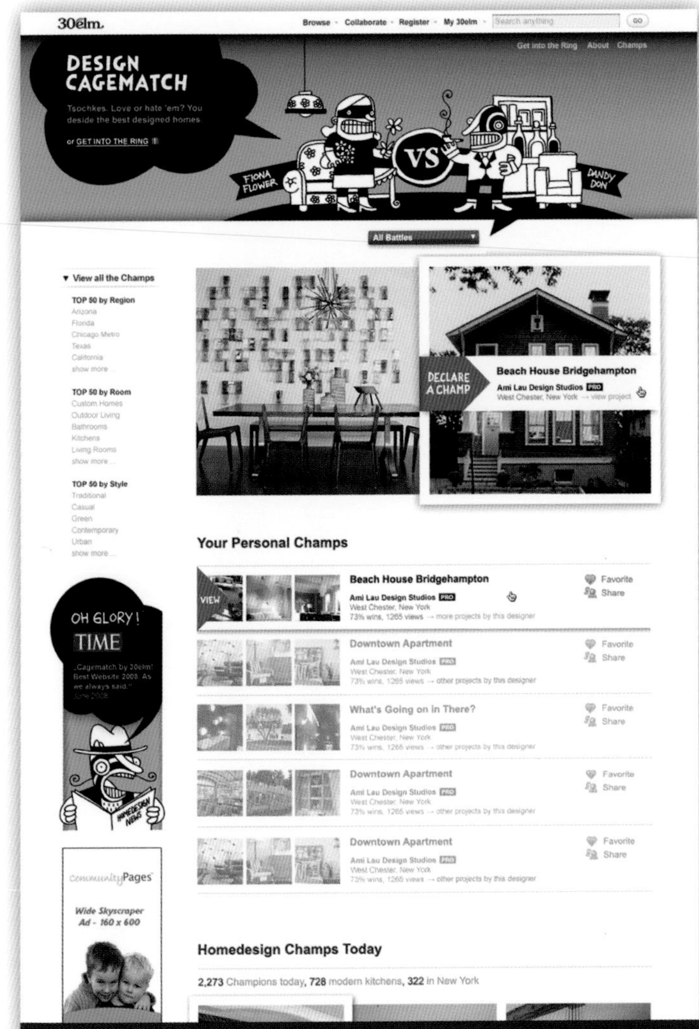

BRONZE
CORPORATE ILLUSTRATION

TITLE
Telefonklotter
ILLUSTRATOR
Tove Hedman
CLIENT
Telia
COUNTRY
Sweden

BRONZE
CORPORATE ILLUSTRATION

TITLE
Sublimation Orchestra
COMPANY
zTy
CLIENT
Sublimation Orchestra
URL
www.sublimation-orchestra.eu
COUNTRY
Germany

BRONZE
CORPORATE ILLUSTRATION

TITLE
YMCA Camps
COMPANY
designersunited.gr
CLIENT
YMCA Thessaloniki
COUNTRY
Greece

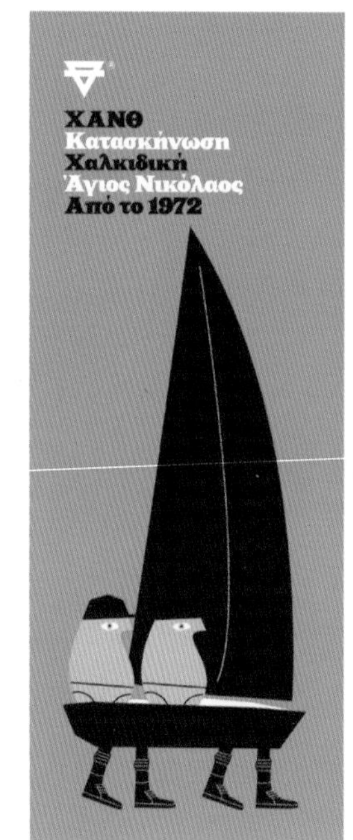

BRONZE
CORPORATE ILLUSTRATION

TITLE
Art circles for Brazil
COMPANY
Tsevis Visual Design
CLIENT
Banco Bradesco Brazil
Neogama BBH, Brazil
COUNTRY
Greece

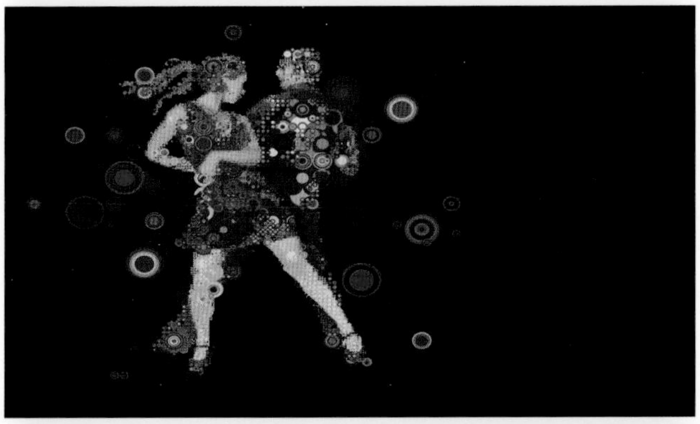

BRONZE
CORPORATE ILLUSTRATION

TITLE
IKEA: Long Live Diversity
ILLUSTRATOR
Tsevis Visual Design
CLIENT
IKEA Sweden
Forsman & Bodenfors
Sweden
COUNTRY
Greece

FINALIST
CORPORATE ILLUSTRATION

TITLE
Global Voice
Annual Report Illustrations
COMPANY
Dara Creative
CLIENT
The Global Voice Group
COUNTRY
Ireland

SELF-PROMOTION

GOLD
PRINTED SELF PROMOTION

TITLE
Beveelt de heer T. Verbeek aan bij Uw kennissen
COMPANY
Thijs Verbeek grafisch ontwerp
DESIGNER
Thijs Verbeek
ART DIRECTOR
Thijs Verbeek
CREATIVE DIRECTOR
Thijs Verbeek
ILLUSTRATOR
Thijs Verbeek
PHOTOGRAPHER
Arjan Benning
COUNTRY
Netherlands

Visual designers can fully meet their clients' expectations by grading messages and making visual decisions without qualms. But the hardest job for designers is self-promotion, requiring great detachment and choices that sometimes prove impossible. So they often bypass the decisions, give up the project, or make do with a bare minimum that is sometimes incomprehensible. Why not explore the frontiers of tinyness with a micro-book a few millimetres high. A few pages, and you have the ideal promotional object to keep close to hand. The jury approved.

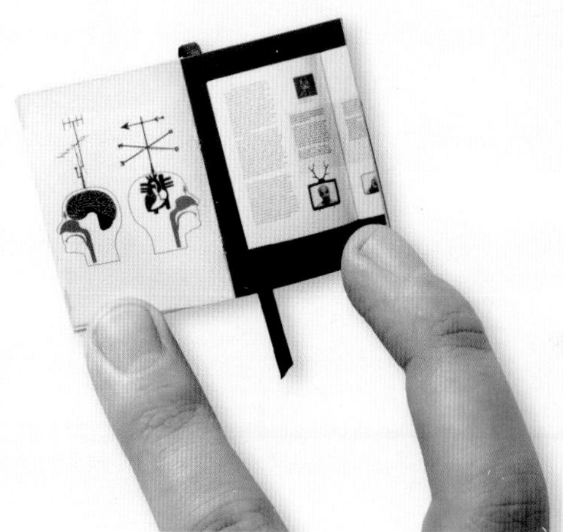

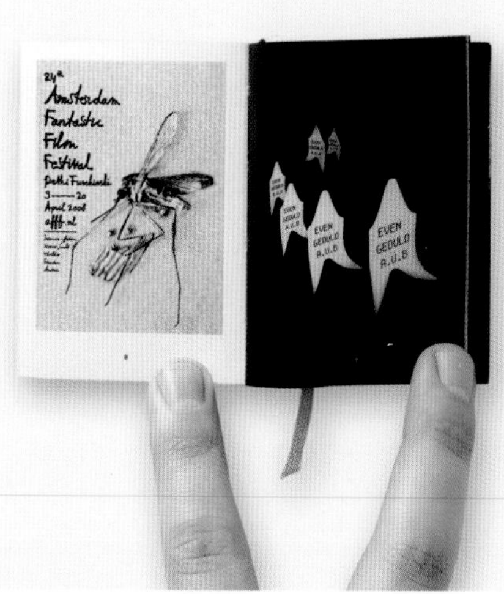

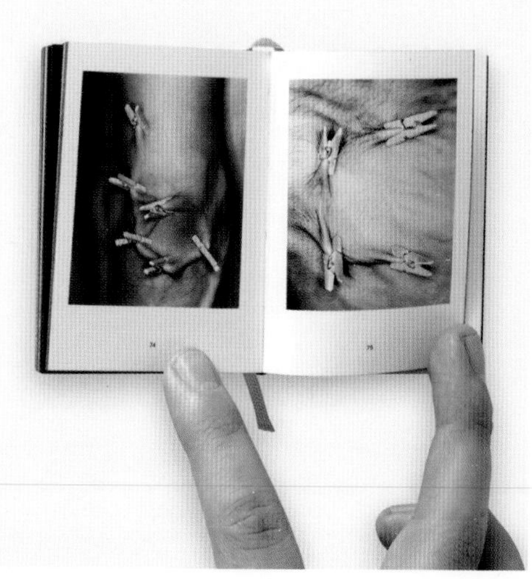

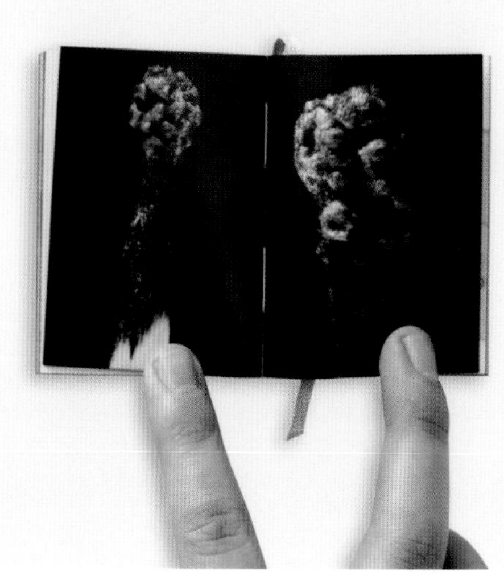

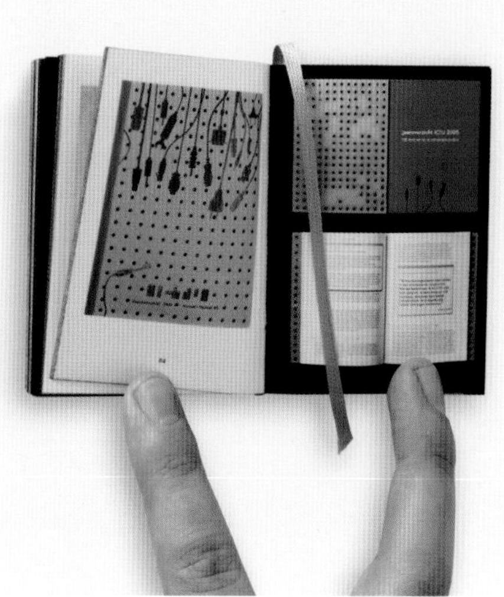

GOLD
PRINTED SELF PROMOTION

TITLE
Impossibles possibles
COMPANY
Enric Jardí disseny gràfic
CLIENT
Arts Gràfiques Orient
DESIGNER
Enric Jardí
WRITER
Teresa Domingo
COUNTRY
Spain

To keep its place in the face of an ever-wider digital offering, print must retain its dimension as a material object that can be collected, lent, given, exchanged, lost and thrown away. Modern printers have upscaled their facilities, and today no book or magazine goes without their techniques of lacquering, cutting out, embossing, hot stamping, and so on. The jury was particularly receptive to the close collaboration between printer and studio for Impossibles Possibles, which has produced a measured and elegant result. The technique's high performance is presented without the extravagance often found in this type of document. This section of entries was particularly rich and generated long, intense discussion among the jury, so consistently high was the standard.

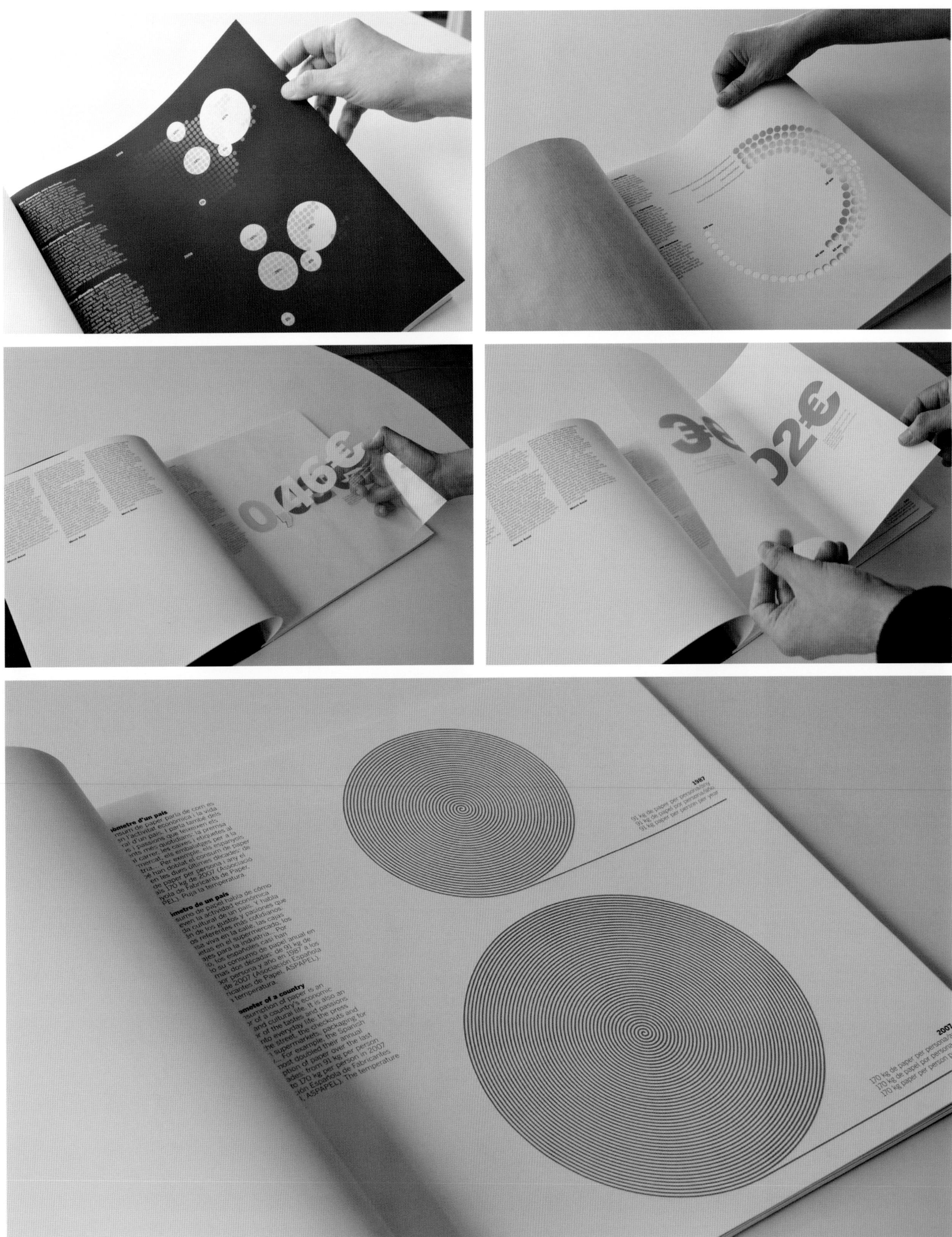

SILVER
PRINTED SELF PROMOTION

TITLE
Christmas Card 2008
COMPANY
Fuenfwerken Design AG
COUNTRY
Germany

Genug Geld
vernichtet!
Ab 2009
nachhaltig
investieren.
Unterstützen Sie
www.
gestaltBildung
.com/stiftung.
Kto. 100 369 222
BLZ 510 500 15

SILVER
PRINTED SELF PROMOTION

TITLE
Lorem Ipsum
COMPANY
studio FM milano srl
DESIGNER
studio FM milano srl
EDITOR
BIS Publishers
COUNTRY
Italy

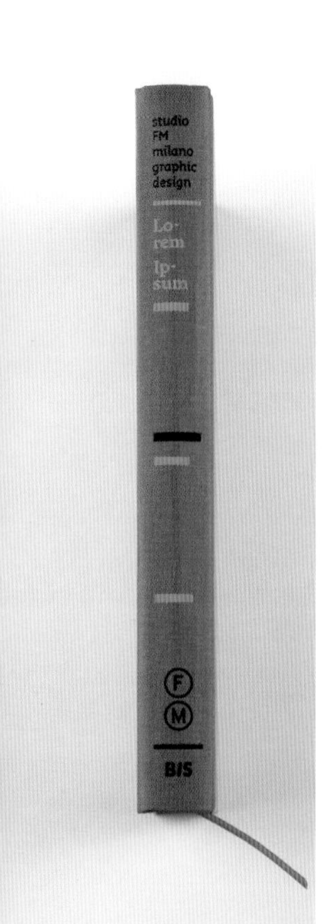

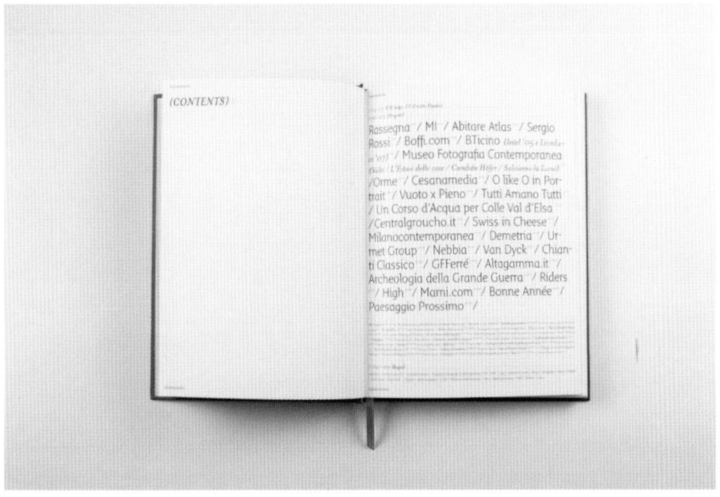
{CONTENTS}
Rassegna / MI / Abitare Atlas / Sergio
Rossi / Boffi.com / BTicino
/ Museo Fotografia Contemporanea
/Orme / Cesanamedia / O like O in Por-
trait / Vuoto x Pieno / Tutti Amano Tutti
/ Un Corso d'Acqua per Colle Val d'Elsa
/ Centralgroucho.it / Swiss in Cheese /
Milanocontemporanea / Demetra / Ur-
met Group / Nebbia / Van Dyck / Chian-
ti Classico / GFFerré / Altagamma.it /
Archeologia della Grande Guerra / Riders
/ High / Mami.com / Bonne Année /
Paesaggio Prossimo

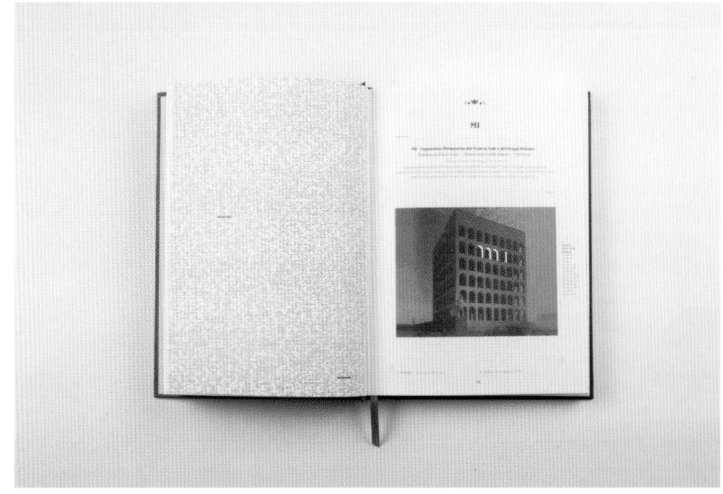
MI

International Herald Tribune
Wednesday, July 26, 2006.
3
Cesanamedia

Van Dyck

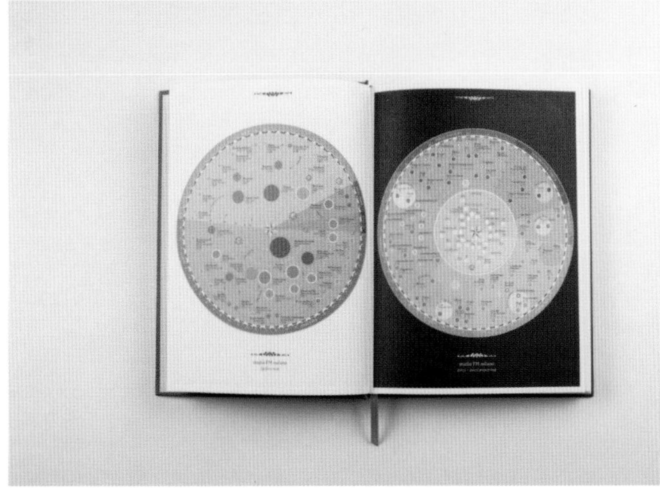

BRONZE
PRINTED SELF PROMOTION

TITLE
New Year's Greetings
COMPANY
Moniteurs GmbH
COUNTRY
Germany

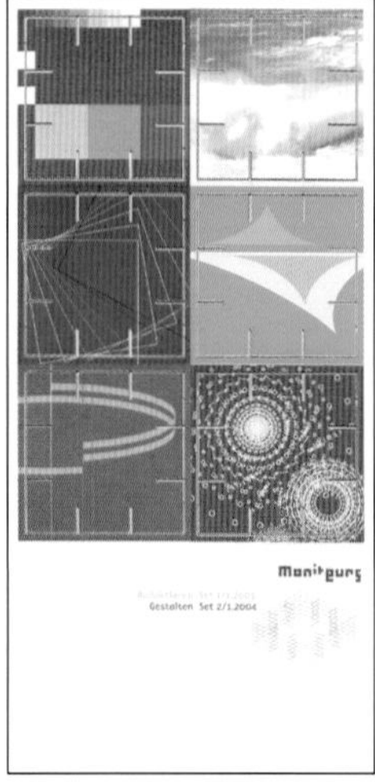

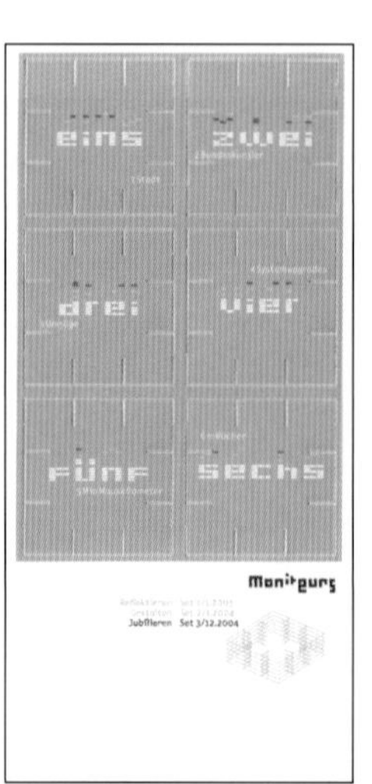

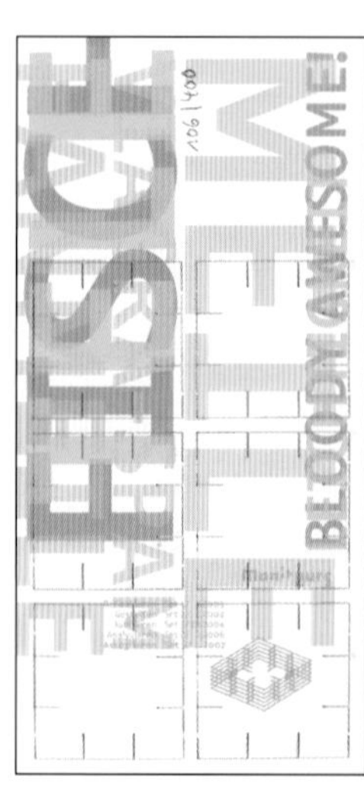

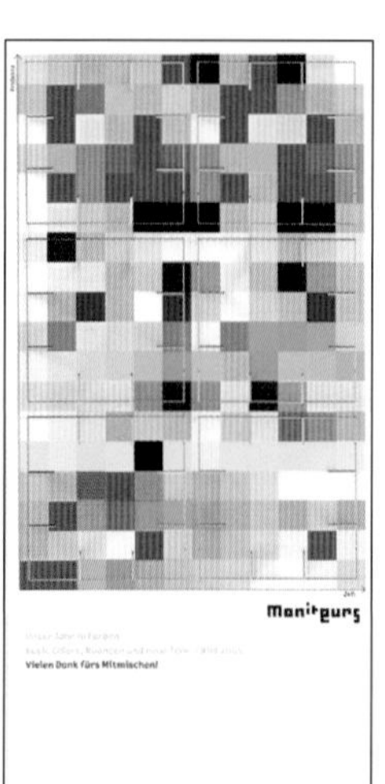

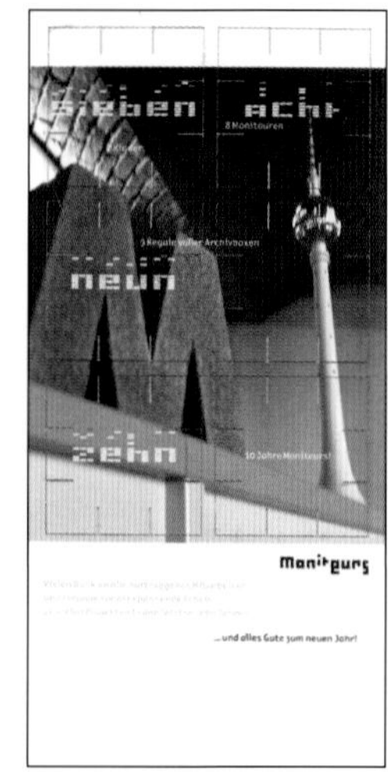

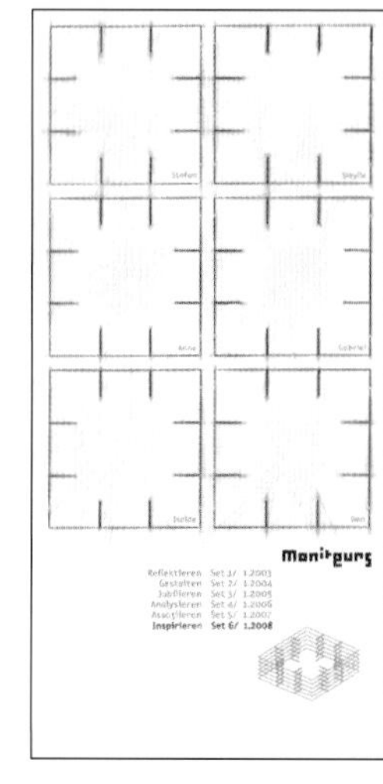

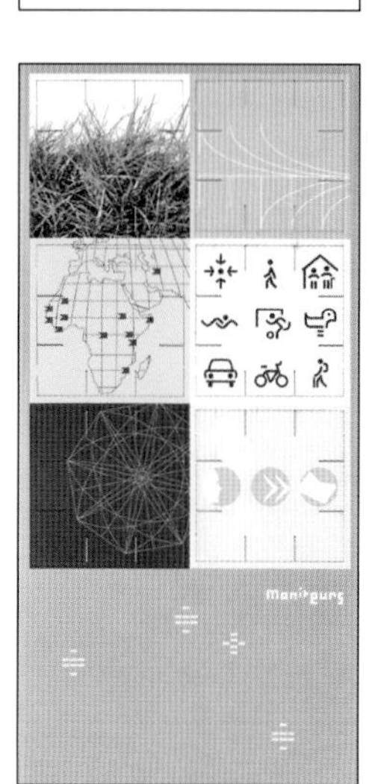

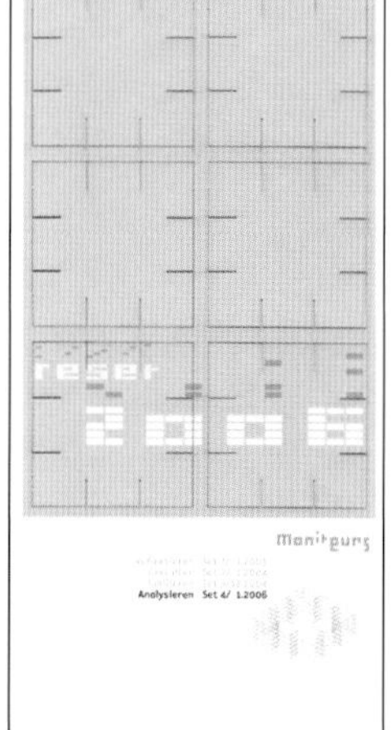

BRONZE
PRINTED SELF PROMOTION

TITLE
Sweet 2009
COMPANY
Kanella Arapoglou
COUNTRY
Greece

BRONZE
PRINTED SELF PROMOTION

TITLE
Christmas
COMPANY
Delikatessen Agentur fuer Marken und Design GmbH
COUNTRY
Germany

BRONZE
PRINTED SELF PROMOTION

TITLE
GVA Studio Selected Projects
COMPANY
GVA Studio
COUNTRY
Switzerland

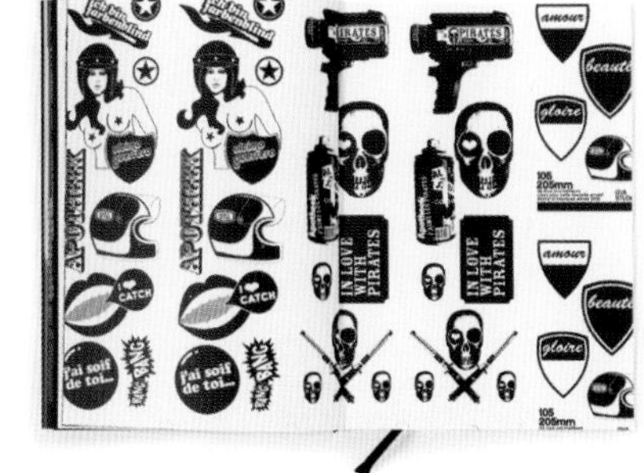

BRONZE
PRINTED SELF PROMOTION

TITLE
Annual Reports
COMPANY
Claus Koch Identity GmbH
COUNTRY
Germany

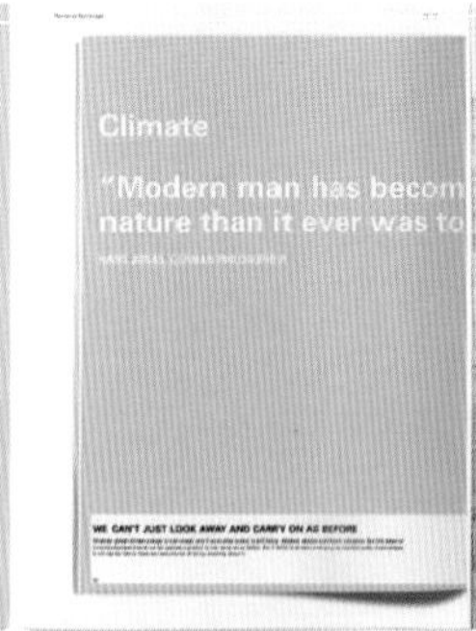

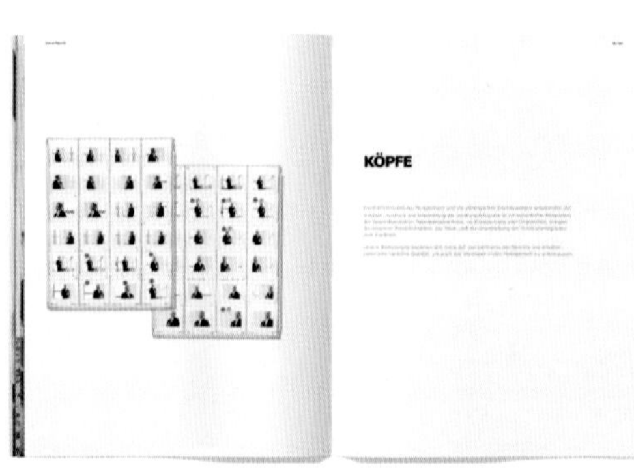

BRONZE
PRINTED SELF PROMOTION

TITLE
Self promotion Wine
COMPANY
Studio Rasic
COUNTRY
Croatia

BRONZE
PRINTED SELF PROMOTION

TITLE
Dare to Weare
COMPANY
Van Riet Ontwerpers
COUNTRY
Netherlands

BRONZE
PRINTED SELF PROMOTION

TITLE
Bitte – Danke
COMPANY
molter & sartor | zweizueins
COUNTRY
Germany

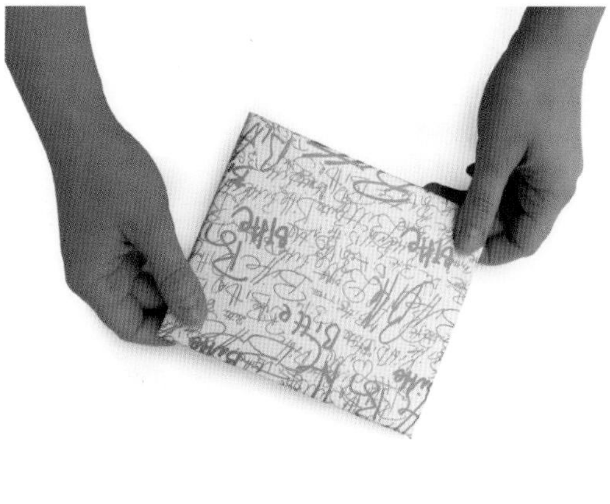

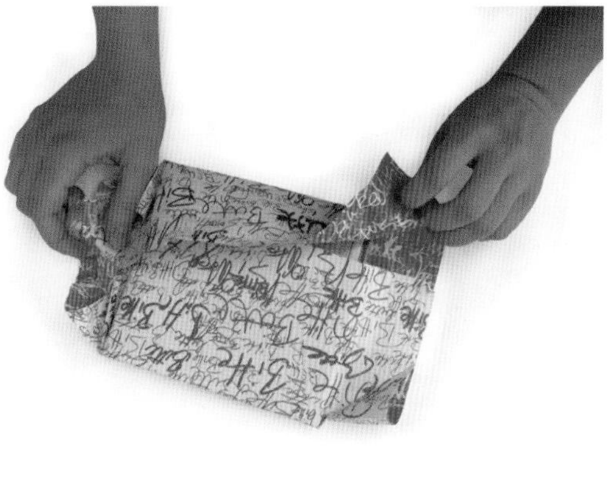

Follow your inner moonlight; don't hide the madness

Bleed

exhibition.bleed.no

Norway

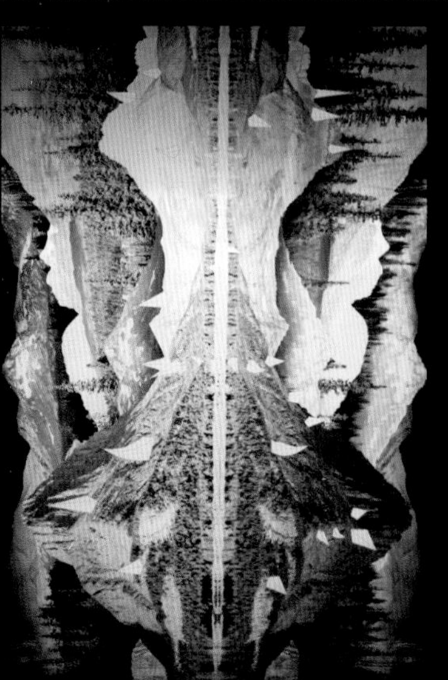

BRONZE
PRINTED SELF PROMOTION

TITLE
courier brochure
COMPANY
bauer konzept
& gestaltung gmbh
COUNTRY
Austria

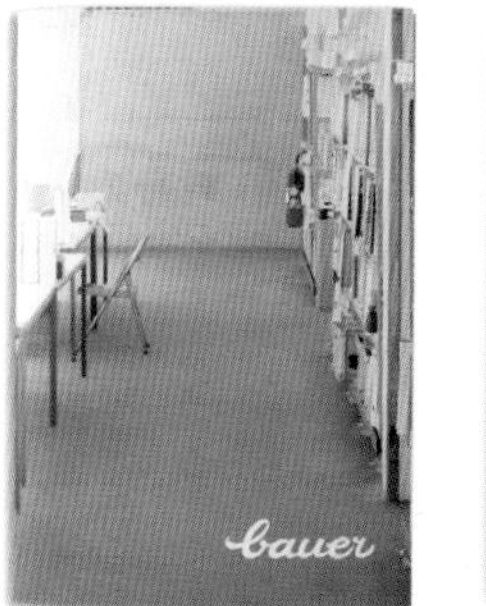

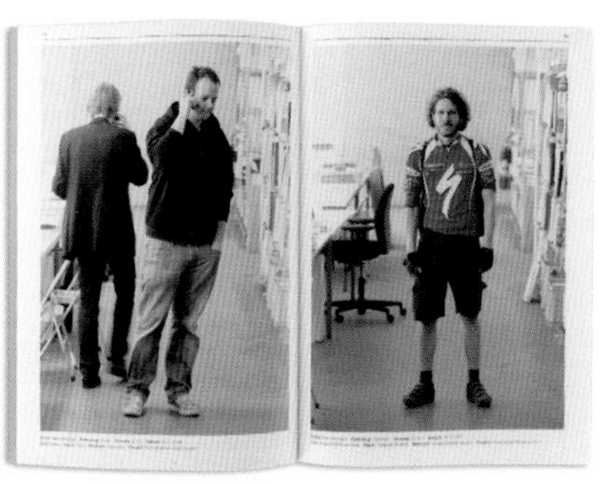

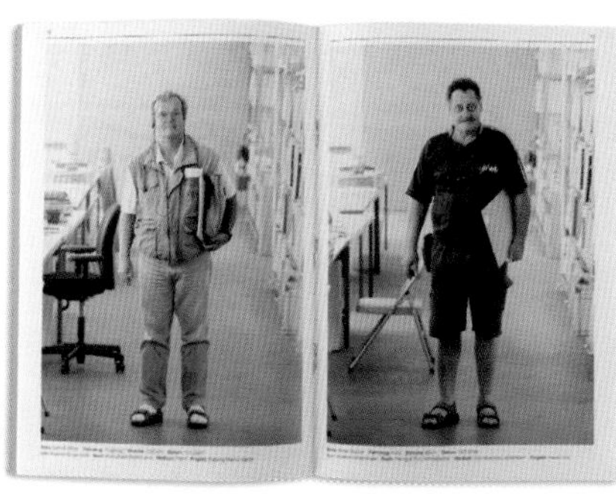

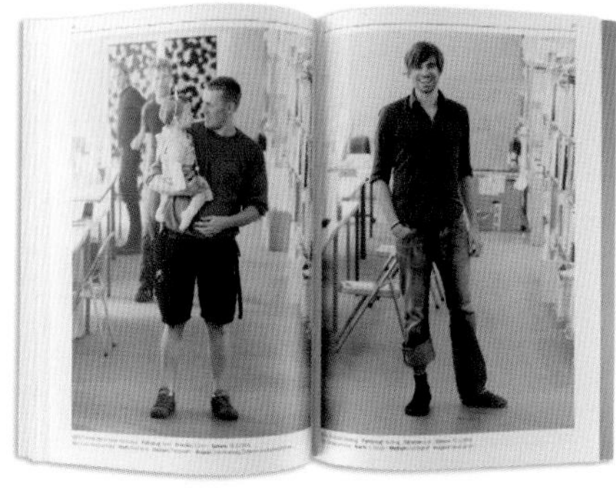

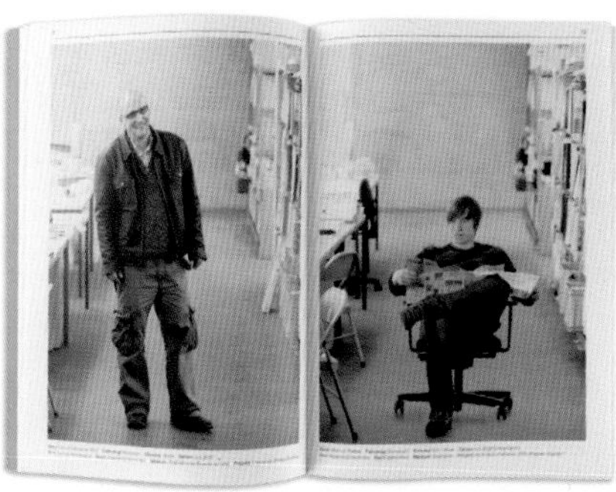

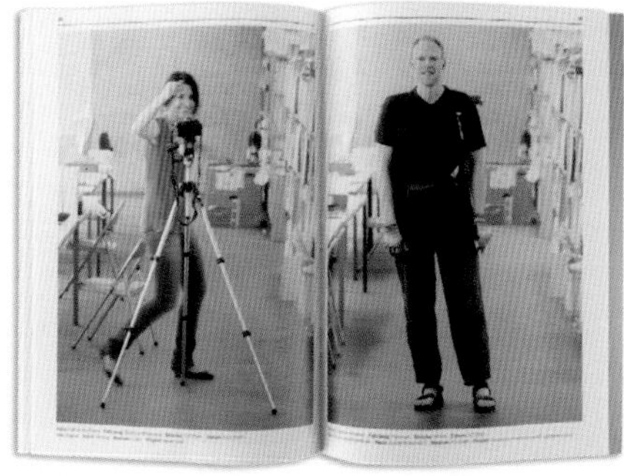

BRONZE
PRINTED SELF PROMOTION

TITLE
A book full of spam (or how to catch glory)
COMPANY
Bendita Gloria
COUNTRY
Spain

GAIN
MEGA HUGE
DIMENSIONS!

IMPRESS THE LADIES, AMAZE YOR FRIENDS, AND QUIETLY PROVE TO YOUR BUSINESS AS-

SOCIATES THAT YOU HAVE ARRI-VED ON LUXURY AND CLASS FOR JUST 10$.

BECOME A SUPER-MAN!

GET READY TO MAKE HER HAPPY!

THIS MAY TURN OUT TO BE THE MOST IM-PORTANT TEXT YOU WILL EVER READ IN YOUR FINANCIAL LIFE.

SMART PEOPLE BUY PILLS ONLINE.

THIS OFFER IS NOT FOR EVERYONE.

IF YOU CAN'T SEE JUST HOW EXCELENT THE RISK/REWARD RATIO IN THIS OFFER IS, THEN THERE IS NOTHING I CAN DO FOR YOU.

IF YOU TAKE OFFENSE TO THIS BOOK SIMPLY VI-SIT US AT: WWW. BENDITAGLORIA. COM

TO:
SAM MALLETT

TO:
PATRIC

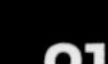

01.

Hartobalotof

ChrisTrivizas | Design

Greece

02.

Not anonymous wishes

Avantgarde Design

Poland

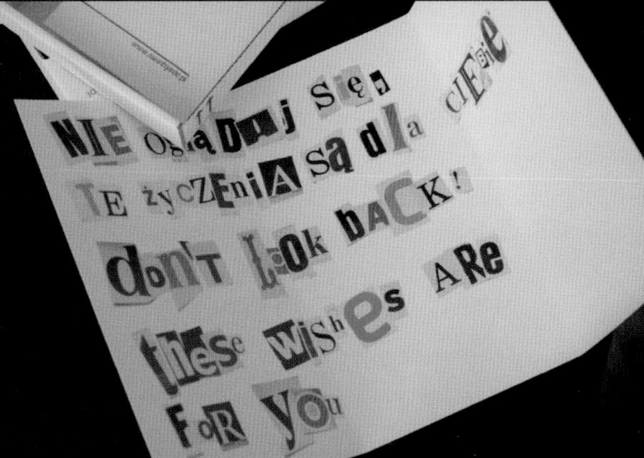

A CLOUD OF IDEAS

We all know that the 21st century will be about knowledge-based industries. And the further we travel into the era of dematerialisation, the more we must build systems and languages that enable us to understand its values and benefits. Visual-design agencies are at the vanguard of this challenge, because it is the essence of their profession. KMS convinced the jury by devising a film that helps you understand a team's creative potential using a simple rectangle and a sustained tempo that eschews excess.

KMSTEA
Maske Corporate Des
A CLOUD OF IDEAS
LOGO SYSTEM
KMS TEAM
Zeil
LOGO SYSTEM
KMS TEAM
LOGO SYSTEM
OFFICE BRANDING
OFFICE BRANDING
STATIONERY
STATIONERY
STATIONERY
KMS TEAM Architecture
KMS TEAM Birgit Rose Vogel
K4 New York
INTERNET
INTERNET

SILVER
DIGITAL SELF PROMOTION

TITLE
S&V Harmonice Mundi
COMPANY
Scholz & Volkmer GmbH
ART DIRECTOR
Nicoletta Gerlach
CREATIVE DIRECTOR
Nicoletta Gerlach
WRITERS
Jin Jeon
Tim Sobczak
Annette Jans
SOUND DESIGNER
Jens Fischer
TECHNICAL DIRECTOR
Peter Reichard
PROGRAMMERS
Marc Storch
Raphael Wichmann
Peter Reichard
CONCEPT
Peter Reichard
Nicoletta Gerlach
PROJECT MANAGER
Sabine Schmidt
SCREEN DESIGNERS
Susanne Wilhelm
Melanie Lenz
Michael Geissler
VIDEO EDITING
Mohshiour Hossain
Till Nowak
URL
www.s-v.de/projects
/Harmonicemundi/en
COUNTRY
Germany

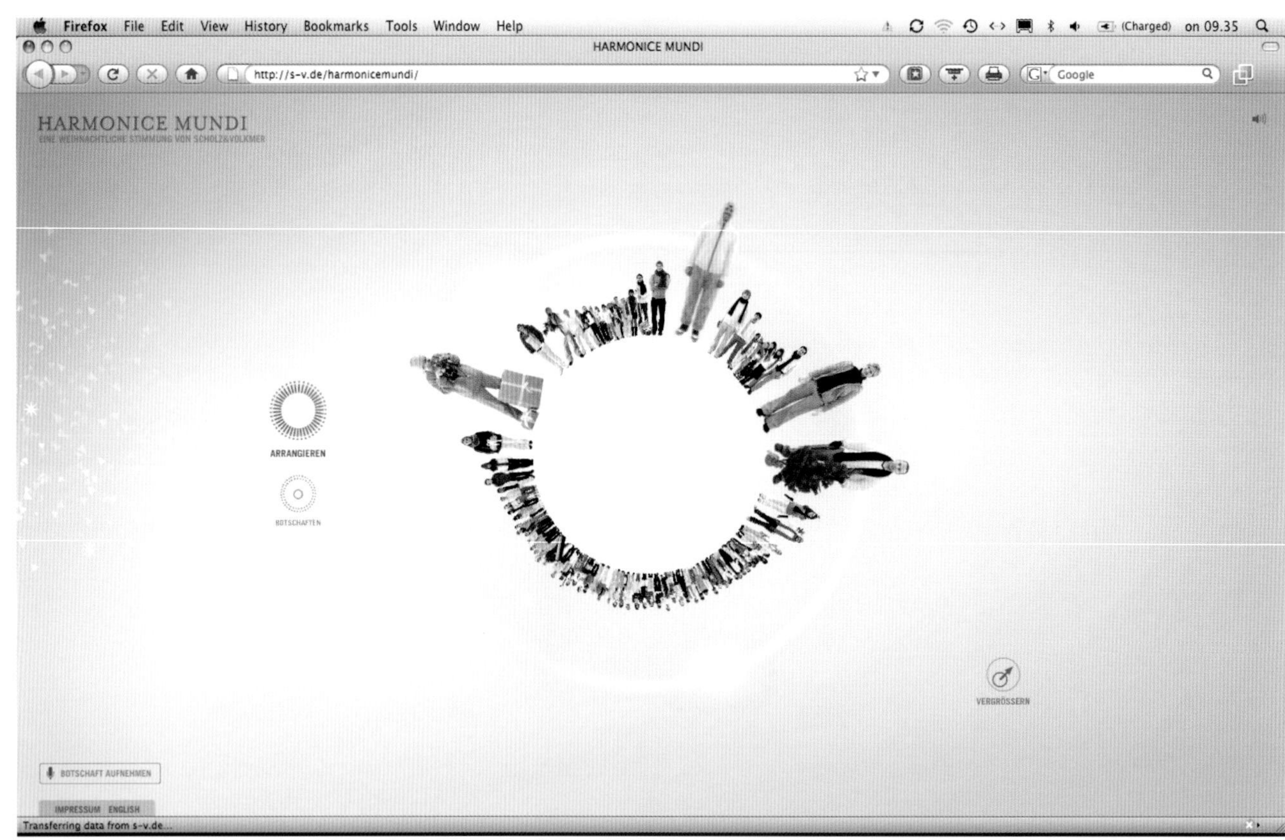

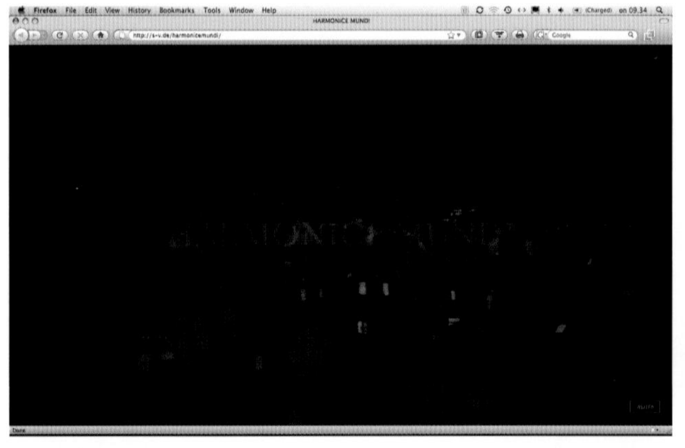

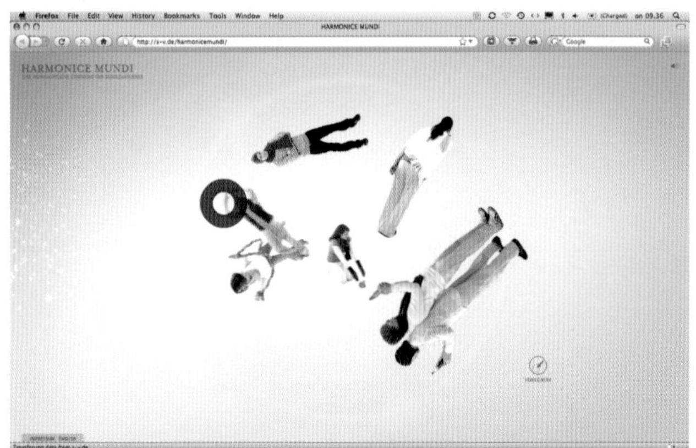

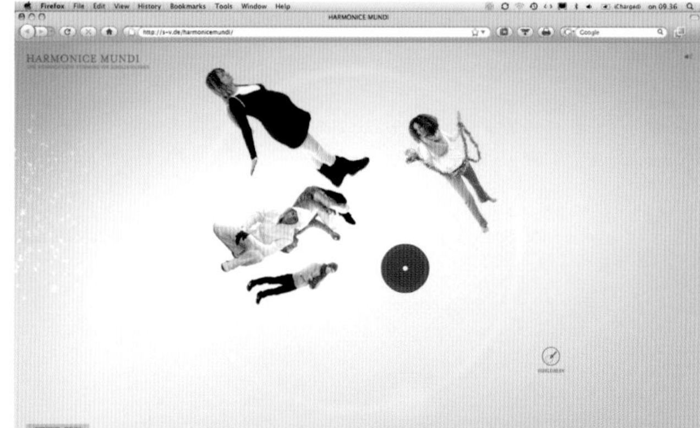

BRONZE
DIGITAL SELF PROMOTION

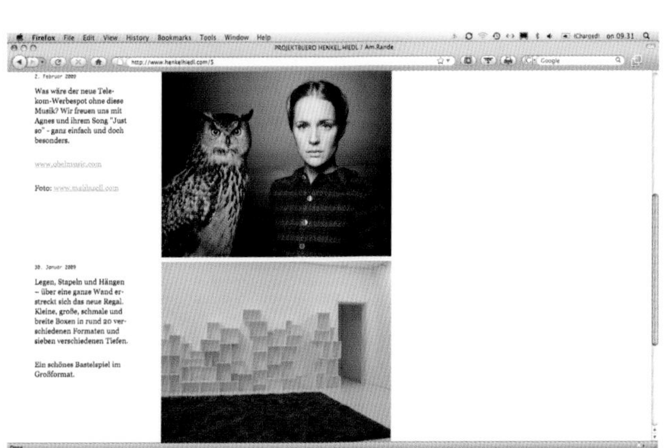

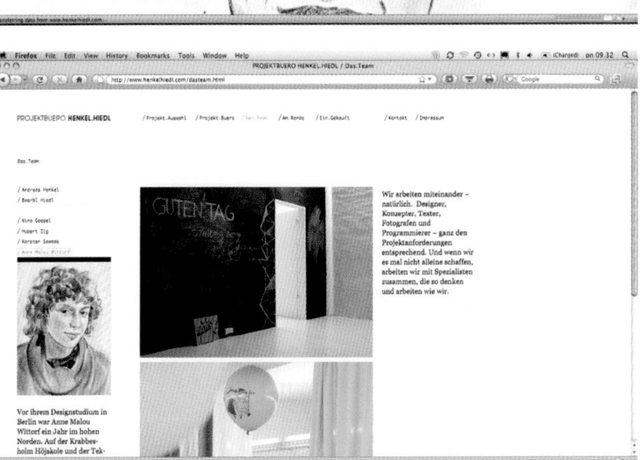

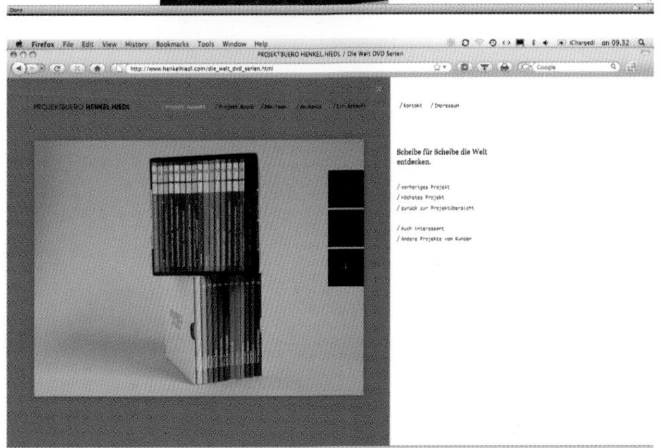

TITLE
Relaunch of www.henkelhiedl.com
COMPANY
Projektbuero Henkel.Hiedl
URL
www.henkelhiedl.com
COUNTRY
Germany

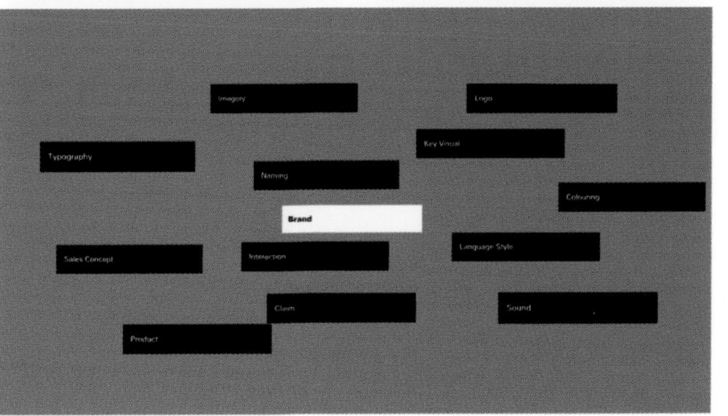

TITLE
Film Tiefendesign
COMPANY
KMS TEAM GmbH
URL
www.kms-team.de/Tiefendesign_en.html
COUNTRY
Germany

GOLD
SELF INITIATED PROJECTS

TITLE
See before reading!
CLIENT
HS Anhalt / Department of Design
DESIGNERS
Susanne Stahl
André Gottschalk
COUNTRY
Germany

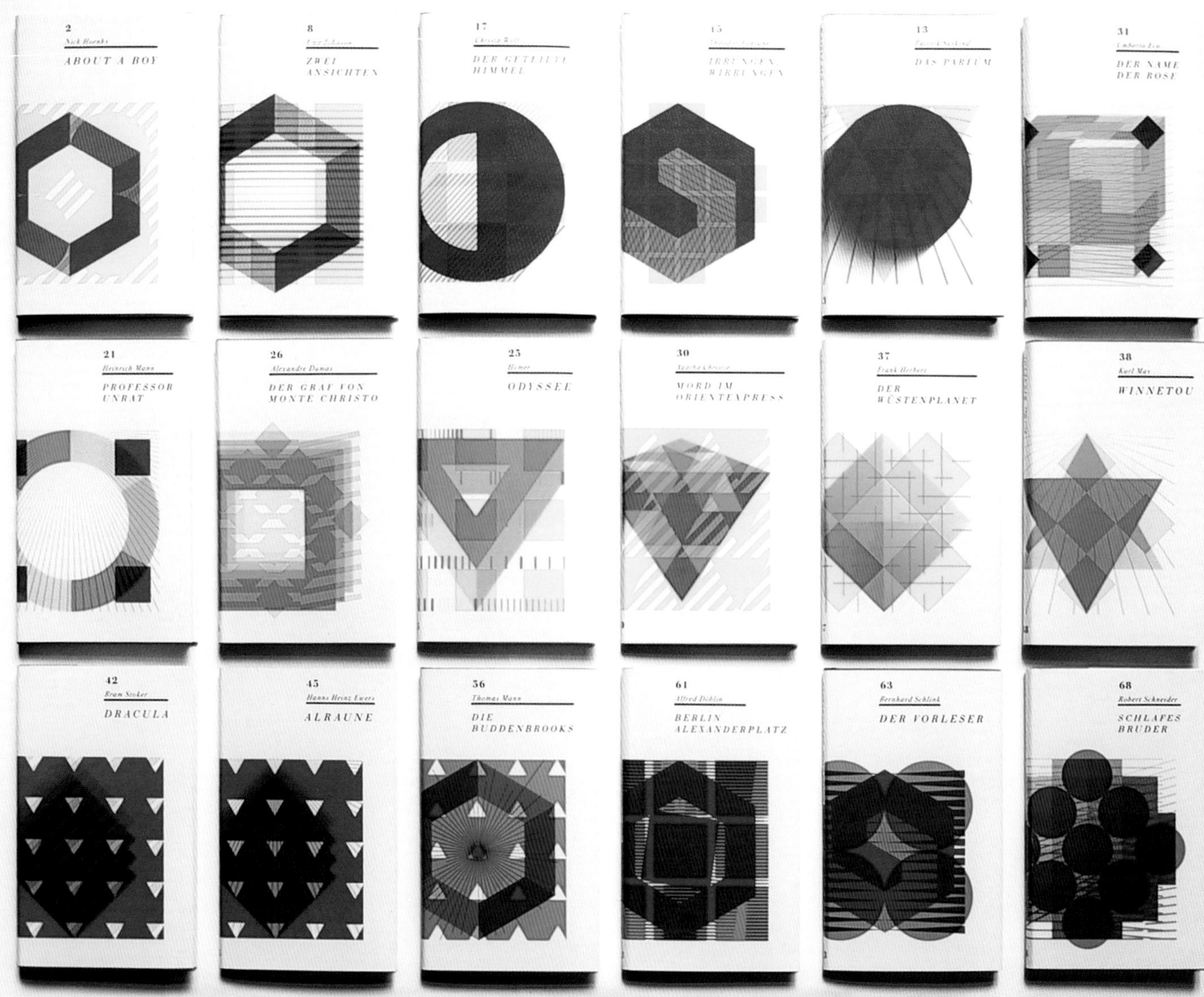

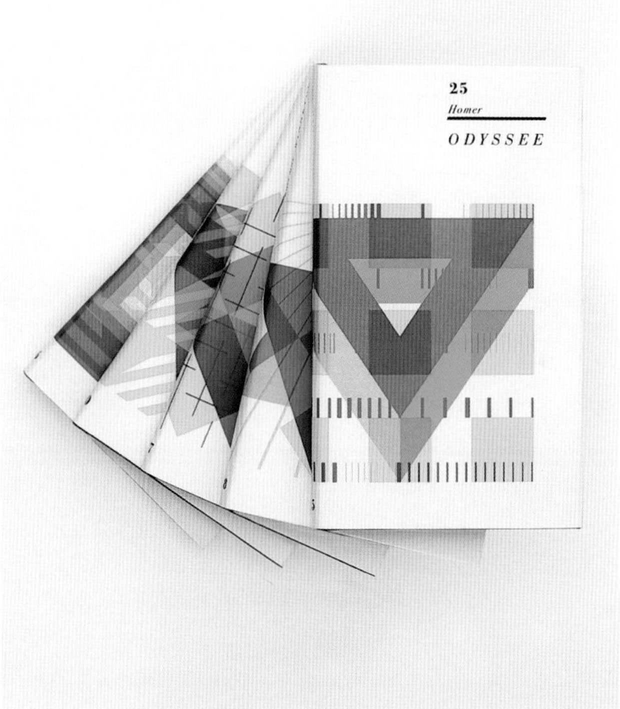

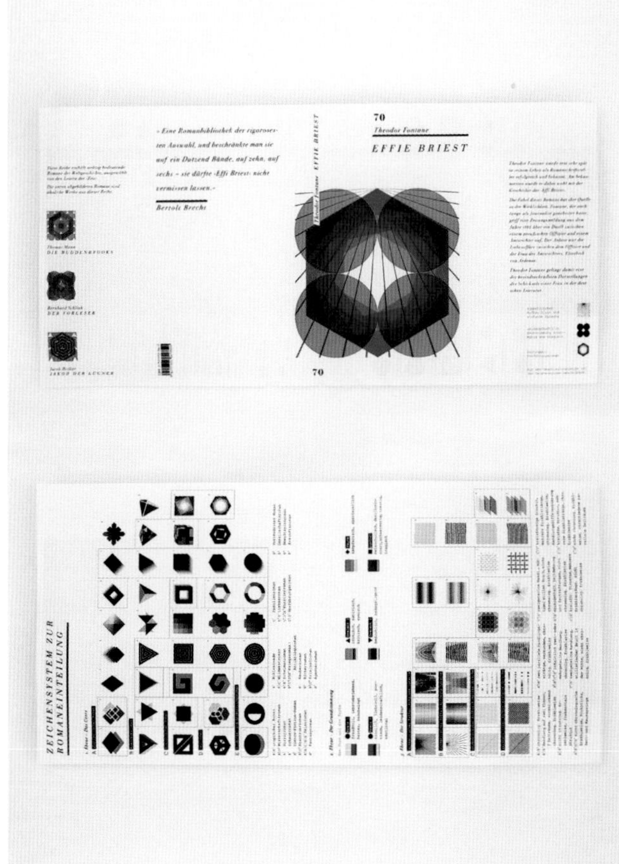

An image is worth a thousand words. Some designers think in a hyper-normative way, their great disappointment often being never to have invented a universal visual language based on a few coded signs that can be combined using a simple grammar. This is the difficult assignment tackled by two students: conveying a book's content through an image. They defined three families of codes comprising geometric symbols, colours and screens, which conjugate as per a simple grammar; they thus find the way to give a distinctive look to each cover in a series of books with diverse contents. The jury acknowledged their implacable logic.

SILVER
SELF INITIATED PROJECTS

TITLE
Surveillance Map of the World
CLIENT
University of Applied Sciences and Arts Dortmund
DESIGNER
Raul Mandru
CODING
Raul Mandru
Tim Gatzky
COUNTRY
Germany

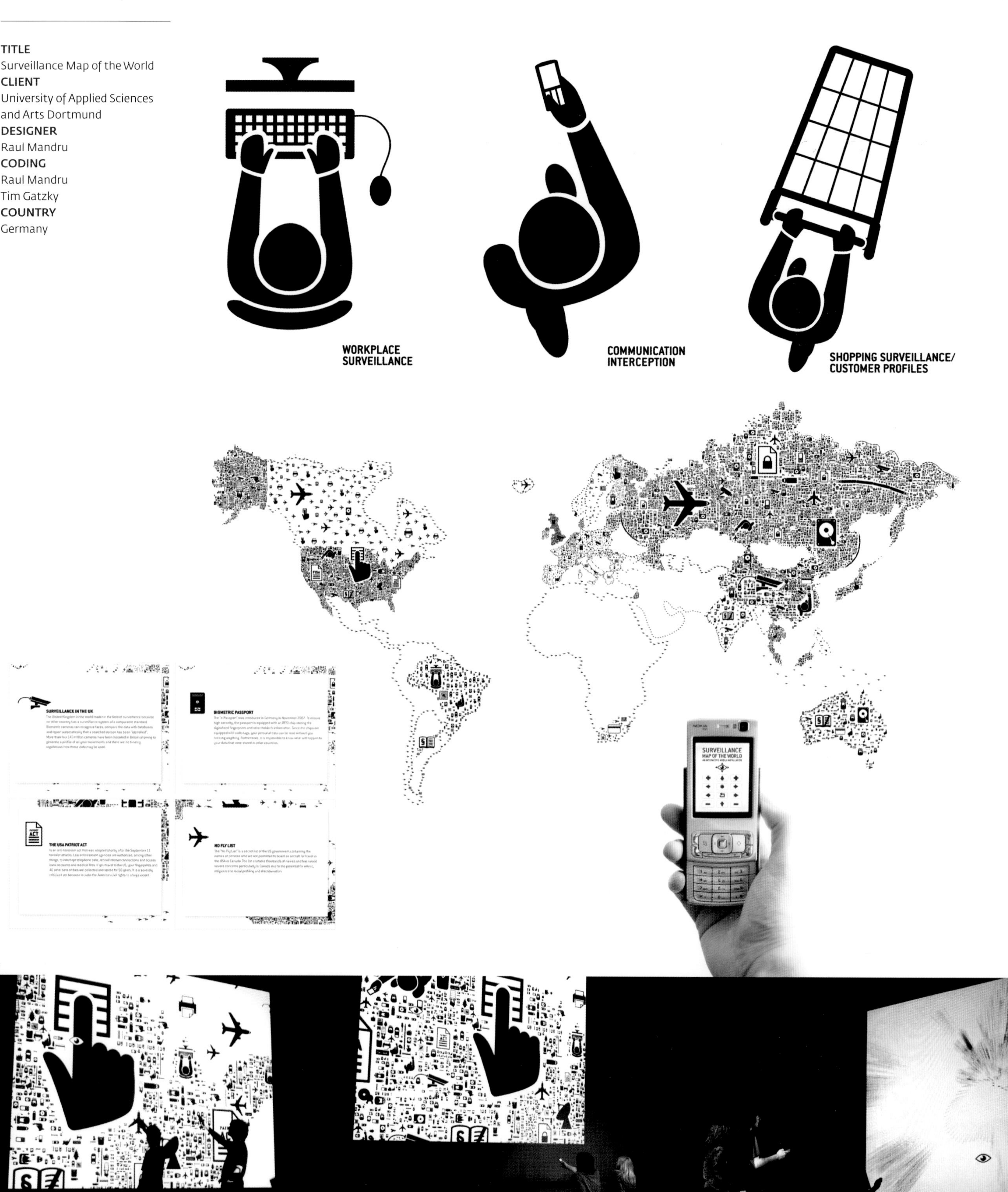

SILVER

SELF INITIATED PROJECTS

TITLE
Czarodziejska Kura
COMPANY
Les Soeurs
CLIENT
Les Soeurs
DESIGNER
Robert Czajka
ART DIRECTOR
Robert Czajka
CREATIVE DIRECTOR
Łukasz Kaniewski
DESIGN DIRECTOR
Robert Czajka
ILLUSTRATORS
Robert Czajka
Mateusz Kaniewski
EDITOR
Łukasz Kaniewski
WRITERS
Łukasz Kaniewski
Joanna Rudniańska
Zbigniew Machej
Ciocia Myszka
Mikołaj Łoziński
OTHER
Ewa Pszczołowska
COUNTRY
Poland

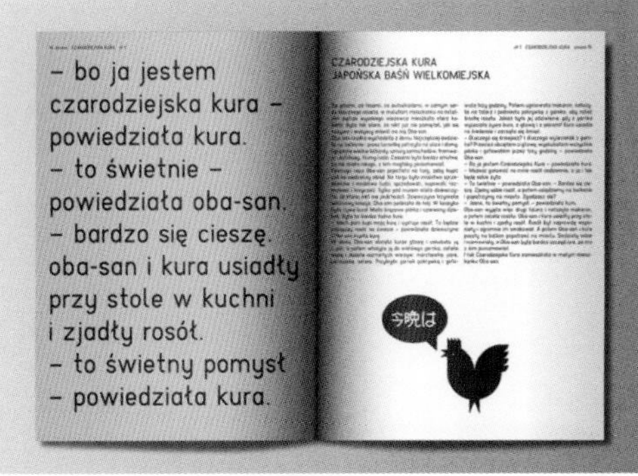

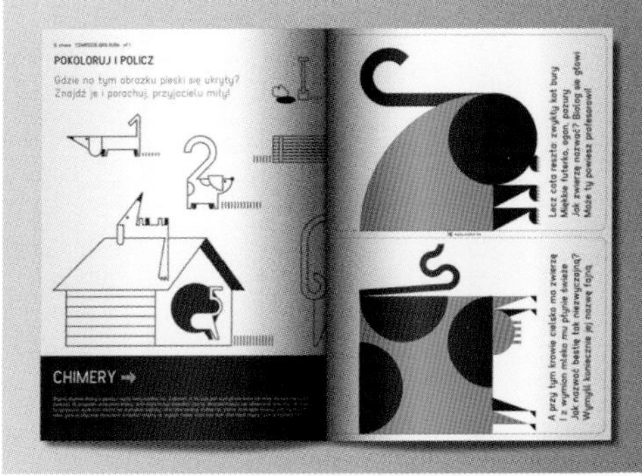

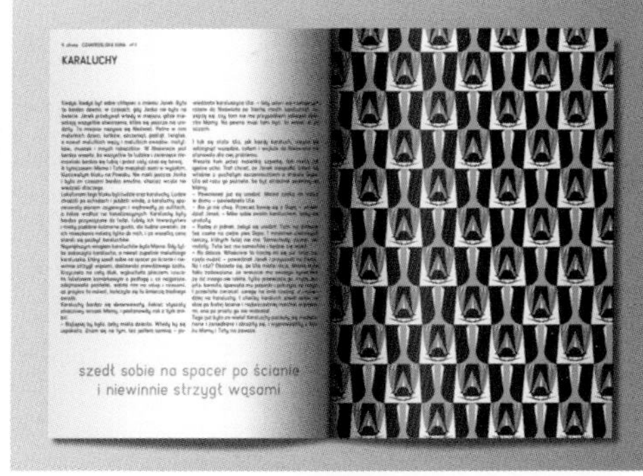

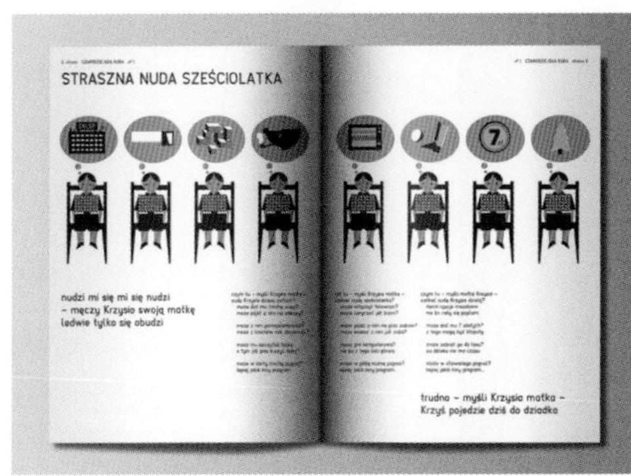

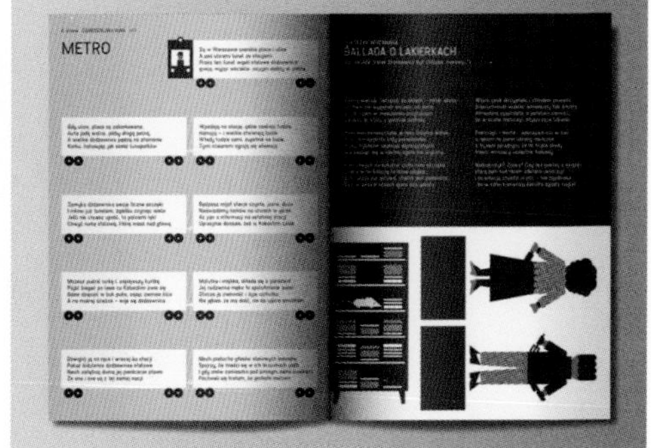

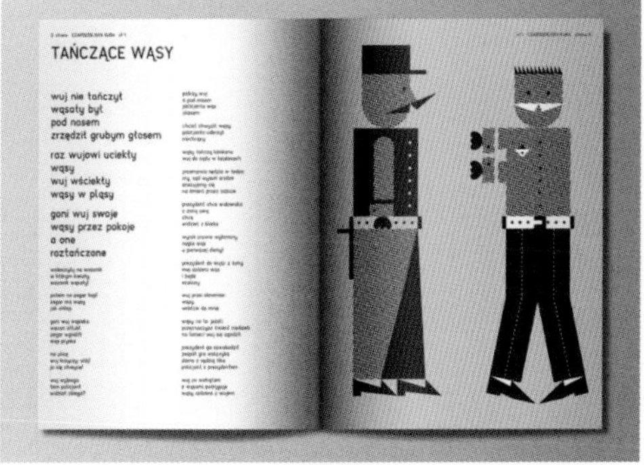

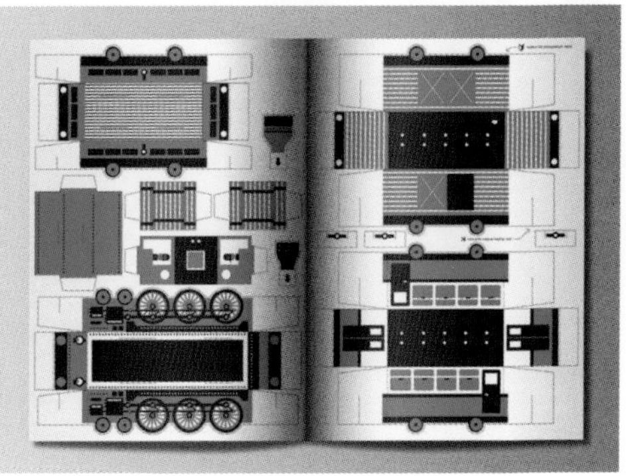

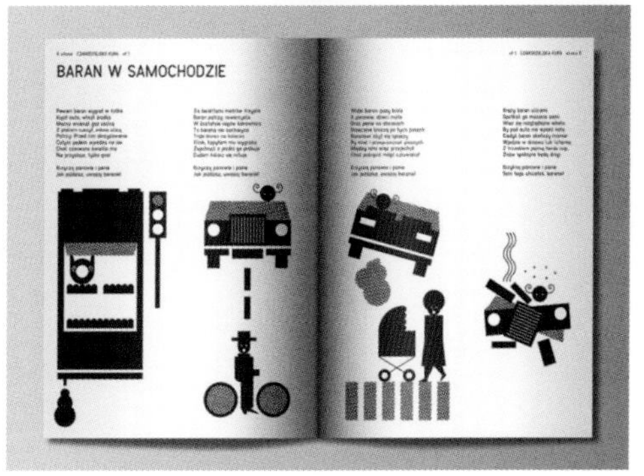

SILVER
SELF INITIATED PROJECTS

TITLE
Emotion diary
COMPANY
2D3D
DESIGNERS
Tiemen Harder
Guido van Gerven
Ilona Hoogeveen
CREATIVE DIRECTOR
Tiemen Harder
ILLUSTRATORS
Tiemen Harder
Guido van Gerven
Ilona Hoogeveen
COUNTRY
Netherlands

BRONZE
SELF INITIATED PROJECTS

TITLE
tube - Handmade Unicums
COMPANY
cubegrafik GmbH
URL
www.tube.ch
COUNTRY
Switzerland

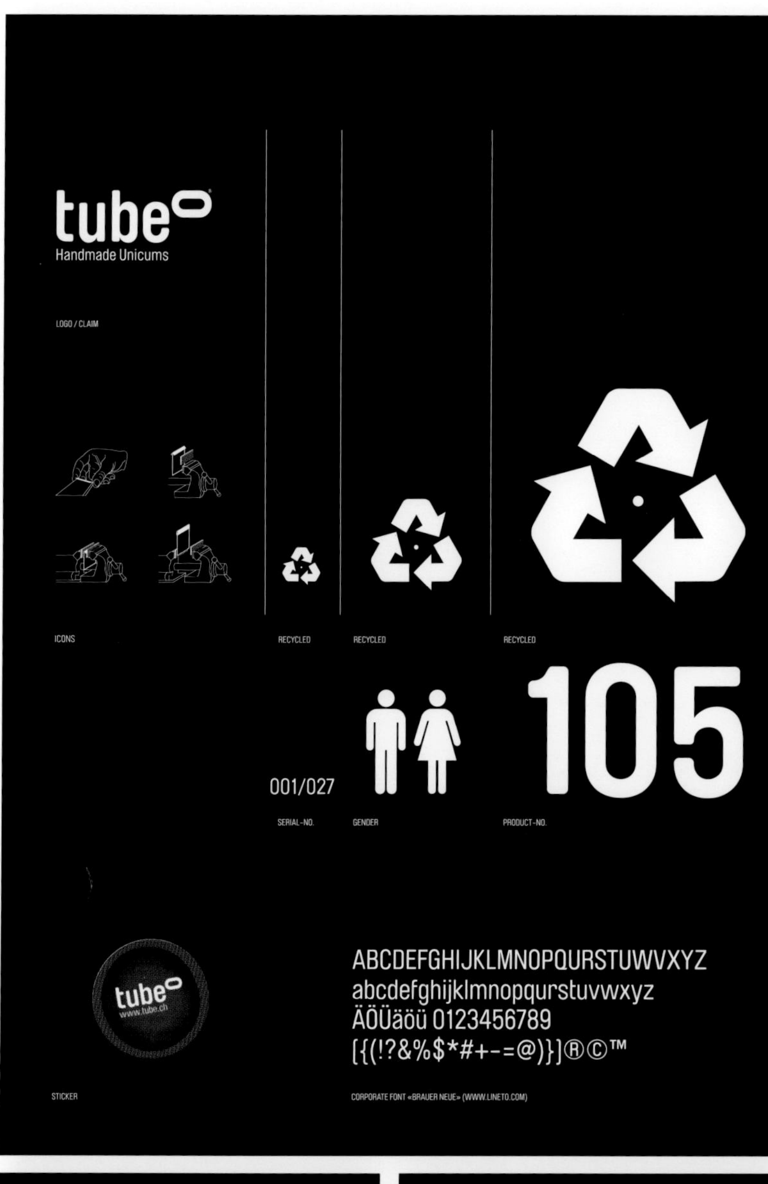

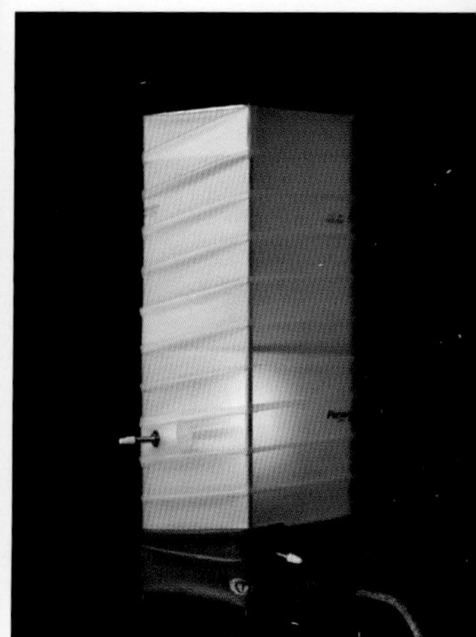

BRONZE
SELF INITIATED PROJECTS

TITLE
Stereotype
DESIGNER
Dennis Dominguez
COUNTRY
Germany

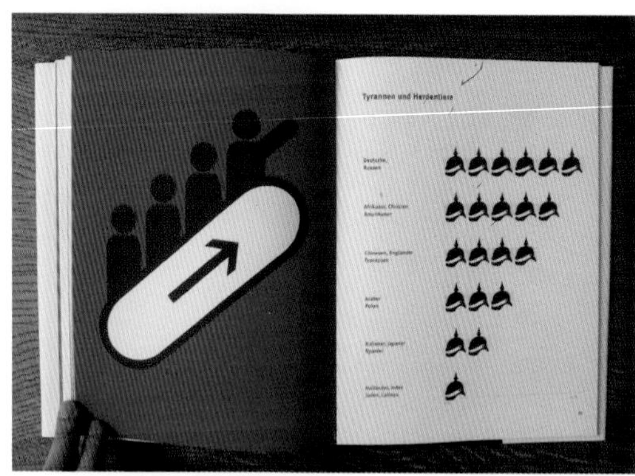

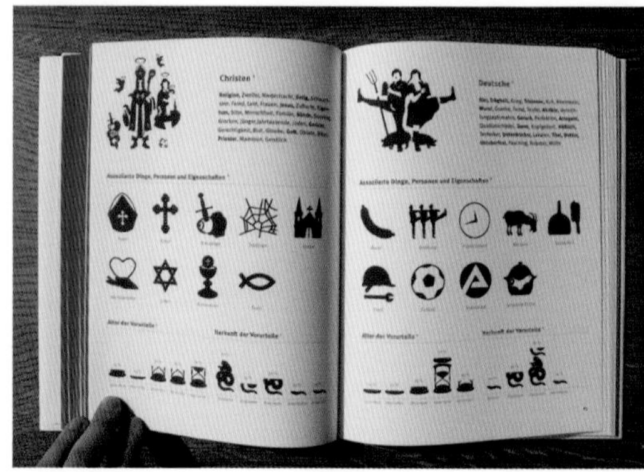

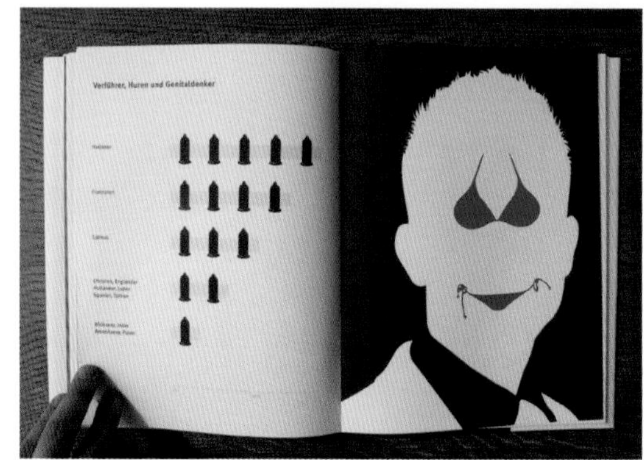

BRONZE
SELF INITIATED PROJECTS

TITLE
Weare scarf
COMPANY
Moving Brands
COUNTRY
United Kingdom

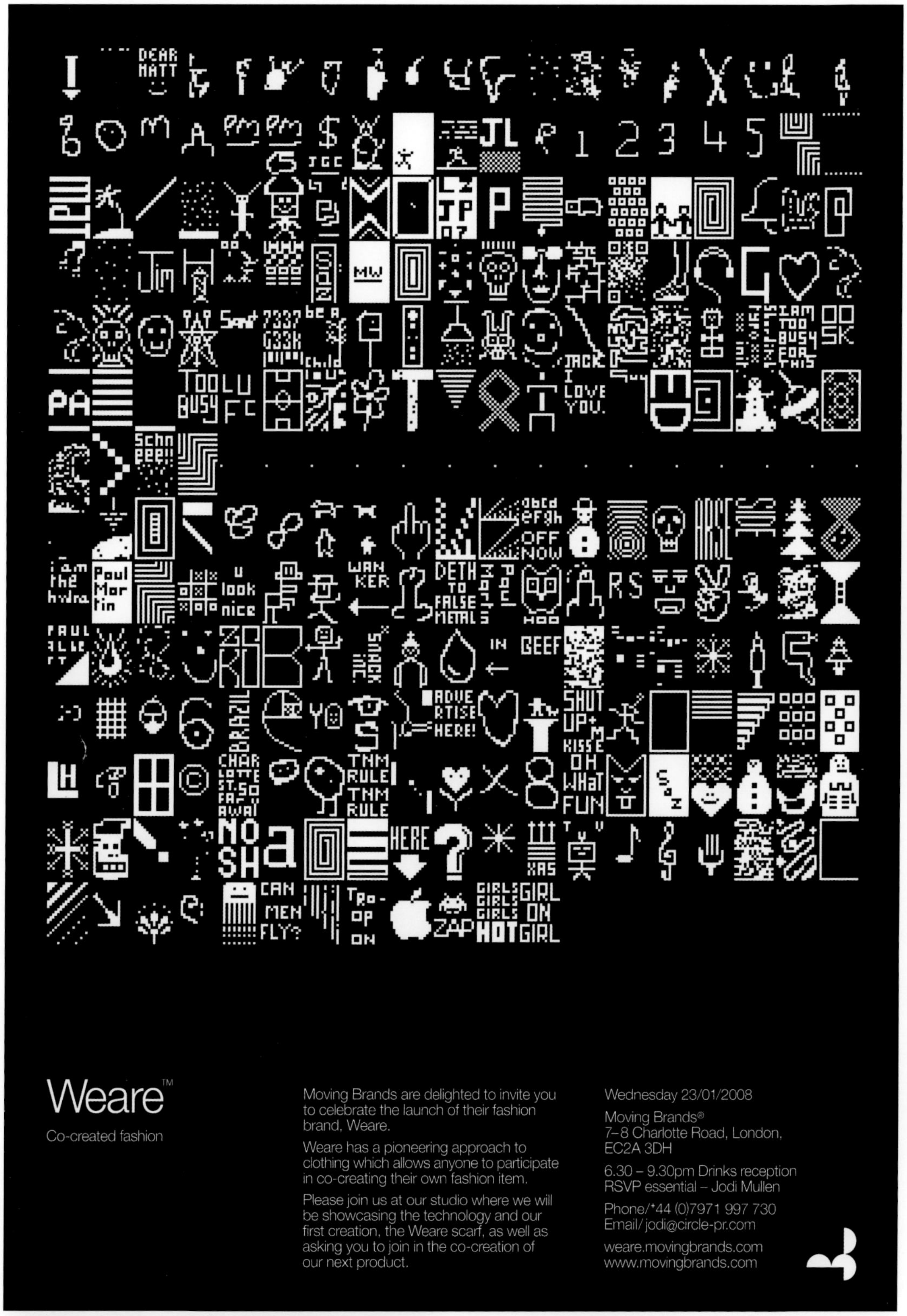

Weare™
Co-created fashion

Moving Brands are delighted to invite you to celebrate the launch of their fashion brand, Weare.

Weare has a pioneering approach to clothing which allows anyone to participate in co-creating their own fashion item.

Please join us at our studio where we will be showcasing the technology and our first creation, the Weare scarf, as well as asking you to join in the co-creation of our next product.

Wednesday 23/01/2008

Moving Brands®
7–8 Charlotte Road, London,
EC2A 3DH

6.30 – 9.30pm Drinks reception
RSVP essential – Jodi Mullen

Phone/+44 (0)7971 997 730
Email/ jodi@circle-pr.com

weare.movingbrands.com
www.movingbrands.com

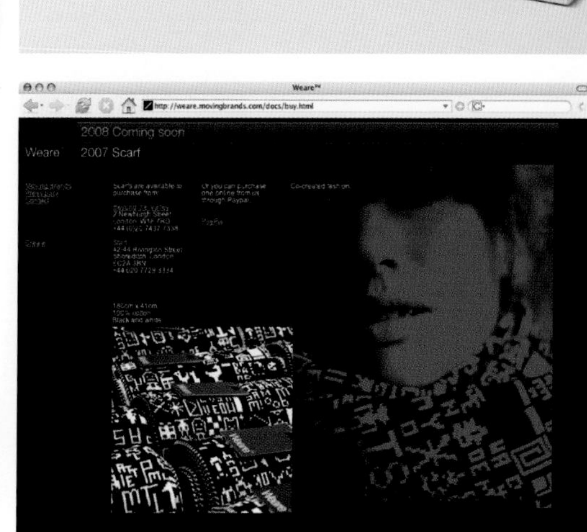

BRONZE
SELF INITIATED PROJECTS

TITLE
Good 50x70 2008
COMPANY
Pasquale Volpe
& Tommaso Minnetti
CLIENT
Good 50x70
URL
www.good50x70.org/2008/
COUNTRY
Italy

Catalogues

Exhibition, Triennale Design Museum, Milan (Italy) 10.06.2008

Exhibition, Triennale Design Museum, Milan (Italy) 10.06.2008

Exhibition, Triennale Design Museum, Milan (Italy) 10.06.2008

Exhibition, Triennale Design Museum, Milan (Italy) 10.06.2008

Exhibition, Piazza dell'anfiteatro romano, Aosta (Italy) 10.10.2008

Exhibition, Triennale Design Museum, Milan (Italy) 10.06.2008

Exhibition, Museo del Acero- UDEM, Monterrey (Mexico) 07.10.2008

Exhibition, Piazza S.Oronzo, Lecce (Italy) 25.10.2008

Exhibition, Triennale Design Museum, Milan (Italy) 10.06.2008

BRONZE
SELF INITIATED PROJECTS

TITLE
message on the bottle
COMPANY
ondesign
COUNTRY
Germany

message
on the
Bottle ...

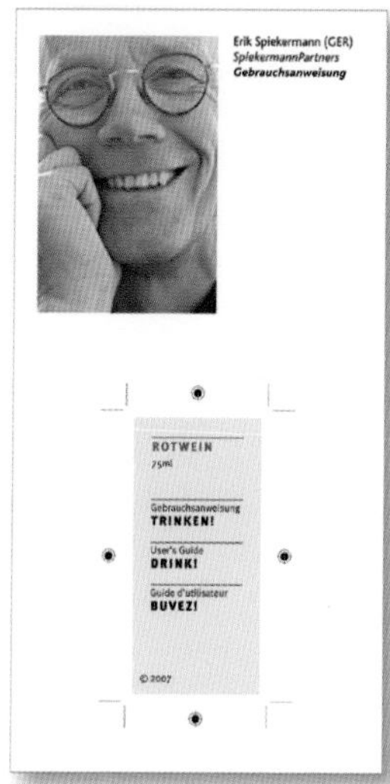

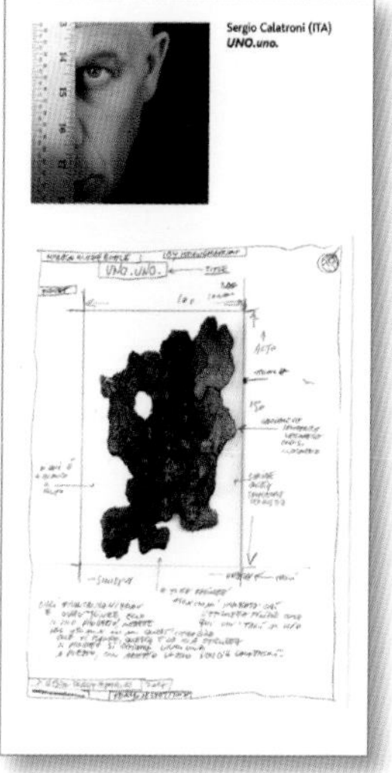

VARIOUS

GOLD
ORIGINAL TYPEFACE

TITLE
Comenia - School Typeface System
COMPANY
Suitcase Type Foundry
CLIENT
Štorm Type Foundry
Suitcase Type Foundry
DESIGNERS
Tomáš Brousil
Radana Lencová
František Štorm
COUNTRY
Czech Republic

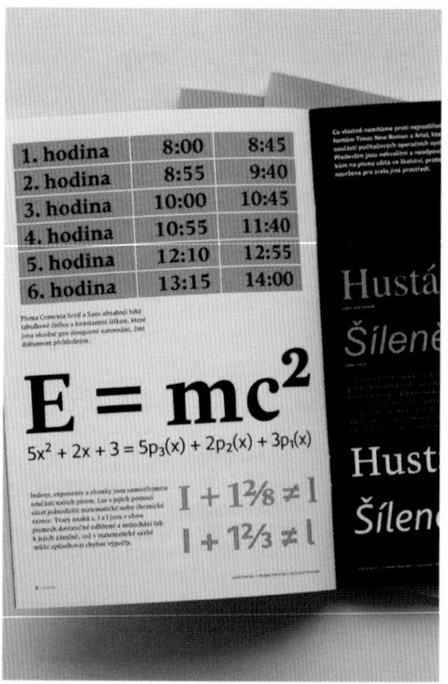

Comenia
School Typeface System

BROUSIL / LENCOVÁ / ŠTORM

The design of a body-text typeface must address a delicate issue: the visible/invisible paradox. A face is designed to ease reading and access to the meaning of the text it represents. If too emphatically distinctive, it will affect readability; if conventional, it would ultimately bore the reader and dull the reading matter. Few people perceive these nuances in the design and choice of typeface for a book. It is often a sensibility that develops when one starts learning to read, and continues throughout one's studies. School books often treat this aspect in scarce detail, unfortunately. By proposing new aesthetic standards to improve reading, Suitcase's project easily garnered the vote of the jury, who wanted to support the work's generosity and relevance.

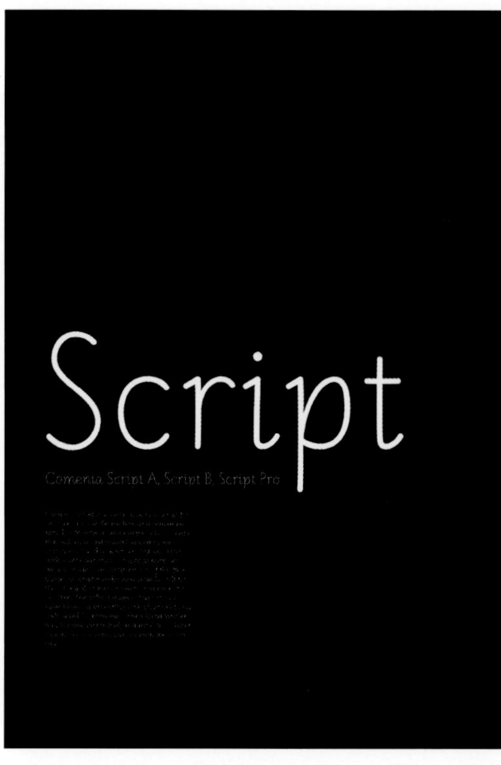

Místo narození **Jana Amose Komenského** není známo, jako pravděpodobná místa se uvádějí Uherský Brod[1] (jak je napsáno v Naardenu na náhrobní desce) nebo Nivnice (Komenský v některých dokumentech připojoval k podpisu Nivanus, Nivnicensis[2]). Občas se zmiňuje i Komňa (z čehož by mohlo vzniknout příjmení Komenský, Comenius), odkud pocházela rodina.[3] Žil s rodiči v Uherském Brodě (pocházel z měšťanské rodiny). Po jejich smrti (1604) se o něj starala

SERIF 18/21 PT

jeho teta ve Strážnici, kde začal studovat. Roku 1608 nastoupil studia na latinské škole v Přerově, odkud odešel na vysokou školu do Herbornu a Heidelbergu v Německu. Již při studiu začal psát dvě velká díla: POKLAD JAZYKA ČESKÉHO, což měl být velký slovník, a dále encyklopedii DIVADLO VEŠKERENSTVA VĚCÍ. Tato díla nedokončil. Po ukončení školy působil v letech 1614–16 v Přerově jako rektor latinské školy. Roku 1616 byl vysvěcen na kazatele a odešel do Fulneku, kde působil jako rektor tamější školy a jako kazatel jednoty bratrské. Ve Fulneku poznal i svou první ženu Magdalénu Vizovskou. V této době píše spis LISTOVÉ DO NEBE.
Po porážce stavovského povstání (1621) byl J. A. Komenský nucen opustit Fulnek a skrýval se na různých místech v Čechách a na Moravě, protože odmítal konvertovat ke katolictví. Po roce ukrývání (roku 1622) mu zemřela jeho žena a dvě děti na mor. Pod vlivem událostí píše filosofické spisy TRUCHLIVÝ a HLUBINA BEZPEČNOSTI. V roce 1624 působil v Brandýse nad Orlicí, kde se také seznámil se svojí druhou ženou Marií Dorotou.
V roce 1628 odešel do exilu do polského Lešna, které se stalo centrem bratrské víry. Zpočátku doufá, že se brzy vrátí zpět do vlasti, proto píše česky. Začal psát učebnice a připravoval plán na zlepšení organizace školství, např. v díle NAVRŽENÍ KRÁTKÉ O OBNOVĚ ŠKOL V KRÁLOVSTVÍ ČESKÉM. V Lešně byl zvolen biskupem a písařem, brzy se stal i zástupcem rektora gymnázia, což vedlo k jeho zájmu o pedagogiku. V tomto období vznikla velká část jeho děl, především pak z oblasti pedagogiky, jako např. VELKÁ DIDAKTIKA. Ta měla být původně součástí velkého díla, které chtěl nazvat RÁJ ČESKÝ. Obsahem měla být teoretická, didaktická a praktická část, která by sloužila rodičům a učitelům. Napsal DIDAKTIKU ČESKOU, kterou později přepracoval do latinské podoby DIDACTICA MAGNA. Postupně se jeho díla jako BRÁNA JAZYKŮ OTEVŘENÁ a INFORMATORIUM ŠKOLY MATEŘSKÉ stala známa po nekatolické Evropě a byl zván na různá

SERIF 10/12 PT

místa na univerzitách, nabídky však odmítal. První významnou nabídku přijal až roku 1641, kdy se rozhodl přijmout pozvání anglického parlamentu na přednáškové turné, během něhož vystoupil i před Královskou akademií věd. V této době vyjádřil své myšlenky ve spise VIA LUCIS. Po odchodu z Anglie dostal řadu dalších nabídek, Komenský si zároveň v tuto dobu uvědomil, že právě prostřednictvím těchto nabídek může rozšířit svůj vliv a svoje myšlenky.
Roku 1642 odešel do Švédska kam ho pozvali, aby jim vytvořil učebnice. Vzniká zde spis NEJNOVĚJŠÍ METODA JAZYKŮ. Učebnice nakonec neudělal. Roku 1648 se vrací zpět do Lešna, kde působí jako biskup. V tomto roce mu také zemřela jeho druhá žena, již o rok později (1649) se oženil potřetí, tentokrát s Janou Gajusovou. Když byl v roce 1648 uzavřen vestfálský mír a tím skončila třicetiletá válka, skončily též naděje českých exulantů na návrat do vlasti. Komenský se loučí s vlastí a církví spisem KŠAFT UMÍRAJÍCÍ MATKY JEDNOTY BRATRSKÉ.
Roku 1652 přijímá nabídku uherského knížete Zikmunda Rákocziho, kde měl u jeho dvora organizovat pansofickou školu (sedmiletá). Poprvé měl tedy možnost ověřit si své názory v praxi. Otevřeny byly ovšem jen 3 třídy, jenž byly nazvány Vestibulum, Janua a Atrium. Pro své žáky vytvořil příručku PRAVIDLA MRAVŮ a také zde vznikla učebnice SVĚT V OBRAZECH a ŠKOLA HROU.
V letech 1654–1658 Komenský opět pobývá v Lešně. Roku 1656 při požáru Lešna přichází Komenský o všechen majetek i cenné rukopisy jako ČESKO-LATINSKÝ SLOVNÍK, na kterém pracoval prakticky celý život a který považoval za stěžejní dílo. Tuto ztrátu nesl velice těžce a prakticky se z ní nikdy nevzpamatoval. Na pozvání svého přítele Louise De Geera odjíždí do Amsterdamu. Konec svého života strávil v Holandsku. Zde vydává soubor svých 43 spisů pod názvem OPERA DIDACTICA OMNIA. Vznikají zde i menší díla a dílo JEDNO POTŘEBNÉ bývá považováno za jeho závěť lidstvu. Zemřel 15. listopadu 1670 a byl pohřben v kostelíku v Naardenu. Místo narození Jana Amose Komenského není známo, jako pravděpodobná místa se uvádějí Uherský Brod1 (jak je napsáno v Naardenu na náhrobní desce) nebo Nivnice (Komenský v některých dokumentech připojoval k podpisu Nivanus, Nivnicensis2). Občas se zmiňuje i Komňa (z čehož by mohlo vzniknout příjmení Komenský, Comenius), odkud pocházela rodina.3 Žil s rodiči v Uherském Brodě (pocházel z měšťanské rodiny). Po jejich smrti (1604) se o něj starala jeho teta ve Strážnici, kde začal studovat. Roku 1608 nastoupil studia na latinské škole v Přerově, odkud odešel na vysokou školu do Herbornu a Heidelbergu v Německu. Již při studiu začal psát dvě velká díla: poklad jazyka českého, což měl být velký slovník, a dále encyklopedii divadlo veškerenstva věcí. Tato díla nedokončil. Po ukončení školy působil v letech 1614–16 v Přerově jako rektor latinské školy. Roku 1616 byl vysvěcen na kazatele a odešel do Fulneku, kde působil jako rektor

SERIF 8/10 PT

Místo narození **Jana Amose Komenského** není známo, jako pravděpodobná místa se uvádějí Uherský Brod[1] (jak je napsáno v Naardenu na náhrobní desce) nebo Nivnice (Komenský v některých dokumentech připojoval k podpisu Nivanus, Nivnicensis[2]). Občas se zmiňuje i Komňa (z čehož by mohlo vzniknout příjmení Komenský, Comenius), odkud pocházela rodina.[3] Žil s rodiči v Uherském Brodě (pocházel z měšťanské rodiny). Po jejich smrti (1604) se o něj starala jeho teta ve Strážnici, kde začal

SANS 18/21 PT

studovat. Roku 1608 nastoupil studia na latinské škole v Přerově, odkud odešel na vysokou školu do Herbornu a Heidelbergu v Německu. Již při studiu začal psát dvě velká díla: POKLAD JAZYKA ČESKÉHO, což měl být velký slovník, a dále encyklopedii DIVADLO VEŠKERENSTVA VĚCÍ. Tato díla nedokončil. Po ukončení školy působil v letech 1614–16 v Přerově jako rektor latinské školy. Roku 1616 byl vysvěcen na kazatele a odešel do Fulneku, kde působil jako rektor tamější školy a jako kazatel jednoty bratrské. Ve Fulneku poznal i svou první ženu Magdalénu Vizovskou. V této době píše spis LISTOVÉ DO NEBE.
Po porážce stavovského povstání (1621) byl J. A. Komenský nucen opustit Fulnek a skrýval se na různých místech v Čechách a na Moravě, protože odmítal konvertovat ke katolictví. Po roce ukrývání (roku 1622) mu zemřela jeho žena a dvě děti na mor. Pod vlivem událostí píše filosofické spisy TRUCHLIVÝ a HLUBINA BEZPEČNOSTI. V roce 1624 působil v Brandýse nad Orlicí, kde se také seznámil se svojí druhou ženou Marií Dorotou.
V roce 1628 odešel do exilu do polského Lešna, které se stalo centrem bratrské víry. Zpočátku doufá, že se brzy vrátí zpět do vlasti, proto píše česky. Začal psát učebnice a připravoval plán na zlepšení organizace školství, např. v díle NAVRŽENÍ KRÁTKÉ O OBNOVĚ ŠKOL V KRÁLOVSTVÍ ČESKÉM. V Lešně byl zvolen biskupem a písařem, brzy se stal i zástupcem rektora gymnázia, což vedlo k jeho zájmu o pedagogiku. V tomto období vznikla velká část jeho děl, především pak z oblasti pedagogiky, jako např. VELKÁ DIDAKTIKA. Ta měla být původně součástí velkého díla, které chtěl nazvat RÁJ ČESKÝ. Obsahem měla být teoretická, didaktická a praktická část, která by sloužila rodičům a učitelům. Napsal DIDAKTIKU ČESKOU, kterou později přepracoval do latinské podoby DIDACTICA MAGNA. Postupně se jeho díla jako BRÁNA JAZYKŮ OTEVŘENÁ a INFORMATORIUM ŠKOLY MATEŘSKÉ stala známa po nekatolické Evropě a byl zván na různá místa na univerzitách, nabídky však odmítal. První významnou nabídku přijal až roku 1641, kdy se rozhodl přijmout pozvání anglického parlamentu na přednáškové turné, během něhož vystoupil i před Královskou akademií věd. V této

SANS 10/12 PT

době vyjádřil své myšlenky ve spise VIA LUCIS. Po odchodu z Anglie dostal řadu dalších nabídek, Komenský si zároveň v tuto dobu uvědomil, že právě prostřednictvím těchto nabídek může rozšířit svůj vliv a svoje myšlenky.
Roku 1642 odešel do Švédska kam ho pozvali, aby jim vytvořil učebnice. Vzniká zde spis NEJNOVĚJŠÍ METODA JAZYKŮ. Učebnice nakonec neudělal. Roku 1648 se vrací zpět do Lešna, kde působí jako biskup. V tomto roce mu také zemřela jeho druhá žena, již o rok později (1649) se oženil potřetí, tentokrát s Janou Gajusovou. Když byl v roce 1648 uzavřen vestfálský mír a tím skončila třicetiletá válka, skončily též naděje českých exulantů na návrat do vlasti. Komenský se loučí s vlastí a církví spisem KŠAFT UMÍRAJÍCÍ MATKY JEDNOTY BRATRSKÉ.
Roku 1652 přijímá nabídku uherského knížete Zikmunda Rákocziho, kde měl u jeho dvora organizovat pansofickou školu (sedmiletá). Poprvé měl tedy možnost ověřit si své názory v praxi. Otevřeny byly ovšem jen 3 třídy, jenž byly nazvány Vestibulum, Janua a Atrium. Pro své žáky vytvořil příručku PRAVIDLA MRAVŮ a také zde vznikla učebnice SVĚT V OBRAZECH a ŠKOLA HROU.
V letech 1654–1658 Komenský opět pobývá v Lešně. Roku 1656 při požáru Lešna přichází Komenský o všechen majetek i cenné rukopisy jako ČESKO-LATINSKÝ SLOVNÍK, na kterém pracoval prakticky celý život a který považoval za stěžejní dílo. Tuto ztrátu nesl velice těžce a prakticky se z ní nikdy nevzpamatoval. Na pozvání svého přítele Louise De Geera odjíždí do Amsterdamu.
Konec svého života strávil v Holandsku. Zde vydává soubor svých 43 spisů pod názvem OPERA DIDACTICA OMNIA. Vznikají zde i menší díla a dílo JEDNO POTŘEBNÉ bývá považováno za jeho závěť lidstvu. Zemřel 15. listopadu 1670 a byl pohřben v kostelíku v Naardenu. Místo narození **Jana Amose Komenského** není známo, jako pravděpodobná místa se uvádějí Uherský Brod[1] (jak je napsáno v Naardenu na náhrobní desce) nebo Nivnice (Komenský v některých dokumentech připojoval k podpisu Nivanus, Nivnicensis[2]). Občas se zmiňuje i Komňa (z čehož by mohlo vzniknout příjmení Komenský, Comenius), odkud pocházela rodina.[3] Žil s rodiči v Uherském Brodě (pocházel z měšťanské rodiny). Po jejich smrti (1604) se o něj starala jeho teta ve Strážnici, kde začal studovat. Roku 1608 nastoupil studia na latinské škole v Přerově, odkud odešel na vysokou školu do Herbornu a Heidelbergu v Německu. Již při studiu začal psát dvě velká díla: POKLAD JAZYKA ČESKÉHO, což měl být velký slovník, a dále encyklopedii DIVADLO VEŠKERENSTVA VĚCÍ. Tato díla nedokončil. Po ukončení školy působil v letech 1614–16 v Přerově jako rektor latinské školy. Roku 1616 byl vysvěcen na kazatele a odešel do Fulneku, kde působil jako rektor tamější školy a jako kazatel jednoty bratrské. Ve Fulneku poznal i svou první ženu Magdalénu Vizovskou. V této době píše spis LISTOVÉ DO NEBE.
Po porážce stavovského povstání (1621) byl J. A. Komenský nucen opustit Fulnek a skrýval se na různých místech v Čechách a na Moravě, protože odmítal konvertovat ke katolictví. Po roce ukrývání (roku 1622) mu zemřela jeho žena a dvě děti na mor. Pod vlivem událostí

SANS 8/10 PT

Místo narození Jana Amose Komenského není známo, jako pravděpodobná místa se uvádějí Uherský Brod1 (jak je napsáno v Naardenu na náhrobní desce) nebo Nivnice (Komenský v některých dokumentech připojoval k podpisu Nivanus, Nivnicensis2). Občas se zmiňuje i Komňa (z čehož by mohlo vzniknout příjmení Komenský, Comenius), odkud pocházela rodina.3 Žil s rodiči v Uherském Brodě (pocházel z měšťanské rodiny). Po jejich smrti (1604) se o něj starala jeho teta ve Strážnici, kde začal studovat. Roku 1608 nastoupil

COMENIA SCRIPT 18/21 PT

studia na latinské škole v Přerově, odkud odešel na vysokou školu do Herbornu a Heidelbergu v Německu. Již při studiu začal psát dvě velká díla: poklad jazyka českého, což měl být velký slovník, a dále encyklopedii divadlo veškerenstva věcí. Tato díla nedokončil. Po ukončení školy působil v letech 1614–16 v Přerově jako rektor latinské školy. Roku 1616 byl vysvěcen na kazatele a odešel do Fulneku, kde působil jako rektor tamější školy a jako kazatel jednoty bratrské. Ve Fulneku poznal i svou první ženu Magdalénu Vizovskou. V této době píše spis listové do nebe.
Po porážce stavovského povstání (1621) byl J. A. Komenský nucen opustit Fulnek a skrýval se na různých místech v Čechách a na Moravě, protože odmítal konvertovat ke katolictví. Po roce ukrývání (roku 1622) mu zemřela jeho žena a dvě děti na mor. Pod vlivem událostí píše filosofické spisy truchlivý a hlubina bezpečnosti. V roce 1624 působil v Brandýse nad Orlicí, kde se také seznámil se svojí druhou ženou Marií Dorotou.
V roce 1628 odešel do exilu do polského Lešna, které se stalo centrem bratrské víry. Zpočátku doufá, že se brzy vrátí zpět do vlasti, proto píše česky. Začal psát učebnice a připravoval plán na zlepšení organizace školství, např. v díle navržení krátké o obnově škol v království českém. V Lešně byl zvolen biskupem a písařem, brzy se stal i zástupcem rektora gymnázia, což vedlo k jeho zájmu o pedagogiku. V tomto období vznikla velká část jeho děl, především pak z oblasti pedagogiky, jako např. velká didaktika. Ta měla být původně součástí velkého díla, které chtěl nazvat ráj český. Obsahem měla být teoretická, didaktická a praktická část, která by sloužila rodičům a učitelům. Napsal didaktiku českou, kterou později přepracoval do latinské podoby didactica magna. Postupně se jeho díla jako brána jazyků otevřená a informatorium školy mateřské stala známa po nekatolické Evropě a byl zván na různá místa na univerzitách, nabídky však odmítal. První významnou nabídku přijal až roku 1641, kdy se rozhodl přijmout pozvání anglického parlamentu na přednáškové turné, během něhož vystoupil i před Královskou akademií věd. V této době vyjádřil své myšlenky ve spise via lucis. Po odchodu z Anglie dostal řadu dalších nabídek, Komenský si zároveň v tuto dobu uvědomil, že právě prostřednictvím

COMENIA SCRIPT 10/12 PT

těchto nabídek může rozšířit svůj vliv a svoje myšlenky.
Roku 1642 odešel do Švédska kam ho pozvali, aby jim vytvořil učebnice. Vzniká zde spis nejnovější metoda jazyků. Učebnice nakonec neudělal. Roku 1648 se vrací zpět do Lešna, kde působí jako biskup. V tomto roce mu také zemřela jeho druhá žena, již o rok později (1649) se oženil potřetí, tentokrát s Janou Gajusovou. Když byl v roce 1648 uzavřen vestfálský mír a tím skončila třicetiletá válka, skončily též naděje českých exulantů na návrat do vlasti. Komenský se loučí s vlastí a církví spisem kšaft umírající matky jednoty bratrské.
Roku 1652 přijímá nabídku uherského knížete Zikmunda Rákocziho, kde měl u jeho dvora organizovat pansofickou školu (sedmiletá). Poprvé měl tedy možnost ověřit si své názory v praxi. Otevřeny byly ovšem jen 3 třídy, jenž byly nazvány Vestibulum, Janua a Atrium. Pro své žáky vytvořil příručku pravidla mravů a také zde vznikla učebnice svět v obrazech a škola hrou.
V letech 1654–1658 Komenský opět pobývá v Lešně. Roku 1656 při požáru Lešna přichází Komenský o všechen majetek i cenné rukopisy jako česko-latinský slovník, na kterém pracoval prakticky celý život a který považoval za stěžejní dílo. Tuto ztrátu nesl velice těžce a prakticky se z ní nikdy nevzpamatoval. Na pozvání svého přítele Louise De Geera odjíždí do Amsterdamu. Konec svého života strávil v Holandsku. Zde vydává soubor svých 43 spisů pod názvem opera didactica omnia. Vznikají zde i menší díla a dílo jedno potřebné bývá považováno za jeho závěť lidstvu. Zemřel 15. listopadu 1670 a byl pohřben v kostelíku v Naardenu. Místo narození Jana Amose Komenského není známo, jako pravděpodobná místa se uvádějí Uherský Brod1 (jak je napsáno v Naardenu na náhrobní desce) nebo Nivnice (Komenský v některých dokumentech připojoval k podpisu Nivanus, Nivnicensis2). Občas se zmiňuje i Komňa (z čehož by mohlo vzniknout příjmení Komenský, Comenius), odkud pocházela rodina.3 Žil s rodiči v Uherském Brodě (pocházel z měšťanské rodiny). Po jejich smrti (1604) se o něj starala jeho teta ve Strážnici, kde začal studovat. Roku 1608 nastoupil studia na latinské škole v Přerově, odkud odešel na vysokou školu do Herbornu a Heidelbergu v Německu. Již při studiu začal psát dvě velká díla: poklad jazyka českého, což měl být velký slovník, a dále encyklopedii divadlo veškerenstva věcí. Tato díla nedokončil. Po ukončení školy působil v letech 1614–16 v Přerově jako rektor latinské školy. Roku 1616 byl vysvěcen na kazatele a odešel do Fulneku, kde působil jako rektor tamější školy a jako kazatel jednoty bratrské. Ve Fulneku poznal i svou první ženu Magdalénu Vizovskou. V této době píše spis listové do nebe.
Po porážce stavovského povstání (1621) byl J. A. Komenský nucen opustit Fulnek a skrýval se na různých místech v Čechách a na Moravě, protože odmítal konvertovat ke katolictví. Po roce ukrývání (roku 1622) mu zemřela jeho žena a dvě děti na mor. Pod vlivem událostí píše filosofické spisy truchlivý a hlubina bezpečnosti. V roce 1624 působil v Brandýse nad Orlicí, kde se také seznámil se svojí druhou ženou Marií Dorotou.
V roce 1628 odešel do exilu do polského Lešna, které se stalo centrem bratrské víry. Zpočátku doufá, že se brzy vrátí zpět do vlasti, proto píše česky. Začal psát učebnice a připravoval plán na zlepšení organizace školství, např. v díle navržení krátké o obnově škol v království českém. V Lešně byl

COMENIA SCRIPT 8/10 PT

TITLE
Malabar Latin & Devanagari Type Family
DESIGNER
Dan Reynolds
CLIENT
University of Reading
COUNTRY
Germany

Malabar Latin and Devanagari - देवनागरी

abcdefghijklmnopqrstuvwxyz
ABCDEFGHIJKLMNOPQRSTUVWXYZ

abcdefghijklmnopqrstuvwxyz
ABCDEFGHIJKLMNOPQRSTUVWXYZ

abcdefghijklmnopqrstuvwxyz
ABCDEFGHIJKLMNOPQRSTUVWXYZ

abcdefghijklmnopqrstuvwxyz
ABCDEFGHIJKLMNOPQRSTUVWXYZ

abcdefghijklmnopqrstuvwxyz
ABCDEFGHIJKLMNOPQRSTUVWXYZ

abcdefghijklmnopqrstuvwxyz
ABCDEFGHIJKLMNOPQRSTUVWXYZ

1234567890 (.,;:?!@&-$£€) 1234567890 [$£€]
1234567890 (.,;:?!@&-$£€) 1234567890 [$£€]

1234567890 (.,;:?!@&-$£€)
1234567890 (.,;:?!@&-$£€)

Karel Martel (23. srpna 686 - 22. října 741) byl franský majordomus. Ač byli oficiálními držiteli královského titulu příslušníci rodu Merovejců, bylo jejich postavení spíš formálního charakteru a skutečným vládcem franské říše byl právě Martel. 25. října 732 zastavil v bitvě u Poitiers útok Saracénů. Tím zastavil postup Arabů a zachránil tak křesťanskou kulturu před náporem islámu. Papež Řehoř III. ho po tomto vítězství požádal, aby se stal ochráncem římské říše. I když byl vliv Karla Martela ob-

फ्रांस के नए राष्ट्रपति निकोला सार्कोज़ी ख़ुद को आधुनिकतावादी विचारों वाला नेता मानते हैं और उनकी पृष्ठभूमि देश के परंपरागत शासक तबके से अलग है. छह मई को हुए चुनाव में देश की सोशलिस्ट पार्टी के साथ उनका कड़ा मुक़ाबला हुआ था और सोशलिस्ट उम्मीदवार सेगोलीन रोयाल से भी उनकी कड़ी टक्कर हुई. निकोला सार्कोज़ी को धुर दक्षिणपंथी तो नहीं लेकिन मध्यमार्गीदक्षिणपंथी विचारधारा वाला नेता माना जाता है. उन्होंने आव्रजन के मुद्दे पर कड़ा रुख़ अपनाकर फ्रांस में एक नई बहस छेड़ी. 2005 में हुए दंगों के दौरान पेरिस के बाहरी इलाक़ों में रहने वाले युवाओं को उन्होंने

Berlin जलंधर

The x-height is very high, a deliberate choice that make the most important parts of lowercase letters visibly larger in tiny text. The height of the capital letters is also rather diminutive, allowing for better character fit as well as eliminating

Diacritical marks and additional alphabetic forms required by many Western, Central, and Eastern European languages are naturally a part of the character set, including those needed in the Baltic states, for Romanian, and for Turkish. Malabar's accents

Why an oldstyle axis?

Malabar is a new multi-lingual type family for extensive text. With both Latin and Devanagari, Malabar supports two of the most widely-spokenlanguages in the world - English and Hindi - as well as a host of others, including the majority of European and several Indian languages, such as Marathi, Nepali, and Sanskrit. Malabar's design is intended for newspapers. In recent years, newspapers have increasingly

Contemporary typeface

Additionally, Malabar may interest publishers of bilingual works. One of the typeface's strengths is the harmony between the Latin and Devanagari components; each was designed to work alongside the other, as well as stand firmly alone. Malabar's 'Roman' characters are seriffed and of the oldstyle genre. A strong diagonal axis is apparent within the curves of the letterforms. Sturdy serifs help strengthen the line of text in small point sizes, as

And a **bold** and ***bold italic*** for emphasis.

CHARLES MARTEL (688–741)
The Hammer
Mayor of the Palace, titular ruler of the Franks
Victor at Tours
Progenitor of the Carolingian dynasty
GRANDFATHER
of Charlemagne - Carolus Magnus -
Frankish King & Imperator Augustus.
चार्लस मार्टेल
perhaps HISTORY'S FIRST utterance
of the phrase
"Stop, Hammertime!"
महाराष्ट्र, भारत
Ich hab' noch einen Koffer in
BERLIN
ohne Besonderheiten & Merkmale
Eine Mischung aus
हिन्दी मराठी नपाली
Karl der Große, sein Opa und die ganze Familie
Es tut mir Leid,
aber von DEINER ARBEIT bekomme ich manchmal
»echt Bauchweh«
जर्मनी यूरोप महाद्वीप में स्थित एक देश है।
Facebook
Antworte auf alle typografische Fragen
en promo chez Linotype
फॉंट्स कोई पेड़ों पर नहीं लगते।

English

Charles "The Hammer" Martel (Latin: *Carolus Martellus*) (ca. 688 - 22 October 741) was proclaimed Mayor of the Palace and ruled the Franks in the name of a titular King. Late in his reign he proclaimed himself Duke of the Franks (the last four years of his reign he did not even bother with the *façade* of a King) and by any name was de facto ruler of the Frankish Realms. In 739 he was offered an office of Roman consul by the Pope, which he rejected possibly not to conflict with Theodatus Ursus who already occupied the office by appointment of the Byzantine emperor Leo III the Isaurian. He expanded his rule over all three of the Frankish kingdoms: Austrasia, Neustria and Burgundy. Martel was born in Herstal, in present-day Belgium, the illegitimate son of Pippin the Middle and his concubine Alpaida (or Chalpaida). He is best remembered for winning the Battle of Tours in 732, which has traditionally been characterized as an event that halted the Islamic expansionism in Europe that had conquered Iberia. "Charles's victory has often been regarded as decisive for world history..." In addition to being the leader of the army that prevailed at Tours, Charles Martel was a truly giant figure of the Middle Ages. A brilliant general, he is considered the forefather of western heavy cavalry, chivalry, founder of the Carolingian Empire (which was named after him), and a catalyst for the feudal system, which would see Europe through the Middle Ages. Although some recent

Above: Text from wikipedia.org and bbc.co.uk/hindi

Danish

Karl Martell - (Martell = *hammeren*) - (23. august 686 i Herstal - 22. oktober 741 i Quierzy-sur-Oise) var rigshovmester og reelt konge over de tre frankiske kongedømmer. Han er især berømt for at vinde slaget ved Poitiers i 732, hvor han standsede et muslimsk plyndringstogt ledet af guvernøren af al-Andalus. Med denne sejr satte han en stopper for videre muslimsk plyndring i Frankrig. Martell blev født i Herstal, beliggende i Wallonien i det nuværende Belgien som en uægte søn af Pipin af Herstal og dennes konkubine Alpaida. Selv om han først og fremmest huskes som lederen af den kristne hær, der vandt ved Tours, er Karl Martell i øvrigt en gigantisk personlighed i den

French

Charles Martel (Herstal, v.688 - Quierzy-sur-Oise, 21 ou 22 octobre 741), fut duc d'Austrasie, puis maire du palais de 737 à 741 et souverain de facto du royaume des Francs (*dux et princeps Francorum*, duc et prince des Francs). À la mort de son père, Pépin de Herstal dit *Pépin le Jeune* (714), Charles de Herstal qui a déjà 29 ans est tout désigné pour reprendre la charge de maire du palais qu'occupait le défunt, ses deux demi-frères Drogon de Champagne et Grimoald II étant eux aussi morts. Mais Charles était un enfant illégitime, et Plectrude, la femme de Pépin, fit tout pour l'écarter du pouvoir et préserver l'avenir de son petit-fils Théodebald (ou Thibaut, Thiaud), le fils de Grimoald

Finnish

Kaarle Martel (lat. Carolus Martellus, "Kaarle Vasara") (n. 685-741) oli frankkilainen ylimys. Kaarle Martel tuli isänsä Pipin Heristalilaisen kuoltua 714 Austrasian major domukseksi eli hovimestariksi. Hän voitti kilpailevan Neustrian major domuksen sisällissodassa, ja hänestä tuli 720 koko Frankkien valtakunnan major domus ja tosiasiallinen hallitsija. Kaarle Martel soti menestyksekkäästi germaaneja vastaan ja voitti maurit Toursin taistelussa lähellä Poitiersia vuonna 732. Jälkimmäinen taistelu toi hänelle liikanimen Vasara. Kaarlen voiton katsottiin pysäyttäneen muslimien laajentumispyrkimykset. Hän oli Kaarle Suuren isoisä. Germaanit ovat indoeu-

Hungarian

Martel (másképp Martell) Károly (686. augusztus 23. - Quierzy, 741. október 21/22.) a Frank Királyság teljhatalmú majordomusa, a Karoling-dinasztia névadója volt. Nevéhez fűződik az arabok nyugat-európai előretörésének megállítása a 732-es poitiers-i csatában. Ragadványneve, melyet számos sikeres hadjáratával érdemelt ki, a latin *martellus* (= kalapács) szóból ered. Apja az austrasiai királyságot Neustria felett győzelemre vezető Heristali Pipin majordomus volt, édesanyja, Alpaïde de Bruyères azonban nem Pipin törvényes asszonya volt. Így történt, hogy amikor Pipin 714-ben meghalt, felesége, Plectrude szembeszállt egyetlen életben

8/13pt samples. Text from wikipedia.org and esakal.com

Latvian

Karla Martela dēls, mažordoms Pipins Īsais (741.-768.g.), tāpat kā tēvs izcēlās ar veiksmi karos pret arābiem, līdz sagrāba varu valstī un kronējas Suasonā par karali (valda: 752-768). Viņa dēls ir Kārlis Lielais, kurš 43 valdīšanas gados pakļāva gandrīz vai visu kristīgo Eiropu. Tūlīt pēc kāpšanas tronī viņš apspiež sadumpojušos baskus un bretoņus. Tad sāka ekspansiju uz sakšu zemēm (karš ar pārtraukumiem ilga 30 gadus). 772. g. franki noposta sakšu zemes līdz Vezerai un nocērt to svēto ozolu Irminsulu. 774. g. franki pakļauj langobardus (Kārlis sevi sāk dēvēt par "franku un langobardu valdnieku"). Pāvests tam piešķir Romas katoļu valsts aizstāvja titulu. 776. g. tiek

Portuguese

Carlos Martel ou Carlos Martelo (c. 688, Herstal - 15 de Outubro de 741, Quierzy-sur-Oise) foi prefeito do palácio e duque dos francos (seja quais forem os títulos, ele governou os reinos francos). Ele expandiu seu domínio sobre os três reinos francos: Austrásia, Nêustria e Borgonha. Carlos Martel era filho ilegítimo de Pepino de Herstal com sua concubina Alpaida e nasceu em Herstal, no que agora é a Valônia, na Bélgica. Ele é melhor lembrado por ter vencido a Batalha de Poitiers (ou batalha de Tours) em 732, que tem sido tradicionalmente considerada com a ação que salvou a Europa do expansionismo muçulmano que já havia conquistado a Península Ibérica. "Não houve mais

Marathi

नवी दिल्ली - संयुक्त पुरोगामी आघाडीला पाठिंबा दिल्याबद्दल काँग्रेस अध्यक्षा श्रीमती सोनिया गांधी यांनी आज (शुक्रवारी) समाजवादी पक्षाचे आभार मानले आहेत. "या निर्णयाचे आम्ही स्वागत करतो. डाव्या पक्षांनी पाठिंबा काढून घेतल्याबद्दल आम्हाला खेद जरूर वाटतो. पण, पुढच्या काळाकडेही पाहिले पाहिजे," असे सूचक वक्तव्य श्रीमती गांधी यांनी केले आहे. "डाव्यांनी पाठिंबा काढून घेण्यापूर्वी पंतप्रधान म्हणाले होते की संसदेला विश्वासात घेतल्याशिवाय अणूकरार अमलात येणार नाही. आम्ही या भूमिकेशी ठाम आहोत," असेही त्या म्हणाल्या. "विश्वासदर्शक ठराव लवकरच मांडण्याची सरकारची इच्छा आहे. त्यामुळे लोकसभेचे विशेष अधिवेशनही लवकरच बोलाविले जाईल," असे श्रीमती गांधी यांनी स्पष्ट केले. विमान जामनगरहून मुंबईकडे आले होते. त्यावेळी त्यातून पाण्याची गळती होत

Swedish

Karl Martell, född 23 augusti 686, död 22 oktober 741, var son till Pippin av Heristal och Alpheid. Han var merovingernas major domus. Hans betecknande binamn Martell betyder "Hammaren". Han segrade 732 vid Tours och Poitiers över en arabisk ryttarhär som invaderat Frankerriket. Han förenade Austrasien i öster och Neustrien i väster med Burgund till ett enhetligt frankiskt välde. Gift med Chrotrudis, död 724. Maior domus (rikshovmästare) var adminstratörer inom Frankerriket, tillsatta av den frankiska kungaätten merovingerna. "De långhåriga merovingerna" stred mest med varandra om makten, och överlät skötsel och administration åt sina

BRONZE
ORIGINAL TYPEFACE

TITLE
Bree
COMPANY
Type-Together
COUNTRY
United Kingdom

Ritmo

More classical **alternate letters** *available*

Upright Italic

Headlines

Logotypes

Que

Branding trends

BRONZE
ORIGINAL TYPEFACE

TITLE
FC Autobahn
COMPANY
Autobahn
CLIENT
Graphic Design Festival Breda (GDFB)
COUNTRY
Netherlands

ABCDEFGHIJKL

MNOPQRSTUV

WXYZ

abcdefghijklm

nopqrstuvwxyz

1234567890

! @ # ( ) : ; < > , .

Planeta

Dani Klauser Grafik Design

Switzerland

ABCDEFGHIJK
LMNOPQ
RSTUVWXYZ
abcdefghijk
lmnopqrstuvwxyz
1234567890
!?@&ß...«»[.,:;]
(---)#*/€$£%™

Planeta-Light 24/29pt.

ABCDEFGHIJK
LMNOPQ
RSTUVWXYZ
abcdefghijk
lmnopqrstuvwxyz
1234567890
!?@&ß...«»[.,:;]
(---)#*/€$£%™

Planeta-Medium 24/29pt.

**ABCDEFGHIJK
LMNOPQ
RSTUVWXYZ
abcdefghijk
lmnopqrstuvwxyz
1234567890
!?@&ß...«»[.,:;]
(---)#*/€$£%™**

Planeta-Bold 24/29pt.

**ABCDEFGHIJK
LMNOPQ
RSTUVWXYZ
abcdefghijk
lmnopqrstuvwxyz
1234567890**
!?@&ß...« »[.,:;]
(---)#*/€$£%™

Planeta-Plakat 24/29pt.

AB EFG
CD HIJ
KLM
NOP

mno yz0
pqr 123
stu 456
vwx 789

QRS abc
TUV def
WXY ghi
Z jkl

.,:;!? " ' ' " „ ‚
{[()]} ‹ › « »
$ £ € © ® ™
@%& ¼ ½ ¾

METHODS OF DETECTING EXTRASOLAR PLANETS

TITLE
Nabil type family
DESIGNER
Emanuela Conidi
CLIENT
MATD University of Reading
COUNTRY
Italy

WONDERFUL, RARE, KNOWLEDGE.

The number one.

zizzania

ولما كان تناسي حقوق

In need of good and beautiful things

QUISQUILIARE

فِي السُّوقِ مُرِيْدِيْنَ أَنْ تَشْتَرِيَ كِتَابَ فِقْهٍ

560 & 890

KÖÖPENHAMINASSA

Ready to take centre stage

لمّا كان الاعتراف بالكرامة المتأصلة في جميع أعضاء الأسرة البشرية

oggigiorno

UN VERO E PROPRIO QUI PRO QUO

že uznání přirozené

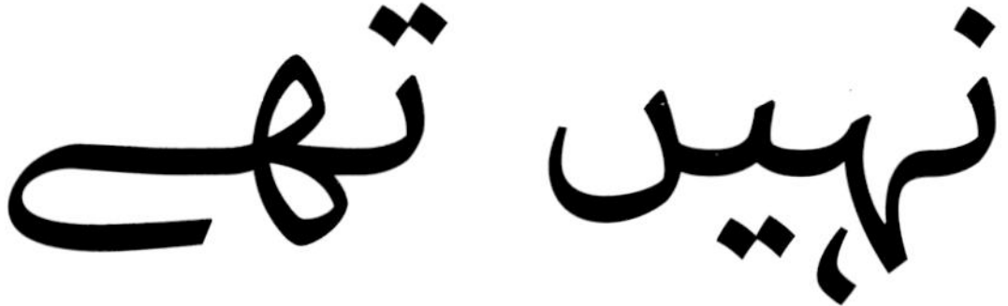

The difficulties accompany its progress

"YOU WILL SEE"

گاجاع پیش های

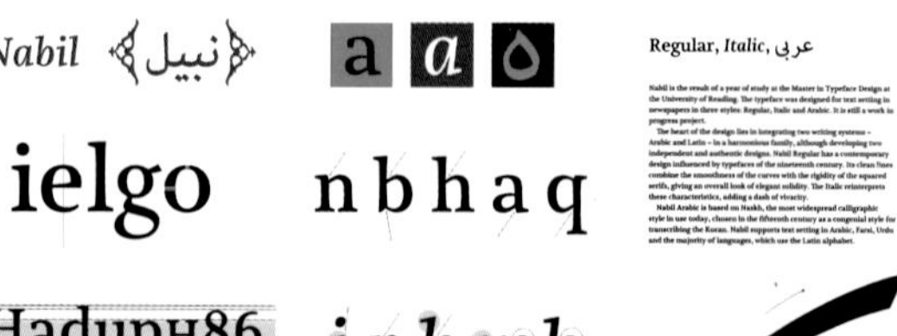

Regular, *Italic*, عربي

Nabil is the result of a year of study at the Master in Typeface Design at the University of Reading. The typeface was designed for text setting in newspapers in three styles: Regular, Italic and Arabic. It is still a work in progress project.

The heart of the design lies in integrating two writing systems – Arabic and Latin – in a harmonious family, although developing two independent and authentic designs. Nabil Regular has a contemporary design influenced by typefaces of the nineteenth century. Its clean lines combine the smoothness of the curves with the rigidity of the squared serifs, giving an overall look of elegant solidity. The Italic reinterprets these characteristics, adding a dash of vivacity.

Nabil Arabic is based on Naskh, the most widespread calligraphic style in use today, chosen in the fifteenth century as a congenial style for transcribing the Koran. Nabil supports text setting in Arabic, Farsi, Urdu and the majority of languages, which use the Latin alphabet.

Hadupн86 *iphwk*

arnjy olp ٥ l م

ŔáÔêŰűl· اس ع ه ب

è ž ö

ITALIAN 10/13 PT
Ogni individuo accusato di un reato è presunto innocente sino a che la sua colpevolezza non sia stata provata legalmente in un pubblico processo nel quale egli abbia avuto tutte le garanzie necessarie per la sua difesa.

HUNGARIAN 10/13 PT
Minden személynek teljesen egyenlő joga van arra, hogy ügyét független és pártatlan bíróság méltányosan és nyilvánosan tárgyalja, s ez határozzon egyrészt jogai és kötelezettségei felől, másrészt minden ellene emelt bűnügyi vád

CZECH 10/13 PT
že uznání přirozené důstojnosti a rovných a nezcizitelných práv členů lidské rodiny je základem svobody, spravedlnosti a míru ve světě, že zneuznání lidských práv a pohrdání jimi vedlo k barbarským činům, urážejícím svědomí lidstva,

PORTUGUESE 10/13 PT
TODOS SÃO IGUAIS PERANTE A LEI E, SEM DISTINÇÃO, TÊM DIREITO A IGUAL PROTECÇÃO DA LEI. TODOS TÊM DIREITO A PROTECÇÃO IGUAL CONTRA QUALQUER DISCRIMINAÇÃO QUE VIOLE A PRESENTE DECLA-

FINNISH 10/13 PT
JULISTUKSEN ILMAISKAPPALEITA ON SAATAVANA YK: N KÖÖPENHAMINASSA SIJAITSEVASTA POHJOISMAISESTA TIEDOTUSTOIMISTOSTA YK: N VIRALLISILLA KIELILLÄ, POHJOISMAISILLA KIELILLÄ JA RAJALLINEN MÄÄRÄ MUILLA KIELILLÄ.

FRENCH 10/13 PT
Tous les êtres humains naissent libres et égaux en dignité et en droits. Ils sont doués de raison et de conscience et doivent agir les uns envers les autres dans un esprit de fraternité. Chacun peut se prévaloir de tous les

ű Ã î

Whereas recognition of the inherent dignity and of the equal and inalienable rights of all members of the human family is the foundation of freedom, justice and peace, in the world,

Whereas disregard and contempt for human rights have resulted in barbarous acts which have outraged the conscience of mankind, and the advent of a world in which human

11/15 AND 11/21 PT

لما كان الاعتراف بالكرامة المتأصلة في جميع أعضاء الأسرة البشرية وبحقوقهم المتسا وية الثابتة هو قد أفضيا أساس الحرية والعدل والسلام في العالم. ولما

Whereas recognition of the inherent dignity and of the equal and inalienable rights of all members of the human family is the foundation of freedom, justice

Whereas disregard and contempt for human rights have resulted in barbarous acts which have outraged the conscience of mankind, and the advent of a world in which

16/20 AND 16/28 PT

لما كان الاعتراف بالكرامة المتأصلة في جميع أعضاء الأسرة البشرية وبحقوقهم المتسا وية الثابتة هو قد أفضيا أساس الحرية والعدل والسلام في العالم. ولما

Whereas recognition of the inherent dignity and of the equal and inalienable rights of all members of the human family is the foundation of freedom, justice and peace, in the world,

Whereas disregard and contempt for human rights have resulted in barbarous acts which have outraged the conscience of mankind, and the advent of a world in which human beings shall enjoy freedom

24/26 AND 24/41 PT

لما كان الاعتراف بالكرامة المتأصلة في جميع أعضاء الأسرة البشرية وبحقوقهم المتسا وية الثابتة هو

alignement QUOSQUE přesvědčení

finally!

ے پاس ہے یا نہیں گلخانه ای برپا

OTTOMAN DOME OF THE ROCK *Koffiee & zucker*

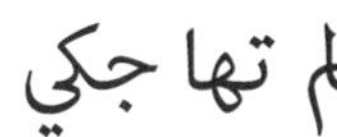

لم تها جكي *määräaikaisilla* ١٣٤٨٠٤٦٥٣

killilersugaanngitsumillu lunedì KULTŪRĄ LĖMĖ

skúlptúrsaðferð في م ث فِيْهِ بِعِزَّتِهِ عَمْرًا. أَلْقُضَاةُ

ÎNVĂȚĂTURĂ «8008.9657» uggioso

BRONZE
ORIGINAL TYPEFACE

TITLE
Kina Type Family
COMPANY
Francesca Bolognini
CLIENT
KABK
Type and Media
COUNTRY
United Kingdom

[...] dopo quarant'anni che scriv[...]on, dopo aver esplorato varie strade e co[...] esperimenti diversi, è venuta l'ora c[...]erchi una definizione complessiva pe[...]o lavoro; proporrei questa: la mia ope[...]e è stata il più delle volte una sottrazione [...]so; ho cercato di *togliere peso ora alle figure umane, ora ai corpi celesti, ora alle citta*; soprattutto ho cercato di togliere peso alla struttura del racconto e al linguaggio [...]

Italo Calvino,
Lezioni Americane

La leggerezza

A-Z

{[(-: 0123456789 ;-)]}

Aa Bb Cc Dd Ee Ff Gg Hh
Ii Jj Kk Ll Mm Nn Oo Pp Qq Rr
Ss Tt Uu Vv Ww Xx Yy Zz

Aa Bb Cc Dd Ee Ff Gg Hh
Ii Jj Kk Ll Mm Nn Oo Pp Qq Rr
Ss Tt Uu Vv Ww Xx Yy Zz

"Th fi fj fl fk fh fb ?!"
.,;:*&@+ -/-

Kina Black & *Italic*

Kina Black Roman and Kina Black Italic are display typefaces and are designed to be used in big sizes,

157 pt.

I imagine it in magazine, as a

headline

But I can think of many other applications, like *brochures, packaging, flyers, posters, logos,* and more...

¶ Extreme moments in life grab attention, demand reflection, and get remembered. What one person finds extreme another may not, *but there are many things in the world that people agree are extreme.* My interest in visual extremes informed the design of Kina: a typeface family meant for magazines that *I designed at the Royal Academy of Art in The Hague.* To develop Kina, I experimented in juxtaposing visual extremes...

I'll give some examples:

Experimenting with extreme weights was the core activity in Kina's development. I started by drawing the thin type because I had a lot of ideas to begin with and I needed to express and record them quickly. Some of these ideas had elements that were meant for both the thin type and the black type that I would develop later, such as the basic structure, and the general shape of the serifs. I started the black type as soon as I arrived at a thin type that I was happy to leave and come back to. I wanted very bold, uniform shapes without contrast in form. But I found the initial results too heavy. So, after trying out a few other unsuccessful ideas, I produced letters which weren't uniform in thickness.

That was one example of how my ideas developed by juxtaposing visual extremes. There are also examples of how my general understanding of typography developed by the same means. For instance, the more letter shapes I drew, the more I realized the importance of the contrast between black and white. It was not easy to reach an overall harmony between all the individual shapes made by the black text cutting into the white paper. I am sure that the complex workings of this relationship will continue to throw-up surprises as my career progresses.

Kina regular came at the very end. I had started work on an italic for each extreme weight, but with the project deadline on the horizon, I decided to focus on a text face. After working with the two extremes I felt fairly confident in confronting the middle-weight.

The Kina family was designed with magazines in mind. But I think it can be used in many different contexts, such as flyers, brochures, posters, or packaging. Kina Thin and Kina Black are designed to be seen in relatively large sizes, such as for headlines or pull-quotes. The two work nicely together, and they are supported by the regular weight for longer text.

At the moment I'm working on the italics for each of the three weights. Kina was designed as a final project for the t]m post-graduate program at the Royal Academy of Art, Den Haag 2008.

A-Z

{[(-: 0123456789 ;-)]}

Aa Bb Cc Dd Ee Ff Gg Hh
Ii Jj Kk Ll Mm Nn Oo Pp Qq Rr
Ss Tt Uu Vv Ww Xx Yy Zz

Aa Bb Cc Dd Ee Ff Gg Hh
Ii Jj Kk Ll Mm Nn Oo Pp Qq Rr
Ss Tt Uu Vv Ww Xx Yy Zz

"¿¡Th fi fj fl fk fh fb?!"
« ...,;:¶*&@ | —+-/_ »

ÀàÁáÈèÉéÌìÒòÓóÙùÚú

Kina Thin & *Italic*

¶ KinaThin is a display typeface designed to be used in a relatively big size. *But it is so well hinted* that you can use it as small as 10 point size.

I imagine it in a magazine, as a headline or pull-quote.
But I can think of many other applications, like brochures, packaging, flyers, poster and logos. Kina can also work very well in short text.

Kina Thin is my first approach in the design of a new typeface. When I started with the early sketches, I knew that I wanted two extremes, the black and the thin. It was difficult to figure out at first what the black should look like, so I started with things that were easy for me to draw. The early sketches where much more lively, and I was targeting the shapes to a feminine audience. The more I drew the more a strong character began to emerge. My aim was to achieve femininity without using flourishes.

14/17.5 pt

11/13 pt

A-Z

{[(-: 0123456789 ;-)]}

Aa Bb Cc Dd Ee Ff Gg Hh
Ii Jj Kk Ll Mm Nn Oo Pp Qq Rr
Ss Tt Uu Vv Ww Xx Yy Zz

ß Ð Þ þ Ł ł ð
Àà Áá Ââ Ãã Ää Åå Èè Éé Êê Ëë
Ìì Íí Îî ÏïÑñ Òò Óó Ôô Õõ Öö Ùù
Úú Ûû Üü Ýý Šš Žž
"¿¡Th fi fj fl fk fh fb?!"
« ....,;:*†‡&@¶|~»
\# +−±÷=/_¼ ½ ¾¹²³'" <>
$€£¥¢

Kina Medium

Kina Medium is a text typeface designed to be used with the rest of the Kina family: Thin, Black, Roman and Italic. It has the all the distinguishing characteristics of the Kina family. It retains the modern contrast, and uses the same 'physiology' of letter forms and serifs. But these characteristics have been tuned and adapted to allow it to perform as any readable text should.

24/27.5 pt

Per qualsiasi singolo "Documento Esteso", l'utente può solo o (a) Installare tale Documento Esteso ad un numero illimitato di singoli destinatari ma non deve estrarre informazioni da più di cinquecento (500) singole richieste di tale

14/17.5 pt

Si le Logiciel est une mise à niveau ou une mise à jour d'une version antérieure du Logiciel, vous devez détenir une licence en vigueur pour cette version antérieure pour pouvoir utiliser la mise à niveau ou la mise à jour. Après avoir installer une telle mise à niveau ou mise à jour, vous pouvez continuer d'utiliser une

11/13 pt

El Software es una mejora o actualización de una versión anterior del Software de Adobe, usted debe poseer una licencia válida de dicha versión anterior para poder utilizar dicha mejora o actualización. Una vez que usted haya instalado dicha mejora o actualización, podrá continuar utilizando la versión anterior de conformidad con su contrato de licencia de usuario final únicamente si (a) la mejora o actualización y todas las versiones anteriores son instaladas en el mismo dispositivo, (b) las versiones anteriores o las copias de éstas no son transferidas a otra parte o dispositivo salvo que todas las copias de la mejora o actualización también

08/10.5 pt

BRONZE
ORIGINAL TYPEFACE

TITLE
Texteron
COMPANY
Cape Arcona Type Foundry
COUNTRY
Germany

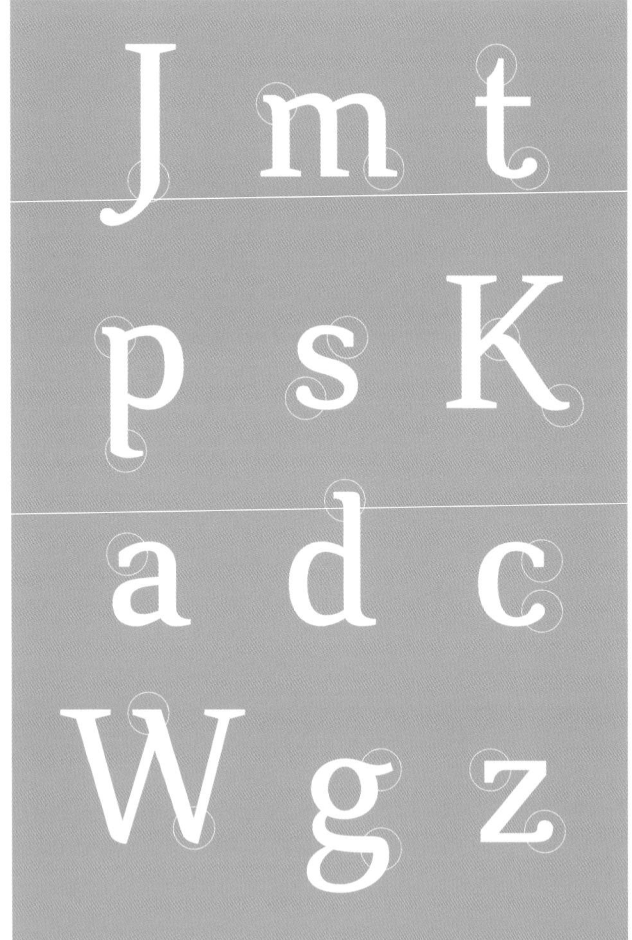

Glyph Set

OPENTYPE FEATURES

LIGATURES
ﬁ ﬂ ﬁ ﬀ ﬃ ﬄ

OLDSTYLE FIGURES
0 1 2 3 4 5 6 7 8 9 0
»in the year 1972«

LINING FIGURES
0 1 2 3 4 5 6 7 8 9 0
5 4 7 2 3 9 1 3 5 4 7

Texteron is an OpenType font family and contains more characters than are directly accessible through the keyboard.

By default Texteron will set numbers as medieval numerals in adaptive width, but you may also decide to use upright monospaced lining figures, by chosing the corresponding opentype option in your layout program.

REGULAR (30 PT)

a b c d e f g h i j k l m n o p
q r s t u v w x y z ß
A B C D E F G H I J K L M N
O P Q R S T U V W X Y Z

0 1 2 3 4 5 6 7 8 9
0 1 2 3 4 5 6 7 8 9

. , : ; - – — _ ' " „ “ ” « » ‹ › · • ! ? ¡ ¿ …
@ & ( ) [ ] { } / | \ § † ‡ ¶ ❦ ℗ ©
√ ◊ ∞ ∆ Ω ∅ ℮ ∏ π ∑ ∂ µ ∫
% ‰ ½ ¼ ¾ ¹ ² ³ + − × ÷ ± ≥ ≤ ≠ ≈ ° ® ™ ª º
ﬁ ﬂ ﬁ ﬀ ﬃ ﬄ

á â ä à å ã æ ā ă ǻ ą ǽ ć ĉ č ċ ď đ ĕ é ê ë è ē ĕ ė ę
ĝ ğ ġ ģ ĥ ħ í î ï ì ĩ ī ĭ į ı ĳ ȷ ĵ ķ ĸ ĺ ľ ļ ł ñ ń ň ņ ŉ ŋ
ó ô ö ò õ ō ŏ ő ǿ ŕ ŗ ř š ś ŝ ş ș ť ţ ŧ
ú û ü ù ũ ū ŭ ů ű ų ẁ ẃ ŵ ẅ ý ÿ ỳ ŷ ž ź ż
Á Â Ä À Å Ã Ā Ă Ǻ Ą Ǽ Æ Ç Ć Ĉ Č Ċ Ď Đ Đ
É Ê Ë È Ĕ Ē Ĕ Ė Ę Ĝ Ğ Ġ Ģ Ĥ Ħ Ĩ Ī Ĭ İ Į Ĳ Í Î Ï Ì Ĵ
Ķ Ĺ Ľ Ļ Ŀ Ł Ń Ň Ņ Ñ Ŋ Ó Ô Ö Ò Õ Ō Ŏ Ő Ø Ǿ
Œ Ŕ Ř Ŗ Ś Ŝ Ş Ș Š Ť Ţ Ŧ Ũ Ū Ŭ Ů Ű Ų Ú Û Ü
Ù Ẁ Ẃ Ŵ Ẅ Ý Ÿ Ỳ Ŷ Ź Ż Ž
€ £ ƒ ¥ $ ¢

4

Weights

BOLDNESS

S
C

REGULAR
BOLD
HEAVY

REGULAR (16 PT)

a b c d e f g h i j k l m n o p q r s t u v x y z ß
A B C D E F G H I J K L M N O P Q R S T U V
W X Y Z 0 1 2 3 4 5 6 7 8 9 @ & . , ? ! € $ £

My help squeezed in and joined the weavers again before six o'clock. Portez ce vieux whisky au juge blond qui fume. Høj bly gom vandt fræk sexquiz på wc. Albert osti fagotin ja töräytti puhkuvan melodian. Pójdź w loch zbić małżeńską gęś futryn! Franz jagt im komplett verwahrlosten Taxi.

BOLD (16 PT)

a b c d e f g h i j k l m n o p q r s t u v x y z ß
A B C D E F G H I J K L M N O P Q R S T U V
W X Y Z 0 1 2 3 4 5 6 7 8 9 @ & . , ? ! € $ £

My help squeezed in and joined the weavers again before six o'clock. Portez ce vieux whisky au juge blond qui fume. Høj bly gom vandt fræk sexquiz på wc. Albert osti fagotin ja töräytti puhkuvan melodian. Pójdź w loch zbić małżeńską gęś futryn! Franz jagt im Taxi.

HEAVY (16 PT)

a b c d e f g h i j k l m n o p q r s t u v x y z ß
A B C D E F G H I J K L M N O P Q R S T U V
W X Y Z 0 1 2 3 4 5 6 7 8 9 @ & . , ? ! € $ £

My help squeezed in and joined the weavers again before six o'clock. Portez ce vieux whisky au juge blond qui fume. Høj bly gom vandt fræk sexquiz på wc. Albert osti fagotin ja töräytti puhkuvan melodian. Pójdź w loch zbić małżeńską gęś futryn!

ITALIC (16 PT)

a b c d e f g h i j k l m n o p q r s t u v x y z ß
A B C D E F G H I J K L M N O P Q R S T U V
W X Y Z 0 1 2 3 4 5 6 7 8 9 @ & . , ? ! € $ £

My help squeezed in and joined the weavers again before six o'clock. Portez ce vieux whisky au juge blond qui fume. Høj bly gom vandt fræk sexquiz på wc. Albert osti fagotin ja töräytti puhkuvan melodian. Pójdź w loch zbić małżeńską gęś futryn! Franz jagt im komplett verwahrlosten Taxi quer durch Bayern.

BOLD ITALIC (16 PT)

a b c d e f g h i j k l m n o p q r s t u v x y z ß
A B C D E F G H I J K L M N O P Q R S T U V
W X Y Z 0 1 2 3 4 5 6 7 8 9 @ & . , ? ! € $ £

My help squeezed in and joined the weavers again before six o'clock. Portez ce vieux whisky au juge blond qui fume. Høj bly gom vandt fræk sexquiz på wc. Albert osti fagotin ja töräytti puhkuvan melodian. Pójdź w loch zbić małżeńską gęś futryn! Franz jagt im komplett verwahrlosten Taxi.

SMALL CAPS (16 PT)

A A B C D E F G H I J K L M N O P Q R S T U V X Y Z
0 1 2 3 4 5 6 7 8 9 @ & . , ? ! € $ £

MY HELP SQUEEZED IN AND JOINED THE WEAVERS AGAIN BEFORE SIX O'CLOCK. PORTEZ CE VIEUX WHISKY AU JUGE BLOND QUI FUME. HØJ BLY GOM VANDT FRÆK SEXQUIZ PÅ WC. ALBERT OSTI FAGOTIN JA TÖRÄYTTI PUHKUVAN MELODIAN. PÓJDŹ W LOCH ZBIĆ MAŁŻEŃSKĄ GĘŚ FUTRYN! FRANZ JAGT IM TAXI.

6

Hamburgefontsiv
REGULAR

Hamburgefontsiv
BOLD

Hamburgefontsiv
HEAVY

Hamburgefontsiv
ITALIC

Hamburgefontsiv
BOLD ITALIC

HAMBURGEFONTSIV
SMALL CAPS

BRONZE
ORIGINAL TYPEFACE

TITLE
Fedra Hindi
COMPANY
Typotheque
COUNTRY
Netherlands

Type design is a relatively small industry. As it takes a considerable amount of time to develop a typeface, many designers try to find a niche market, hoping that licensing of their font will eventually repay the months or possibly years invested in their work. It probably comes as no suprise that most of their efforts are concentrated on creating Latin typefaces, selling the fonts in the Western world. That unfortunately ignores parts of the world where Latin script is not used. Creating 'Non-Latin' fonts (an unfortunate, almost colonial but industry-accepted word for those other writing scripts) is simply not profitable. Most Non-Latin fonts are either made by software giants to support their operating systems, or made as exclusive corporate fonts for global companies (but only for that company's exclusive use), or made as student projects (with little hope of finding commercial distribution). Typotheque attempts to give as much attention to Non-Latin as to Latin fonts. Having already created Кириллица (Cyrillic), Ελληνικά (Greek), العربية (Arabic), and Հայերեն (Armenian) fonts, this) project now presents the most ambitious extension of the Fedra type family — हिंदी (Hindi). By doing so, Fedra now supports over 190 languages, spoken by over 3.5 billion people.

प्रतियोगिता

देश की आर्थिक राजधानी में 26 नवम्बर को आतंकियों की ओर से मुम्बई आतंकवाद निरोधक दस्ते (एटीएस) के चीफ हेमंत करकरे सहित 16 पुलिसकर्मियों को निशाना बनाए जाने के बाद अहमदाबाद क्राइमब्रांच के रायखड में गायकवाड़ हवेली स्थित कार्यालय की किलेबंदी कर दी गई है. यहां बेरीकेट बनाकर सशस्त्र जवान को तैनात किया गया है, इसके अलावा प्रवेश द्वारों पर भी सशस्त्र जवान वॉच टावर पर तैनात किए गए हैं. सूत्रों के अनुसार क्राइमब्रांच के कार्यालय पर आतंकी हमला कर सकते हैं.

महात्मा गांधी की अस्थियों का विसर्जन किया गया

पहले निर्धारित स्थान पर आपको अपने विषय में जानकारी देनी होगी. उसके बाद बीबीसी और इसको सेवाएं देने वाली संस्थाओं की उन सुविधाओं का लाभ आप उठा पाएँगे जिनका चयन आपने किया होगा. आपके द्वारा दी गई जानकारी का उपयोग हम इस नीति के तहत

अमावश्या की गहन निशा के अंधकार में तुम अपना मस्तक तनिक आत्मगौरव के साथ ऊँचा उठाकर तो देखो, विश्व के गगनमंडल में तुम्हारी कलित कीर्ती के असंख्य दीपक जल रहे हैं. **दक्षिण भारत में आंध्र प्रदेश के वारंगल ज़िले में पुलिस ने तीन लड़कों को गोली मार दी. इन लड़कों को शुक्रवार को दो लड़कियों पर तेज़ाब फेंकने के आरोप में गिरफ़्तार किया गया था.**

आपकी रुचि के समा
आतंकवाद से निपटने के लिए मिलकर का
भारत जीत से 256 रन
महात्मा गांधी
की अस्थियों
ग्रामीण परिवेश की फ़िल्मों में तानाशाह जमींदार और सूदखोर महाजन खलना
कलाकारों का चयन महत्व
प्रतियोगि
शशिधर मुखर्जी की 1943 में प्रदर्शित 'क़िस्मत' में अपराधी का पात्र ही नायक रहा
अशोक कुमार ने उसे अभिनीत किया था. यह एंटी नायक छवि की पहली फ़िल्म
विशेषकर उन अधिकारियों को अपना निशाना बन
ब्रिटेन के प्रधान

अ अ आ इ ई उ ऊ ऋ ॠ ऌ ॡ ऍ ऎ ए ऐ ऑ ऒ ओ औ
क ख ग घ ङ च छ ज झ ञ ट ठ ड ढ ण त थ द ध न ऩ प फ ब भ म
य र ऱ ल ळ ऴ व श ष स ह क्ष त्र ज्ञ क़ ख़ ग़ ज़ ड़ ढ़ फ़ य़

1 2 3 4 5 6 7 8 9 0 (: - ? . , ' ')
ॐ

SILVER
CARDS & FLYERS

TITLE
Speed Cooking - Cookery Maps
COMPANY
Rose de Claire, Design
CLIENT
Ministry of Health Luxembourg
DESIGNER
Delphine Forcher
ART DIRECTOR
Delphine Forcher
CREATIVE DIRECTOR
Albert Seyser
DESIGN DIRECTOR
Albert Seyser
ILLUSTRATOR
Delphine Forcher
EDITOR
National Youth Service
Luxembourg (SNJ)
WRITER
Michel Grevis
COUNTRY
Luxembourg

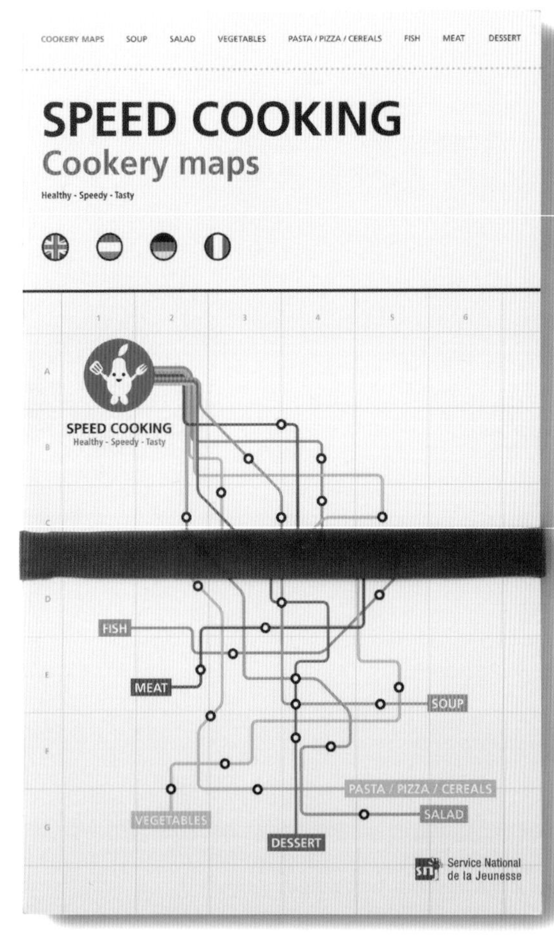

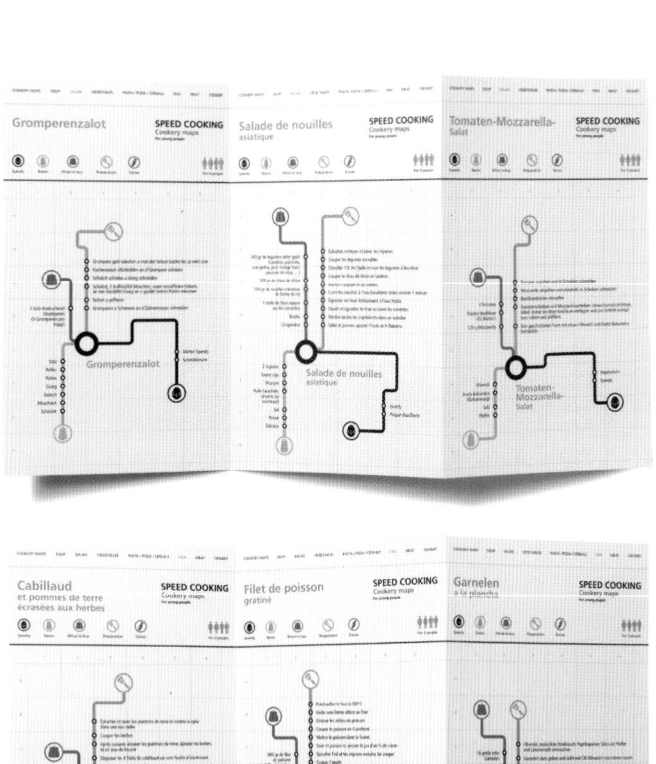

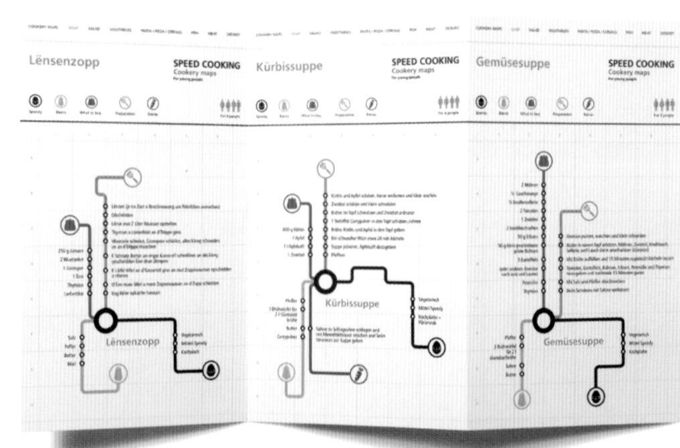

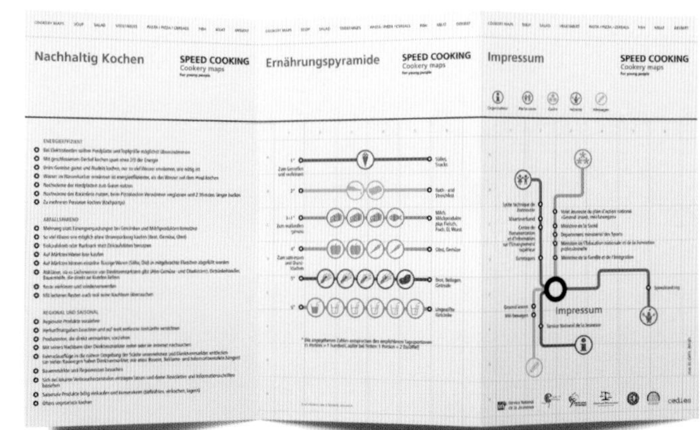

BRONZE
CARDS & FLYERS

TITLE
Wedding Invitation
COMPANY
beetroot design group
CLIENT
Tasos & Despina
COUNTRY
Greece

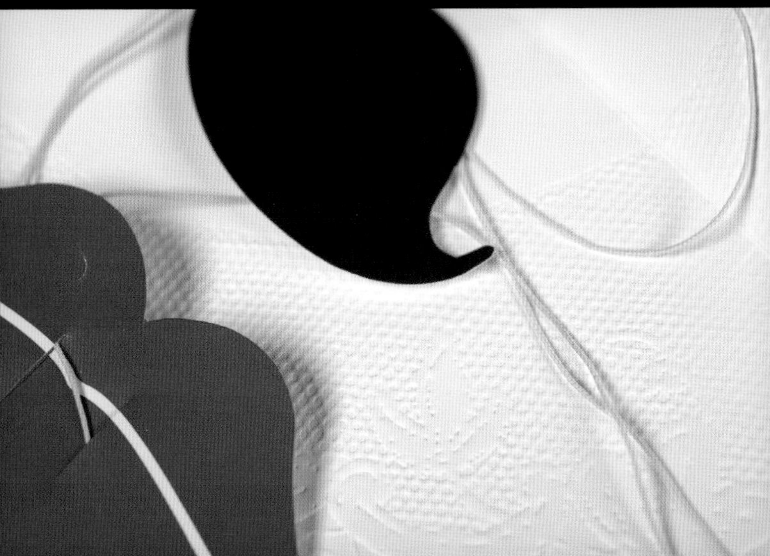

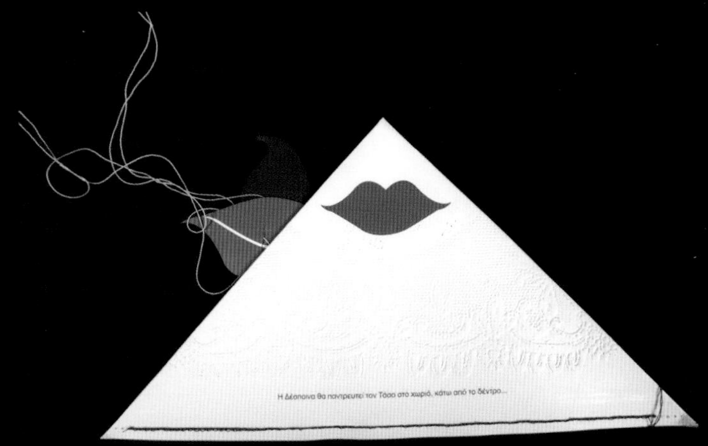

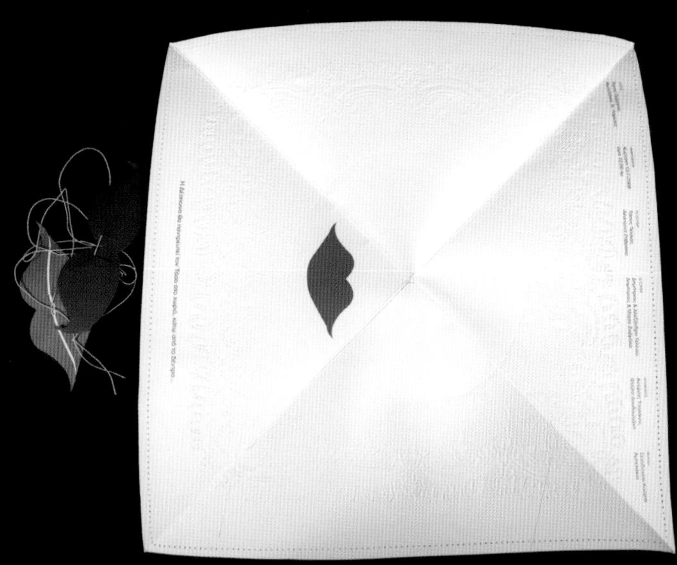

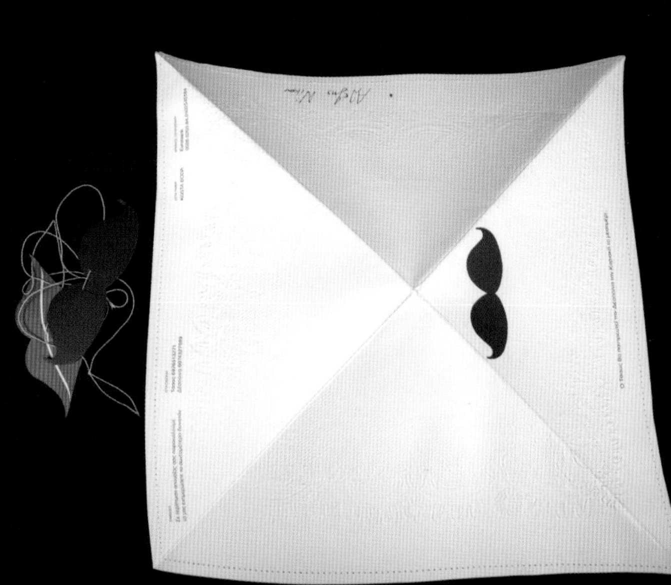

BRONZE
CARDS & FLYERS

TITLE
MVRDV
COMPANY
beetroot design group
CLIENT
Cyprus Architects Association
COUNTRY
Greece

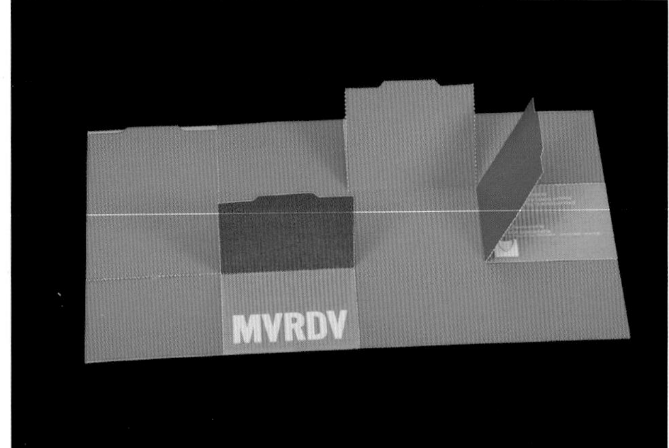

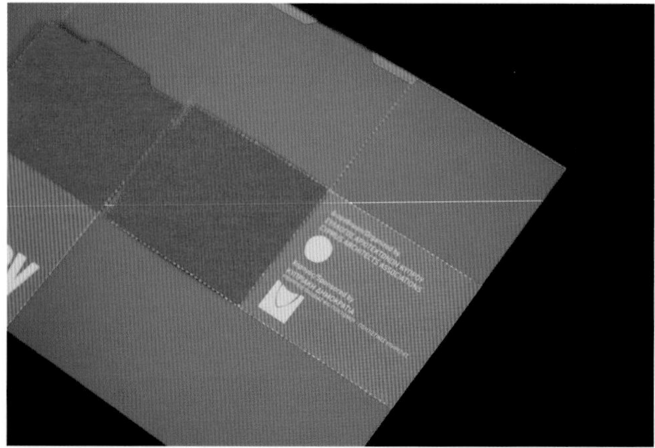

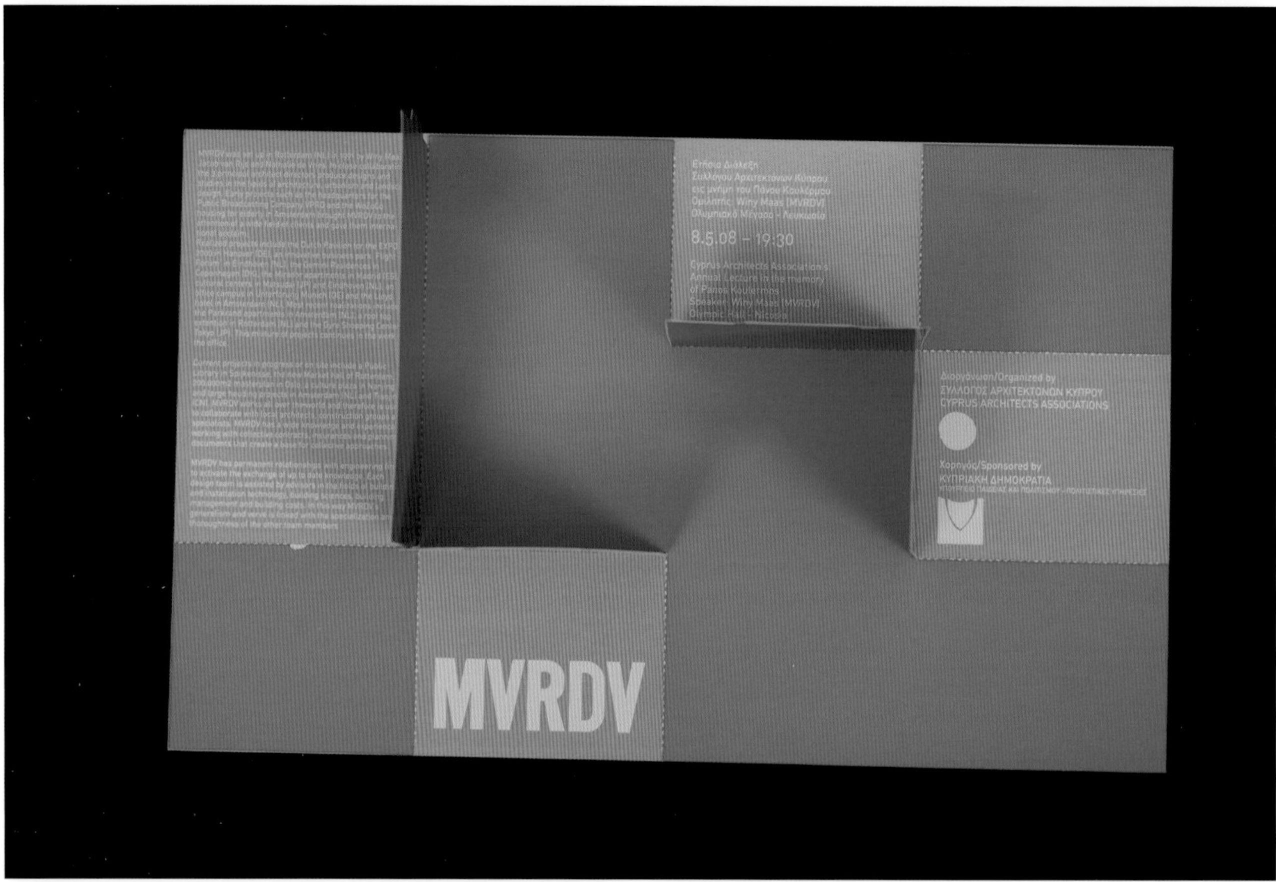

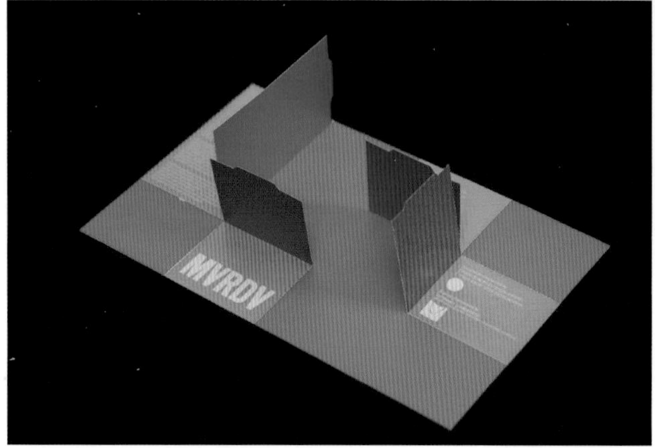

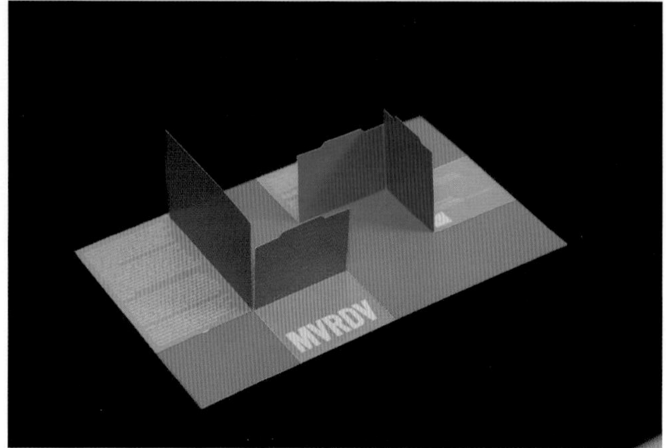

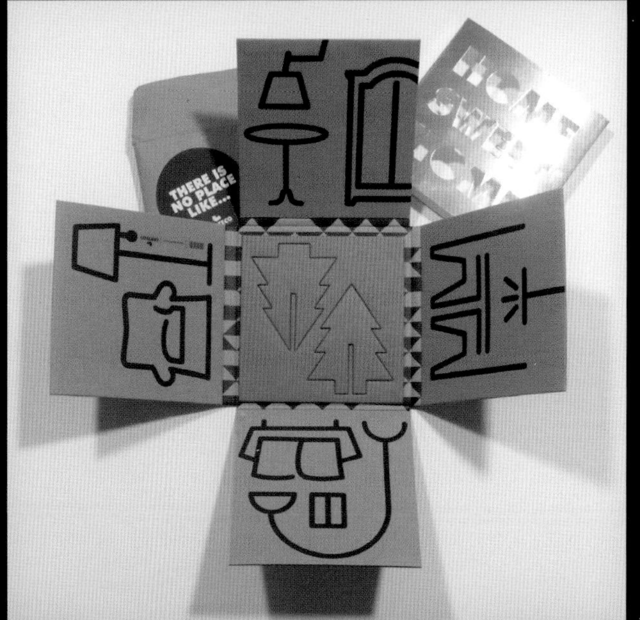

TITLE
Carteco Xmas card
COMPANY
busybuilding
CLIENT
Carteco
COUNTRY
Greece

BRONZE
CARDS & FLYERS

TITLE
4 oktober
Company
Obed Vleugels
CLIENT
Willem en Liene
COUNTRY
Belgium

BRONZE
CARDS & FLYERS

TITLE
invitation card
IsolaMarras f/W 2008
COMPANY
studio paolo bazzani
CLIENT
Isola Marras
COUNTRY
Italy

GOLD
CALENDAR

TITLE
Walking Calendar
COMPANY
Graphic design studio by Yurko Gutsulyak
CLIENT
Huggies
DESIGNER
Yurko Gutsulyak
ART DIRECTOR
Yurko Gutsulyak
COUNTRY
Ukraine

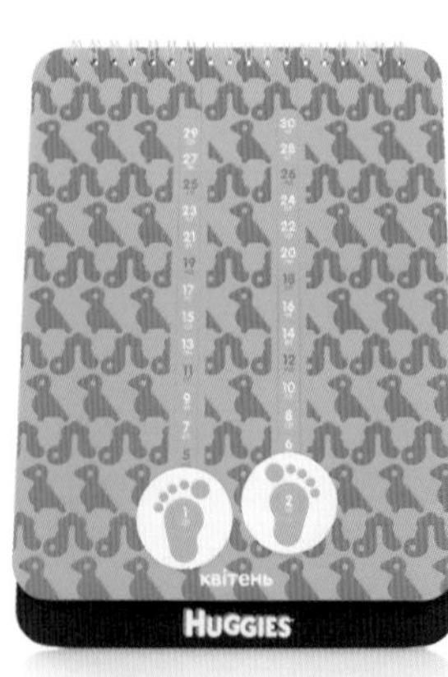

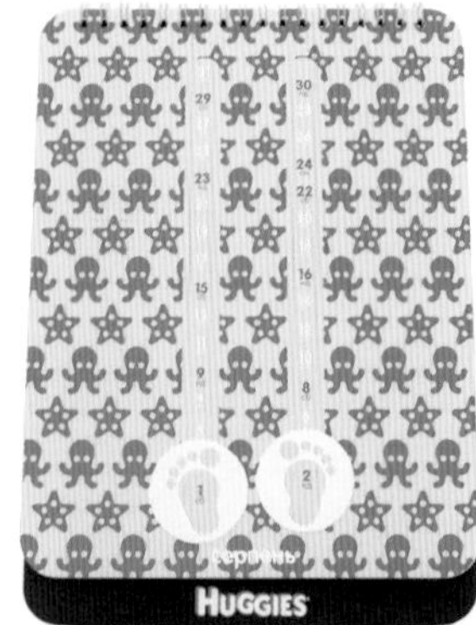

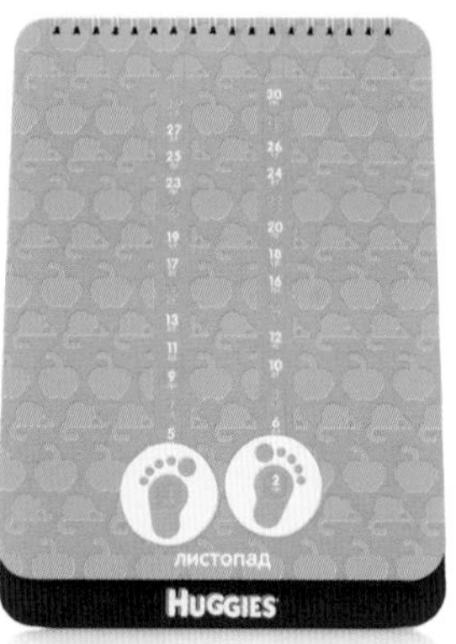

Young children have no notion of time. They live in the present, and the future is even more unclear than yesterday, which is just a vague memory. The winning calendar is an appealing solution to materially mark time by linking it to that unit of human measurement: the step.

GOLD
CALENDAR

TITLE
Verstand op Nul
Blik op Oneindig
COMPANY
Ando bv
CLIENT
Ando bv
DESIGNER
Ontwerphaven
ART DIRECTOR
Fokko Tamminga
CREATIVE DIRECTOR
Suzanne Hertogs
WRITER
Nicole Ros
COUNTRY
Netherlands

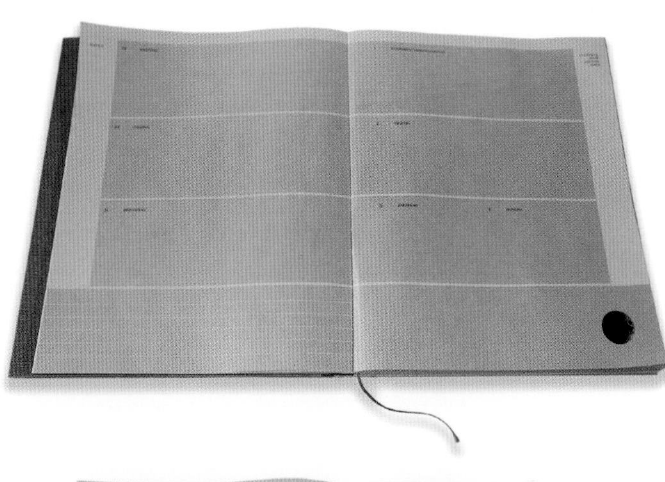

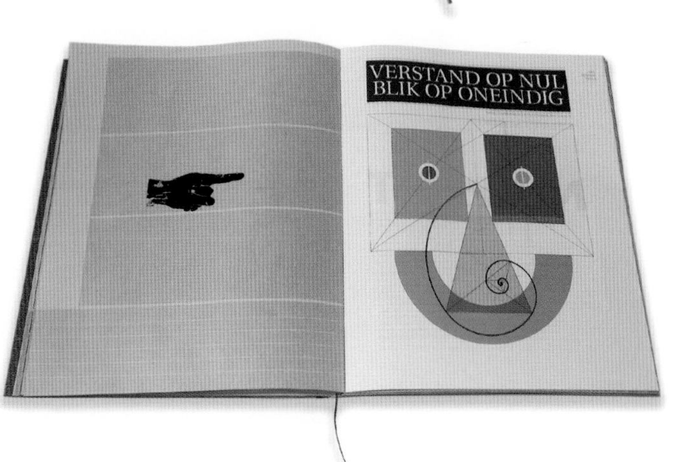

Calendar and diary are measures of time. They also provide milestones of passing time. For appointments or unmissable events, they are the scrupulous stewards of our histories and future memories. With time now speeding by, this abridged form of the journal of yesteryear deserves excellent craftwork. And in our electronic age, Ando's diary plays graciously with forms and materials to give each moment a sense of plenitude.

BRONZE
CALENDAR

TITLE
Best of Blue
COMPANY
brand.david
Kommunikation GmbH
CLIENT
BluePrint AG
COUNTRY
Germany

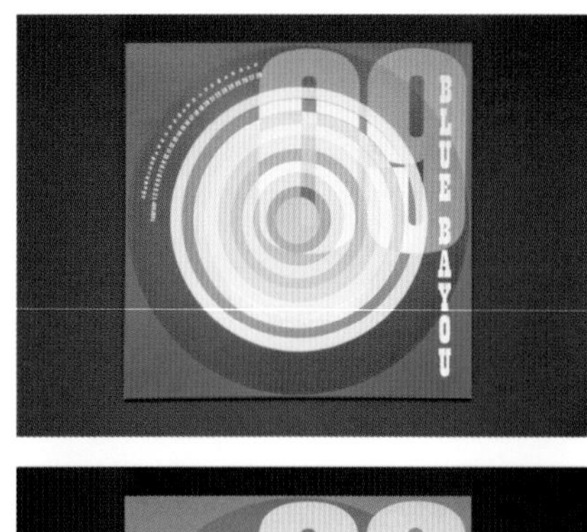

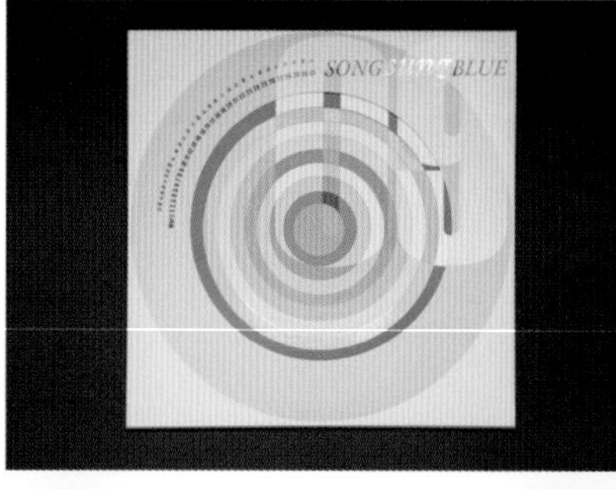

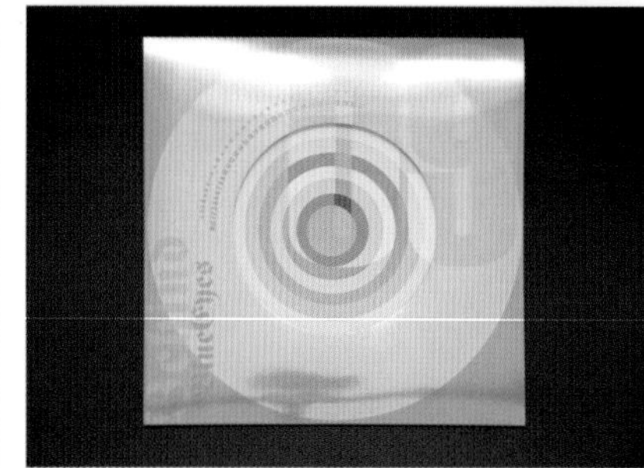

BRONZE
CALENDAR

TITLE
Hionidis 2009
COMPANY
beetroot design group
CLIENT
Hionidis mens fashion
COUNTRY
Greece

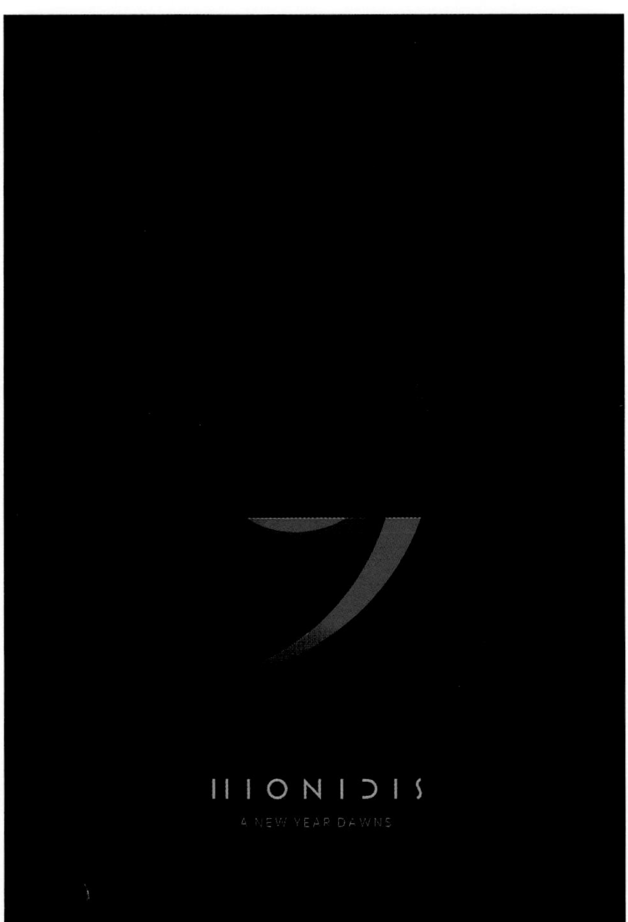

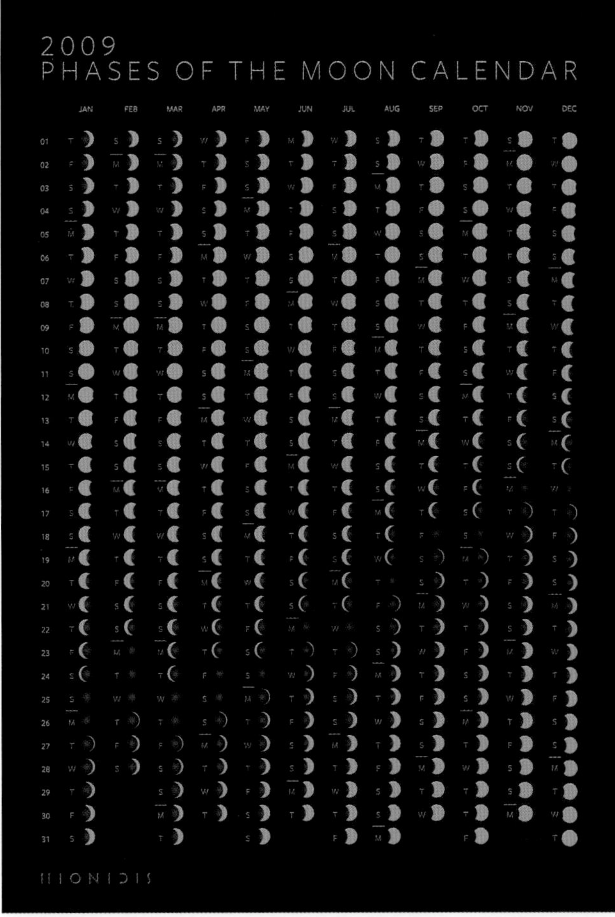

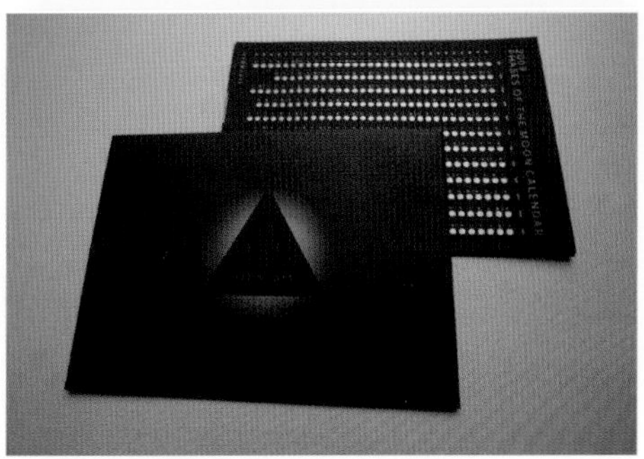

BRONZE
CALENDAR

TITLE
Igepa
COMPANY
Bruketa&Zinic OM
CLIENT
Igepa Plana Papers
COUNTRY
Croatia

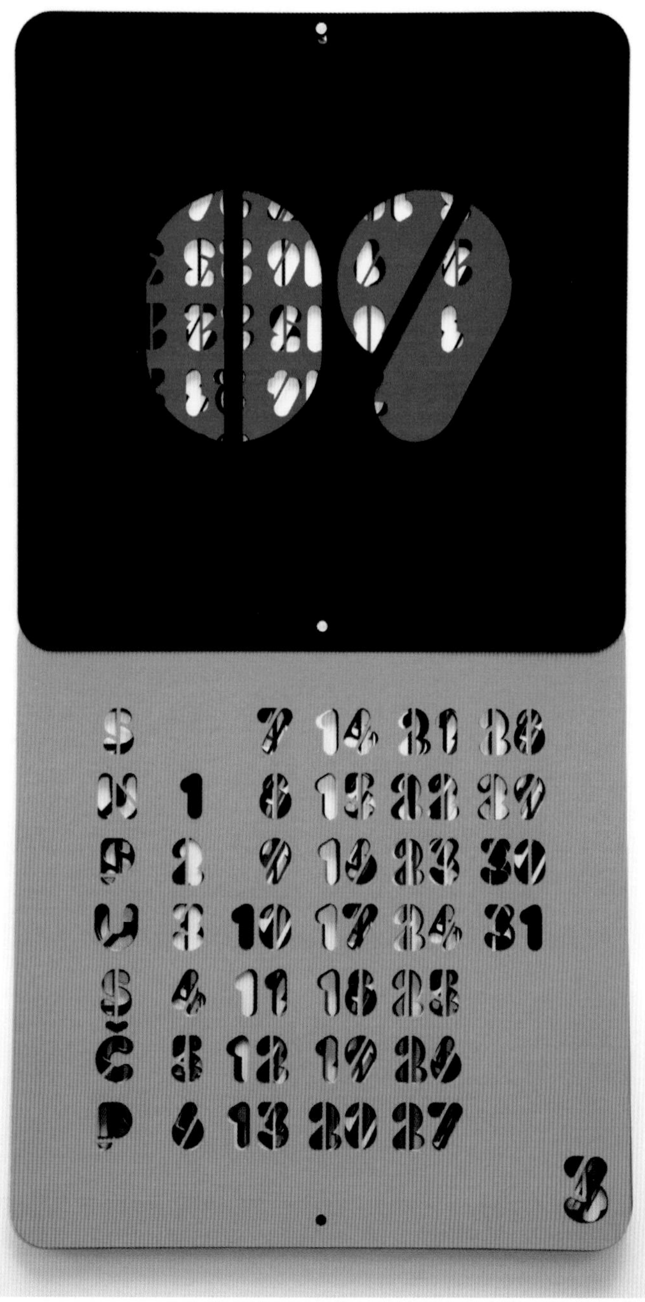

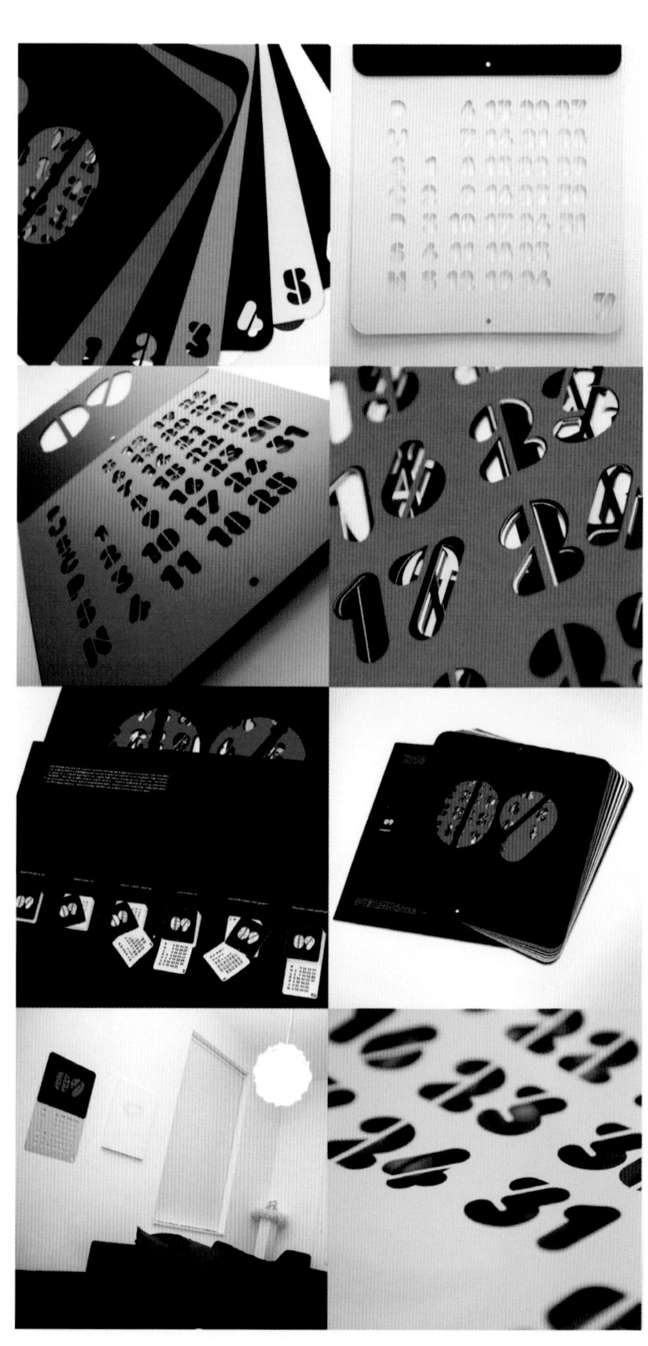

FINALIST
CALENDAR

01.

TITLE
Que Calendar
DESIGNER
Selin Estroti
CLIENT
Que
COUNTRY
Turkey

02.

TITLE
Sberbank calendar
COMPANY
fastway
CLIENT
Volgo-Vyatskiy Sberbank
URL
http://ideasthatrock.ru/portfolio/design/sberbank/calendar2009
COUNTRY
Russia

SILVER
SINGLE POSTER

José González – In Our Nature Tour

Zwölf Medien

2fortheroad booking
Berlin

Stefan Guzy
Björn Wiede

Stefan Guzy
Björn Wiede

Germany

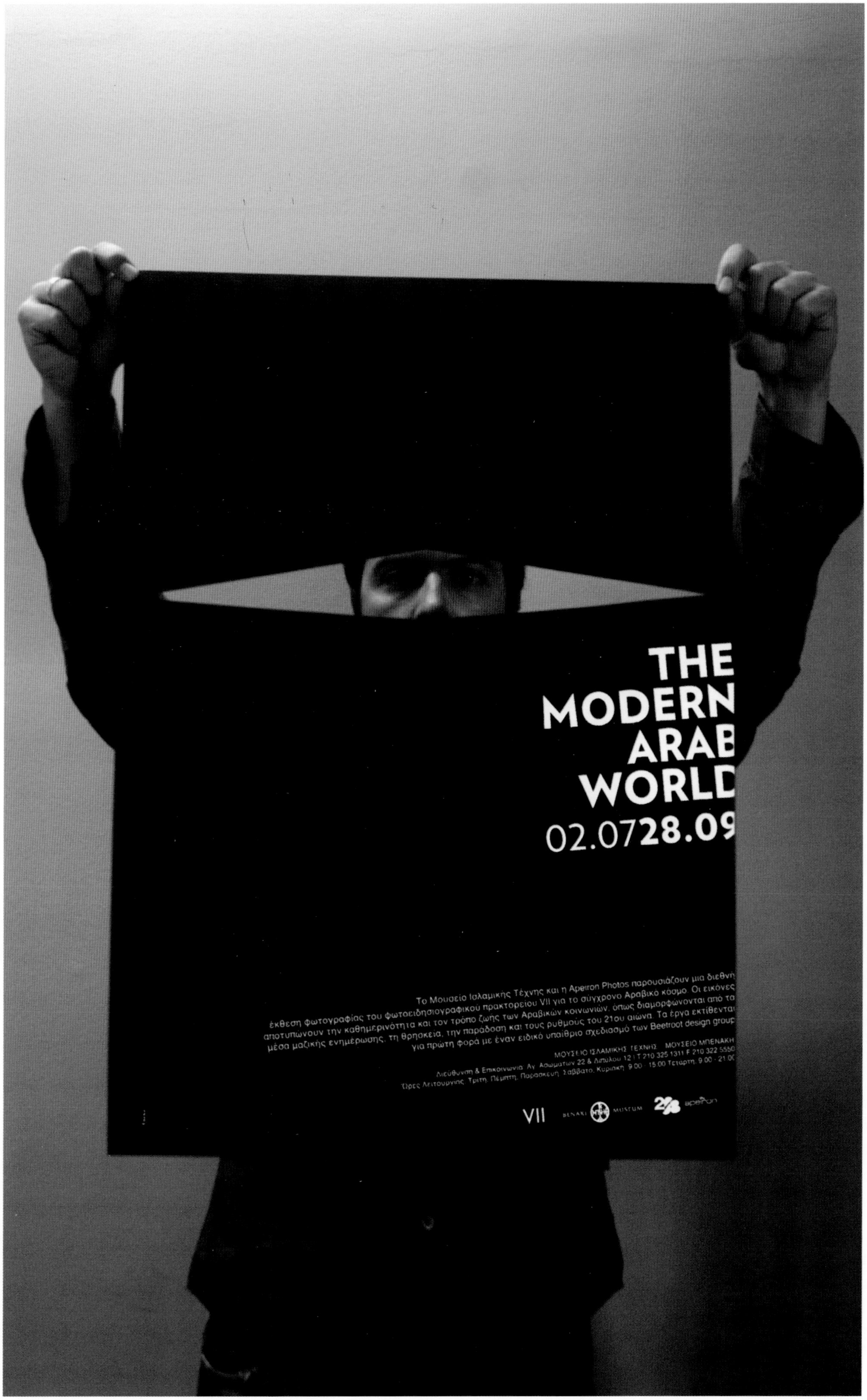

SILVER
SINGLE POSTER

TITLE
Arab world
COMPANY
beetroot design group
CLIENT
Apeiron photos / VII / Benaki Museum
DESIGNERS
Michalis Rafail
Ilias Pantikakis
ART DIRECTORS
Vagelis Liakos
Alexis Nikou
CREATIVE DIRECTOR
Yiannis Charalambopoulos
COUNTRY
Greece

Papierkomplizen

Viola Zimmermann
Madeleine Stahel

Sonderegger AG
Fischer Papier
Buchbinderei Burkh

Switzerland

BRONZE
SINGLE POSTER

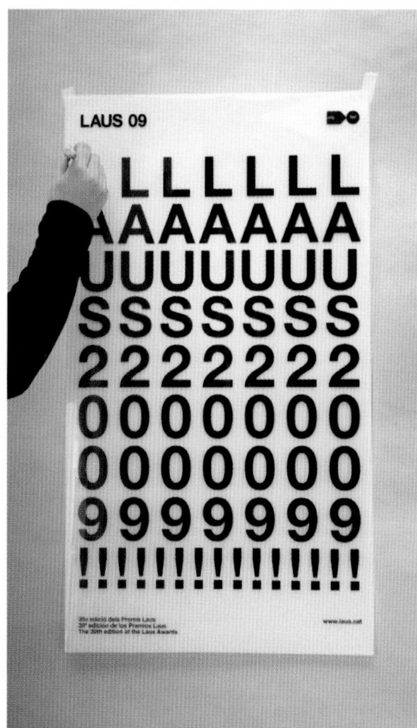

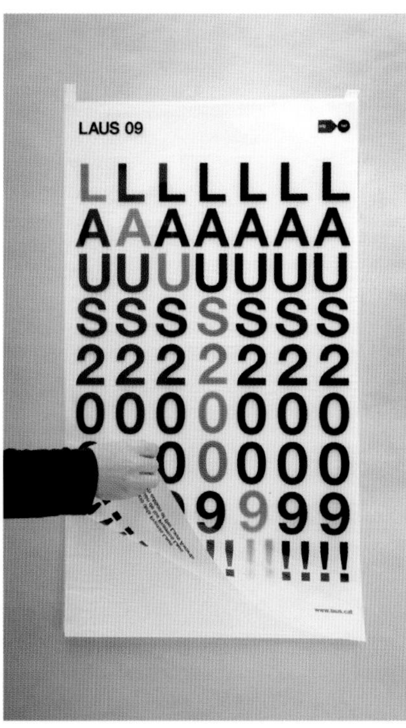

01.
TITLE
Laus Rub-ons
COMPANY
Dfraile
CLIENT
Adg-Fad
COUNTRY
Spain

02.
TITLE
Footstation
COMPANY
CCRZ
CLIENT
Ufficio Cultura di chiasso
COUNTRY
Switzerland

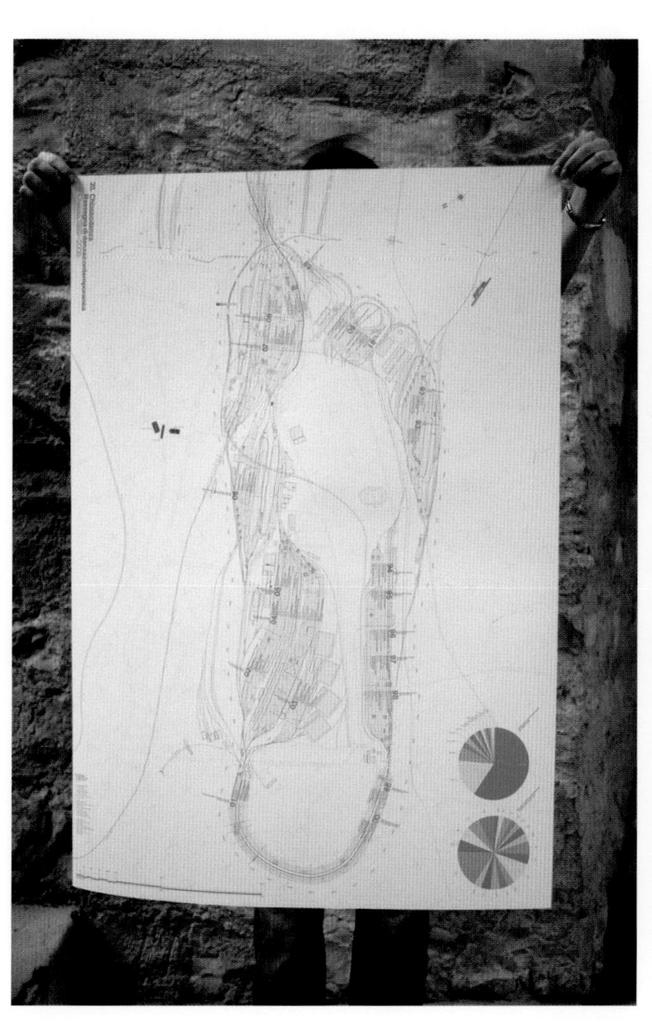

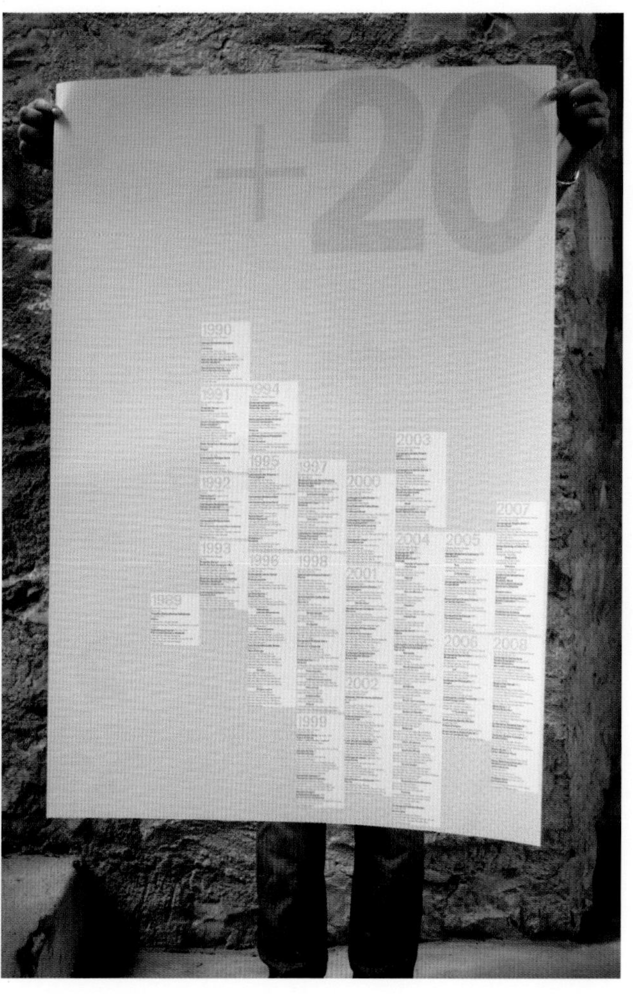

BRONZE
SINGLE POSTER

01.
TITLE
EEE OOO Greek renaissance
COMPANY
pi6 communication design
CLIENT
Apeiron Photos
COUNTRY
Greece

02.
TITLE
Evolution Creates Diversity
COMPANY
gewerk
CLIENT
VolkswagenStiftung
COUNTRY
Germany

BRONZE
SINGLE POSTER

03.
TITLE
The Long Night of Muses and Museums
COMPANY
KW Neun Grafikagentur
CLIENT
Kulturbüro der Stadt Augsburg
COUNTRY
Germany

04.
TITLE
Beyondrisør
COMPANY
Bleed
CLIENT
Risør kommune
COUNTRY
Norway

BRONZE
SINGLE POSTER

05.
TITLE
Distance
COMPANY
David Torrents
CLIENT
Arjowiggins
COUNTRY
Spain

06.
TITLE
Damien Hirst
COMPANY
Bleed
CLIENT
Studio Hugo Opdal
COUNTRY
Norway

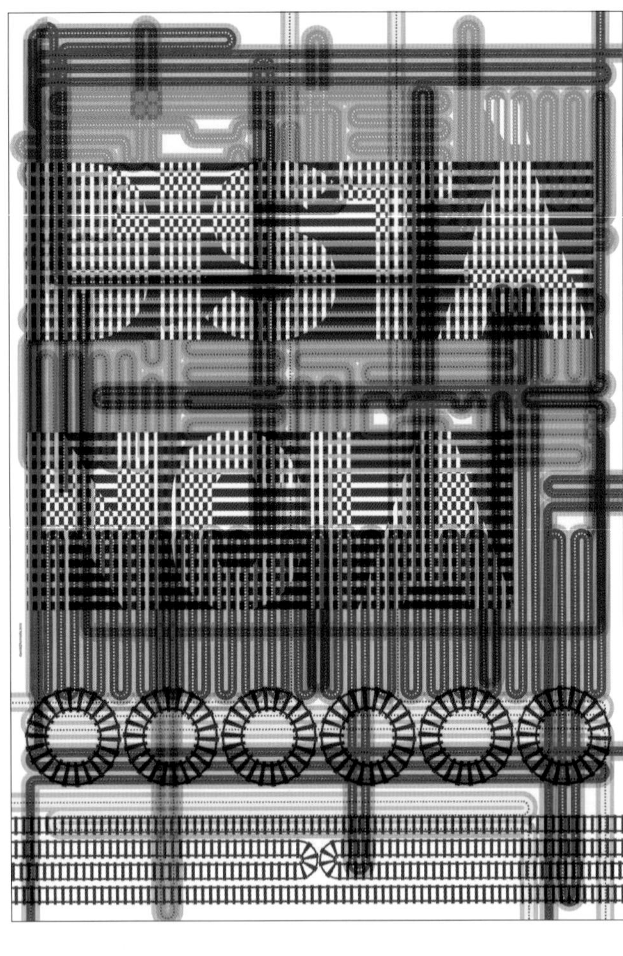

BRONZE
SINGLE POSTER

07.
TITLE
Solid Coded
COMPANY
KW Neun Grafikagentur
CLIENT
FH Augsburg
COUNTRY
Germany

08.
TITLE
bauer'08
DESIGNERS
Simone Ciotola with Francesca Ceccoli
CLIENT
cfp Bauer (public design and photography school)
COUNTRY
Italy

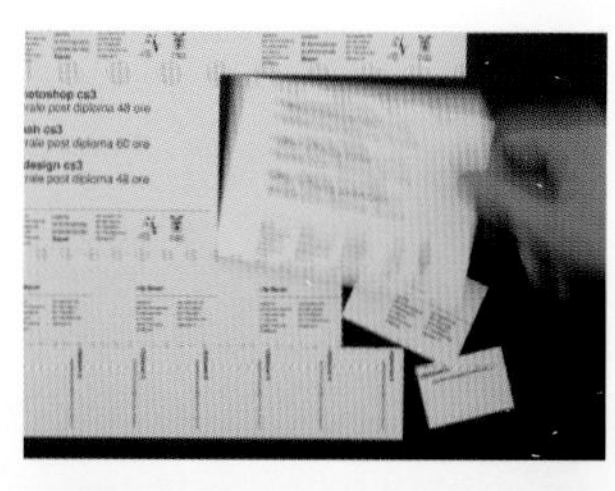

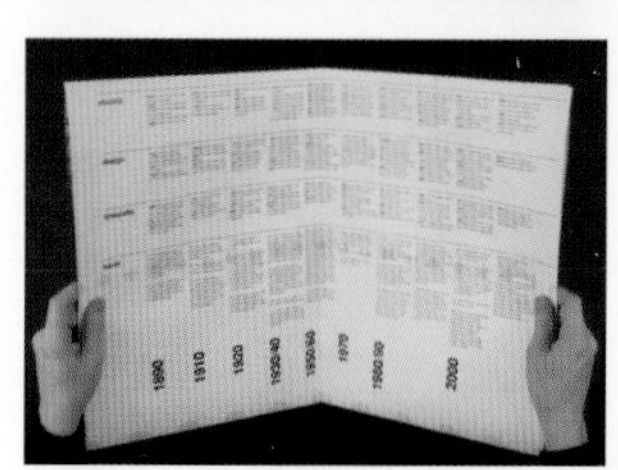

GOLD
POSTER SERIES

TITLE
Stevie Wonder tribute party
COMPANY
Bendita Gloria
CLIENT
El Refugi
DESIGNERS
Alba Rosell
Santi Fuster
ART DIRECTORS
Alba Rosell
Santi Fuste
CREATIVE DIRECTORS
Alba Rosell
Santi Fuster
COUNTRY
Spain

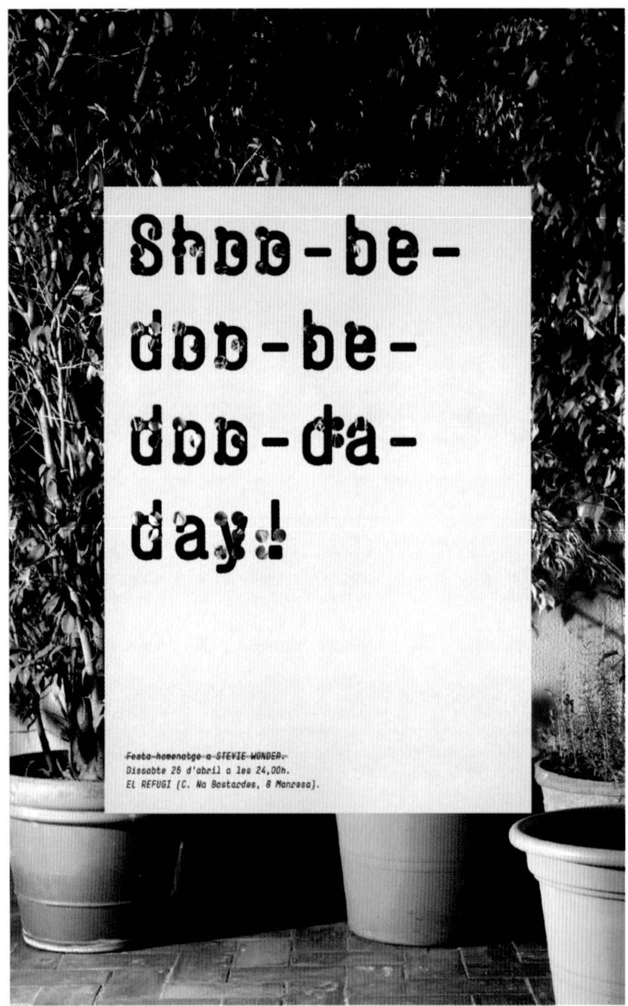

A picture reveals itself in the course of a discovery that engages emotions and knowledge. A poster must more typically communicate its message in one stunning moment. In this series of posters for a concert of music by Stevie Wonder, the designer aptly deployed several ideas: with the titles of universally-known songs; with the dual roman/braille alphabet to signify one of the singer's characteristics; the cut-out braille dots that express absence; and lastly, the monochrome that symbolises the binary quality of seeing and not seeing. It is a poster with an instant message, and which plays on the senses.

Isn't
she
lovely?
Festa-homenatge a STEVIE WONDER.
Dissabte 26 d'abril a les 24,00h.
EL REFUGI (C. Na Bastardes, 8 Manresa).

SILVER
POSTER SERIES

TITLE
Syzygy
COMPANY
Astrid Stavro
CLIENT
Art Directors Club of Europe
DESIGNERS
Astrid Stavro
Richard Sarson
Ana Domínguez
ART DIRECTOR
Astrid Stavro
CREATIVE DIRECTOR
Astrid Stavro
DESIGN DIRECTOR
Astrid Stavro
COUNTRY
Spain

Nippon Connection 2008

Bergmann Studios

Nippon Connection e. V.

K. Baumann
S. Beck
K. Bergmann
A. J. Nowitzki

K. Baumann
S. Beck
K. Bergmann
A. J. Nowitzki

K. Baumann
S. Beck
K. Bergmann
A. J. Nowitzki

K. Baumann
S. Beck
K. Bergmann
A. J. Nowitzki

K. Baumann
S. Beck
K. Bergmann
A. J. Nowitzki

Germany

BRONZE
POSTER SERIES

TITLE
The DeSoto Caucus
COMPANY
Designbolaget
CLIENT
The DeSoto Caucus
COUNTRY
Denmark

BRONZE
POSTER SERIES

TITLE
MVRDV
COMPANY
beetroot design group
CLIENT
Cyprus Architects Association
COUNTRY
Greece

BRONZE
POSTER SERIES

TITLE
Amsterdam Sinfonietta Poster Series 2008
COMPANY
Studio Dumbar
CLIENT
Amsterdam Sinfonietta
COUNTRY
Netherlands

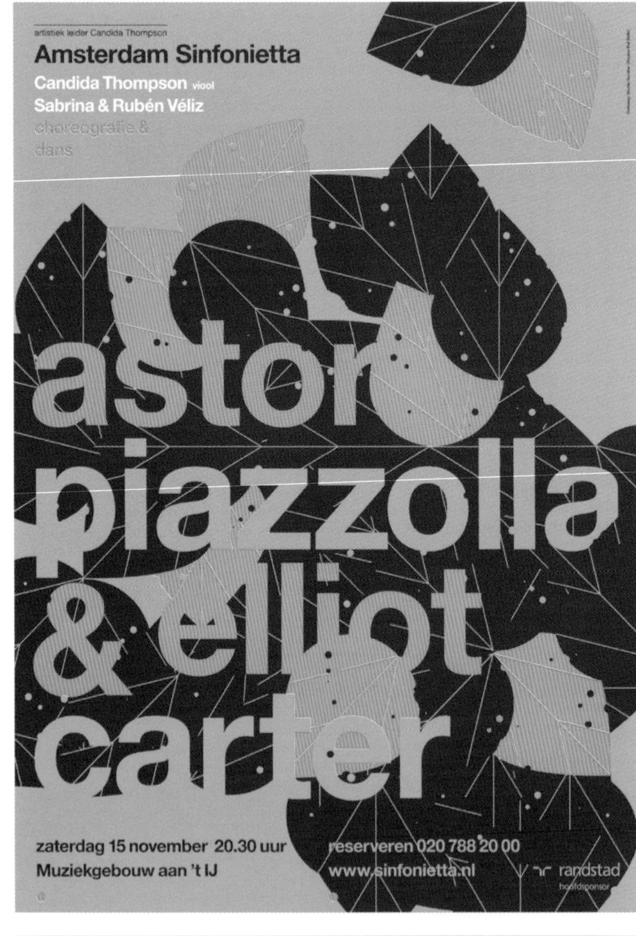

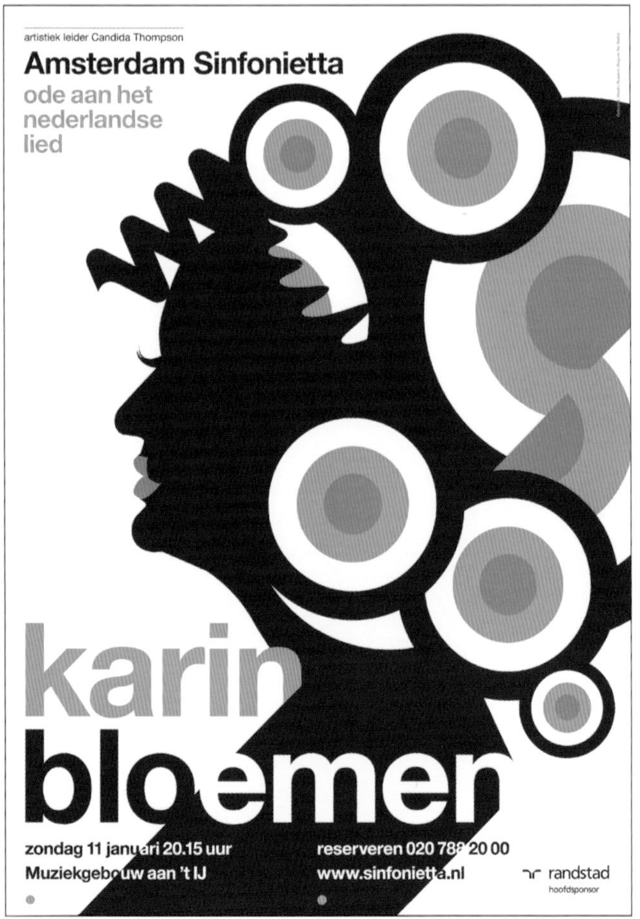

BRONZE
POSTER SERIES

TITLE
The institute
COMPANY
atelier Julian Legendre
CLIENT
Conservatoire/Ville d'Orléans
COUNTRY
France

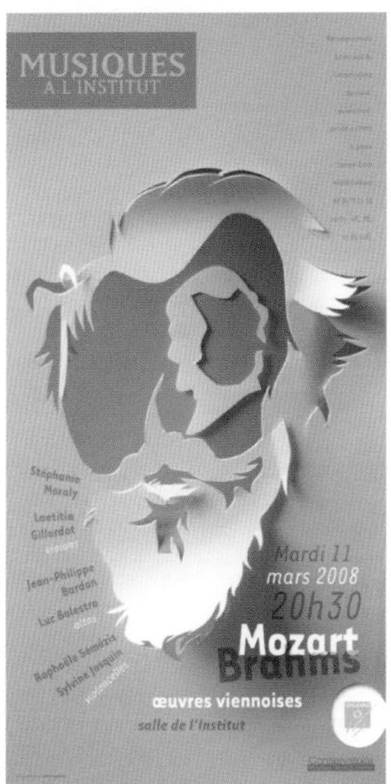

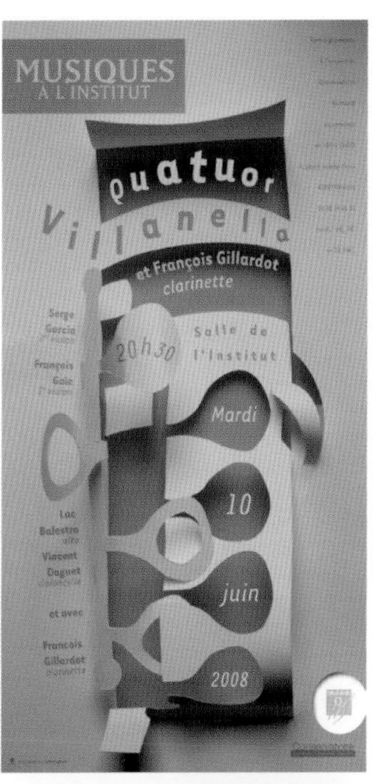

CASSIOPEIA
APRESENTA
→ DE & COM
ALEXANDRE OSÓRIO
I FEEL LIFE
LIKE A
CIRCUS
OF LIES
22 → 25 Fev '08
27 Fev → 1 MAR / 22H → PLANO B
R. CÂNDIDO DOS REIS, 30 PORTO
dgARTES
plano B

CASSIOPEIA
APRESENTA
→ DE & COM
ALEXANDRE OSÓRIO
I FEEL LIFE
LIKE A
CIRCUS
OF LIES
22 → 25 Fev '08
27 Fev → 1 MAR / 22H → PLANO B
R. CÂNDIDO DOS REIS, 30 PORTO
dgARTES
plano B

FINALIST
POSTER SERIES

01.
TITLE
What does your body tells you?
COMPANY
SE IDEA AB
CLIENT
Härnösands ryggklinik
COUNTRY
Sweden

02.
TITLE
radiodialoge
COMPANY
sapp+scheufele OEG
CLIENT
radiofabrik salzburg
URL
www.radiodialoge.at
COUNTRY
Austria

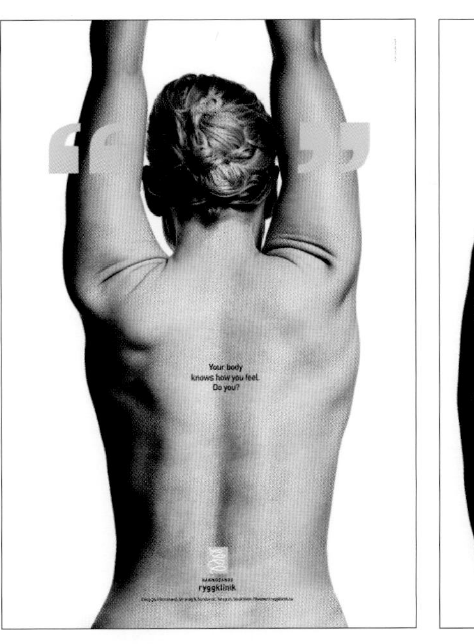

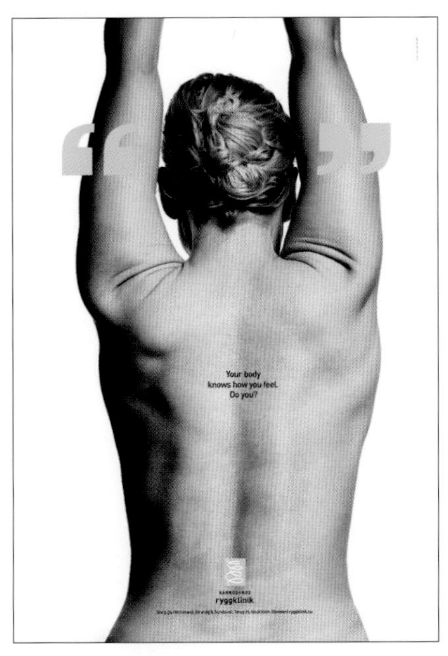

SILVER
SIGNS & DISPLAYS

TITLE
Signage System Muenchner Technologiezentrum
COMPANY
L2M3 Kommunikationsdesign GmbH
CLIENT
Stadtwerke Muenchen
DESIGNERS
Sascha Lobe
Frank Geiger
CREATIVE DIRECTOR
Sascha Lobe
DESIGN DIRECTOR
Sascha Lobe
COUNTRY
Germany

B
B4.12
MANFRED MUELLER CONSULTING
A4.12-A3.14
A4.12-A3.14
COMMUNICATION TECHNOLOGIE
B4.12
A4.12-A3.14
A4.12-A3.14
COMMUNICATION TECHNOLOGIE
B3.12
MANFRED MUELLER CONSULTING
B3.12-B3.14
MANFRED MUELLER-MAIER
SABINE MUSTERMANN
B3.12-B3.14
COMMUNICATION TECHNOLOGIE
A4.12-A3.14
B0.12-B0.14
B0.12
MANFRED MUELLER-MAIER
SABINE MUSTERMANN
B0.12-B3.14
B1.12-B1.14
MANFRED MUELLER
CONSULTING
D
D1.12-A1.14
PETER BEIERHAUSER
IT INNOVATIONS
D1.12-D1.14
MANFRED MUELLER
CONSULTING
D4.12
MANFRED MUELLER CONSULTING
D4.12-A3.14
GREEN IT
D4.12-A3.14
COMMUNICATION TECHNOLOGIE
D0.01-D0.03
D-CONSULTING
D0.12-D0.14
DSF CONSULTING
INTERNATIONAL CONSULTING
D0.12
MANFRED MUELLER-MAIER
SABINE MUSTERMANN
D0.12-D3.14
PEER TO CUSTUMOR
INFORMATIONSSYSTEME
F
F4.12-F3.14
MANFRED MUELLER
CONSULTING
F4.12
MANFRED MUELLER CONSULTING
F4.12-F3.14
GEWWENHORST
F4.12-F3.14
COMMUNICATION TECHNOLOGIE
F4.12
SIMON & SCHLURCH
F4.12-F3.14
SZARDONZKY GMBH
F4.12-F3.14
COMMUNICATION TECHNOLOGIE
F3.12
MANFRED MUELLER CONSULTING
F3.12-F3.14
MANFRED MUELLER-MAIER
SABINE MUSTERMANN
F3.12-F3.14
COMMUNICATION TECHNOLOGIE
F2.12-F2.14
MANFRED MUELLER
CONSULTING
F1.12-F1.14
FORSCHUNGSLABOR
MÜLER & CONG
F1.12-F1.14
MANFRED MUELLER
CONSULTING
H
MANFRED MUELLER
CONSULTING
FORSCHUNGSLABOR
MAURER, BLEICHER & PARTNER
MANFRED MUELLER CONSULTING
MANFRED MUELLER-MAIER
SABINE MUSTERMANN
COMMUNICATION TECHNOLOGIE
MANFRED
MUELLER
CONSULTING
MANFRED MUELLER
CONSULTING
GRÖNINGER & BAUER
MANFRED MUELLER
CONSULTING
SCHMIDT & SÖHNE
MANFRED MUELLER-MAIER
SABINE MUSTERMANN
BLEICHENBACHER DESIGN
A
A4.12-A3.14
MANFRED MUELLER
CONSULTING
A4.12
MANFRED MUELLER CONSULTING
A4.12-A3.14
GESELLSCHAFT FÜR EDV
A4.12-A3.14
COMMUNICATION TECHNOLOGIE
A4.12
COMMUNICATION & BRAND
A4.12-A3.14
GREEN BLUE GMBH
A4.12-A3.14
COMMUNICATION TECHNOLOGIE
A3.12-A3.14
MANFRED
MUELLER
CONSULTING
A2.12-A2.14
MANFRED MUELLER
CONSULTING
A1.12-A1.14
BLU ID
SOFTWARESOLUTIONS
A1.12-A1.14
MANFRED MUELLER
CONSULTING
C
C4.12-C3.14
MANFRED MUELLER
CONSULTING
C3.12
VIVID ANIMATIONS
A4.12
COMMUNICATION IN DESIGN
A4.12-A3.14
GREEN BLUE GMBH
C3.12
MANFRED MUELLER CONSULTING
C3.12-A3.14
MANFRED MUELLER-MAIER
SABINE MUSTERMANN
C3.12-A3.14
COMMUNICATION TECHNOLOGIE
C1.12-C1.14
MANFRED MUELLER
CONSULTING
C0.12-C0.14
BLU ID
SOFTWARESOLUTIONS
C0.12
MANFRED MUELLER-MAIER
SABINE MUSTERMANN
C0.12-C3.14
SOFTWARE IN MOTION GMBH
E
E4.12
MANFRED MUELLER CONSULTING
E4.12-A3.14
BREULER HMBH
IT & NETZWERK GMBH
E4.12-A3.14
COMMUNICATION TECHNOLOGIE
E4.12
SARAGO
LÖSUNG IN MEDIEN
E4.12-A3.14
ATANA
FLUGSICHERUNG
E4.12-A3.14
COMMUNICATION & MORE
E3.12
MANFRED MUELLER CONSULTING
E3.12-A3.14
MANFRED MUELLER-MAIER
SABINE MUSTERMANN
E3.12-A3.14
COMMUNICATION TECHNOLOGIE
E1.12-A1.14
PETERS & PETERS
INTERAKTIVE MEDIEN
MANFRED
MUELLER
E0.12-A0.14
ARTCORPORATOIN
E0.12
GRAFIK UND RAUM
SABINE MUSTERMANN
E0.12-D3.14
OXIDIUM
G
MANFRED MUELLER
CONSULTING
IT & FORSCHUNGS GMBH
FORSCHUNGSLABOR MANNER
COMMUNICATION TECHNOLOGIE

SILVER
SIGNS & DISPLAYS

TITLE
Waiting for the rain
(U iscekivanju kise)
COMPANY
Studio Rasic
CLIENT
Mediterranean
Sculptors' Symposium
DESIGNER
Ante Rasicr
ART DIRECTOR
Ante Rasic
COUNTRY
Croatia

SILVER
SIGNS & DISPLAYS

TITLE
Vai com Deus
COMPANY
R2 design
CLIENT
Dr. Eduardo Fernandes
DESIGNERS
Lizá Ramalho
Artur Rebelo
ART DIRECTORS
Lizá Ramalho
Artur Rebelo
CREATIVE DIRECTORS
Lizá Ramalho
Artur Rebelo
DESIGN DIRECTORS
Lizá Ramalho
Artur Rebelo
COUNTRY
Portugal

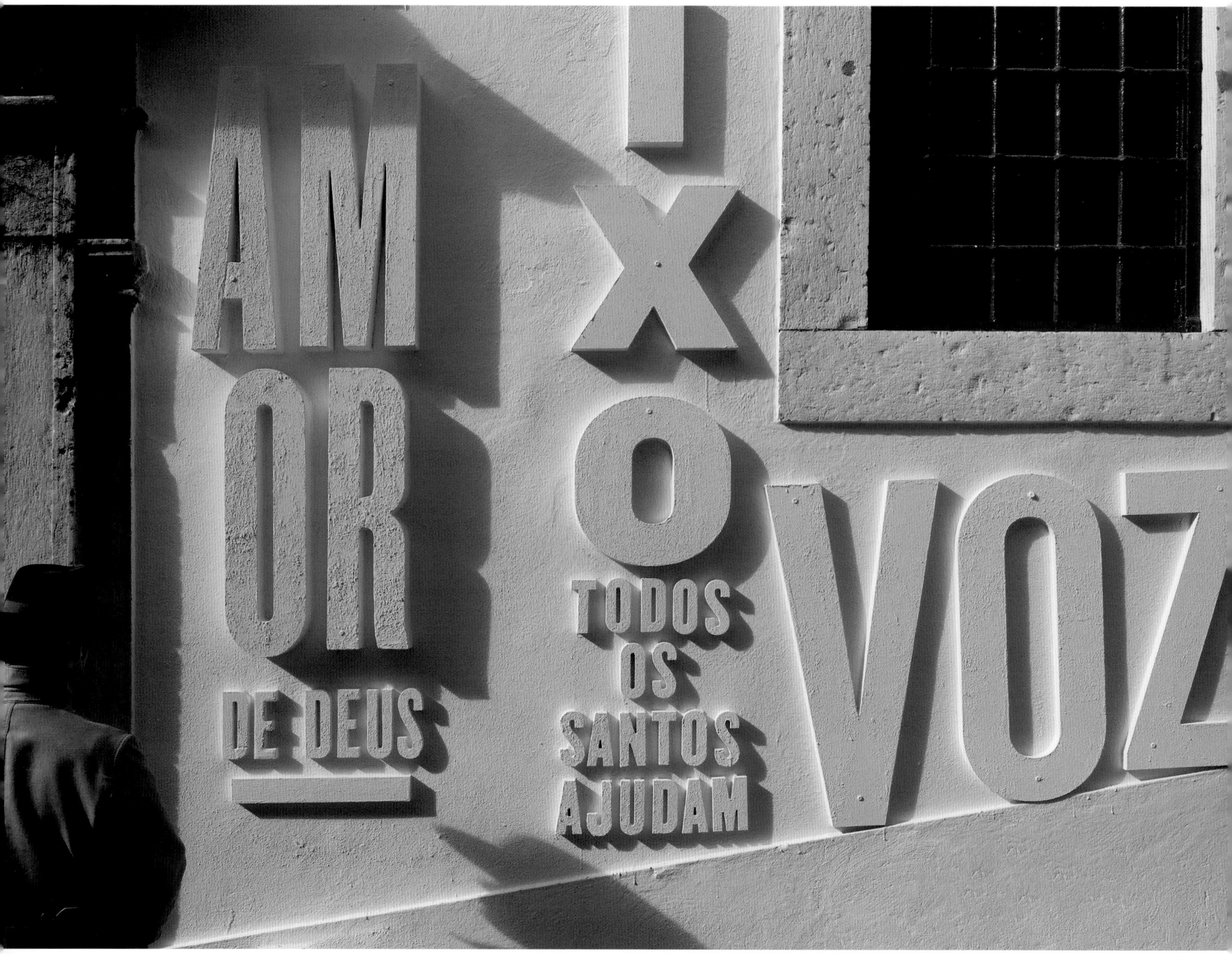

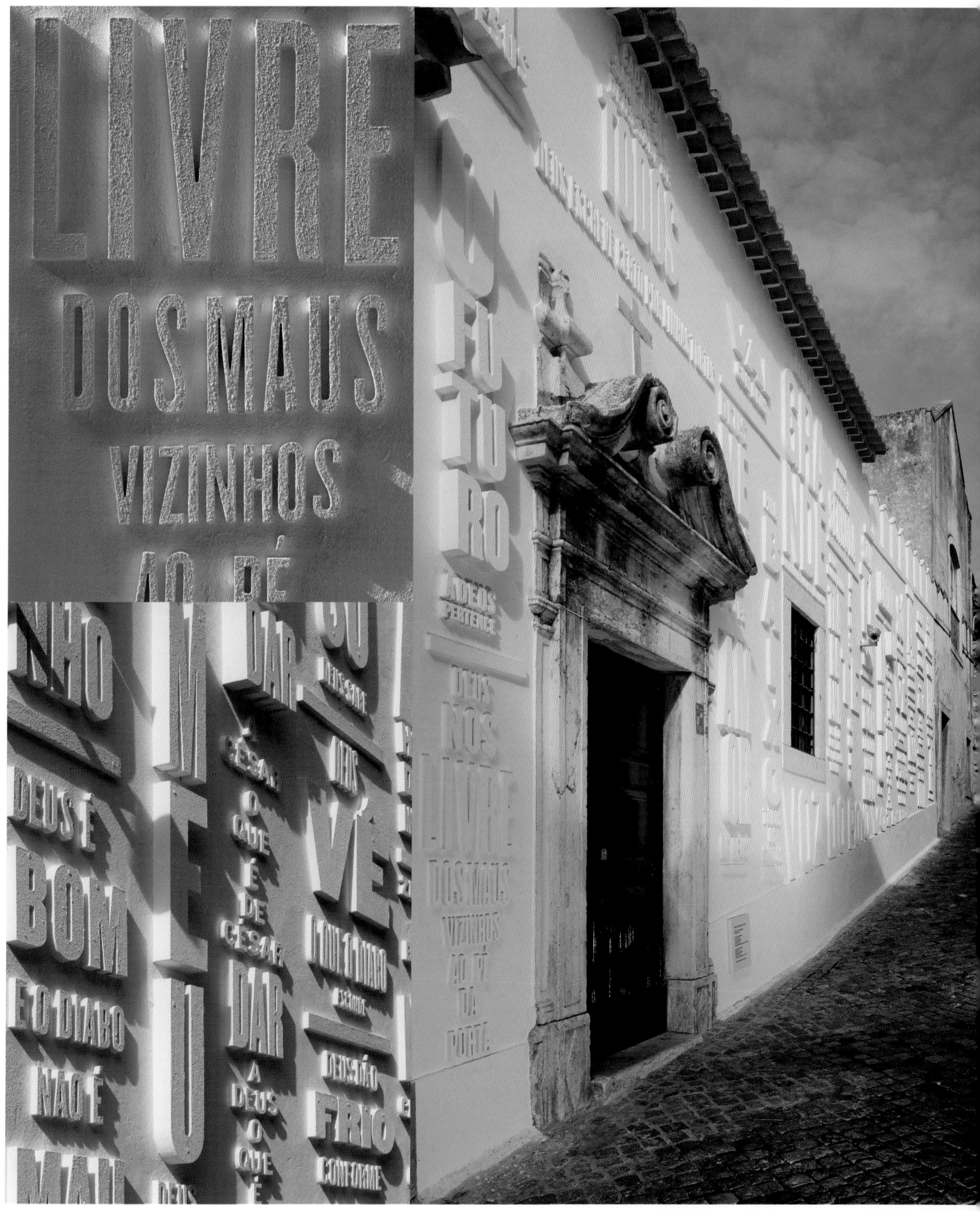
LIVRE
DOS MAUS
VIZINHOS
DEUS É
BOM
E O DIABO
NÃO É
CÉSAR
O
QUE
É
DE
CÉSAR
DAR
A
DEUS
O
QUE
DEUS SABE
DEUS
VÊ
DEUS DÁ O
FRIO
CONFORME
O
FU
TU
RO
A DEUS
PERTENCE
DEUS
NOS
LIVRE
DOS MAUS
VIZINHOS
AO PÉ
DA
PORTA

BRONZE
SIGNS & DISPLAYS

TITLE
Minimetrò
COMPANY
zup associati srl
CLIENT
Minimetrò SpA
COUNTRY
Italy

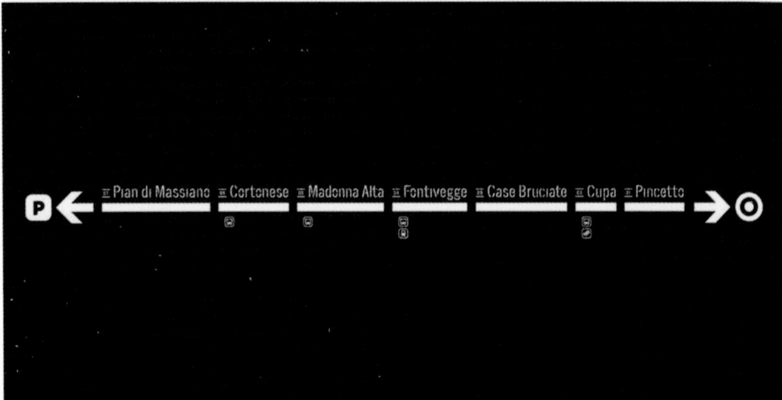

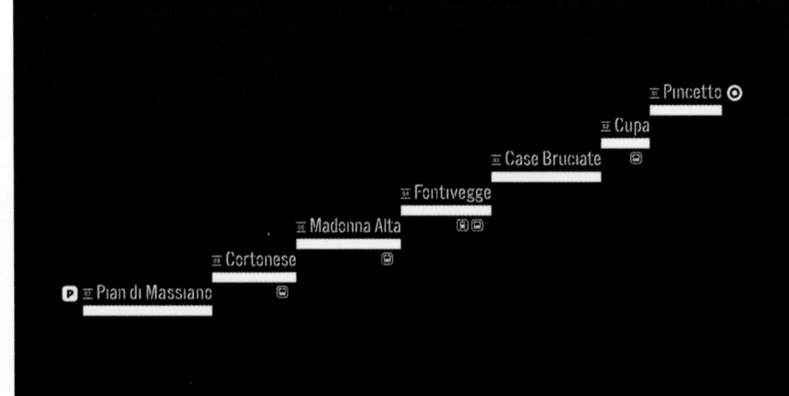

Madonna Alta
05

02 Cupa

uscita / exit

uscita / exit

Pian di Massiano

BRONZE
SIGNS & DISPLAYS

TITLE
MSF
COMPANY
Estudio Diego Feijóo
CLIENT
Médecins Sans Frontières Spain
COUNTRY
Spain

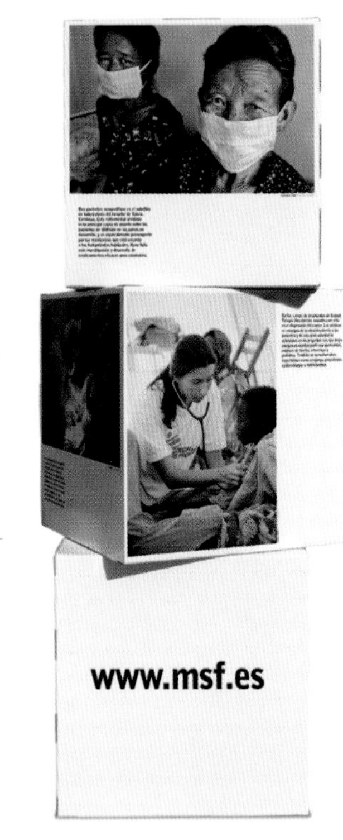

BRONZE
SIGNS & DISPLAYS

TITLE
Signage System GREY Group
COMPANY
KW43 Branddesign
CLIENT
Grey Group
COUNTRY
Germany

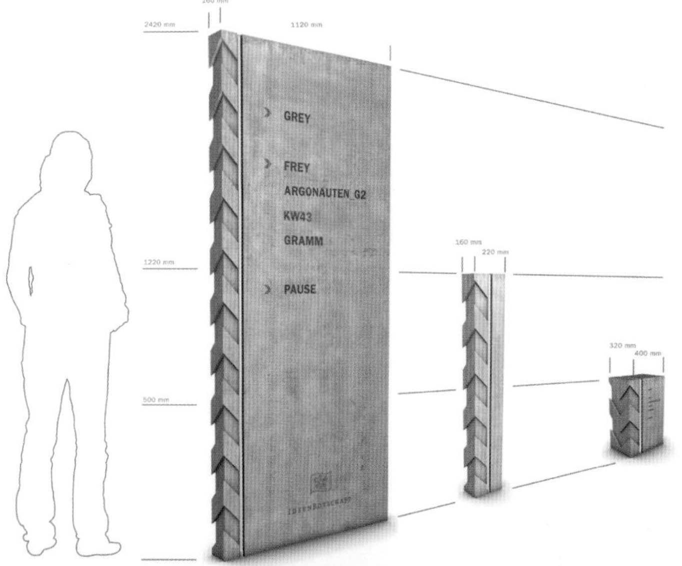

BRONZE
SIGNS & DISPLAYS

TITLE
Signaletik Volksschule Tschaggungs
COMPANY
Sigi Ramoser Sägenvier DesignKommunikation
CLIENT
Gemeinde Tschagguns / Lang Vonier Architekten
COUNTRY
Austria

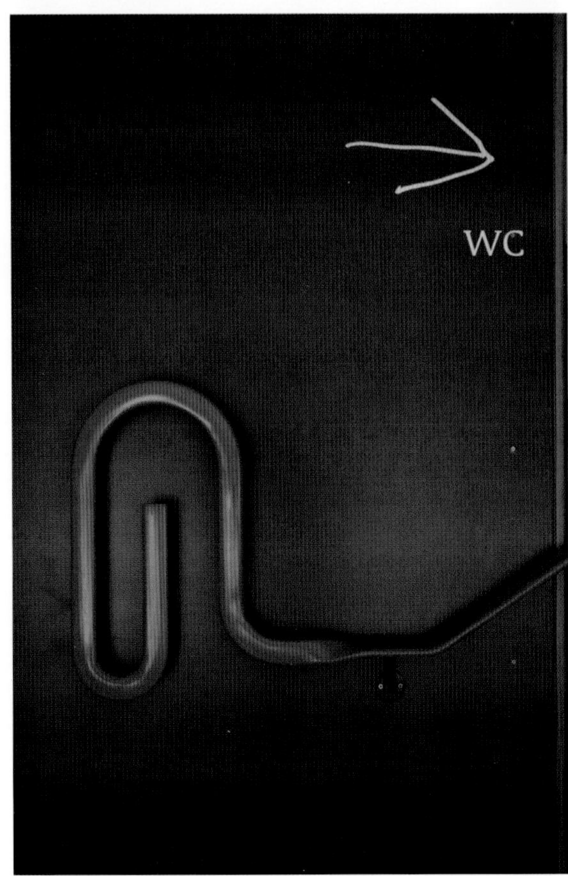

Kürschner
Sozialberaterin
Cutterin Brückenbauer

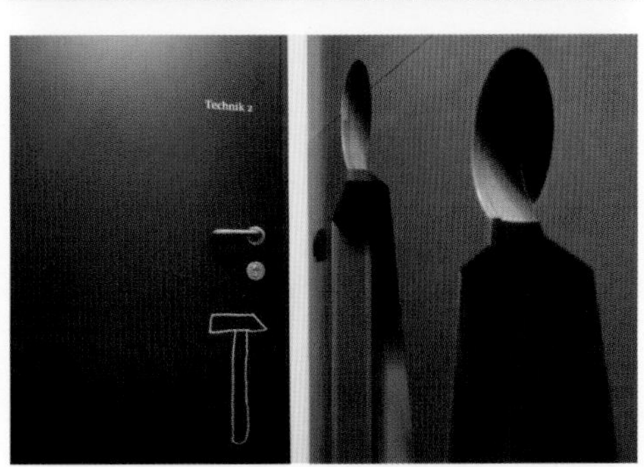

Technik 2

Umkleiden

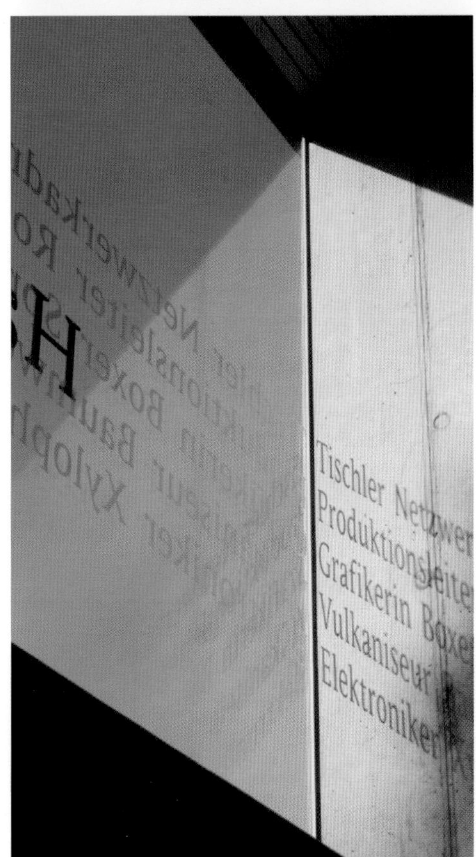

Tischler
Grafikerin
Vulkaniseur
Elektroniker

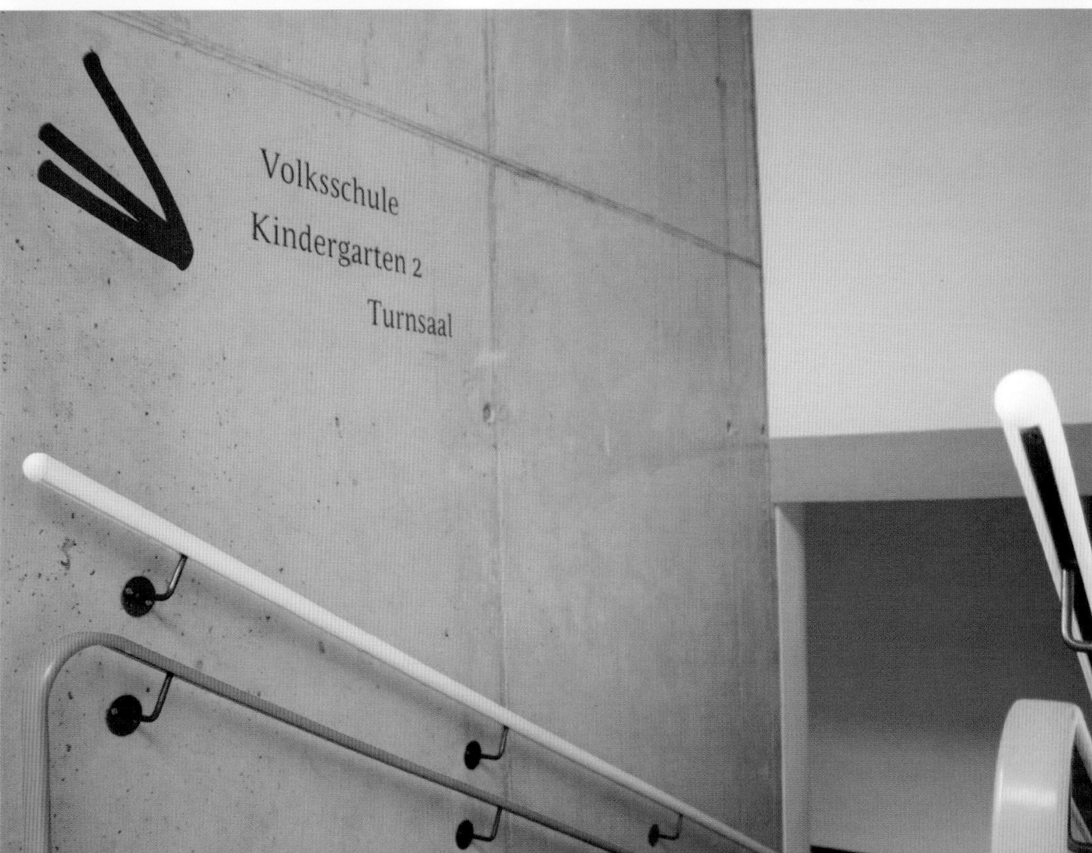

Volksschule
Kindergarten 2
Turnsaal

BRONZE
SIGNS & DISPLAYS

TITLE
TAP
COMPANY
P-06 atelier, ambientes e comunicação, lda
CLIENT
JLCG Architects
COUNTRY
Portugal

-1

DINNG DONNNG
DING DONNNG
DINNG DONNNG
badaboum
tchamtcahtcha tcham
BUM
zin zeegziengzieng
→sortie

accueil
billet terie
scenseurs
bille teri
e
info
mezzanine
auditorium
rest urant

8
log
do
bl

R
rest urant

A

GOLD
MISCELLANEOUS PRINTED

TITLE
MUMOK Placemats
COMPANY
bauer konzept
& gestaltung gmbh
CLIENT
MUMOK Museum
Moderner Kunst Stiftung
Ludwig Wien
DESIGNER
Erwin K. Bauer
PHOTOGRAPHERS
Janto Lenherr
Michael Strobl
COUNTRY
Austria

Besuchen Sie uns, holen Sie sich Ihren Gutschein
für ein ermäßigtes Ticket ins MUMOK von der Rezeption!
Visit the Museum of Modern Art Vienna! Collect your voucher
for a reduced admission from the reception!

MuseumsQuartier
Museumsplatz 1
A-1070 Wien
www.mumok.at

HOTEL
VIENNART
WIEN

17.03.2006 – 21.05.2006 Kontakt – Die Kunstsammlung der Erste Bank-Gruppe | **17.03.2006 – 21.05.2006** Plamen Dejanoff – Planets of Comparison | **05.05.2006 – 16.07.2006** Wiener Aktionismus **bis 17.5.2006** Highlights der Klassischen Moderne | **bis 16.7.2006** Nouveau Réalisme | **09.06.2006 – 1.10.2006** Why Pictures Now? – Fotografie, Film, Video seit 1970

In museums, I sometimes feel as if I am in a shopping mall or in a big brand's flagship store, surrounded by people who walk along, attracted by this or that item in a cavern of treasures. But do they grasp the dimension of the works around them? Temple and consumption are two concepts that nowadays combine in many places – shops, stadia, concert venues, supermarkets, museums, churches, and so on. Mumok's poster series fits the spirit of this dual themes. By referencing the work in the visitor's everyday setting, the museum makes the artistic act closer and more accessible. The metaphorical idea will bring a kindly smile to the faces of the initiated, and kindle a desire for discovery in anyone who is less well versed, and who will at last find out a little more about where they are.

SILVER
MISCELLANEOUS PRINTED

TITLE
Postage stamp mushrooms
COMPANY
Studio't Brandt Weer
CLIENT
TNT Post Nederland
DESIGNERS
Studio't Brandt Weer:
Marenthe Otten
Koen Geurts
ART DIRECTOR
Marenthe Otten
ILLUSTRATOR
Marenthe Otten
PHOTOGRAPHERS
Taylor F. Lockwood
Eric Etman
Chiel Noordeloos
DK Images
COUNTRY
Netherlands

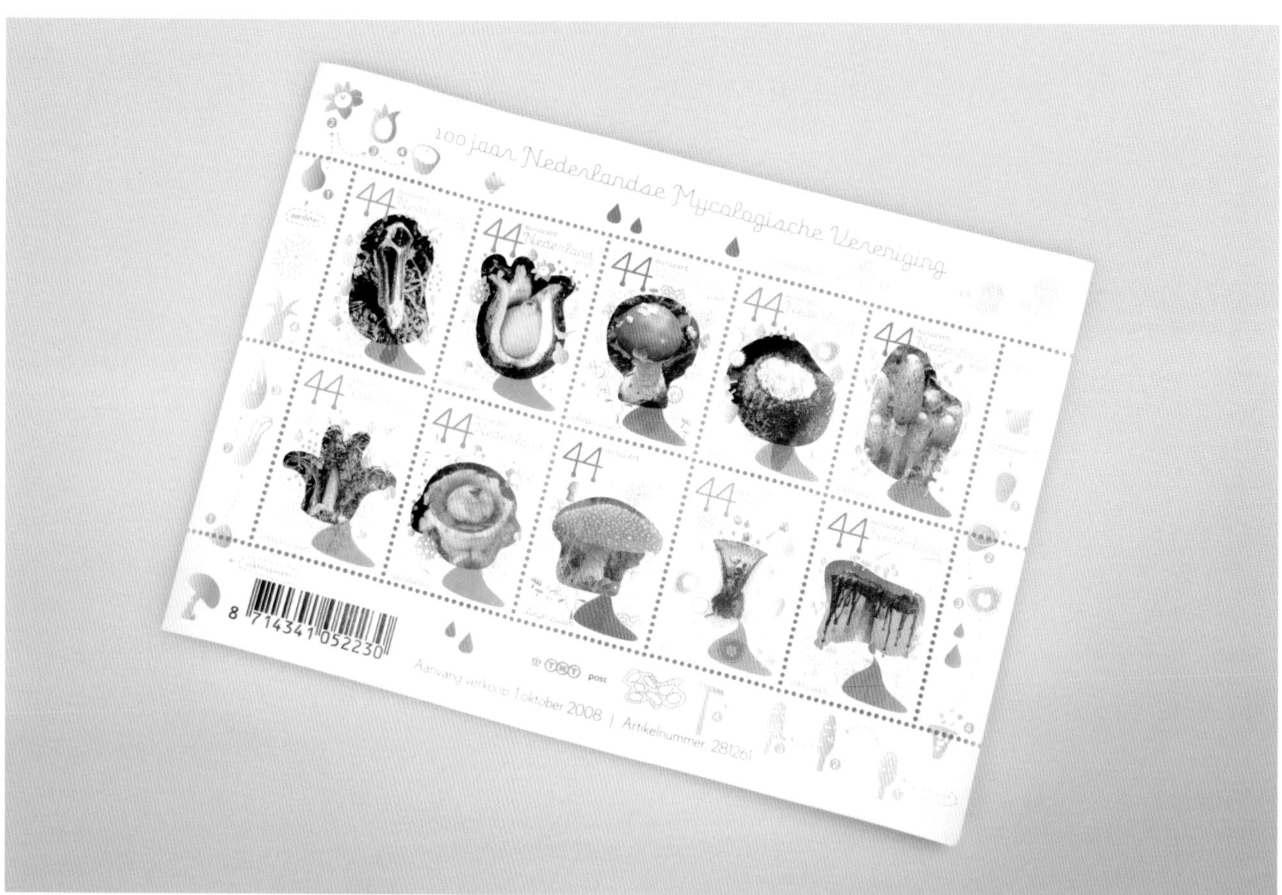

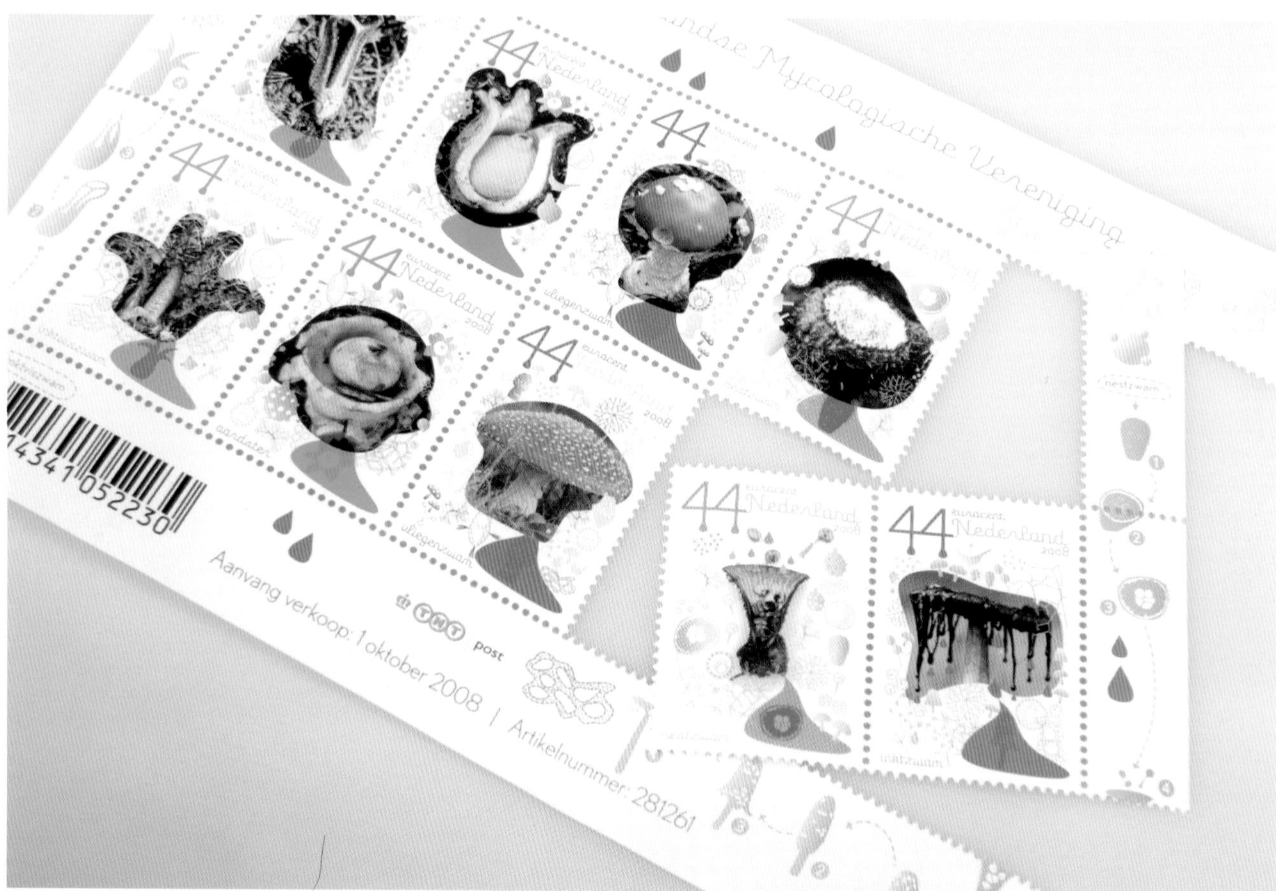

TNT Green Stamps

De Designpolitie

TNT

Designpolitie

Designpolitie

Designpolitie

Designpolitie

Designpolitie

Designpolitie & TNT

Designpolitie

Netherlands

BRONZE
MISCELLANEOUS PRINTED

TITLE
q-type
COMPANY
Kochan & Partner
CLIENT
Forum Typografie e. V.
COUNTRY
Germany

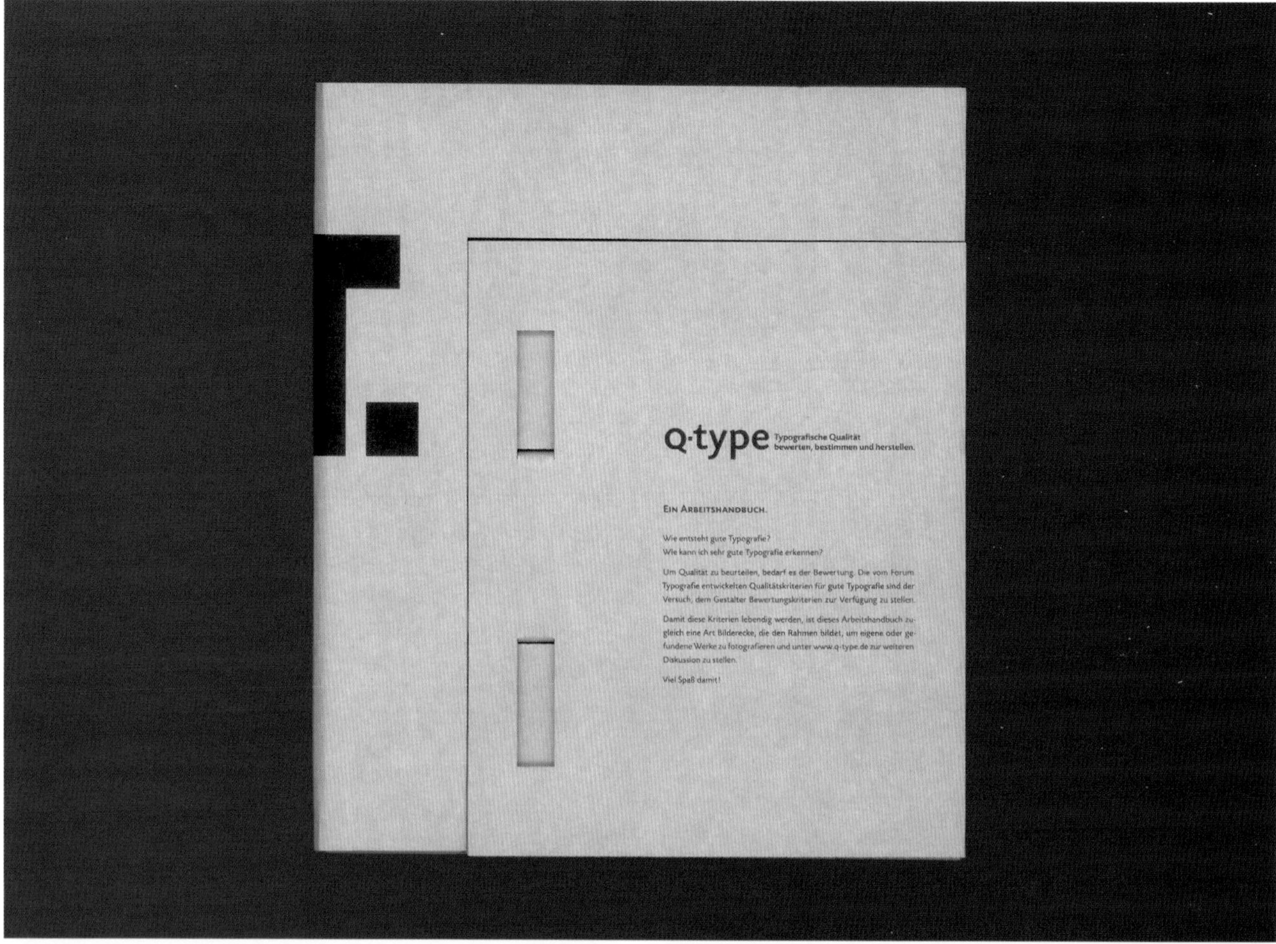

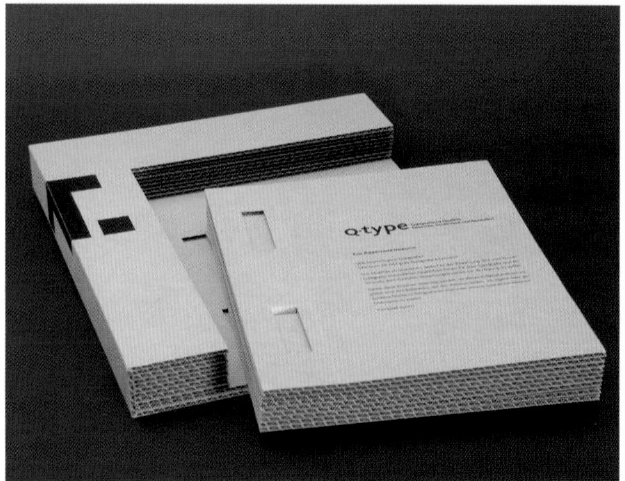

BRONZE
MISCELLANEOUS PRINTED

TITLE
Imagine Peace Tower stamp
COMPANY
Orn Smari slf
CLIENT
Iceland Post
COUNTRY
Iceland

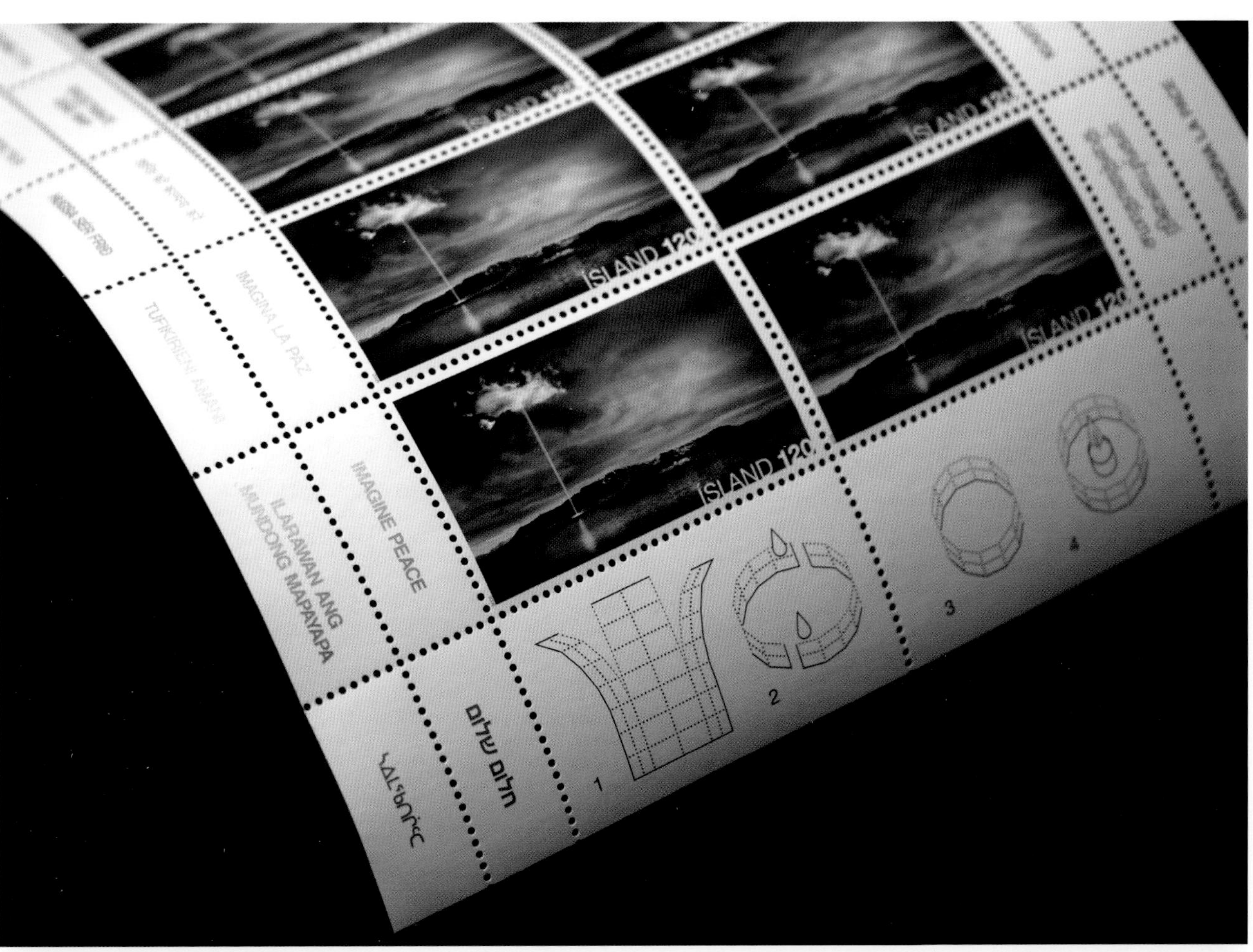

BRONZE
MISCELLANEOUS PRINTED

TITLE
Ordinary stationary
COMPANY
beetroot design group
DESIGNER
Hartovasilion
COUNTRY
Greece

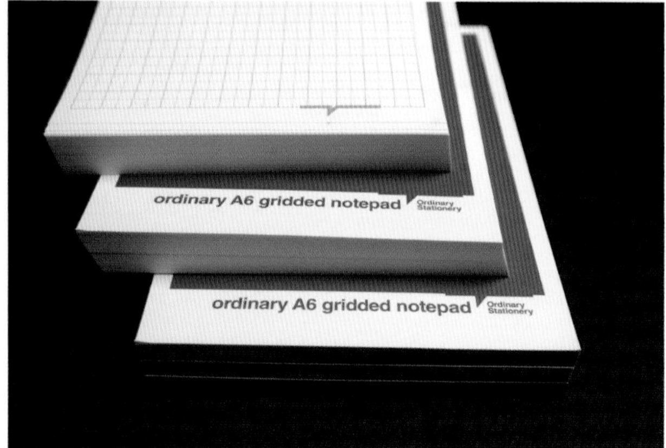

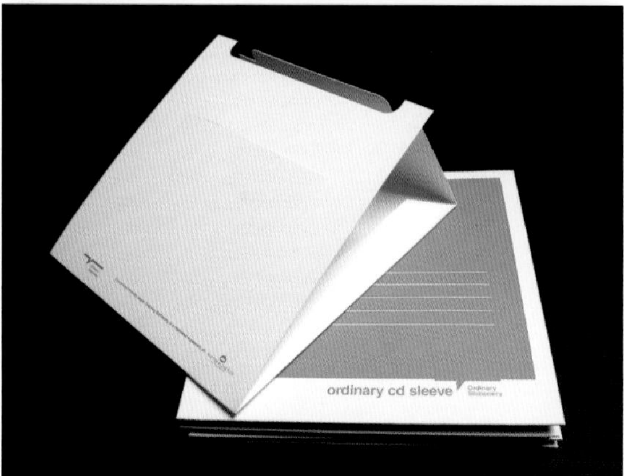

BRONZE
MISCELLANEOUS PRINTED

TITLE
I cook Greek
COMPANY
Mousegraphics
CLIENT
I cook Greek
COUNTRY
Greece

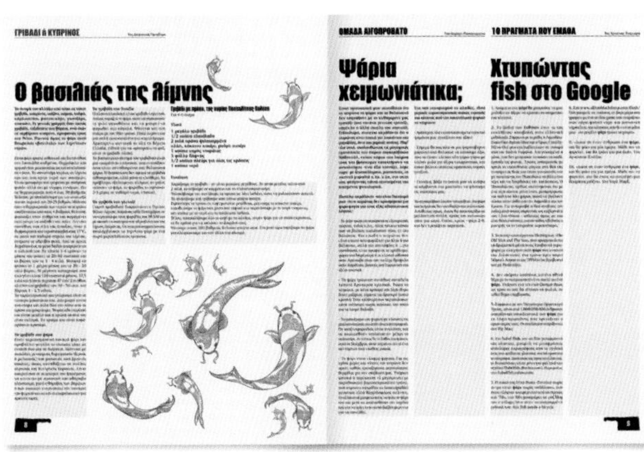

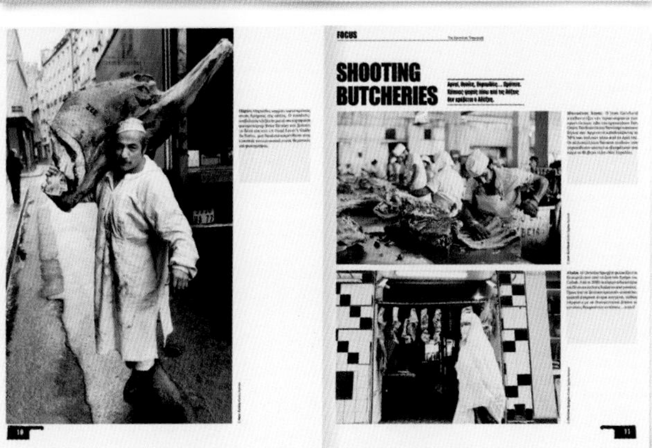

GOLD
JURY PRIZE

TITLE
Comenia - School Typeface System
COMPANY
Suitcase Type Foundry
CLIENT
Štorm Type Foundry
Suitcase Type Foundry
DESIGNERS
Tomáš Brousil
Radana Lencová
František Štorm
COUNTRY
Czech Republic

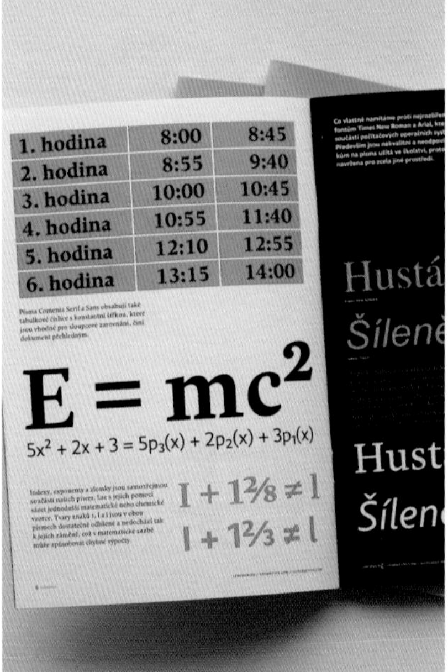

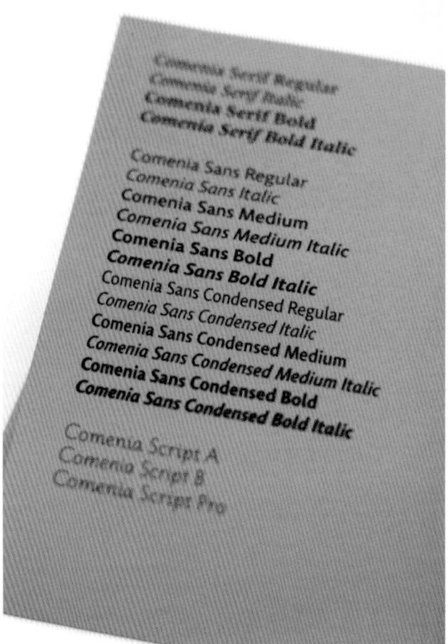

INDEX

G: Gold, S: Silver, B: Bronze, F: Finalist

INDEX

G: Gold, **S:** Silver, **B:** Bronze, **F:** Finalist

PETPUNK
LITHUANIA
www.petpunk.com
S: 158-159

PI6 COMMUNICATION DESIGN
GREECE
www.pi6.gr
B: 300

PROJECTOR
SWEDEN
www.projector.se
B: 140

PROJEKTBUERO HENKEL.HIEDL
GERMANY
www.henkelhiedl.com
B: 151, 261

PUBLICIS YORUM
TURKEY
www.publicisyorum.com
S: 226-227

PUNCHCARD
NETHERLANDS
www.punchcard.nl
G: 168-169, S: 172-173

R2 DESIGN
PORTUGAL
www.r2design.com
S: 318-319, B: 312

RADEK SIDUN, OLGA BENESOVA
CZECH REPUBLIC
www.komfortmag.cz
B: 133

RAUL MANDRU
GERMANY
raul@mandru.de
S: 264

RIVER CRESCO AB
SWEDEN
www.river.se
F: 155

ROEL VENDERBOSCH
NETHERLANDS
www.venderbosch.com
S: 220

ROSAGELB – PINKYELLOW
GERMANY
www.rosagelb.de
B: 40-41

ROSE DE CLAIRE, DESIGN
LUXEMBOURG
www.rosedeclaire.lu
S: 284

ROSEBUD, INC.
GERMANY
www.rosebud-inc.com
S: 62-63

R'PURE STUDIO (RAISON PURE DESIGN GROUP)
FRANCE
www.raisonpure.com
S: 206

SAPP+SCHEUFELE OEG
AUSTRIA
www.sapp.at
F: 313

SCHOLZ & VOLKMER GMBH
GERMANY
www.s-v.de
S: 260

SE IDEA AB
SWEDEN
info@seidea.se
F: 125, 313

SELIN ESTROTI
TURKEY
selinestroti@gmail.com
F: 295

SHUKA
RUSSIA
www.shuka.ru
B: 145

SIGI RAMOSER SÄGENVIER DESIGNKOMMUNIKATION
AUSTRIA
www.saegenvier.at
S: 104, B: 324-325

SILO
NETHERLANDS
www.silodesign.nl
S: 26

SIMON & GOETZ DESIGN GMBH & CO. KG
GERMANY
simongoetz.de
B: 72

SIMONE CIOTOLA WITH FRANCESCA CECCOLI
ITALY
www.simoneciotola.it
B: 303

SOLAR INITIATIVE NETHERLANDS
www.solar.nl
B: 42-43

SOLE 24 ORE SPA
ITALY
il@ilsole24ore.com
G: 126-127

SPECK VISUELLE KOMMUNIKATION
GERMANY
dominic@speckkremin.de
S: 16

STEFANO TONTI DESIGN
ITALY
www.stefanotonti.it
F: 15

STRUKTIV E.U. - OFFICE FOR ADVERTISING ART
AUSTRIA
www.struktiv.at
S: 88-89

STUDIO BEIGE
NETHERLANDS
www.studiobeige.nl
B: 107

STUDIO BLACKBURN
UNITED KINGDOM
www.studioblackburn.com
S: 205

STUDIO DUMBAR
NETHERLANDS
www.studiodumbar.com
S: 84-85, B: 310

STUDIO FM MILANO SRL
ITALY
www.studiofmmilano.it
S: 244-245, B: 53

STUDIO KLUIF
NETHERLANDS
www.studiokluif.nl
S: 66-67, B: 78

STUDIO LAUCKE
NETHERLANDS
www.studio-laucke.com
G: 108-109

STUDIO PAOLO BAZZANI
ITALY
www.paolobazzani.it
B: 289

STUDIO RASIC
CROATIA
www.studio-rasic.hr
S: 316-317, B: 251

STUDIO 'T BRANDT WEER
NETHERLANDS
www.tbrandtweer.nl
S: 330, B: 73

STYLT TRAMPOLI AB
SWEDEN
www.stylt.se
B: 19

SUITCASE TYPE FOUNDRY
CZECH REPUBLIC
www.suitcasetype.com
G: 274-275, 336-337

SUSANNE STAHL ANDRÉ GOTTSCHALK
GERMANY
stahl.susanne@gmail.com
G: 262-263

TGG HAFEN SENN STIEGER
SWITZERLAND
tgg.ch
B: 101

THE DESIGN SHOP
GREECE
www.thedesignshop.gr
S: 118, B: 14, 207

THIJS VERBEEK GRAFISCH ONTWERP
NETHERLANDS
www.thijsverbeek.nl
G: 238-239

TOVE HEDMAN
SWEDEN
tovelisa.blogspot.com
B: 230

TRAPPED IN SUBURBIA
NETHERLANDS
www.trappedinsuburbia.nl
S: 49

TRIDVAJEDAN MARKET COMMUNICATION LTD.
CROATIA
www.tridvajedan.hr
B: 70

TSEVIS VISUAL DESIGN
GREECE
www.tsevis.com
B: 233, 234

TURNER DUCKWORTH: LONDON & SAN FRANCISCO
UNITED KINGDOM
www.turnerduckworth.co.uk
B: 184, 214

TYPE-TOGETHER
UNITED KINGDOM
www.type-together.com
B: 277

TYPOTHEQUE
NETHERLANDS
www.typotheque.com
B: 283

UNIT9
UNITED KINGDOM
unit9.com
B: 139

VALLADARES, DISEÑO Y COMUNICACION
SPAIN
www.valladaresdc.net
B: 182

VAN RIET ONTWERPERS
NETHERLANDS
vanrietontwerpers.nl
B: 252

VIDALE-GLOESENER SARL
LUXEMBOURG
www.vidalegloesener.lu
G: 12, B: 52, F: 15

VIER FÜR TEXAS
GERMANY
www.vier-fuer-texas.de
G: 76, B: 229

VIOLA ZIMMERMANN, MADELEINE STAHEL
SWITZERLAND
viola.ch
S: 298

VIRGEN EXTRA
SPAIN
virgen-extra.com
S: 17

VLADAN SRDIC / STUDIO 360
SLOVENIA
www.studio360.si
B: 216

WEEHSEL - FREDERIK LINKE
SWITZERLAND
www.weehsel.com
B: 80, 97

WEMAKE
SPAIN
www.wemake.org
B: 165

WORTWERK
AUSTRIA
www.wortwerk.at
S: 128-129

XHOCH4
GERMANY
www.xhoch4.de
S: 110-111, B: 106

ZTY
GERMANY
www.iamzty.com
B: 231

ZUP ASSOCIATI SRL
ITALY
www.zup.it
S: 210, B: 28-29, 320-321

ZWÖLF MEDIEN
GERMANY
www.zwoelf.net
S: 296

CREDITS

European Design Ltd
Sokratous 157
176 73 Kallithea
Athens
Greece
T +30 210 9593033
F +30 210 9523607
info@europeandesign.org
www. europeandesign.org

ISBN 978-960-98284-1-3

Texts by Michel Chanaud

Layout and design by busybuilding

www.europeandesign.org